John Wilson

Lectures on our Israelitish Origin

John Wilson

Lectures on our Israelitish Origin

ISBN/EAN: 9783743347885

Manufactured in Europe, USA, Canada, Australia, Japa

Cover: Foto ©Lupo / pixelio.de

Manufactured and distributed by brebook publishing software (www.brebook.com)

John Wilson

Lectures on our Israelitish Origin

LECTURES

ON

OUR ISRAELITISH ORIGIN.

PRINTED BY BALLANTYNE AND COMPANY
EDINBURGH AND LONDON

LECTURES

ON

OUR ISRAELITISH ORIGIN.

BY

THE LATE JOHN WILSON,

AUTHOR OF "TITLE-DEEDS OF THE HOLY LAND," "WORLD TO COME," "MISSION OF ELIJAH," "BEING OF GOD," "WATCHMEN OF EPHRAIM," ETC. ETC.

"The gifts and calling of God are without repentance."—ROM. xi. 29.

Fifth Edition, Revised and Enlarged.

LONDON:
JAMES NISBET & CO., 21 BERNERS STREET.
MDCCCLXXVI.

" And as it is owned the whole scheme of Scripture is not yet understood, so if it ever comes to be understood before the *restitution of all things* (Acts iii. 21), and without miraculous interpositions, it must be in the same way as natural knowledge is come at—by the continuance and progress of learning and liberty, and by particular persons attending to, comparing, and pursuing intimations scattered up and down it, which are overlooked and disregarded by the generality of the world. For this is the way in which all improvements are made, by thoughtful men tracing on obscure hints, as it were dropped us by nature accidentally, or which seem to come into our minds by chance."—Bishop Butler's "*Analogy of Religion,*" ch. iii.

PREFACE.

THE following lectures are intended to prove that the God of Abraham, Isaac, and Jacob, who is verily a God of truth, is fulfilling His Word with regard to the multitudinous seed, the many nations to come of the house of Ephraim, as truly as He has accomplished His purpose in giving the One seed Christ to come of the house of Judah. These nations have, from the beginning, been in a state of training for their high and important destiny— that of showing forth the praise of Jehovah, who is the God of nature and of providence as well as of redemption, and whose wondrous wisdom is manifest in all.

The author holds, with many modern students of prophecy, that the prophecies must be literally fulfilled, and that Judah must mean Judah, and Israel mean literally Israel. At the same time, he agrees with those who apply to these Christian nations many of the prophecies respecting Israel, believing, as he does, that these nations have not merely come into the place of ancient Israel, but are truly the seed of Abraham according to the flesh—are of the so-called "lost house of Israel," the leading tribe of which was Ephraim. These nations have been brought forth at the time and in the place predicted; they are the modern nations of Europe, and especially those of Saxon race, whose glorious privilege it now is to "preach the gospel for a witness unto all nations ere the end come."

How the promised seed has come to be sown in these countries, is accounted for in the latter part of the course; but the author earnestly requests a careful perusal of the first eight lectures, as it is upon the scriptural foundation there laid that his after-conclusions chiefly rest. These he has supported by proof, as various in kind and great in quantity as he trusts will be requisite to substantiate the truth of the view he has been led to entertain. The plan of the lecturer has been to look on the subject in all points of view, but especially in the light of God's Word. In that light would he ever rejoice to look upon all around him— upon the world and its inhabitant, man; and the wondrous course of God's providence, which all hath respect to His people of Israel, of whom He hath said in truth, "I have chosen thee, and not cast thee away." Even after they were seemingly cast away, the God of Abraham still declared by His prophet Jeremiah—

"I am a Father to Israel,
And Ephraim is my Firstborn."

J. W.

Edge-Hill, Liverpool,
August 1840.

PREFACE TO THE FOURTH EDITION.

AFTER considering the subject for more than a quarter of a century, and having the truth of his views tried in many ways, the author of "Lectures on Our Israelitish Origin" sees nothing to shake his confidence in that which he has so long maintained, that "Israel's grave was the Saxon's birthplace;" that the English, although not Jews, are yet sprung from the outcasts of Israel, after whom the Word of God was sent to the north country, and to these "isles afar off." He still holds that the Christian people of these islands are of that "fulness of the Gentiles" promised to come of Ephraim, unto whom, through the cross, was appointed the birthright and the power of ministering blessing to all the nations of the earth. Let us be faithful to our trust, and no man may with impunity interpose to prevent our freely exercising this right, as in the hand of God. May we indeed arise to the dignity of our high calling of God in Christ Jesus!

September 1867.

PREFACE TO THE FIFTH EDITION.

In response to the growing desire for an edition of "Our Israelitish Origin" better adapted for studious readers, ranging over the last one-and-twenty years, when the first edition became altogether unprocurable, and in remembrance of the many friends of all ranks, ages, and conditions of life now "fallen asleep," who by their wise sympathy and large-hearted encouragement did what they could to cheer the late author in his laborious efforts to fulfil his mission, with the very gravest sense of responsibility, the issue of this new form of the work has been undertaken.

Thanks are due to those who have so faithfully exerted their influence in its behalf during the long delay. Meanwhile, a new circle of readers has arisen, for whom the same difficulties do not exist, general knowledge being more extensive, and the Church having been energised. "The enunciation of our origin apparently has been the touchstone of truth to change historic chaos into orderly sequence."

In reviewing the names of those who actively interested themselves in "The Mission of Elijah," "The Watchmen of Ephraim," as well as the former editions of this work, and are not here to bid the present volume "God-speed," the thought presents itself, that for each of *us* the time of personal service, and power of testimony to the covenanted faithfulness of "the God of all the families of Israel in their generations," must be limited.

Some abler pen might have been found for the preparation of the present volume; but it is doubtful whether any now living are in such full possession of the various details required, or of the author's desires with regard to it.

Ample and acknowledged use has been made in the following pages of the labours of collateral or subsequent investigators, most of whom were stirred up to their researches by the earlier editions. As walking in the light of that City on whose gates are written "the names of the twelve tribes of the children of Israel," let us compare these far-scattered records of the omniscience and omnipresence of Jehovah, with His revealed Promises to the Fathers, confirmed to us by the doings, death, and resurrection of Messiah; and refreshed by these evidences of the divine government and foreknowledge, let us become diligent followers of those "who through faith and patience inherit the Promises." As it was to the revered author, so is our Israelitish origin to the present writer—a solemn reality, of the highest significance, whether as regards the present life, or that to come.

BRIGHTON, 1876.

ERRATA

The careful reader is requested to make the following *Errata* before using this book :—

Page 56, line 32, for בן read בני.
,, 131, line 1 of note, omit comma after Rufus.
,, 139, insert as footnote—" See Sinianca's Papers, published by the Rolls' Office : Spanish Series."
,, 142, line 27, for "Jewish," read "Hebrew."
,, 159, insert as footnote—" See ' Perranzabuloe,' by Rev. C. J. C. Trelawney, M.A., 5th Edition, 1843. Rivingtons."
,, 166, line 4 of note, for "to root up" read "to root out."
,, 174, line 3 of note, for "MSS." read "MS."
,, 175, at end of last line insert " Vol. vii., § 429."
,, 365, line 12, should be *Ammim*, עמים.
,, 365, line 14, should be *Yishi*, ישי.
,, 365, last line but one, should be *Yishuathi*, ישועת.

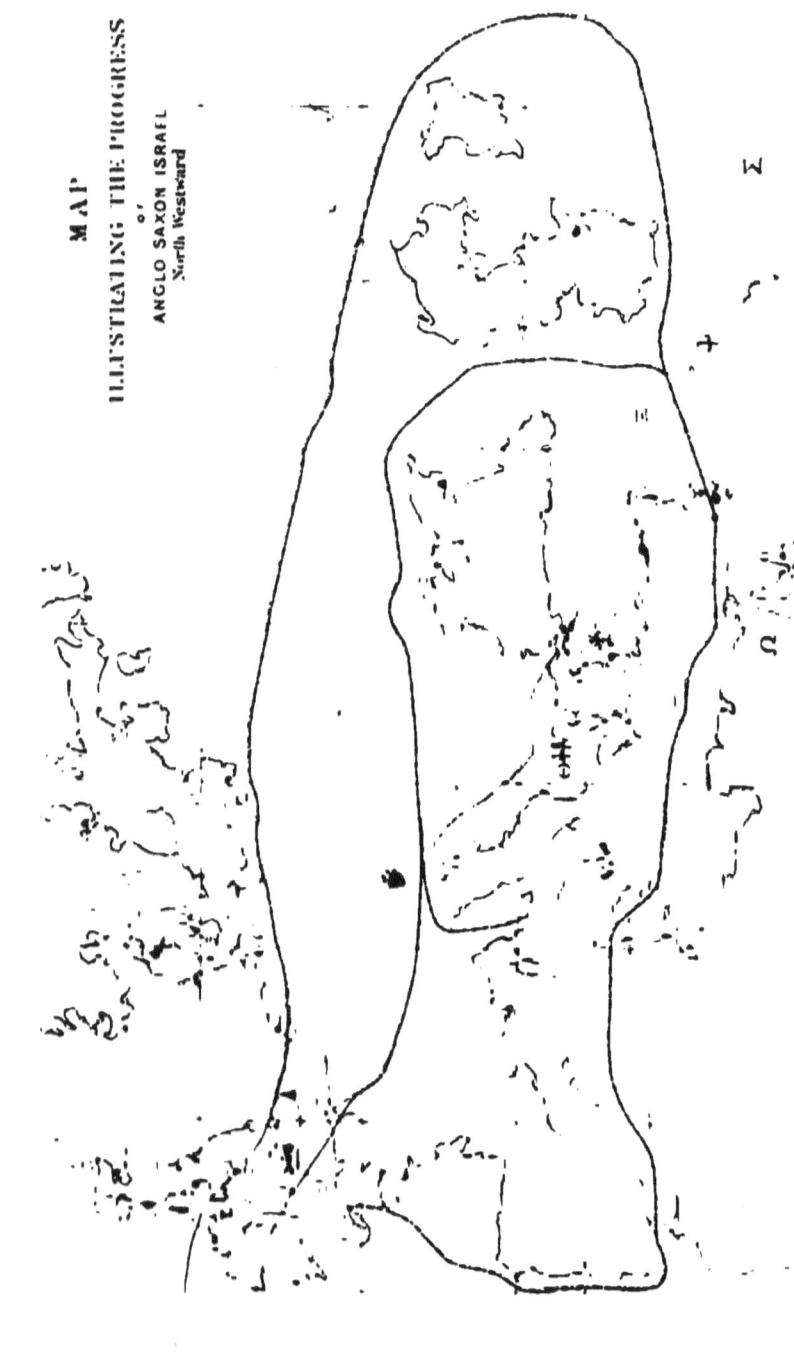

KEY TO THE MAP.

To Illustrate Rev. i. 16.

(See MISSION OF ELIJAH, pp. 175-6; and WATCHMEN OF EPHRAIM, vol. i. p. 102).

Mercy-Seat	{ England, or "Isles afar off."
Altar of Incense	Roman Territory.
Table of Shewbread	Greece.
Golden Candlestick	{ Asia Minor (seven Apocalyptic Churches).
Brazen Laver	Mesopotamia.
Altar of Burnt-Offering	{ Palestine, Jerusalem.

To Illustrate Genesis xv. 9 17.

(LECTURES ON OUR ISRAELITISH ORIGIN, p. 1.)

Divided Heifer	{ Israel in Persia and Asia Minor.
,, She-Goat	{ Israel in Grecian Empire.
,, Ram	{ Israel in Roman Empire.
,, Turtle-Dove and Young Pigeon	Israel in British Isles.
Burning Lamp passing between these Pieces	{ Apostolic Ministry of the Gospel.

To Illustrate Isaiah xi. 6 8.

(SEE TITLE DEEDS, p. 3.)

△	"The *Wolf* shall dwell with the Lamb"	{ Fourth Beast, or Roman Empire of Dan. vii.
○	"The *Leopard* with the Kid"	Third Beast, or Grecian Empire.
☌	"The *Bear* with the Cow"	{ Second Beast, or Persian Empire.
♆	"The *Lion* with the Ox."	{ First Beast, or Babylonian Empire.
⌶	"The Sucking Child shall play with the Asp."	{ Assyrian Empire.
Ω	"The Weaned Child shall put his hand on the *Cockatrice* den"	{ Egyptian Empire.

The UPPER (BLUE) Line represents the stream of Israel escaping from the region of the Araxes in Assyria, southward through Media and Parthia, and eastward of the Caspian Sea: through Scythia, Sarmatia, Dacia, Northern Germania, Gallia, and Belgæ, to Britannia and America.

A SECOND (BLUE) Line represents another stream from the same region, between the Caspian and Euxine Seas; through Armenia, Dacia, Illyricum, Southern Germania, and Gallia, to Britannia.

A THIRD (BLUE) Line proceeds from the coast of Palestine along the Mediterranean, through the Pillars of Hercules, the Atlantic Ocean, and the Bay of Biscay, to these "Isles afar off," &c.

A FOURTH Line proceeds from Palestine, through Syria, Asia Minor, Greece, Italy, Southern Germany, "round about unto Illyricum," showing the course of the *Gospel of Jesus Christ* in a north-westerly direction.

A WAVY Line shows the *Travels of St Paul* in the same direction.

CONTENTS.

LECTURE	PAGE
I. INTRODUCTORY LECTURE—THE VISION OF ABRAHAM	1
II. RELATION OF ABRAHAM'S POSTERITY TO THE THREE GRAND RACES OF MANKIND	18
III. THE LAND OF ISRAEL	32
IV. THE PROMISES MADE TO THE FATHERS	51
V. THE TRAINING AND EDUCATION OF THE PATRIARCHS	70
VI. TRAINING OF ISRAEL UNDER THE JUDGES AND KINGS	84
VII. ISRAEL AND JUDAH	99
VIII. CERTAINTY OF THE RECOVERY OF ISRAEL	114
IX. THE ESCAPED OF ISRAEL	137
X. THE EARLY CONNECTION OF BRITAIN WITH EASTERN LANDS	157
XI. HISTORICAL CONNECTION OF THE LANGUAGES OF EUROPE	179
XII. BREAKING UP OF THE ASSYRIAN EMPIRE	198
XIII. THE PROGRESS OF ISRAEL WESTWARD	212
XIV. "SET THEE UP WAYMARKS"	229
XV. THE STATE OF EUROPE SUBSEQUENT TO THE NORTHERN INVASIONS OF ROME	246
XVI. ISRAEL'S GRAVE THE SAXON'S BIRTHPLACE	267
XVII. SOCIAL AND POLITICAL RELATIONS OF THE ANGLO-SAXONS	290
XVIII. ANGLO-SAXON ARTS OF PEACE AND WAR	316

LECTURE	PAGE
XIX. FRENCH TESTIMONY AS TO THE ENGLISH CONSTITUTION AND HISTORY.	337
XX. RESUMÉ OF THE EVIDENCE FOR OUR ISRAELITISH ORIGIN.	366
XXI. PROVIDENCE AND PROPHECY.	350

THE RE-DISCOVERY OF OUR ISRAELITISH ORIGIN.	411
INDEX OF BOOKS, AUTHORS, AND SUBJECTS	443
INDEX OF SCRIPTURE TEXTS .	449

OUR ISRAELITISH ORIGIN.

I.

INTRODUCTORY LECTURE—THE VISION OF ABRAHAM.

"The Mystery of God," Rev. x., Not Anything New—Intimated in Isaiah xxix.—The Vision of All, Gen. xv.—Ministration of Mercy and Judgment—The Land Promised to Abraham's Seed, in the line of Isaac, greater in extent than has ever been Possessed by his Descendants—The Covenant being made before the Law, and Confirmed by Christ, ensures to the Believing Children of Abraham the Fulfilment of the Promises—The Stranger who believingly takes hold of the Lord's Covenant is to have Inheritance with Israel, Isaiah lvi.

"THE MYSTERY OF GOD" (Rev. x. 1-7), which was to be "finished in the days of the voice of the seventh angel, when he shall begin to sound," must refer to some important working of God, which would be ripe for disclosure in "the last days." That which is revealed, however, is not anything new, but rather the opening up of what "He hath declared unto His servants the prophets."

"THE MYSTERY" to be disclosed upon the opening of "the Book," is very clearly intimated by the prophet Isaiah, chap. xxix. But "a very little while" before Lebanon should be "turned into a fruitful field"—before the curse should be taken from the Land, and the People of Promise restored thereto in blessing, "the deaf" were to "hear the words of the Book;" and thereupon the God of Israel is found to have been a covenant-keeping God. Not another people in their place, whether Jews or Gentiles, but the very Children of Promise themselves have been found, when "the manifestation of the sons of God" has taken place (Rom. viii. 19-25).

"Therefore thus saith the Lord, who redeemed Abraham, concerning the house of Jacob; Jacob shall not now be ashamed, neither shall his face now wax pale. But when he seeth his children, THE WORK OF MY HANDS, in the midst of him, they shall sanctify My name, and sanctify the Holy One of Jacob, and shall fear the God of Israel."

The preceding part of Isaiah xxix. is remarkably connected with our subject. The woful case to which "the city where David dwelt" would be subjected is described. The ASSYRIANS encamped against it round about; but were allowed to proceed no further. The BABYLONIANS were permitted to "lay siege against her with a mount," and prevailed to the taking of the city and removing therefrom of the strength and beauty of the Jewish people, whose sufferings did not thus end; for after seventy years' captivity, their enemies were powerful round about. Yea, the words were literally fulfilled in Jerusalem herself, "And I will raise forts against thee."

At length, by the power of the ROMANS, the threatening was accomplished, "and thou shalt be brought down;" since which the predictions respecting the deep degradation of Jerusalem have been abundantly verified—(ver. 4)—"Thou shalt speak out of the ground, and thy speech shall be low out of the dust, and thy voice shall be as of one that hath a familiar spirit, out of the ground, and thy speech shall whisper out of the dust."

When the inhabitants of Jerusalem had debased Christianity, the city fell into the hands of the SARACENS, the children of Hagar, "*the stranger*," of whom it is here said, "Moreover the multitude of thy strangers shall be like small dust." Next came the TURKS, "the multitude of the terrible ones;" and they "shall be as chaff that passeth away: yea, it shall be at an instant suddenly." The Lord will cleanse Jerusalem—"Thou shalt be visited of the Lord of Hosts with thunder, and with earthquake, and great noise, with storm and tempest, and the flame of devouring fire." When she is cleansed, then shall she be defended. Yea, already have all those nations which have burdened themselves with her been cut to pieces; and so, most signally, will it be with regard to the last great invasion—"And the multitude of all the nations that fight against Ariel, even all that fight against her and her munition, and that distress her, shall be as a dream of a night vision."

Not only the avowed enemies of Zion have been dreaming—her own children have been in a stupor; they stumble on as in the dark. And so it follows, "Stay yourselves, and wonder; cry ye out, and cry! Take your pleasure and riot. They are drunken, but not with wine; they stagger, but not with strong drink." The reason is then alleged—"For the Lord hath poured out upon you the spirit of deep sleep, and hath closed your eyes; the prophets and your heads, the seers hath He covered. And the VISION OF ALL is become unto you as the words of a Book that is sealed" (Isa. xxix.)

The First Vision in the Bible (Gen. xv.) seems to be that here alluded to, and contains a view of the whole course of Divine Providence, both in judgment and mercy, with regard to Abraham's posterity, especially respecting that portion which was afterwards spoken of as ALL ISRAEL.

If we have come to *the Time for opening the Book*, then are we also come to the Time when the Vision should "speak," Hab. ii. 3. It was THE VISION OF ALL (Lect. xviii.) which, even in Isaiah's time, had become "as the words of a Book that is sealed."

Let us hear the words addressed to Abram. We can only be blessed along with that Father of the Faithful, who, as we are told, "believed God, and it was counted to him for righteousness." "Now it was not written for his sake alone that it was imputed to him, but for us also, to whom it shall be imputed, if we believe on Him that raised up Jesus our Lord from the dead" (Rom. iv. 23, 24.)

"After these things the word of the Lord came unto Abram in a Vision, saying, Fear not, Abram, I am thy Shield and thy Exceeding Great Reward." Let us connect with these words the declaration of our great High Priest and Apostle, Christ Jesus, Rev. i. 17, 18 ; "Fear not, I am the First and the Last." He who was presented to Abram as the Object of his faith, in the first recorded Vision of the Bible, is the same who was presented to John in the last great Vision with which the Sacred Volume ends. What He is as our Shield—hath been, and ever will be— is also declared : "I am He that liveth and was dead; and, behold, I am alive for evermore." He hath life in Himself : He died for our sins ; He rose again for our justification ; and He ever liveth to make intercession for us. As our Exceeding Great Reward He is the "AMEN, and hath the keys of Hades and of death ;" and it is through His giving "the Amen" to the supplications of His saints, that they know God to be "the Rewarder of them that diligently seek Him." As the Great AMEN—the Fulfiller of the Promises—He will Himself be presented in answer to the earnest cry of His waiting people, "Come, Lord Jesus, come quickly!" Then will God "give reward unto His servants the prophets, and to them that fear Him, both small and great."

"And Abram said, Lord God, what wilt Thou give me, seeing I go childless; and the steward of my house is this Eliezer of Damascus?" He longed for the *sign* of the fulfilment of the promise already given, with regard to a SEED who should inherit the land, chap. xii. 7. "And Abram said, Behold, to me Thou hast given no seed; and, lo, one born in my house is mine heir." God condescended to assure him that not merely an *adopted* posterity should inherit the promises: "And, behold, the word of the Lord came unto him, saying, This shall not be thine heir; but he that shall come forth of thine own bowels shall be thine heir."

And surely the birth of Isaac, in the circumstances, was the assured pledge or sign to Abram that all else would be accomplished, according to the word of the Lord: that through Christ, the One Seed already promised, a numerous posterity would at length be brought forth to inherit with him the promised blessing. These are they who, in the present dispensation being employed in turning many to righteousness, "shall shine as the stars for ever and ever" in the period of reward, Dan. xii. 3. And so it follows (ver. 5), "And He brought him forth abroad, and said, Look now toward heaven, and tell the stars if thou be able to number them. And He said unto him, So shall thy seed be." As an example to the numerous seed who thus will be lifted up, first in grace and then in glory, it is declared with regard to Abram, unto whom the Lord had been presented as his "Shield and Exceeding Great

Reward," that "he believed the Lord, and He counted it to him for righteousness."

The Lord recognises not only the truth of the promise respecting Abram's seed, but also of that relating to the LAND. He had not taken from Abram the lesser gift because He had given him the greater (ver. 7). "And He said unto him, I am the Lord that brought thee out of Ur of the Chaldees, to give thee this LAND, to inherit it." Abram was not so indifferent with regard to this land as many of his descendants have been; and, that he might be in no doubt as to what had been spoken, he even asked a sign, saying, "Lord God, whereby shall I know that I shall inherit it?" That which was given to him appears to have been also a sign for us. To him was presented the symbol, "the mystery" of which has been accomplished in his descendants. They have been in the same "gross or great darkness" (Isa. lx. 2), so that they have not seen "afar off." But, when they do see, they will find that our God has not neglected to give evidence of His intention to fulfil all His word (ver. 9); "And He said, Take me an heifer of three years old, and a she-goat of three years old, and a ram of three years old, and a turtledove, and a young pigeon. And he took unto him all these, and divided them in the midst, and laid each piece one against another; but the birds divided he not. And when the fowls came down upon the carcases, Abram drove them away." Until our own day, these have never been effectually frayed away from preying upon the torn carcase of Judah. That people, therefore, do not seem to be symbolised by these divided "carcases."

"For the divisions of Reuben," the natural first-born of Jacob, there were to be "great searchings of heart" (Judges v. 15, 16). "The Lord sent a word into Jacob, and it hath lighted upon Israel" (Isa. ix. 8). "The word of God is quick and powerful, and sharper than any two-edged sword, piercing even to the dividing asunder of soul and spirit, and of the joints and marrow, and is a discerner of the thoughts and intents of the heart. Neither is there any creature that is not manifest in His sight; but all things are naked and opened to the eyes of Him with whom we have to do." These latter words are quoted from the Epistle addressed to the Hebrews, chap. iv. 12, 13; and it is to be observed that, whilst it is admitted that every creature is naked and open before the eyes of Omniscience, yet the dividing of the "carcases" had a special reference to the Hebrews—the descendants of Abram, unto whom the word of the Lord was "sent," and upon whom it was to "light."

The seed of Jacob, more especially of the HOUSE OF ISRAEL, appear to be the people represented by these "carcases," which, although divided, were not to be given as a prey to the fowls of heaven, Hos. ii. 18. They were of tender concern to Abram. His posterity, with regard to whom he had expressed so deep an interest in the preceding part of the chapter, were indeed divided according to the word of the Lord; more especially through the instrumentality of the Assyrians, who were allowed to take or drive them away in two or three great captivities. Of those led away captive, many appear to have settled along the borders of the Black Sea, the banks of the Danube, and the north-western parts of Europe; whilst, of those which "escaped," as fleeing from the coast of Palestine down the Mediterranean by the ships of Tyre, settlements seem to have been formed "over against" them, along the northern borders of that sea and in these "isles afar off."

Thus the great bodies of Israel were divided and subdivided. "But the birds divided he not;" and it is remarkable, that in Isa. xi. 6, 7, when the young of these tame animals—the heifer, the she-goat, and the ram—are spoken of as being gathered into the sanctuary along with the previously wild animals, no mention is made of the turtle-dove or young pigeon.

"The WOLF," by which was represented the fourth or Roman Empire, "shall dwell with the lamb," the young of the last of the animals divided by Abram. "And the LEOPARD," which was used to represent the Grecian Empire (Dan. vii.), "shall lie down with the kid"—the young of the she-goat. The young of the heifer is then adverted to: "And the calf, and the young lion, and the fatling together, and a little child (קטן *katon*) shall lead them." The same tame animal in another stage of existence is spoken of in connection with PERSIA, when it is said, "The cow and the BEAR shall feed: their young ones shall lie down together." The same kind of animal, as not only full grown, but also powerful and strong for labour, is spoken of as having assimilated to it the LION which represented the BABYLONIAN Empire: "And the lion shall eat straw like the ox." Then, as if alluding to the Caspian Sea which bounded ASSYRIA northward, it is prophesied: "The sucking child (יונק *yonek*) shall play on the hole of the ASP;" and, lastly, as turning to Egypt, "The weaned child shall put his hand on the COCKATRICE' den."

"They"—the EGYPTIAN and ASSYRIAN—"shall not hurt," nor shall the BABYLONIAN lion, nor the PERSIAN bear, nor the GRECIAN leopard, nor the ROMAN wolf, "destroy in all My holy mountain." For the earth—or land—see Lect. iii.,—shall be full of the knowledge of the Lord, as the waters cover the sea." Their evil nature will have been taken away by the knowledge of the Lord. The "sanctuary" will have been cleansed; and even as the different animals naturally opposed to each other assembled peaceably in the ark prepared by Noah, so will the Lord assemble into His prepared place many out of these nations, as being "joined" unto His people of Israel. "And in that day there shall be a root of Jesse which shall stand for an Ensign of the peoples (עַמִּים *ammim*): to it shall the Gentiles or nations seek (גוֹיִם *Gōyim*), and His rest shall be glory."

But previous to this "glory" being made manifest, there was to be a period of great "darkness" upon both land and people, adverted to in Isa. lx., where the call is given to Zion: "Arise, shine, for thy light is come; and the glory of the Lord is risen upon thee." It is added, "For, behold, darkness shall cover the earth (or land, Lect. iii.), and gross darkness the peoples (אֻמִּים *ammim*); but the Lord shall arise upon thee; and His glory shall be seen upon thee. And the Gentiles (גוֹיִם *Gōyim*) shall come to thy light, and kings to the brightness of thy rising."

Immediately before the departure of Israel from the land, Ephraim is represented as "a silly dove without heart" (Hos. vii. 11). "They call to Egypt; they go to Assyria. When they shall go, I will spread My net upon them: I will bring them down as the fowls of heaven; I will chastise them as their congregation hath heard." But, though at that time sorely reduced, they will return in beauty and with blessing as promised, "Though ye have lien among the pots . . . the wings of a dove covered with silver, and her feathers with yellow gold!" (Ps. lxviii. 13). And accordingly when the question is asked, "Who are these that fly as a cloud, and as the doves to their windows?" it is answered, "Surely the isles shall wait for Me, and the ships of Tarshish first; to bring My sons from far, their silver and their gold with them, unto the name of the Lord thy God, and to the Holy One of Israel" (Isa. lx. 8).

Then, when "the voice of the turtle shall be heard in the land," will the sign be given of fast approaching blessing. A long deep sleep, and fearful "darkness," were, however, to precede this gladsome breaking of the light, the sign of which "mystery" fell upon Abram. And it has been fulfilled even in his believing children, evidenced by their almost studied inattention to the word of prophecy, "unto which ye do well that ye take heed, as unto a light that shineth in a dark place" (2 Pet. i. 19). How fearful has been the "darkness" that has for many ages hung over the case of the people of promise, and over God's great working in Providence in regard to them! As looking forward to the long dreary time of Israel's hiding, truly the prophets might well exclaim, "Who hath believed our report, and to whom is the arm of the Lord revealed?" It was so dark that they knew not even the Son of God—the long-expected Messiah—when He appeared in the very place, time, and circumstances appointed from the days of old. This case of Abram's descendants was thus shadowed forth: "And when the sun was going down, a deep sleep fell upon Abram; and, lo! an horror of great darkness fell upon him;" fulfilled in that "spirit of deep sleep" and covering of the seers referred to in Isa. xxix. 10.

The dark and deeply distressed state of Israel in Egypt, their deliverance therefrom under the hand of Moses, their espousal to the Lord in the wilderness, and their entrance to the land under the captain of the Lord's host, spoke of greater things yet to come: "And He said unto Abram, Know of a surety that thy seed shall be a stranger in a land that is not theirs, and shall serve them, and they shall afflict them four hundred years; and also that nation whom they shall serve will I judge: and afterwards shall they come out with great substance." The pledge that this would be was also given to his immediate descendants: "And thou shalt go to thy fathers in peace; thou shalt be buried in a good old age" (ver. 15).

Referring to the deliverance from the Egyptian bondage it is said, "But in the fourth generation they shall come hither again; for the iniquity of the Amorites is not yet full" (ver. 16). Then, going forward to the period following their expulsion from the land (represented by the divided carcases, deep sleep, and horror of great darkness), it follows with regard to the ministration of judgment and mercy going forth from Jerusalem in the case of the Jews: "And it came to pass, that when the sun went down, and it was dark, behold, a smoking furnace and a burning lamp that passed between those pieces" (ver. 17). These we are told, in Isa. xxxi. 9, were in Jerusalem. The Assyrian, who had been the instrument of separating "the carcases" of Israel, was not allowed to accomplish the same for Judah, with regard to whom the Lord had a further purpose to serve. And so the word was fulfilled, "And he shall pass over to his stronghold for fear, and his princes shall be afraid of the ensign, saith the Lord, whose fire is in Zion, and His furnace in Jerusalem."

But when the Jews had filled up "the measure" of their iniquity in the land, then was the word of God (which is a light to our feet and a lamp to our path) sent in ministration away from Jerusalem, down through Asia Minor, Greece, and Rome, in the midst of the divided "carcases"—the expatriated and scattered children of Israel. Then was the Great High Priest—who had been rejected in Jerusalem —found "in the midst of the seven golden candlesticks," as removed to the cities of Asia Minor (Rev. i., ii.) There, in the ministration of the word was He beheld, whose "eyes are as a flame of fire," and who "searcheth the reins and the heart." To search out and consume the heart-wickedness of His people, by that which truly maketh manifest, Israel had been parted and thus placed along the great line in which hath come the ministration of that word by believing Jews such as Paul "from Jerusalem, round about unto Illyricum." It was by "the lamp of fire" from Jerusalem, supplied by our great superintending High Priest, that mercy visited us who sat in darkness, "to guide our feet into the way of peace."

The ministration of judgment hath also thus come. As in the believing Jews, who were "made light in the Lord," was displayed "the burning lamp," so hath been fulfilled in the unbelieving Jews the figure of "the smoking furnace." The Romans, who laid Jerusalem waste, and led them away captive in their last great captivity, drew them down north-westward in the same direction as had previously come the ministration of the Word of life. They have been an exemplification of the curse upon those who reject Him, in whom alone blessing can be found; and they have been a constant and loudly attesting witness to the truth of the Gospel.*

Not in the Jews alone have these witnesses been made apparent. Not only "from Jerusalem round about unto Illyricum," but even straight onward in the direction of our own islands, the case of every other people has been made to witness to the truthfulness of God either in mercy or by judgment. Nor will the witness here terminate. Nay, hence it has in a measure spread out unto "the uttermost

---

* As to the uses which the "remnant" from Jerusalem was to serve us to "the outcasts of Israel," see Ezek. xiv. 22, 23.

parts of the earth;" whence it will come together in unity and strength when the children of promise shall in the light, "as the stones of a crown, be lifted up as an ensign upon His land" (Zech. ix. 16).

Then will the Lord accomplish His covenant mercy of which He spake to Abraham, saying, "UNTO THY SEED HAVE I GIVEN THIS LAND, FROM THE RIVER OF EGYPT UNTO THE GREAT RIVER, THE RIVER EUPHRATES." The country then inhabited by "the Kenites, and the Kenizzites, and the Kadmonites, and the Hittites, and the Perizzites, and the Rephaims, and the Amorites, and the Canaanites, and the Girgashites, and the Jebusites," is now empty for returning Israel. So truly as they have multiplied in "the ends of the earth," has their own central land been made empty for them; but they that are left of the nations around shall yet say, "This land that was desolate is become like the Garden of Eden; and the waste, and desolate, and ruined cities, are become fenced, and are inhabited! Then the heathen that are left round about you, shall know that I, the Lord, build the ruined places, and plant that that was desolate: I the Lord have spoken, and I will do it."

Yes; there shall yet come the voice from the throne, saying, "It is done:" "The Mystery of God is finished!" "The face of the covering which was cast over all nations" is destroyed. "The glory of the Lord shall be revealed, and all flesh shall see together."

Now will have come "the manifestation of the sons of God;" the waiting for God's Son from heaven, and the great proclamation of the Gospel of the kingdom.

"Brethren," saith the Apostle of the Gentiles (Gal. iii. 15-29), " I speak after the manner of men; Though it be but a man's covenant, yet, if it be confirmed, no man disannulleth, or addeth thereto. Now, to Abraham and his seed were the promises made." When he was first led into the land which he was afterwards to receive for a possession (Gen. xii. 7), the Lord—who then gave the free promise—said not "to seeds," as of many, but "unto thy SEED will I give this land:" which one Seed is Christ. It is as being in Him that the inheritance can be enjoyed by the people: it is as being one with Him who is the Head, that the members of the body of Christ can be blessed as was promised; and the blessing in Christ was freely promised to a multitudinous seed to be brought forth of the posterity of Abraham, in the line of Joseph, and especially of Ephraim. See Gen. xlviii. 15–20; xlix. 22–26.

The covenant, given upon oath to Abraham, and confirmed to Ephraim, cannot be made void. "And this I say, the covenant that was confirmed before of God in Christ, the law—which was four hundred and thirty years after—cannot disannul, that it should make the promise of none effect. For if the inheritance be of the law, it is no more of promise. But God gave it to Abraham of promise. Wherefore then serveth the law? It was added because of transgression, till the Seed should come to whom the promise was made."

The entering into that which was promised was to be by "the key of David;" by the fulness of the Spirit's ministration; "by angels in the hand of a Mediator," in whose right hand are "the seven stars, the angels of the seven churches." All power of ministering is His, who is not only of men—one of the parties concerned in the covenant—He is also God, who will not go back from His word, nor break the oath which He sware unto the fathers. Through the fulness of the Spirit's ministration, received by faith, He will introduce us to the fulness of blessing.

"Is the law, then, against the promises of God? God

forbid: for if there had been a law which could have given life, verily righteousness should have been by the law. But the Scripture hath concluded all under sin, that the promise by faith of Jesus Christ might be given to them that believe. But before faith came" (and Christ is our faith), "we were kept under the law, shut up unto the faith that should afterwards be revealed," as He was in His first coming, and shall be much more gloriously in His second appearing. "Wherefore the law was our schoolmaster unto Christ, that we might be justified by faith. But after that faith is come, we are no longer under a schoolmaster. For ye are all the children of God by faith in Christ Jesus." He is the One Son of God, in whom the many sons of God are found accepted in His sight. "For as many of you as have been baptized into Christ have put on Christ. There is neither Jew nor Greek, there is neither bond nor free, there is neither male nor female: for ye are all one in Christ Jesus."

As to ministration in the Church, it is true there is some difference between male and female, just as there is between different members of the body. So is there also between "the Church of the First-born" Ephraim (Jer. xxxi. 9), and the other portions of Israel. Peculiar advantages are bestowed upon some, by whom particular duties are required to be performed, which are not so expected from those upon whom the like favours have not been bestowed. But none is excluded from the Body because of his natural descent or earthly position. There may be variety of capacity, opportunity, and office, and also some difference as to the degrees of reward; but there is oneness of Headship, of Body, and of Spirit; and we are also "called in one hope of our calling." "And if ye be Christ's"—members of the Body of Christ who is the Son of Abraham—" then are ye Abraham's seed, and heirs according to the promise."

The Lord, " who keepeth truth for ever," is indeed true to the free promises made respecting the posterity of Abraham; but when He makes the promised discovery of the long-lost children of Rachel, and of His marvellous grace unto them, so that the nations shall know " He hath not dealt so with any people," the stranger is not to say, " The Lord hath utterly separated me from His people." The word of the Lord is, Isa. lvi. 6-8, " The sons of the stranger that join themselves to the Lord," submitting themselves to the first commandment, " Thou shalt have no other gods before Me ; " " to serve Him," obeying the second, which forbids the service of images; " and to love the name of the Lord, to be His servants," being obedient thus in heart and life to the third, which forbids the taking the name of the Most High in vain : " every one that keepeth the Sabbath from polluting it, and taketh hold of My covenant," which points forward to the day of the Lord when redemption shall be completed, as the fourth commandment also commemorates the finishing of the work of creation : " even them will I bring to My holy mountain, and make them joyful in My house of prayer; their burnt-offerings and their sacrifices shall be accepted upon Mine altar; for Mine house shall be called an house of prayer for all people. The Lord God, which gathereth the outcasts of Israel, saith, Yet will I gather to him beside those that are gathered unto him." The Lord will prove faithful to " the outcasts of Israel," and He will also show kindness to " the dispersed of Judah;" but not exclusively to either or to both : He will also be " for salvation unto the ends of the earth."

The opening up of the Book of the Covenant was to be

through the ministration of the Spirit, by the Lamb after He had been slain, and previous to His coming forth in kingly power to take possession of the inheritance (Rev. v.) Then shall He inherit all nations, and it will be found that "Jacob is the lot" (cord, cable, or measuring line) "of His inheritance" (Deut. xxxii. 8, 9).

The progress of God's great revelation of His purposes with regard to the promised Inheritance, especially to the one Seed, Christ, is given, Rev. v.-viii. The sealing thereof to the (מלא־הגוים, *melo ha-Gōyim*) multitude of nations, and the recognition of the lost children of Ephraim, who were to obtain in Him the birthright blessing, we find in Jer. xxx., xxxi.[1]

We are now come to the time when the Son of God, through the ministration of the Spirit, was to open the Book of their Inheritance to the Children of Promise, previous to His coming forth in fulness of power to take the dominion, and give them possession. "He that spared not His own Son, but delivered Him up for us all, how shall He not, with Him, freely give us all things?" (Rom. viii. 32).

---

[1] See "Title-Deeds of the Holy Land," by the same Author.

II.

RELATION OF ABRAHAM'S POSTERITY TO THE THREE GRAND RACES OF MANKIND.

The Adamic Dispensation—The Flood—Covenant with Noah—Babel—Tartar, Negro, and Caucasian Races—The European Family—The Prophecy of Noah—Contrast of the European Family with the most anciently civilised Portions of the Three Grand Races—Designs with regard to Israel—God shall enlarge, or persuade, Japhet.

GOD MADE MAN UPRIGHT — made him "in His own image"—and he was equally happy as he was holy. His will was in unison with that of the Framer and Sustainer of all things; and thus, being in harmony with universal nature, it suffered not those painful collisions to which, in consequence of sin, it is now so constantly exposed.

As man became alienated from God—from the True Good—the Light of Jehovah's countenance—so did he become subject to that wretchedness which results from his possession of active powers adapted for communion with the spiritual world, but undirected to their proper Object.

In this low estate man was not left by Him who alone could help him. God manifested Himself unto Adam in a manner fitted to his fallen condition. Salvation through the Great Atoning Sacrifice was then revealed. It was promised that "the Seed of the woman" should bruise the serpent's head (Gen. iii. 15), and, in place of the insufficient covering of his own workmanship, with which Adam in his first emotions of shame had covered himself, he was clothed with the skins (as we suppose) of the animals slain in sacrifice at the first institution of that new mode of worship which was then appointed for him, as requiring to be redeemed by the blood-shedding of the Lamb of God, and clothed with the righteousness of Him in whose Name alone we may approach the Father.

The "good seed" being thus sown in the first family of mankind, they were allowed to "multiply and replenish the earth." But even in that early period of history there was a distinction of races. The descendants of Cain were emphatically "wicked;" whilst the sons of Seth are called "THE SONS OF GOD" (Gen. vi. 2). In process of time these two races intermingled, and the result was a powerful progeny; but their power was not consecrated to the Lord. Men, as they grew mighty, became monsters in wickedness; and as they replenished the earth, they equally filled it with violence. Their enormities called for vengeance from Heaven. The waters of the Flood were sent to quench the fire of their lust, and to sweep them with their works of wickedness from the face of the earth.

Of all the families of mankind only one was spared—the family of Noah; which, together with the individuals who had intermarried therewith, was preserved in the ark that Noah was directed to prepare during the hundred and twenty years he testified against that ungodly generation, and preached righteousness, pointing to the "rest that remaineth for the people of God," of which the ark was a type.

It has been remarked that from the creation of man God was preaching righteousness, and had been writing His Gospel in even the names of Noah and his progenitors.

Thus, ADAM means *red earth*, out of which man was formed; or it may be from the other Hebrew word signifying *image*; and, made of *earth*, man was formed after the *image* of God, which we lost in "the first Adam who is of the earth earthy," but have it restored in "the second Adam, who is the Lord from Heaven." SETH, the son of Adam, hath his name meaning *placed*. Man, made of *earth* and in the *image* of God, was *placed* in Eden by his Maker; but by his sin he *placed* himself in a wilderness of thorns and briers. And then ENOS means *mortal*, referring to the *deathful* state into which man was precipitated by his fall into sin. CAINAN means *lamentation*, the result of that state of spiritual death to which man had then fallen. But MAHALALEEL brings into view the Lord, the Saviour; this name meaning *God to be praised*, which the Word was even before He came down to earth to accomplish our redemption. His humbling Himself is taught in the next name, JARED meaning *He shall descend*. He dedicated Himself to take upon Him the form of a servant, and to become a messenger to those who received His message with the utmost despite. This service is expressed in the next name, ENOCH, which means *dedicated*. The ministry which He fulfilled, until the time of His being offered up, was that of a "Teacher come from God." "Never man spake like this man," and the subject of His teaching to His chosen disciples much related to "the decease He should accomplish at Jerusalem;" which seems to be the object pointed at by the next name, METHUSELAH, meaning *He sent His death*. "He died for our sins, and rose again for our justification." And then did He who said, "I am not *sent* but to the lost sheep of the House of Israel," *send* forth His apostles with power to preach "the good tidings of great joy." LAMECH means *to the afflicted;* and to the "*afflicted*, tossed with tempest and not comforted"—"the desolate woman" (Isa. liv.), the lost House of Israel—was the Gospel more especially *sent*. The name NOAH describes the character of the message which hath proceeded from Jerusalem, through Judea, through Samaria, through Asia Minor, through Greece, and still more north-westward, until, having reached these "isles afar off," it is being spread out unto "the uttermost ends of the earth." It is REST or *consolation*. It is "Comfort ye, comfort ye My people, saith your God." It is an invitation to enter into *rest;* into the enjoyment of perfect peace, whatever troubles may abound: to take refuge in the Ark of safety, of which that built by Noah was a faint shadow.

Thus, in the first names of the godly seed—the ten generations between Adam and Noah—we have most distinctly written the great purpose of Jehovah with regard to mankind generally, and Israel in particular. The names together, as given in 1 Chron. i. 1–4, without the assistance of any interposing words, read:—"Man—placed—mortal—lamentation—God to be praised—shall descend—dedicated—He sent His death—to the afflicted—rest or consolation." "The afflictions of Joseph" (Amos vi. 6) and the fact that the blessings of the Gospel have been mainly addressed to his descendants, and through them to the world, will hereafter engage our attention.

With NOAH a new covenant was made. It was that no such sudden destruction by the waters of a flood should end the present dispensation. His children might therefore with confidence go forward to multiply and replenish the earth; and "the bow in the cloud" was appointed to be a token of this covenant: that when they looked upon it they might think upon God as remembering His promise—that the showers should fall in measure—that the clouds should be girt, as it were, with the band of the Almighty, and no more burst upon the world with the waters of a universal deluge.

The family of Noah seem to have left the mountains and come down to the more inviting plain of Shinar. Here on the site of Babylon—the first of the tyrant list of empires which have so sought to lord it over men—did they seek to centralise the human race in a grand confederacy against the will of Heaven. Early did Babylon oppose itself to the King of Salem who "hath chosen Zion, and desired it for His habitation," saying, "this is My rest for ever: here will I dwell, for I have desired it." The Lord confounded the folly of these early founders of a universal empire independent of Him who alone hath a right to reign. He forced the rebels to disperse; and the three families of Noah, according to the divine appointment, were scattered abroad upon the face of all the earth.

Like the Adamic dispensation, that of Noah went into utter apostasy; and the whole world was being covered with idolatry. But God remembered His covenant with Noah, and brought not such an overwhelming judgment as the Flood to sweep away all his posterity from the face of the earth; and adopted another method of dealing with mankind. He chose one, to whom and to whose posterity He would show especial favour, upon whom He would bestow a very superior training, and who should be the depositary of His lively oracles, as well as those through whom He would communicate blessing to the other families of mankind.

Before proceeding farther to trace the purposes of God with regard to this chosen race, and to identify them among the nations, it may be well to understand what the general masses of mankind are from whom they are to be distinguished, and among whom they were to be a blessing.

There are three Grand Races of mankind. These have been distinguished from each other by form of head and other physical marks, as well as by intellectual and moral character. Not that any one of them has qualities of which the others are entirely deficient, but each race possesses in very different degrees and modifications those qualities which are common to all. In the masses the races may be clearly marked out from each other, and are known as the CALMUC-TARTAR, the CAUCASIAN, and the NEGRO.

THE CALMUC-TARTAR races seem to have been appointed the northern portion of the globe. There they exist in very different conditions. As Laplanders in the extreme north, they differ much from their brethren traversing the great wilds between Russia and China, still less do they resemble the Chinese, who, as being most stationary, seem to have retained more of the ancient civilisation of the race, as received from the first fathers of mankind. Europe appears to have been anciently possessed by this race; and, on the discovery of America by the modern possessors of Europe, it was found to be considerably peopled by them. Except in the case of China, the JAPHETIC races are generally found very thinly spread over a wide territory.

The races we are describing have much breadth of face and width between the eyes. The cheek-bones are wide asunder and prominent, and the whole head is in general very broad; corresponding with their general restless and roving character. In many cases they are addicted to violence and war, as well as impatient of restraint, and ambitious of a proud independence. The warlike propensities, and those which principally tend to muscular activity, having their organs situated on the side of the head, occasion the breadth described. The physiognomy otherwise is correspondent. The features are harsh, the parts not well proportioned according to our ideas of beauty, the hair is long and straight, and the beard scanty. In the North American Indians, it scarcely exists. This, however, seems to be partly produced by art; just as, in the case of the Caribs, the breadth of head has been aggravated by pressure in infancy. The complexion is somewhat of an olive hue; and varies, from that of the dun Laplander to the colour of the Red Indian traversing his wide-spreading wilds; where the physical powers must of course obtain freer expansion than amid the snows of Lapland, or as being cooped up so closely as in China.

Correspondent to their form of head, these races have in general manifested considerable mechanical skill, and have frequently made extensive conquests. These, however, they more easily make than retain. They can execute, but seem rather wanting in masterly wisdom; and require a superior moral and intellectual power to guide their great force to a proper end. They do not sufficiently care for those under them. China seems to be rather an exception; but even there the exposure of children is allowed. This—the Japhetic—race has less care for children than either of the others; and it may easily be observed that in them generally there is less of a projection over the cerebellum, in the region of the head allotted to that propensity which gives an interest in the young.

On the opposite side of the globe, and chiefly in the vast continent of Africa, we have the NEGRO RACES, the supposed descendants of HAM. These in general have the head elongated behind, forming in this respect a considerable contrast to the Japhetic races; and the Negroes are as remarkable for their love of children and fondness for nursing, as the Tártar tribes are for their indifference in these respects. The forehead is narrower, and, perhaps, also lower, correspondent to their deficiency in reasoning power and mechanical ingenuity. The upper and middle part of the head, where is the organ of veneration, is generally high; but there is a deficiency in that which gives a tendency to form ideas respecting the spiritual world, and to hold communion therewith. Consequently, the mind is left more to the influence of objects of sense; and worship is apt to be rendered to the sensible creature rather than to the unseen Creator. They more easily become subject to others. They have intelligence; but seem to have little forethought or power of planning, and require to be cared for like children. They can more easily be seduced into unreasonable acts; but they have much gentleness and affection, and power of being made useful when properly trained. Their mildness is indicated by a comparative narrowness of the head over the ears. The wide-headed Japhetic races cannot be so easily managed.

It need scarcely be remarked that the NEGRO races are generally distinguished by prominence of the lower part of the face, especially the mouth. They have black, woolly, strongly-curled hair; and the blackness of the skin is about as uniform with regard to the children of Ham, as the brown colour is to the descendants of Japhet, which, however, seems mainly occasioned by climate. In some countries the children of HAM are comparatively white.

These races appear to have early taken possession of the

lands in which the families of Abraham were first to be planted. Thus, CUSH inhabited Arabia destined for Ishmael; and CANAAN took possession of the very Land of Promise itself; and even north-eastward of these countries, in ill-fated Babylon, we find NIMROD, the "mighty hunter before God," erecting the throne of his empire. This central position was not, however, designed for the descendants of HAM; and they have long been expelled from their usurped domain.

The children of SHEM, generally called the CAUCASIAN race, occupy the central position, and chiefly inhabit southern Asia. We find them spread over Armenia, Persia, Arabia, and the thickly peopled regions of India. The Jews are an improved specimen of this race; and so also are "the chief of the nations" (Jer. xxxi. 7), the modern inhabitants of Europe. These people are generally characterised by an oval face, with regular features. The head is more remarkable for height than either for length or breadth, although it has in general a goodly proportion of both. The reflective region is especially well developed, and so also is the imaginative. They have the largest proportion of those powers which regard the spiritual world, and which tend to give an elevated and refined exercise to the intellect. When allowed to grow, the beard is abundant in this race. The hair is softer and more pliant than in any of the other families. Stature and complexion seem to be greatly modified by climate. In some quarters, as in the burning plains of India, this race may be found quite black; while in more elevated situations, and in temperate climes, they are found fair and still fairer, until in Europe we find them with the lily hand and rosy cheek, the azure eye and flaxen hair; corresponding with

Jeremiah's description of what his people once were, Lam. iv. 7:—

> "Her Nazarites were purer than snow,
> They were whiter than milk,
> They were more ruddy in body than rubies,
> Their polishing was of sapphire."

This race may more generally be characterised as having the head elevated and elongated in front, with delicacy of texture and beautifully proportioned features. But although the head is more finely formed (representing a greater proportion of the reflective faculties, imaginative powers, and religious sentiments), yet, altogether, the mind has less force, indicated by the comparative smallness of the head. The brain is better in quality and form, but less in quantity. The Jews and modern possessors of Europe are exceptions to the latter part of this rule, in whom the head is not only more beautifully formed than in even the other branches of the Semitic family; but it is also greater in volume than in the case of either the Negro on the one hand, or of the Tartar on the other.

It may be remarked that the European branch of the SEMITIC race is rapidly spreading Westward. From the East they came into the maritime parts of Europe, and have gradually pushed the people to "the ends of the earth" who previously possessed these countries; or have taken them up, to become one people with them, and make with them partakers of the same blessings. After renewing their strength in these islands (Isa. xlix. 1), this improved family of the Semitic race has launched out on the great Atlantic. The tide of emigration has rolled over that world of waters still farther west, encroaching upon the Japhetic race in America, as it did in Europe; and appears destined to spread, until the wilderness be wholly inhabited, and "the desert rejoice and blossom as the rose" (Isa. xxxv. 1). With all their faults they seem to be eminently "a seed which the Lord hath blessed" (Isa. lxi. 9).

In Gen. ix. 25-27, there is a remarkable prophecy by Noah with regard to his three sons. We there find Ham punished in his seed (ver. 25), a point in which, judging from his race, he would be most likely to feel: whilst Shem is blessed in the Object of his religious regard (ver. 26), and in his descendants the religious sentiments are the strongest; while Japhet, whose name means *persuasion* or *enlargement*, was promised emancipation or an introduction to the tents of Shem. And, although long shut out from the peculiar privileges of the people of God, at length more especially with regard to them was "the middle wall of partition" to be broken down (Eph. ii. 14), and free access to be had into the liberty wherewith Christ doth make His people free, persuading them by His grace to become fellow-heirs of the kingdom. Much mingled with the posterity of Shem, the descendants of Japhet "dwell in their tents," filling the place of upper servants: whilst not only has Canaan been "cursed," but the lower place—that of the mere slave—has been generally left to the other children of Ham. God has especially manifested Himself and His great salvation to the posterity of SHEM, who have even, as we have seen, the greatest natural capacity for that kind of knowledge. Not only has the true religion been more abundant with the SEMITIC race, but false religions have also abounded.

The truth, however, will prevail; and then, indeed, shall SHEM be "blessed," and be given still more fully his place at the head of the human family. JAPHET, intermingled with SHEM, will occupy the place of a servant born in the house; whilst, the curse being removed from CANAAN, he will be blessed through the ministration of SHEM, and the whole human family, taking refuge in the Ark of the Covenant, will become the blissful family of God.

A singular contrast may be observed between the European family and even the most civilised portions of each of these three Grand Races. Besides their nomadic branches—which as being too far separated from the main stems to retain the full advantages of ancient civilisation possessed by the immediate descendants of Noah, or who in consequence of other changes have been thrown into a state of utter barbarism, and seem quite incapable of regaining what they have lost—there seems to have been a portion of each, which, as being more stationary in the original seats of mankind, has retained a sufficient knowledge of nature and of art to procure for it the appellation of "civilised."

Thus, of the same race with the wandering Tartars, we have the Chinese; of the Semitic or Caucasian race, we have the Hindoos; and of the children of Ham—of the same general race with the Negroes—we have the most anciently civilised empire of Egypt and their kindred along the coast of Palestine. These three nations—the Chinese, the Hindoos, and the Egyptians—appear to have with difficulty retained what they have had from time immemorial. In some instances they seem rather to have lost than gained; and the practice of the arts they have often retained without knowing the principle according to which the effect they aim at is produced.

Not so the European family, and especially that of Anglo-Saxon origin. They had lost all, and were "stripped naked as in the day they were born," when they presented themselves here in the West (Hos. ii. 3); but they have not remained as those generally do who are thus left destitute. They have evidently been given a principle of life—an onward and upward tendency—which is not merely of use to themselves, but in general gives an impetus to all with whom they come into contact; who must either yield to its influence, or be broken down by it. Theirs is not merely a retentive capacity, but also an inventive genius. Theirs is not a contentment with empirical practices: they must know the principles of the arts they practise, by the knowledge of which not only is retention of the arts ensured, but also way opened up for new improvements and discoveries. The great work of self-instruction is ever going forward. They are not bound down to the limits of the knowledge possessed by their fathers: they are wiser than all their teachers among men (Ps. cxix. 99), for God Himself has been their Instructor, both in nature and in grace; and He hath given them a capacity to receive His instruction and communicate it to others, above what any nation or number of nations has ever possessed.

This is no matter of chance. We shall see that it is according to the original purposes and whole course of God's procedure with regard to Israel; which are very fully expressed in that remarkable song of Moses (Deut. xxxii.), were we are told that

"When the Most High divided to the nations their inheritance;
When He separated the sons of Adam,
He set the bounds of the people
According to the number of the children of Israel."

Why should the Lord thus set "the bounds" of other nations according to the number of a people not yet born into the world? Because this people were intended to compass these nations; which they could not do, unless their numbers were proportionate to "the bounds of the people" they were intended to encompass. And so it follows :—

> "For the Lord's portion is His people,
> And Jacob is the lot—[*i.e., cord* or *measuring line* הבל *chebel* or *cable.—See Parkhurst*] of His inheritance."

Then follows a description of the careful training by which they were to be so far fitted for the important purposes which God had in view with regard to them. And there is an extended prophecy, clearly recognising the fact, that the purpose of their creation was not accomplished during their former sojourn in the Land. Nor indeed could it be, without their going forth to encompass the various nations which the Lord intended to bring within His fold. When this end is accomplished, then goes forth the joyful invitation with which the song concludes :—

> "Rejoice, O ye Nations (גוים *Goyim*) His People ; (עמו *Ammo*)
> For He will avenge the blood of His servants,
> And will render vengeance to His adversaries ;
> And will be merciful to His Land and to His People !" עמו.

III.

THE LAND OF ISRAEL.

Interesting Scenes and Objects to be passed in a Voyage to the Land of Promise—Tyre—Important Transactions connected with the Land identified with Eden in Ezek. xxviii. and xxxi.—Central Position by Land and Water—Central relation to the British Empire, and all varieties of Mankind—Description of it from Scripture, and correspondent human testimony—Present State—Future Renovation, as described, Zech. xiv., Joel iii., Ezek. xxxviii.-ix., xlvii., Isaiah xxx., Ps. xlvi.—The Land doubly lost and won—Terms Earth and World considered—The great Empires Conquered but did not Enjoy the Land—Practical Results of this Enquiry.

THE LAND OF ISRAEL is situated in the very centre of the three Grand Families of mankind; whilst it may be said of the nations of Europe in relation thereto—" They are at hand." In general they may reach it either by land or water. Our course is by the Mediterranean; as we ascend which, what interesting scenes open upon our view!

In GIBRALTAR, at the very entrance, we are presented with one of the grand positions which have been given to Britain for the transmission of truth and establishment of righteousness all over the globe. Alas, that as regards the purposes for which they have been designed by the God of Israel, these should have hitherto been so feebly occupied! Here, also, in Spain on the one side and in Morocco on the other, we behold the scenes of intense suffering and attempted deep degradation of our kinsmen the Jews.

As we ascend, Rome on the left hand, and Carthage on

the right, remind us of important events connected both with ancient heathen story and the history of the Christian Church. Meantime we may be passing over the treasures from the temple at Jerusalem, since rifled from Rome, but now lying with much other treasure at the bottom of this sea.

In MALTA, our nation has been given another most important position in relation to these interesting portions of the globe. We pass Greece, where so much of an enduring nature was written and acted in the days of old; and whither the Apostle Paul was directly led by the Spirit of God, being allowed to diverge neither to the right hand nor the left, until he had reached the western extremity of Asia, when he was in vision called by a man of Macedonia to come over into Europe (Acts xvi. 9).

As we proceed, on the left side we have the site of the Seven Churches of Asia, towards which in the Apocalypse we have our attention called by the Spirit of Prophecy in its first movement north-westward; whilst on the right hand we have emptied into this sea the Nile—the great river of Egypt—on the banks of which were transacted some of the most remarkable events recorded in the first books of the Bible.

And now we have arrived at the coast of the LAND OF ISRAEL. Here was TYRE, the root of that great maritime confederacy which in early ages connected such distant parts of the globe, which even thousands of years ago brought the British Isles — "the Isles afar off" — "the Isles of Tarshish"—into commercial alliance with the Land of Israel, and which, in the Providence of God, was given the greatest facilities for transmitting the "escaped" of Israel westward (Isa. lxvi. 19), just as Assyria was appointed to carry into captivity the body of the people northward (Isa. x. 5–15). Each of these—Tyre and Assyria—was the most fitting instrument for the work to which it was appointed; although we may believe that nothing was farther from their hearts than to accomplish God's good pleasure to His "first-born" Ephraim, and thereby to the world.

We now enter upon the mountains of Israel, where wandered the Patriarchs Abraham, Isaac, and Jacob; where ministered "Melchizedek, priest of the Most High God;" to which were conducted God's ancient people by the Cloud of Glory and the ministry of Moses and Joshua; where was erected the Throne of David; where was reared the Temple of Solomon; where the Prophets delivered the counsels of Jehovah; where the High Priest of the nation was allowed to come into the presence of the God of Israel; where in our very nature the Lord of Glory Himself condescended to tabernacle among men; where the Great Atonement was offered; whence our Great High Priest "ascended up into the Holiest of All;" and upon which so copiously descended "the former rain," when, having "ascended up on high, He received gifts to give unto men, yea, for the rebellious also" (that is, the backsliding house of Israel), "that the Lord God might dwell among them" (Ps. lxviii. 18).

This land, so distinguished in the Word and Providence of God, must be at least near that which was the most early favoured. It seems worthy of remark, that both Tyre and Assyria are spoken of in Scripture as bordering upon "Eden—the Garden of God;" and the land which bordered upon these two states in common, being situated between them, was the LAND OF ISRAEL, so marked as the theatre of God's grand manifestations to man. TYRE is on the western coast of the Land of Israel; and in Ezek. xxviii. 13 it is said of the prince or king of Tyrus:—

"Thou hast been in EDEN, the GARDEN OF GOD." "Thou wast upon the HOLY MOUNTAIN OF GOD" (ver. 14). "I will cast thee as profane out of the MOUNTAIN OF GOD" (ver. 16). TYRE, be it remarked, is close to Mount Lebanon, one of the most distinguished and elevated portions of the LAND OF ISRAEL.

Let us now pass over to Assyria, the north-eastern boundary of the land, and we shall find a country, equally with Tyre, spoken of as being in the immediate neighbourhood of "Eden," or "the Garden of God," and also as being connected with Lebanon. Thus, in Ezek. xxxi., the Lord, by the prophet, addressing the king of Egypt (to the south-west of the Land of Israel) speaks of Assyria, at the north-eastern border, saying—

"Behold the Assyrian,
 A cedar in Lebanon, with fair branches, and with a shadowing shroud,
 And of an high stature ; and his top was among the thick boughs ;
 The waters made him great.
 The deep set him up on high,
 With her rivers running round about his plants ;
 And sent out her little rivers unto all the trees of the field."—ver. 3, 4.

"The cedars in the GARDEN OF GOD could not hide him.
 Nor any tree in the GARDEN OF GOD was like unto him in his beauty.
 I have made him fair by the multitude of his branches,
 So that all the trees of EDEN that were in the GARDEN OF GOD envied
  him."—ver. 8, 9.

"I made the nations to shake at the sound of his fall,
 When I cast him down to hell with them that descend into the pits.
 And all the trees of EDEN, the choice and best of Lebanon,
 All that drink water, shall be comforted in the nether part of the
  earth."—ver. 16.

Then, speaking of Pharaoh himself, the prophecy concludes (ver. 18) :—

"To whom art thou thus like in glory and in greatness among the trees
 of EDEN ?

> Yet shalt thou be brought down with the trees of EDEN;
> Unto the nether parts of the earth:
> Thou shalt lie in the midst of the uncircumcised,
> With them that be slain with the sword.
> This is Pharaoh and all his multitude, saith the Lord God."

Thus are the trees of EDEN and of Lebanon spoken of, as if the same thing were meant by either expression; and thus is the case of Assyria illustrated to Egypt, by imagery derived from THE GARDEN OF GOD, which as we suppose lay between them, and the advantages of which highly favoured position they both in part enjoyed. Even with regard to that portion of this intermediate space which is now most remarkably under the curse, it is said (Gen. xiii. 10), "And Lot lifted up his eyes, and beheld all the plain of Jordan, that it was well watered everywhere, before God destroyed Sodom and Gomorrah, even as the garden of the Lord, the land of Egypt, as thou comest unto Zoar." Even more eastward in the land of Arabia, Mount Horeb is called "the mountain of God," and the ground there was said to be "holy ground" (Exod. iii. 5). There the Lord condescended to speak with man, and there the law was promulgated and the tabernacle set up; and there it was that the rod of Moses drew water from the rock to give drink to the hosts of Israel; a pledge that streams will yet abundantly refresh that burning desert, when claimed by their King as belonging to the portion of Israel.[1]

As being situated between Assyria and Egypt, THE LAND

---

[1] In the Egyptian "Hymn to Amen" (composed about B.C. 1400), on No. 17 of the Boulaq Papyri, ver. 3, has been thus translated by M. Mariette:—"Supporter of affairs above every good; in whose goodness the gods rejoice; to whom adoration is paid in the great house; crowned in the house of flame; whose fragrance the gods love; when he comes from Arabia; prince of the dew, traversing foreign lands; benignly approaching the Holy Land (Palestine or Arabia)."

of Israel is most centrally placed with regard to all other lands: on the side of Egypt all Africa being stretched out from it to the south and west; on the side of Assyria the still greater portion of our hemisphere in Asia; and Europe on the other hand, from every part of which it is not too much to suppose that highways will yet be cast up, whereby an easy conveyance will be prepared for all to flow unto it—" to the name of the Lord, to Jerusalem" (Jer. iii. 17). Hither these highways can most conveniently converge, supposing them to reach out unto Africa. See "*Title Deeds of the Holy Land*," p. 96.

Westward, by the Mediterranean, Syria and Palestine have not only a connection by sea with the coasts of Africa and Europe, but also with the great Atlantic Ocean; and thereby with America, the more distant portion of our globe to the west.

South-eastward of the Land, we have the Red Sea, by which we reach out to the great Indian Ocean, and thereby gain Australia and New Zealand, the counterpart of South America, as the islands northward are of the West India Islands, and as the eastern part of Asia, if separated from the westward portion, would be the counterpart of North America. Beside these, we have the Persian Gulf stretching out to the coasts of India and China.

We must indeed see that THE LAND OF ISRAEL is most centrally placed. Here our brethren in America, Australia, New Zealand, the Cape of Good Hope, and India, may most conveniently meet with the inhabitants of Britain, the sunburnt Indian with the inhabitants of Iceland, and the wanderer of the desert with the children of Erin's green isle. Without any of them feeling as if he went far from his home to meet his brother, the inhabitants of all countries may here join in sweet fellowship. Where the Most High hath appointed, may most appropriately be placed the throne of universal empire; and however widely scattered may be their possessions, this is best fitted for being the common *home* of the human race.[1]

The MIND that appointed this, when the relations of this land to the more distant parts of the globe were to man unknown, must have been that of our Father in heaven—the God of that grace which was hence sent forth to collect "the scattered" into one (Ezek. xxxiv. 12, 13)—the God of that glory which shall be enjoyed when He shall reign as described, Ps. xlvii. 8, 9 :—

" God reigneth over the heathen (גוים *Gōyim*);
God sitteth upon the throne of His holiness:
The princes of the peoples (עמים *Ammim*) are gathered together;
The people (עם *Am*) of the God of Abraham:
For the shields of the earth belong unto God;
He is greatly exalted."

When Israel were about to be given possession of this land under that covenant which they almost immediately and continuously broke, it was thus characterised (Deut. viii. 7-10) :—

" The Lord thy God bringeth thee into a good land (ארץ *eretz*).
A land of brooks of water,
Of fountains and depths
That spring out of valleys and hills;

" A land of wheat and barley,
And vines, and fig-trees, and pomegranates;
A land of oil-olive and honey;
A land wherein thou shalt eat bread without scarceness.

---

[1] *Canon Tristram* found on Hermon "two English winter birds, with the horned lark of Persia, the chough of the Alps; and, just below, a finch related to the Himalayan birds, and a warbler related to the Central African *Dessonornis*."

> " Thou shalt not lack anything in it:
> A land whose stones are iron,
> And out of whose hills thou mayest dig brass.
> When thou hast eaten and art full,
> Then thou shalt bless the Lord thy God,
> For the good land that He hath given thee."

Naturalists have said that the fecundity of this land was owing to "several circumstances; such as, the excellent temperature of the air, which was never subject to excessive heat or cold; the regularity of the seasons, especially the former and latter rain; and the natural fatness and fertility of the soil, which required no manuring.

"It was famous for its large and delicious grapes;[1] for its palm-trees and dates; and for its balsam-shrubs, which produced the celebrated balm of Gilead; for the constant verdure of its fruit-trees, its citrons, and oranges. Its vines yielded grapes twice, and sometimes thrice, in the year. Its honey was abundant. Its inhabitants cultivated sugarcanes with great assiduity: their cotton, hemp, and flax, were mostly of their own growth, and manufacture. Its vicinity to Lebanon afforded them an ample supply of cedar, cypresses, and other stately and fragrant trees. They fed large herds of cattle, and flocks of sheep; and their hilly country afforded them, not only variety and plenty of pasture, but also abundance of water, which descended thence into the valleys and lowlands, which it fertilised. They had plenty of fish; and they had salt, which *Galen* affirms to have been preferable to any other. The fecundity of Palestine has been extolled, even by Julian the Apostate; who frequently, in his epistles, mentions the perpetuity, excellence, and abundance of its fruits and produce."—*Rees' Cyclopedia.*

Such was the land, even after it had lost the bloom of

---
[1] See "Watchmen of Ephraim," vol. i. 323.

Eden; but now, the visible effects of the Divine displeasure have been so long upon it, that the far greater part is reduced to a mere desert; and the author who supplies the foregoing description, concludes by saying, "If we were to judge by its present appearance, nature itself has rendered it incapable of cultivation." This is exactly correspondent to what was prophesied would be the case during the scattering of "the holy people." Lev. xxvi. 43:—

> "The land also shall be left of them,
> And shall enjoy her Sabbaths,
> While she lieth desolate without them."

Immediately before this (ver. 42), the Lord hath said,

> "Then will I remember My covenant with Jacob,
> And also My covenant with Isaac,
> And also My covenant with Abraham will I remember;
> And I will remember the land."

Then will that land which hath indeed been made "utterly desolate" be again and far more abundantly found blooming with beauty and teeming with plenty. One of the principal means of blessing seems to be its being cleft with rivers, preceded by an earthquake "such as was not since men were upon the earth, so mighty an earthquake and so great." Compare Rev. xvi. 18 with Isa. xxx. 25; Ezek. xxxviii. 20, xlvii. 1-12; Joel iii. 16-18; Zech. xiv. 4, 8; Ps. xlvi. 1-4. This will be upon the approaching Restoration, when it has again been carefully cultivated and rendered fruitful far beyond what it now is. Then will the despot of the north, having gathered to him "many nations," come up to make a prey of the restored and prosperous people. This earthquake, such as the Jews had previously experienced in the days of King Uzziah, although disastrous to the enemy, will be the cause of blessing to Israel. The land is to be lifted up, and the valley into which the Mount of Olives had been rent is to be the bed of the river; which like that of EDEN is to go forth eastward to water the GARDEN OF GOD. Thus it is said, Zech. xiv. 8-10,

> "And it shall be in that day that living (or *running*) waters shall go out from Jerusalem;
> Half of them towards the former sea (*as flowing in the valley eastward*):
> And half of them towards the hinder sea (or *Mediterranean*);
> In summer and in winter shall it be.
> And the Lord shall be King over all the earth:
> In that day shall there be one Lord,
> And His name One.
> All the land shall be turned as a plain,
> From Geba to Rimmon, south of Jerusalem:
> And it shall be lifted up, and inhabited in her place."

Doubtless this lifting up will of itself help to lift the land out of its burning barrenness into a temperature more conducive to health.

> "And there shall be no more utter destruction,
> But Jerusalem shall be safely inhabited."

The same matters are also foretold explicitly by Joel in the end of his prophecy, ch. iii. 9-18:

> "Assemble yourselves and come all ye heathen (כל הגוים, *Kol-ha-Gōyim*)
> And gather yourselves together round about;
> Thither cause thy mighty ones to come down, O Lord;
> Let the heathen (הגוים, *Ha-Gōyim*) be wakened,
> And come up to the valley of Jehoshaphat (*the Lord shall judge*),
> For there will I sit to judge all the heathen (כל הגוים, *Kol-ha-Gōyim*) round about."

The valley of Jehoshaphat lies between the Mount of Olives and Jerusalem; and is thus the more immediate scene of that awful convulsion intimated in Zechariah, in which the Mount of Olives is to be cleft in twain. Then are the wicked, as it were, cut down, and thrown into "the great wine-press of the wrath of God" (ver. 13-18),—

> "Put ye in the sickle, for the harvest is ripe:
> Come, get you down, for the vats overflow,
> For their wickedness is great.
> Multitudes, multitudes, in the valley of decision:
> For the day of the Lord is near in the valley of decision.
> The sun and the moon shall be darkened,
> And the stars shall withdraw their shining.
> The Lord also shall roar out of Zion,
> And utter His voice from Jerusalem;
> And the heavens and the earth shall *shake:*
> But the Lord will be the hope of His people,
> And the strength of the children of Israel.
> So shall ye know that I am the Lord your God,
> Dwelling in Zion, My holy mountain;
> Then shall Jerusalem be holy,
> And there shall no strangers pass through her any more.
> And it shall come to pass in that day
> That the mountains shall drop down new wine,
> And the hills shall flow with milk,
> And all the rivers of Judah shall flow with waters,
> And a fountain shall come forth of the house of the Lord,
> And shall water the valley of Shittim."

The same river and the paradisaical character of its banks, are still more minutely described in Ezek. xlvii.: as the preceding events, connected with the destruction of the despot of the north and all his multitude, at the time of the great earthquake and grand deliverance of Israel, are described in xxxviii. 20, 21, and xxxix. 21, 22:—

> "All the men that are upon the face of the earth,
> Shall shake at My presence,
> And the mountains shall be thrown down,
> And the steep places shall fall,
> And every wall shall fall to the ground.
> And I will call for a sword against him,
> Throughout all My mountains, saith the Lord God:
> Every man's sword shall be against his brother."

"And I will set My glory among the heathen (בגוים, *ba-Gōyim*),
And all the heathen (בל־הגוים, *Kol-ha-Gōyim*) shall see
My judgment, that I have executed,
And My hand that I have laid upon them.
So the house of Israel shall know
That I am the Lord, their God,
From that day, and forward."

The same things are frequently adverted to in Isaiah, as in ch. xxx. 25, 26:—

"And there shall be upon every high mountain,
And upon every high hill,
Rivers and streams of water,
In the day of the great slaughter,
When the towers fall."

—Here it is added, that a wonderful change shall also take place in the atmosphere, so that,—

"The light of the moon shall be as the light of the sun,
And the light of the sun be sevenfold,
As the light of seven days,
In the day that the Lord bindeth up the breach of His people,
And healeth the stroke of their wound."

So also, speaking of the great deliverance of Israel, it is said (ch. xxxiii. 20, 21):—

"Look upon Zion!
The city of our solemnities;
Thine eyes shall see Jerusalem a quiet habitation,
A tabernacle that shall not be taken down;
Not one of the stakes thereof shall ever be removed,
Neither shall any of the cords thereof be broken."

The same things are frequently adverted to in the book of Psalms. Thus, in Ps. xlvi., after describing the great earthquake by which "the mountains are carried into the midst of the sea," and during which "the God of Jacob" is found a sure Refuge for His people, the discovery of blessing is made:—

"A river!
The streams whereof shall make glad the city of God,
The holy place of the tabernacles of the Most High!"

The destruction of the enemy, and consequent deliverance and peace of Israel are in the same Psalm described as taking place at that time.

In this land was Adam placed in innocence, and Israel when "holiness to the Lord." In this land did both Adam and Israel break the Covenant whereby they held possession, and thence were they both driven to till the common ground; and because of the sin of the one and of the other "hath the curse devoured the earth." In this land did the Prince of Glory condescend to bear the shame, here will He condescend to bear the glory, and sway His sceptre over the renewed earth. As yet will be accomplished that which is written, Isa. ii. 2-5,—

> "And it shall come to pass in the last days,
> The mountain of the Lord's house shall be established
> In the top of the mountains,
> And shall be exalted above the hills;
> And all nations (כל הגוים, *Kol-ha-Gōyim*) shall flow unto it,
> And many peoples (עמים, *Ammim*) shall go and say, Come ye,
> And let us go up to the mountain of the Lord,
> To the House of the God of Jacob,
> And He will teach us of His ways,
> And we will walk in His paths;
> For out of Zion shall go forth the Law,
> And the Word of the Lord from Jerusalem.
> And He shall judge among the nations (הגוים, *ha Gōyim*),
> And shall rebuke many peoples (עמים, *Ammim*);
> And they shall beat their swords into plough-shares,
> And their spears into pruning-hooks:
> Nation shall not lift up sword against nation (גוי אל גוי, *Goyi-el-Goy*),
> Neither shall they learn war any more.
> O house of Jacob, Come ye,
> And let us walk in the light of the Lord."

Then, through the same redeeming love whereby the outward blessings have been recovered, will Israel be given an inward beauty and moral fruitfulness correspondent to the goodness which the Lord will manifest to the mountains and plains, the streams and the sea-coasts of the land which had been promised to their fathers, and which are to be given in everlasting possession (Hos. xiv. 4-7):—

> "I will heal their backslidings,
> I will love them freely:
> For Mine anger is turned away from him.
>
> "I will be as the dew unto Israel:
> He shall grow as the lily,
> And cast forth his roots as Lebanon.
>
> "His branches shall spread,
> And his beauty shall be as the olive-tree,
> And his smell as Lebanon.
>
> "They that dwell under his shadow shall return:
> They shall revive as the corn, and grow as the vine,
> The scent thereof shall be as the wine of Lebanon."

We are apt to look upon the terms "earth" and "world" as exactly synonymous. They appear, however, in several parts of Scripture to have a considerable distinction of meaning. The Hebrew word (ארץ, *eretz*), from which it is likely our *earth* is derived, seems to be more specially applied to that distinguished portion of the globe which is so much the subject of promise. The term תבל, *thevel* or *world*, seems not to be so applied, except when the other parts of the globe are meant also to be included.

The two are distinguished both as to creation and redemption. In Ps. xc. 2, God is said to have "formed the EARTH and the *world;*" and in Ps. xxiv., referring to the Lord's return when He comes to claim His own, it is said, "The EARTH is the Lord's, and the fulness thereof; the *world*, and they that dwell therein." It is upon the "EARTH," more especially, that the physical changes preparatory to the establishment of the Millennial kingdom are to take place, as intimated in Isa. xxiv. The *eretz*, earth or land, will be dreadfully convulsed; after which the dry deserts will be found well watered, and blooming with perennial beauty. At the close of the Millennium, not only will the barren land have been thus recovered from barrenness, but great revolutions having also occurred in the world abroad, the very sea will be made to give way to scenes of greater beauty and more full of goodness to man. Then, as is expressed in Rev. xxi. 1, " there shall be no more sea."

It is before that time of the *world's* entire recovery, and at the commencement of the Millennium, that the LAND OF ISRAEL is to be so entirely changed, which, it is intimated (Heb. xi. 8-16), was clearly understood by the Patriarchs. Abraham is there said to have been called to "go out into a place which he should *afterwards* receive for an inheritance;" and "he sojourned in the Land of Promise as in a strange country." It was indeed the Land of Promise,—the time was not yet come for possession. To the Patriarchs it was as yet only "a strange country," wherein at that time they sought no permanent dwelling; and there Abraham with Isaac, heirs of the same promise, dwelt in " tabernacles."

Abraham looked for something farther than was yet in the land. " He looked for a city which hath foundations, whose builder and maker is God." These Patriarchs, it is expressly said, "all died in faith, not having received the promises, but having seen them afar off; and were persuaded of, and embraced them, and confessed that they were strangers and pilgrims on the earth. For they that say such things, declare plainly that they seek a country." They looked for a more blessed state of things than was then to be enjoyed. They looked for the land as it shall be, when the will of God shall be done on earth as it is in heaven. "They desired a better country, that is, a heavenly: wherefore God is not ashamed to be called their God," as if He had failed in His promise to them; for even after they had died without having received the promises, He still calls Himself *their* God,—"the God of Abraham, Isaac, and Jacob;" and why? Because He will perform to them the promises. "*He hath prepared for them a city,*" "the New Jerusalem that cometh down from God out of heaven," and which is to be the seat of dominion under the whole heaven. Then will Abraham be found "the heir," not merely of the land, but also "of the world." The promise of THE LAND may indeed be said to imply that of *the world;* just as the possession of a throne implies the possession of the empire over which that throne is placed.

It is remarkable, that a spot so eminently fitted for being the throne of universal empire should never yet have been so occupied by any of the great powers which since the rise of the Assyrian Empire have aimed at the sovereignty of the world. True these three great states of ancient times—Tyre, Egypt, and Assyria—were on its several bounds; but the eligibility of the land itself seems not to have been observed.

THE ASSYRIAN, with a force like that of his own mighty river, swept over it, carrying away the house of Israel captive (2 Kings xvii. 23), and threatening also the destruction of Judah. But he stayed not in the land, and left only the wreck of some conquered nations in the place of captive Israel.

THE BABYLONIAN came next, and completed the removal of the people of promise, by taking away Judah also (2 Kings xxiv.) But he seems not to have thought of occupying this glorious position, from which to issue his arbitrary mandates to " all people, nations, and languages, that dwell upon the face of all the earth."

The Medes and Persians next bore sway. They gave so far release to Judah, as to allow him to return to the the land of his fathers (Ezra i. 3), not thinking that they were thus parting with the throne of the world.

The Macedonian conqueror passed over the land of Israel as one not knowing its value, and took up his abode in Babylon, which was to be destroyed. Three of the great kingdoms into which his empire was divided bordered upon this land—north, south, and east; but though much disturbed by two of these, Egypt on the south and Syria to the north, still the throne of the earth was left comparatively empty.

The Romans came next, throwing their desolating wings over the oppressed Jews, and at length filled with desolation the land of Immanuel. But they thought not of making this the throne of their glory, although ultimately they removed the chief seat of their empire eastward as far as Byzantium. These two last, the Macedonians and Romans, as coming by sea and drawing the people out to them, seem to have been the "fishers" that it was prophesied (Jer. xvi. 16) would "fish" Israel out of their land.

Afterwards came "the hunters" who were to "hunt" them. These were the Arabians or Saracens on the one hand, and the Turks on the other. The former swept over it from south to north; and northward erected some principal seats of their empire, as in Bagdad and Aleppo. The Turks "hunted" from east to west, as far as Constantinople (anciently Byzantium), where they erected the throne of that empire which is now tottering to its fall.

It is remarkable that although these nations have in

their turn trodden Jerusalem under foot, and have in all directions swept over the land to further conquests, yet none of them have in truth enjoyed it; and it is as remarkable, that the only kingdom of Jerusalem which has been at all set up since the expulsion of the Jews, is that of the Franks at the time of the Crusades; the only enterprise in which all the Western nations ever fully united. The land, however, was not then prepared for Israel, nor were they prepared for it; and their wisdom will be to wait their being given possession of it through the power of the blood of Jesus.

But doubtless one of the practical results to which our present inquiry should lead, is that a people in Christ have a right to initiate proceedings in this matter, and that they who ought to do this without fear are those whom Providence has of late years brought so remarkably into connection with it, and to whose political, commercial, and more enduring interests, as well as those of the world generally, it is of importance that it should be well occupied.

And when the Lord has accomplished His word to His people,—

> "They that be of Thee shall build the old waste places;
> Thou shalt raise up the foundations of many generations;
> And Thou shalt be called The Repairer of the breach,
> The Restorer of paths to dwell in,—

—when a people spread out to "all the ends of the earth," but especially having their dwelling in the West and their kingdoms in the East, with the Euphrates for a highway whereby they can more rapidly communicate with these; when this people, who already have one of their highways through Egypt and by the Red Sea, have their other highway on the side of Assyria, and when they see to the proper occupation of the land lying between, then will be given additional confirmation to God's prophetic word, which will be an assured sign of the still more important events which are to follow.

So long as Christians despise the birthright, and attribute to the natural birth that which can only come through the being made one with the Son of God, so long must there be comparative darkness, confusion, and weakness. But let the men of Ephraim in Christ exercise the right of the "First-born" (Jer. xxxi. 8), for the benefit of the whole household of God, and then comes the fulfilment of that word (Isa. xviii. 3) :—

> "All ye inhabitants of the world (תֵל *thevel*), and dwellers on the earth (אֶרֶץ *eretz*), see ye ;
> When He lifteth up an ensign on the mountains,
> And when He bloweth a trumpet, Hear ye."

Then will the Lord "set up an ensign for the nations (גוֹיִם *Gōyim*), and assemble the outcasts of Israel, and gather together the dispersed of Judah from the four corners of the earth" (אֶרֶץ *eretz*) (Isa. xi. 12).

IV.

THE PROMISES MADE TO THE FATHERS.

Possession of the Promised Land not to be had through the Law, but in Christ, Rom. iv. 13-18.—Calling of Abraham.—What is meant by "the Seed," to whom the Land was absolutely promised?—The One Seed, Christ.—Whether of Ishmael, or of Isaac, was to come the Multitudinous Seed?—The Three Birthright Blessings distinctly specified, and written in the Names of the Three Great Receivers of the Promises, Gen. xxii.—Promises to Isaac, Gen. xxvi. 2-4.—Isaac Blessing Jacob.—Jacob's Vision at Bethel, and Interview with the Angel of the Covenant.—The Multiplicity more particularly conferred upon the House of Joseph and Tribe of Ephraim.—The returning Prodigal.—Unquestionable evidences of possession of the Birthright Blessings possessed by the Rejoicing Multitude, Rev. vii.

It is worthy of remark that, unlike the Covenant made with the people of Israel, the Promises made to their Fathers were unconditional. As marking this distinction, the Apostle Paul thus argues:—"The promise that he (*i.e.*, *Abraham*) should be the heir of the world, was not to Abraham, or to his seed through the law, but through the righteousness of faith. For if they which are of the law be heirs, faith is made void, and the promise made of none effect" (Rom. iv. 13-18). Why? Because the law utterly failed of securing the heirship to Israel. In place of doing this, "it worketh wrath; for where no law is, there is no transgression. Therefore it is of faith, that it might be ty grace; to the end the promise might be sure to all the seed—not to that only which is of the law (such as the Jews who retained the Mosaic ritual), but to that also which is of the faith of Abraham;" who was justified by a faith which he had before circumcision. The main portion of Abraham's descendants of the House of Israel (who, at the time the Apostle wrote, had been 700 years out of the Land) were already in circumstances similar to his own; and, unknown as Israel, in uncircumcision have been growing up into the promised "multitude of nations." So the Apostle here takes notice, that it was said to Abraham, "I have made thee a father of MANY NATIONS."

"He is the father of us all before Him whom he believed;" although, to the view of *man*, the literal accomplishment of the prophecy has not taken place. Ephraim, the seed of Abraham, of whom the promised "multitude of nations" was emphatically to come, has been accounted dead or non-existent; but God "quickeneth the dead, and calleth those things that be not as though they were" (Rom. iv. 17). Abraham "against hope, believed in hope, that he might become the father of many nations, according to that which was spoken, So shall thy seed be"— *i.e.*, "as the stars of heaven for multitude." And we shall presently see that this was spoken of the "multitude" of a natural seed, even as contrasted with one adopted.

The Promises made to the Fathers, with respect to the heirship of the world, are thus recognised in the New Testament as still standing; and they are "sure to all the seed" of Abraham having faith in the promised Messiah, whether they belong to the circumcision or to the uncircumcision; to the Jews within the wall of separation, as well as to the "branches" of Joseph which have "run over the wall" (Gen. xlix. 22). The blessing is more directly to ISRAEL; and through them to other nations. Our business, therefore, is still with "the Promises made unto the Fathers, Abraham, Isaac, and Jacob."

The first Promise which seems to refer to the ultimate fulfilment spoken of in John xi. 52, when shall be gathered "together in one the children of God that were scattered abroad," is recorded Gen. xii. 1-3: "Now the Lord had said unto Abraham, Get thee out of thy country, and from thy kindred, and from thy father's house, unto a land that I will show thee: and I will make of thee a great nation. And I will bless thee, and make thy name GREAT"—such was the meaning of the name which he then bore; Abram, *Great* or *High father*, or *father of the High One*. "And thou shalt be a blessing: and I will bless them that bless thee, and curse him that curseth thee; and in thee shall all the families of the earth be blessed." The seed of Abram were to have an intimate, powerful, and ultimately a most beneficial influence upon all the families of mankind. Through their instrumentality other nations were to be blessed. Their commission to bless extended to "all the families of the earth;" and those who refused participation in their blessings were to wither away before them. This is their calling from the beginning, of which He who knows the end from the beginning (Isa. xlvi. 10) will not "repent."

Abram obeyed the call of Jehovah, and came into the Land of Canaan (v. 7); and the Lord appeared unto him, and said, "UNTO THY SEED WILL I GIVE THIS LAND." This Promise is full, free, and altogether unconditional. It may be observed that it is intimately connected with the former, that in his seed all the families of the earth would be blessed, that being the most advantageous position from which streams of blessing could be diffused over all the world.

There may be some question as to what is meant by the seed of Abram here spoken of. Is it an individual or many; an adopted or a natural posterity? This is plainly answered in Gal. iii. 16: " Now to Abraham and to his seed were the promises made. He saith not, And to seeds as of many; but as of One, and to thy seed, which is Christ."

To CHRIST then the Land was promised. He is the Head, and only in Him can the Inheritance be enjoyed by the multitudinous seed. None can come into possession except as being viewed in Him. "THOU art worthy," sing the four Living Creatures, and the twenty-four Elders (Rev. v. 8, 9). HE only is worthy to claim the Inheritance, having truly acted the part of a Kinsman Redeemer. But although it is to ONE that the Land is given, yet many come into the enjoyment of it through Him. And, accordingly the song thus concludes:—

"THOU hast made us unto our God kings and priests (Exod. xix. 6): AND WE SHALL REIGN ON THE EARTH."

The question then comes to be whether this multitudinous seed, viewed in the ONE SEED CHRIST, is the *natural* posterity of Abram, or merely an *adopted* family? Abram's circumstances at the time he received the Promise seemed to offer nothing but an adopted heir. The doubt, however, was resolved for him (Gen. xv.) He had been complaining that merely one born in his house was to be his heir. The Lord answers (ver. 4, 5), "This shall not be thine heir; but he that shall come forth out of thine own bowels shall be thine heir. And He brought him forth abroad, and said, Look now toward heaven, and tell the stars, if thou be able to number them: and He said unto him, So shall thy seed be." The Lord evidently distinguishes between a natural and a merely adopted seed, and points to the *multiplicity* of the seed as in contrast to mere human expectation at the time. It is added, "And he believed in the Lord, and it was accounted unto him for righteousness." Abram looked forward to the promised inheritance through the right of the ONE Promised Seed, through whom alone either he or any of his numerous progeny could come into the promised possession; and he stood accepted in Him whose day he saw afar off, and in seeing which he rejoiced (John viii. 56).

A farther distinction is made in Gen. xvii., where the *multiplicity* of the seed is particularly dwelt upon. (ver. 3-6), "And Abram fell on his face, and God talked with him, saying, As for Me, behold My covenant (ברתי *Brithi*) is with thee, and thou shalt be a father of many nations. Neither shall thy name be any more called Abram, but thy name shall be called ABRAHAM; for a father of MANY nations have I made thee. And I will make thee exceeding fruitful; and I will make nations of thee, and kings shall come out of thee."

Then with regard to the *continuance* of God's favour towards the posterity of Abraham: "And I will establish my Covenant between Me and thee, and thy seed after thee, in their generations, for an everlasting Covenant, to be a God unto thee, and to thy seed after thee" (ver. 7). Having through all their changes followed them with His everlasting love, He brings them at last into the Promised Inheritance: "And I will give unto thee, and unto thy seed after thee, the land wherein thou art a stranger; all the land of Canaan for an everlasting possession, and I will be their God" (ver. 8).

Now, the question is, Were this numerous posterity with whom the Lord was to be always, and who were ultimately to be given possession of the Land, to come of Ishmael who had already been born to Abraham—whose posterity is now known to be extremely numerous, and who may be said to have long had actual possession of the Land? Abraham himself seems to have had scarcely any other expectation. But what saith God? "SARAH thy wife shall bear thee a son indeed, and thou shalt call his name ISAAC; I will establish My Covenant with him for an everlasting Covenant, and with his seed after him. My Covenant will I establish with ISAAC, whom Sarah shall bear unto thee at this set time in the next year."

Thus explicit is the promise with regard to the many nations to come, not of Ishmael, however numerous his posterity might be, but of that very son Isaac which should be born of his wife Sarai the following year. And the name of Sarai, *my princess*, is changed to Sarah, THE PRINCESS, as if she was to be the mother in common of those who should inherit the Promises; just as Abram is changed to Abraham, THE FATHER OF A MULTITUDE—"a multitude of nations."

That these Promises might be made doubly sure, God confirmed them with an oath (Gen. xxii. 16-18). Abraham having in purpose offered up his son Isaac—a type of the offering up of the Son of God, the Heir of the Promises by whose death they are all confirmed (Romans xv. 8)— the God of Truth condescended to address him thus:— "By Myself have I sworn, saith the Lord . . . that in blessing I will bless thee, and in multiplying I will multiply thy seed as the stars of heaven, and as the sand which is upon the sea shore; and thy seed shall possess the gate of his enemies; and in thy seed shall all nations (כל גוי *Kol Goyii*) of the earth be blessed."

Here then the three birthright blessings are distinctly

promised to Abraham. These are, the MULTIPLICITY, or double portion; the KINGSHIP, or place of rule; and the PRIESTHOOD, or being made the medium of blessing. The double portion is expressed in the first of these promises, which speaks of the immense multiplicity of the race; while the language in which it is conveyed intimates that they would possess the more elevated portions of the earth and also the sea-shore. And the Land of Promise is one in which they may indeed most eligibly possess this double portion, being most centrally placed as regards both land and water.

The second of these Promises respects the PLACE OF RULE—the Kingship—which is expressed by saying his seed should possess "the gate of his enemies." It was in the gates of the cities that people in old times held their councils and exercised rule. To "possess the gate of the enemy" was thus synonymous with overturning his councils and possessing his power. Now it may be observed that the great enemies of Israel—the Babylonians, Medes, Greeks, and Romans—all proceeded from the north. These empires composed the Great Image described in Dan. ii., as well as the Assyrians who had previously ravaged the Land, and led away the main portion of the people into the north country, where they multiplied as promised, were given possession of "the gate of their enemies," and have gone out by it unto all parts of the world (Mic. ii. 13.)

The third Promise regards the PRIESTHOOD. This seed promised to Abraham is to be the means of conveying blessing unto all the nations of the earth. This is emphatically said of Christ; but it is also true of the other seed of Abraham, who are heirs together with him of the Promise (Gal. iii. 39). Already have these nations who so wonderfully multiplied in the north, and who have been given so far the "gate" of their enemy, been made the instruments of conveying the glorious gospel of the grace of God unto "all the ends of the earth." All blessings are in the first instance put into their hands; through them to be distributed among the nations. "The children of Belial" are here also, and try to mar this ministry. Still the blessing is conveyed through Israel, and this we are given cause to hope will be yet much more abundantly.

These three Promises were written in the names of the three great receivers thereof. The first, referring to their multiplicity, is written in the name ABRAHAM, *the father of a great multitude*, who had also been called Abram, or *high father*. The second, regarding the supplanting and possession of power, is written in the name of his grandson JACOB, *a supplanter*, and ISRAEL, *Prince of God*, or *great prince*. And the third, regarding the communication of blessing, the making known "the good tidings of great joy unto all people," is expressed in the name of Abraham's own son ISAAC, i.e. *laughter;* at whose birth his mother said, "God hath made me to laugh; all that hear will laugh with me."

To ISAAC the Promises were confirmed which had been thus so unequivocally given to Abraham (Gen. xxvi. 2-4).

"And the Lord appeared unto him, and said, Go not down into Egypt; dwell in the land that I shall tell thee of. Sojourn in this land, and I will be with thee, and I will bless thee; for unto thee, and unto thy seed, I will give all these countries. And I will perform the oath which I sware unto Abraham thy father; and I will make thy seed to multiply as the stars of heaven, and I will give unto thy seed all these countries; and in thy seed shall all the nations of the earth be blessed."

Here, again, the Multiplicity, the Dominion, and the

Power of Blessing are expressly connected with the seed of Abraham in the line of Isaac.

But Isaac had two sons, both of the same mother, and born at the same time. Which of these was heir of the Promises? Neither are we here left in doubt. Even before they were born the blessing was promised to JACOB. Isaac wished it in preference to be conveyed to Esau; but his purpose was overruled, and, although by means we cannot altogether approve, the blessing descended to the child of Promise. It is a wonderful example of Divine faithfulness triumphing over human infidelity: of Isaac to his God; of Rebekah to her husband; and of Jacob to his brother. JACOB seems to be a type of the supplanting seed of Abraham who have come into the possession of blessing meant by God for them, but by the human bestowers for another.

And this is the blessing wherewith Isaac blessed Jacob, supposing him to be Esau (Gen. xxvii. 28, 29):—

> "God give thee of the dew of heaven,
> And the fatness of the earth,
> And plenty of corn and wine.
>
> "Let people serve thee,
> And nations bow down to thee.
> Be lord over thy brethren,
>
> "And let thy mother's sons bow down to thee.
> Cursed be every one that curseth thee,
> And blessed be he that blesseth thee."

The heirship of the World is here most distinctly given to JACOB's posterity, even as distinguished from that of Esau, his own twin-brother.

In Gen. xxviii. 12-15, the Promises made to Abraham and Isaac, and which had been unintentionally conveyed to Jacob, are all confirmed to him in a vision which he had of the glorious kingdom of Messiah, and to which our

Saviour seems to allude when, speaking with Nathanael who had made confession of His being the King of Israel, He says, "Hereafter shall ye see heaven opened, and the angels of God ascending and descending upon the Son of man." Here it is said that, Jacob having lighted on a certain place, he took of the stones for his pillows,[1] and laid him down to sleep:

"And he dreamed, and behold a ladder set upon the earth; and the top of it reached to heaven; and behold the angels of God ascending and descending on it. And behold the Lord stood above it, and He said—

> "I am the Lord God of Abraham thy father,
> And the God of Isaac;
>
> "The land whereon thou liest,
> To thee will I give it,
> And to thy seed;
> And thy seed shall be as the dust of the earth;
>
> "And thou shalt spread abroad,
> To the West, and to the East,
> And to the North, and to the South."

This is the very order in which the seed of Israel seem to have spread: first to the West, and then latterly to the East; first to the North, and lately more emphatically to the South. And now seems to be dawning that which is here again said, "And in thee and in thy seed shall all the families of the earth be blessed." Then as regards the good Providence of God until all these things should be accomplished (ver. 15):—

> "And, behold, I am with thee,
> And will keep thee in all places whither thou goest,
> And I will bring thee again into this land,
> For I will not leave thee,
> Until I have done that which I have spoken to thee of."

---

[1] See England, the Remnant of Judah, by Rev. F. R. A. Glover, Longmans.

Notwithstanding all appearances, we believe that God has been true to His promise, in making Israel the subject of His peculiar care (Deut. xiv. 2; 1 Peter ii. 9). He will never leave them until the kingdom of grace be consummated in glory.

At the same place (Bethel, or *House of God*) the Lord met with Jacob on his return from the north country where he had served for a wife (Gen. xxxv. 9-12): "And God appeared unto Jacob, when he came out of Padan-aram, and blessed him. And God said unto him, Thy name is Jacob; thy name shall not any more be called Jacob, but ISRAEL (or prince of God) shall be thy name; and He called his name ISRAEL. And God said unto him, I am God Almighty."

When Israel returns with his numerous posterity, the kingdom under the whole heaven shall be given them. When God has been inquired at to do for them what He hath promised—when they have "wrestled" to obtain the blessing they shall indeed in fulness be made princes in all the earth (Ps. xlv. 16). God condescends to pledge His great Name that He will accomplish these Promises, and adds—

"Be fruitful and multiply;
A nation, *and a company of nations, shall be of thee,*
And kings shall come out of thy loins;
And the Land which I gave Abraham and Isaac,
To thee will I give it,
And to thy seed after thee will I give the Land."

But Jacob had twelve sons. To which of these were the Birthright Promises made? Or were they all made alike to each? They belonged, by the right of custom, to Reuben, the first-born, but, from moral considerations, were taken from him and distributed among three of his brethren. The Priesthood was given to LEVI. The Kingship to JUDAH, of whom, according to the flesh, came Christ, to whom "every knee shall bow." The Double Portion—the Multiplicity—was given to JOSEPH, whose name means *increase;* to which there is abundant reference both as to the number of his posterity, and the amplitude of their possessions, in the blessing which Jacob pronounced upon him, as recorded Gen. xlix. 22-26—

> "JOSEPH is a fruitful bough,
> A fruitful bough by a well;
> *Whose* branches run over the wall :
>
> "The archers have sorely grieved him,
> And shot at him,
> And hated him :
>
> "But his bow abode in strength,
> And the arms of his hands were made strong
> By the hands of the Mighty God of Jacob;
>
> "By the name of the Shepherd, the Stone of Israel;
> By the God of thy father, who shall help thee;
> And by the Almighty, who shall bless thee :
>
> "With blessings of heaven above,
> Blessings of the deep that lieth under,
> Blessings of the breasts and of the womb.
>
> "The blessings of thy father have prevailed
> Above the blessings of my progenitors,
> Unto the utmost bound of the everlasting hills :
>
> "They shall be upon the head of Joseph,
> And on the crown of the head of him
> That was separated from his brethren."

Compare Deut. xxxiii. 13-17. The blessing in its amplitude as to the Double Portion, the Multiplicity of the seed, and all correspondent blessings either in the high places of the earth, or as being masters of the "deep that croucheth beneath," like a camel of the desert ready to convey with speed whithersoever the governor listeth : the full blessing, and blessings beyond those of his progenitors, Jacob here pronounces upon the head of JOSEPH.

It is remarkable, that not only was the blessing more emphatically conveyed to Joseph, but also that between his two sons, Manasseh and Ephraim, a distinction again was made (Gen. xlviii. 3-7). EPHRAIM, the younger, and the meaning of whose name is *I will bring forth fruits*, had the fruitfulness more particularly promised unto him by Jacob; who having referred to the first great Birthright Blessing, the *Double Portion*, as being his in the promise of God, and naturally belonging to Reuben his first-born, or to Simeon his next eldest son, expressly adopts them into its enjoyment. And he blessed JOSEPH, and said—

> "God, before whom my fathers, Abraham and Isaac, did walk,
> The God which fed me all my life long unto this day,
> The Angel which redeemed me from all evil,
>   Bless the lads;
> And let my name be named on them,
> And the name of my fathers, Abraham and Isaac,
> And let them grow into a multitude in the midst of the earth."

The Hebrew expression used in the last part of this blessing implies that they would grow *as fishes do increase*, sending off colonising shoals, as has been the case with regard to the people spoken of in the north country. Thus worthy would they be of the name of their father JOSEPH— *adding* or *increase*.

The line in which was to come the great Multiplicity is still more distinctly pointed out, for when Joseph perceived that his father had crossed his arms, so as to put the right hand upon the head of the younger in place of upon that of Manasseh, he wished to correct the supposed mistake; but his father who had evidently been guided by inspiration in the act, as well as in the words, refused and said (ver. 19 compare with 1 Chron. v. 1, 2; Jer. xxxi. 9)—

> "I know, my son, I know;
> He also shall be a people,
> And he also shall be great;

> But truly his younger brother shall be greater than he;
> And his seed shall become A MULTITUDE OF NATIONS."

Is it so, that a multitude or fulness of nations hath come of this so-called lost portion of the house of Israel? These are *not* mere idle words. And, let it be considered, that "a multitude of nations cannot indeed well be hid in a corner;" nor are they. The same word is translated both "*multitude*" and "*fulness.*" Put *Gentiles* for "nations" (and the words in the translation are used indifferently), and then we have Paul's very expression when, speaking of Israel in Rom. xi. 25, he says, that "blindness, in part, hath happened unto Israel, until the FULNESS OF THE GENTILES (or Nations) be come in"—*i.e.*, until that fulness or "MULTITUDE OF NATIONS," promised by Jacob to come of Ephraim, be brought forth, and are introduced into the Christian Church. "And so ALL ISRAEL shall be saved."

Paul fully recognises the truth of God with regard to Israel, looking far on into futurity, and at the same time tracing back the procedure of God from the days of old when He had called them, and since which He had ever been bestowing upon them gifts according as they were able to bear His kindness, he at length bursts into that exclamation of wonder and praise with which he concludes his reasonings in Romans ix., x., xi., respecting the darkness then hanging over this people. Looking beyond all the troublous darkness to Israel, as coming up "out of the Great Tribulation," and as fully accomplishing their destiny, he exclaims—

> "O the depth of the riches,
> And of the wisdom,
> And knowledge
> OF GOD,
> How unsearchable are His judgments,
> And His ways past finding out!

> "For who hath known the mind of the Lord?
> Or who hath been His counsellor?
> Or who hath first given to Him,
> And it shall be recompensed to him again?
> For of HIM,
> And through Him,
> And to Him are all things;
> To whom be glory for ever—Amen."

It is not necessary that Joseph's posterity should hitherto have been known as Israel. Joseph was not known in Egypt as a son of Jacob, when the Lord made him "fruitful in a strange land." Nay, he had previously called the name of his first-born "Manasseh," as having himself *forgotten* all his toil, and all his father's house.

There was evidence, however, to convince his father and his brethren that Joseph found in Egypt was the very same Joseph who had by his brethren been thought of as lost, and by his father believed to be dead. And, as we shall see, there is abundant evidence to prove equally the identity of his descendants in the "north country," out of which they are as really to be brought as were their fathers out of Egypt.

Under the former dispensation JOSEPH was not a remarkably "fruitful bough." It was through the cross, as being joined to the "Root of David," that Ephraim was to become worthy of his name, "*I will bring forth fruits.*" The kingdom taken from the Jews under the law was, according to the gospel, to be given to "a nation bringing forth the fruits thereof" (Matt. xxi. 43). To what we call the Anglo-Saxon race in these "isles afar off," and hence spread out to all "the ends of the earth," has been given the unspeakable privilege of distributing the Scriptures to all the families of mankind in their own languages. It is ours to testify for Christ and against Antichrist; to proclaim liberty to the captive, and point all men everywhere to the means of health, cure, and blessing. No people have been so liberally dealt with by the God of Providence, whether in respect to material gold, or that which gold represents, or that which is better than gold—the true riches—" His word, His statutes, and His judgments to Israel " (Ps. cxlvii. 19, 20).

Our ancient laws, political constitution, and ecclesiastical arrangements afford evidence of our having been under the training of Moses, and of having been punished and otherwise dealt with as Ephraim was to be when cast out among the Gentiles. To us belongs the responsibility of using aright the privileges of " the first-born." We should have confidence in Him who has so appointed, thank God, and go forward.

And this is how we may best prove our Birthright: by returning in humble penitence to our Father, confessing our unworthiness and guilt in the words of Jer. xxxi. 18, 19, Luke xv., and by learning to be like the Son of God, eminent in self-denying service for the glory of God in the good of man; by acting as Joseph did towards his brethren in Egypt, and as the men of Ephraim did to the Jewish captives who were brought into Samaria (2 Chron. xxviii. 12-15; Luke x. 30-35).

God's great purpose in separating Israel to Himself, as we have seen, was to make them instrumental in conveying good to others. When He promised that Abram should be " the father of a great nation," and be given a great name, the purpose for which this great nation should come into being, and be given this extensive influence was declared in what follows, " And thou shalt be a blessing." THE POWER PROMISED WAS A POWER TO DO GOOD.

When it was intimated that others should have blessing or curse, success or defeat, according as they helped or hindered "the people of the God of Abraham," it was that the law of love might have free development among all mankind. This was the promise: "In thee shall all the families of the earth be blessed." And thus the call of Abraham's posterity was the very opposite of a selfish, narrow pre-eminence. Their "greatness" was to be a GREATNESS OF SERVICE, the widest possible manifestation of the divine power in bestowing blessing through whatever means God might be pleased to work.

This, then, is our Birthright: THE WILL TO WORK FREELY FOR OTHERS; not as either slaves or hirelings, but as the freeborn sons of God in Christ, doing whatsoever our heavenly Father may give us to do for the good of others.

When ISAAC was born, whose name means "*laughter*," his mother, as if in prophetic anticipation, said, "God hath made me to laugh; and all that hear shall laugh with me" (Gen. xxi. 6). ISAAC'S POSTERITY WERE TO CONVEY THE GLAD TIDINGS OF GREAT JOY TO ALL PEOPLE. Unto them were to be entrusted the Oracles of God; not that they might hide these precious talents in a napkin, but that they should open them out for the joy of all the earth.

When Isaac was received back as from the dead, and the Lord was pleased to confirm His promises to Abraham, this was the climax: "And in thy seed shall all the nations of the earth be blessed" (Gen. xxii. 18). All nations are to be made blessed in Christ. And this is the unspeakable happiness of the children of faithful Abraham: THAT BEING FOUND IN CHRIST, THEY ARE NOT ONLY CAUSED TO REJOICE, BUT ARE ALSO GIVEN THE PRIVILEGE OF DIFFUSING HIS JOY ABROAD AMONG ALL NATIONS.

And when, in the lonely solitude of Bethel, with "the stone" for his pillows, and a fugitive from his father's house, long before the birth of any of his children, possession of the Central Land was promised to JACOB, and a wide diffusion therefrom—west, east, north, and south—this is contemplated as the purpose for which Israel was to be raised up and spread abroad: "And in thee and in thy seed shall all the families of the earth be blessed" (Gen. xxviii. 14). THOSE WHO ARE IN CHRIST ARE TO BE FOUND AS HE WAS IN THE WORLD: GOING ABOUT DOING GOOD. If thus found, there is no occasion to ask, "Who is their father?" Undoubtedly they are "the Children of Promise" and "Heirs of the Kingdom."

It is remarkable that in Rev. vii., after the sealing of the limited number "from Juda and his companions" (Ezek. xxxvii. 16), we have the description of another company, who may most clearly be recognised as possessing the three Birthright Blessings promised to ABRAHAM in the line of ISAAC, then in that of JACOB, and, more particularly as to the Double Portion, to the house of JOSEPH in the line of EPHRAIM, the chief of those tribes that had been called "Lost," and which were by the Assyrians carried into the same quarter whence the modern possessors of Europe have come.

First, As to the Multiplicity promised to Abraham, and written in his name: "After this I beheld, and lo, a GREAT MULTITUDE, WHICH NO MAN COULD NUMBER, OF ALL NATIONS, AND KINDREDS, AND PEOPLES, AND TONGUES."[1]

Second, As to their having SUPPLANTED their enemies, and come into the place of honour and power, expressed in the names Jacob and Israel, it is said that they "stood before the Throne, and before the Lamb, clothed with white robes, and PALMS IN THEIR HANDS." They are brought near unto the Supreme, the Source of all Blessing, and are given the tokens of VICTORY.

[1] Watchmen of Ephraim, ii. 56.

Third, As is promised in the name ISAAC, they are full of REJOICING, and call upon all to rejoice with them. Their song is the most blessed which the heart of man can conceive. They "cried with a loud voice, SALVATION TO OUR GOD THAT SITTETH ON THE THRONE, AND UNTO THE LAMB."

Here are the people possessing the Blessings of "the First-born."[1] Although EPHRAIM, who was appointed to the Birthright, is omitted as to a *limited* number previous to the Great Tribulation, we are not to suppose that therefore he had *no* sealed servants of God, correspondent thereto; and it is worthy of remark that the description given of these by the Elder consists of exactly twelve lines, arranged in threes, after the manner of Hebrew poetry, as if they had reference to "the twelve tribes scattered abroad," but which are at the time referred to gathered out of "all nations, and kindreds, and people, and tongues" into the enjoyment of the Blessings of the First-born—

" These have come out of the Great Tribulation,
And have washed their robes,
And made them white in the blood of the Lamb:

" Therefore are they before the throne of God,
And serve Him day and night in His Temple;
And He that sitteth on the throne shall dwell among them.

" They shall hunger no more,
Neither thirst any more;
Neither shall the sun light on them, nor any heat.

" For the Lamb which is in the midst of the throne shall feed them,
And shall lead them unto living fountains of waters;
And God shall wipe away all tears from their eyes."

---

[1] This seems to be that which is called in Heb. xii. 23, "The General Assembly and Church of the First-born, which are written (or enrolled) in heaven."

V.

THE TRAINING AND EDUCATION OF THE PATRIARCHS.

Israel's close Connection with the Three Grand Families of Mankind.—Mingling of Races.—Parental Influence upon Offspring exemplified in the case of Abraham's Posterity.—Care as to the Physical Properties of the Chosen Race.—Religious, Intellectual, and Moral Training of Abraham, Isaac, Jacob, Joseph, and his Brethren.—Of Israel, in Egypt, in the Wilderness.—Conscience.—Accuracy of Measurement and Detail, &c.—Resemblance of Ancient Egyptian Furniture to that of the English.—Anglo-Saxon Chaldron, Ark of the Covenant, &c.—Whence?

HAVING chosen a particular family whereby to exercise a most extensive influence among mankind; having appointed them the most advantageous position from which to dispense to all the ends of the earth the blessings of which in the first place they were to be made partakers; having indubitably secured unto them by reiterated promise the Blessings of the First-born; having chosen Israel to be the "cord, or cable, of His inheritance," the instructors of mankind, and the declarers of His glory unto the nations, the Most High dealt with them accordingly. He brought them "near unto Himself," led them about, and instructed them (Deut. xxxii. 10. As a tender parent with a child, He "took them by the arms, and taught them to go," gradually strengthening them for the service in which they were afterwards to be engaged for their heavenly Father and their brethren of mankind.

He brought them into every variety of situation, thereby

continually enlarging their experience, and giving them a sympathy with universal nature. He qualified them for all climes, and for meeting with every condition of life; for laying hold upon all instrumentality, and for seizing upon every medium through which blessing might be conveyed unto the whole family of Adam.

One of the principal means of improving a people, as well as of enlarging its sympathy, is intercourse with others. The connection of the chosen race with the three Grand Families of mankind is remarkable. The three first generations on both the father's and mother's side were entirely of the race of Shem; but afterwards their connection with the descendants of Ham seems to have been very intimate—Joseph having married an Egyptian princess, and Judah a Canaanitess. Such also seems to have been Tamar, the mother of Phares and Zara. A wholesome restriction was put upon this intercourse. Still it seems to have gone forward, and must have had a considerable influence upon the race, adding to the superior intellectual and moral constitution possessed by the original stock, that strength of domestic affection for which the descendants of Ham are remarkable. Afterwards they were led out, as we shall see, among the more vigorous Japhetic race in the north country, to have the needful energy given to their intellectual power, and those sentiments and affections which they previously possessed.

It is a fact now abundantly ascertained, not only as to the inferior animals and plants, with regard to which the principle has long been acted upon, but also in respect to the human race, that in many cases the dispositions and attainments of the parents have a most important influence upon the capacity and habits of their offspring. The laws which regulate this influence are not yet clearly defined, but there can be no doubt as to the general principle, implied in the very first truths of our religion, in which the moral and intellectual constitution of man is recognised as having been grievously injured by the fall of Adam, our first father.

When we speak of the influence of parents upon their children previous to birth, we must distinguish between natural capacity and special divine grace. We speak now of the natural capacity and disposition; and subordinate although this be to the other, still it is of vast importance to the happiness of the individual, as well as to his usefulness in society. Even where children are of the same parent, there is often a striking coincidence between the varying disposition of the parent, and the permanent character given to his different children. Thus Ishmael, born to Abraham after his conflict with the kings at the valley of Shaveh, has given birth to a race delighting in war; whilst Isaac, born to him in his old age, after his long training and discipline, except in one grand instance, manifested much of that subdued and pious character of mind which might have been expected. And if, as some have supposed, the Brahmins be the descendants of Abraham by Keturah, they most remarkably manifest the self-possession and willingness to sacrifice the affections through religious motives which were so conspicuous in him at the time of his offering up his son Isaac (Gen. xxii.) In them the principle has been misapplied, but the natural feeling may be regarded as the same.

In the choice of the progenitors of the chosen race, even physical strength and beauty were not unattended to. The health of Abraham and Sarah appears to have been sound. The various journeys of Abraham, and the multifarious duties to which he had to attend, must have required a strong physical constitution, and may also have tended to increase it. His agility is remarked, as in the case of entertaining the angels, and the successful pursuit of the captors of his kinsman Lot. The beauty of his wife Sarah, and of Rebecca the beloved wife of Isaac, and of Rachel the best beloved wife of Jacob, is very particularly and repeatedly noticed. And, as in the case of Joseph, of whom the multitudinous seed was to come, we find that this beauty was not lost to the children of these mothers of Israel. From many parts of Scripture we learn that the daughters of Israel were fair and comely; and much is recorded even with regard to the children of Judah, whose beauty is not so much spoken of as is that of Joseph (Lam. iv. 7).

The means taken to preserve health of body, and to season, strengthen, and attune the physical powers, were remarkably adapted for the purposes intended, and certainly argue in the Guide and Lawgiver of Israel a full knowledge of the natural laws. But these we do not now dwell upon.[1] If personal beauty and bodily activity and strength were attended to in choosing the fathers and mothers of this peculiar people, much more may we expect attention would be paid to the improvement and invigoration of their moral and intellectual constitution.

One of the first lessons ABRAHAM had to learn was the proper exercise of *Faith*—an immediate dependence upon the guidance and protection of the unseen God. He was called to go out, "not knowing whither he went" (Heb. xi. 8), nor how he was to be supported and preserved, otherwise than as the Almighty would vouchsafe.

At the same time, the faculty of *Hope* was brought into most healthful exercise, by the many precious promises

[1] See "Laws of Moses" in Watchmen of Ephraim, vols. ii., iii.

given respecting his seed, and especially with regard to Messiah's " day " (John viii. 56), which he was permitted to see afar off; his possession of the Land wherein he was a stranger, and of that " city which hath foundations, whose Builder and Maker is God " (Heb. xi. 10).

Veneration was given abundant occasion for exercise, not more by the need he had for patient submission to the will of God during long delay, and the trials which God in His sovereignty allowed him to endure, than by the call for rejoicing devotion to Him by whom he was ever so signally delivered and so abundantly blessed.

The sentiment of *Justice* was nourished by the sacrifices he was enjoined to offer, as pointing forward to the sacrifice of God's beloved Son for the sins of guilty men. And lessons of *Truth* were equally impressed upon him by his being shown the folly of duplicity, as in denying his wife, and by his Great Teacher so wonderfully fulfilling His word to himself.

By this divine goodness also was *Benevolence* instructed, and in its exercise was he encouraged by his being privileged to entertain " angels unawares." To crown all, he was taught *patience* in waiting, and *perseverance* in action, by his ultimate though long-delayed success. True *dignity*, yet humble and delighted *obedience*, as being made of one mind with the Most High God, who condescended to have fellowship with him, might therefore be expected to characterise Abraham.

At the same time, his INTELLECT must have been greatly cultivated by his being led into such a variety of scenes and circumstances. His *knowledge of localities* must have been greatly enlarged by his travels into such a variety of countries. *Individuality*, or power of observing and distinguishing objects, was given exercise by coming into contact with various nations, as well as with so many individuals. The productions of nature and art in the different countries through which he passed would also help to keep this important mental power abundantly employed.

He must have been well acquainted with civil affairs, and we see that he was neither unskilled in diplomacy, nor unsuccessful in war, although only for the sake of peace does he seem to have turned his attention to the sword. It is likely he had astronomical knowledge with him from Egypt and the east; and in Damascus and Egypt, and the smaller states between, he had opportunity of becoming well acquainted with the arts and their various productions.

Causality must have been well employed in learning the ways of God, which were so much unfolded to him; and *Comparison* in illustrating these to others, while commanding "his children, and his household after him, that they should keep the way of the Lord to do justice and judgment" (Gen. xviii. 19). His powers of intelligence and reflection, no less than the higher sentiments, must indeed have been greatly cultivated; all which training seems to have been not for his own advantage only, but clearly also for the benefit of his numerous posterity, on whose account he was called ABRAHAM—"the father of a multitude"—"a great and mighty nation," through whom all the nations of the earth were to be blessed. It was not until his mind had attained the maturity which all this training was calculated to afford, that Isaac, in whom his seed was to be "called," was born.

In ISAAC there seems to have been a repetition of many of the same trials and travels; the same exercise of faith, hope, veneration, justice, benevolence, and firmness. Many of the very same incidents happened in his case which had occurred to his father; and perhaps, therefore, less is said respecting him. If we may be allowed the expression, in him there seems to have been a conning over the lessons taught to his father. His life passed in greater quietness, and in a calm cultivation of personal piety and of the domestic affections, until their waywardness led him to destroy that domestic peace which he so much valued, by his endeavour to thwart the purposes of God as to the bestowment of blessing.

In addition to the faculties already mentioned in JACOB, another useful class was called into play. He was early called upon to exert *prudence* in the preservation of his life from the wrath of his brother, after he had by stealth procured the Blessing, and also in the acquisition, preservation, and management of his property, as well as in preventing mischief in his numerous family, and assuaging disputes when they arose. The *wisdom* he was thus called upon to exercise, no less than the virtues taught to his fathers, was necessary to be possessed by a people who were to supplant every other, and be made "princes in all the earth;" justifying their title to the two names given to their father, JACOB, "a *supplanter*," and ISRAEL, "a *prince of God.*"

Jehovah seems to have manifested Himself less immediately to man in the case of JOSEPH and his brethren; but He is equally instructive by His providence. What a powerful lesson of virtue is given in JOSEPH, as triumphing over all the unkindness and powerful treachery of brethren and of strangers! Separated from his father's house, and his true origin unknown, he is put into a position of returning good for evil, and of being a succour in trouble to those who had appointed him to death and sold him into bondage.

His firm resistance to the seducements of sin prepared for his being given the control of all that was possessed by the most polished nation then in the world; at the same time, we are shown how his over-faithfulness to Pharaoh, in making the Egyptians slaves for a morsel of bread, is rewarded upon his own posterity, who, under the descendants of these same Egyptians, were long afterwards subjected to cruel bondage. God overruled even that for good. Previously the chosen race had only been accustomed to pasturage or tillage; but as they were designed to plant "cities," and dwell in them, it was necessary they should become more concentrated than could be allowed in pastoral life.

By the position in which JOSEPH was placed in Egypt, where so much depended upon his management, the *Imaginative* or Conceptive powers had been greatly called into exercise, and his power of *planning* seems almost to have developed to the degree of abuse at the time his brethren arrived first in Egypt. Not only was it useful he should be given much exercise of that inventive and improving genius for which his descendants were to be so remarkable, but it was also requisite that the race generally should be broken in, so as to perform the duties and labours of more settled life. Accordingly they are laid hold upon by the Egyptians, and are taught by them those arts which it was now requisite for them to possess, such as making bricks, building cities, &c.[1] They are trained

---

[1] At the Egyptian Hall in London in 1843, there was an exhibition of Egyptian furniture made more than 3000 years before, so very similar to our own household articles—such as chests of drawers, chairs, sofas, tables, &c.—that an English house could have been quite easily furnished from that celebrated country, where Joseph was once the honoured governor, and raised to the highest dignity in that great nation, the cradle of science and general knowledge.

to industry and hardship. By their previous way of life they had acquired a strong physical constitution, and now it is given abundance of exercise, profitable at least to their posterity, if not immediately to themselves. Their moral feelings are at the same time educated, as becoming acquainted with "the heart of a stranger;" so that when given a land of their own, they might know how to deal with him, as they themselves would have chosen to be dealt with in the same situation.

Their patient waiting upon God for the accomplishment of His promises is put to a severe trial. At length God makes bare His holy arm, and seizes upon the simplest means—the rod of a shepherd—to break the sceptre of Egypt, and clear a way for the oppressed through all the difficulties wherewith they are surrounded. They are taught the justice, wisdom, and power of Jehovah, in His safely leading Israel, His "first-born," through the deep, whilst "the enemy sank as lead in the mighty waters." After being taught all the wisdom, and made to *feel* all the power of Egypt, they are made to *see* all such to be of no avail in contravening the purposes of the God of Israel.

In the WILDERNESS another course of training commenced connected with their future destiny. In the most minute particulars they are instructed in their religious, social, and personal duties. They are led about, and habituated to military discipline. They are taught alike personal cleanliness and holiness of heart. They are trained to put away everything hurtful or unseemly, and to be considerate of each other's welfare and happiness. They are given a body of political institutions remarkably calculated to teach them order, and train them up for independence, for the enjoyment and preservation of their public and individual rights. They are initiated into the forms of a popular government, and by the division of their nation into tribes they are taught the principles of the confederation of states.

It may be observed that up to this time there had been a gradual development of the principles of government, according as they were called for by the condition of the people. In the infancy of the race, whilst as a family they lived under Abraham, Isaac, and Jacob, the PATRIARCHAL principle prevailed. Upon the death of Jacob, when twelve brethren were left pretty equal in authority, the ARISTOCRATIC form of government may be said to have existed; and this rule by elders being the heads of families seems to have continued till Israel were brought out into the wilderness, where the DEMOCRATIC principle was added to their political constitution (Deut. i. 9–18). Then were the whole people commanded to "look out from among themselves good men and true," who should be appointed as officers, "rulers of tens, of fifties, of hundreds, and of thousands;" so that every matter, great or small, might be instantly attended to and put to rights by those in whom they had confidence, who, understanding the affairs of the persons they represented, had wisdom to direct, and were men known to have integrity to act according to the best of their knowledge and judgment.

Here also they were given a body of religious rites remarkably calculated to lead them into a minute knowledge of both nature and art. They could not make those distinctions as to clean and unclean animals, and the various parts of the same animal—as to different plants, spices, and ointments—as to metals and precious stones—without becoming extensively acquainted with natural history. And by their regularly recurring Festivals they could not but become well accustomed to chronological and astronomical observation.

At the same time, the acquisitions made in Egypt were not lost. Perfection in the arts was called for in the construction of the Tabernacle and its various important contents, in making dresses for the priests, engraving stones, compounding ointments, and working variously in wood and precious metals. They are taught to work for the Lord, and to feed at His hand. At once do they see Him as the God of Creation, Providence, and Redemption; by whom the ordinary laws of Nature are overruled that the people He had ransomed from the hand of the enemy might be delivered and sustained. God is their Lawgiver, Governor, Judge, and Guide; "a Wall of Fire around them, and the Glory in the midst of them" (Zech. ii. 5).

There, in the quiet of the Desert, with all the world shut out, that so their attention might be the more entirely concentrated upon the words of their Great Teacher, and the visible representations of spiritual truths, which they were as yet too carnal, too much in childhood, otherwise to learn, and which it was important should be impressed upon their imaginations with all the solemnity, brightness, and power that now accompanied them: God drew near, and was Himself their Teacher. What simple sublimity in the scene! How full of meaning the words that were uttered!

The grand course of God's procedure in Providence and Grace is set before them both by word and lively emblem; as when (Exod. xxxiv. 6), hid in a cleft of the rock, their leader saw thus the God of Israel passing by, and proclaiming, "The Lord, the Lord God, merciful and gracious" —which He was at the first advent of His Son, and by the bestowment of His Spirit; and "long-suffering" during the backslidings and wanderings of both the houses of Israel, until His second appearing, when He shall be seen as " abundant in goodness and truth."

The same things were expressed in grand scenic representation when the High Priest with the blood of the Atonement was seen entering into the Most Holy Place, to appear in the presence of God for the people, who were standing without, waiting for his return; when he came forth, not clad in plain raiment as before, but " clothed in garments of glory and beauty, to bless the people in the name of the Lord." So our Great High Priest, the Lord Jesus Christ, after having " entered into the Holiest of All not made with hands," and " not with the blood of others," but with His own blood, though now gone to " appear in the presence of God for us," will, to those who look for Him, appear the second time in glory and in majesty, fully to bestow the blessing He hath gone to procure.

The power of tracing analogies, so essential to them as the intended instructors of mankind, was thus given the highest cultivation. And the whole of their *Reflective faculties* were brought into healthful exercise in thinking upon all that the Lord had done, was doing, and would do with them. They are taught the origin of the world and the past history of man, to see sin as the cause of all evil, and the goodness of God as the source of all good to man. They are put to school to learn in lively emblems the justice and mercy of God, and the future history of their nation and of the world.

Their *sense of Propriety* is educated in the most profitable manner by the minute attention they are taught to pay to the holy service of religion—to useful, social, and most wholesome private observances. The *Observing powers*, which take notice of proportions and measure

F

distances, were especially useful to them as being intended to become the Lord's cable or measuring-line (Deut. xxxii. 9), to compass sea and land for the extension of the divine goodness among men, and the bringing all parts of the world into one grand interchange of blessing.

The provision made for the cultivation of their mental powers is abundantly manifest when, in reading the books of Moses, we observe the minute attention which was to be paid to every sort of measurement, as in the making of the Tabernacle and its contents.

It may justly be questioned whether there be a single profession, trade, art, or science with regard to which profit may not be derived from the diligent perusal and thorough understanding of the Pentateuch. It is short of the truth to suppose that these books had in view only the inculcation of one truth, however important that may be. Evidently Israel in the Wilderness were in a grand course of training and development with regard to everything requisite—whether belonging to their physical, moral, or intellectual constitution—in order that they should be eminently "a seed to serve the Lord," and be strong for labour in diffusing blessings among men.

[Evidently something more than has generally been taken for granted was intended and accomplished by the residence of Israel in Egypt. Where and when did the Anglo-Saxons obtain their chaldron wheat-measure of the time of Edgar the Peaceable, A.D. 959, by the 'quarter' of which their descendants sell wheat to the present day? Certain it is that it is of identically the same capacity as the Hebrew Ark of the Covenant, and the Laver as well as the Coffer found in the King's Chamber of the Great Pyramid of Jeezeh. Modern research has prepared many to appreciate the significance of such an important element in the training of Israel as a lengthened residence in the immediate vicinity of the "immortal sermon in stone," erected apparently for the transmission to latest time of the great moral, astronomical, prophetical, and metrological secrets of which the righteous king, priest, and prophet had been made the depositary.[1]]

[1] See Our Inheritance in the Great Pyramid, by C. Piazzi Smyth, 2d edition, 1874. Isbister & Co.

VI.

TRAINING OF ISRAEL UNDER THE JUDGES AND KINGS.

Balaam's Prophecy—The Three Grand Principles of Government successively developed—Israel in the Land, under the Judges, and the Kings—All have failed, in the very respects in which they excelled—Israel Trained to Maritime Affairs, preparatory to going forth among the nations—God's Purposes with regard to Israel, and for which He had been training them, not accomplished during their former residence in the Land—Will be fully accomplished in the Promised Kingdom—The Good Samaritans.

WE have shown the fitness of the LAND OF ISRAEL for being the seat of universal dominion, and the important fact that, although the Great Empires have all possessed this part of the globe, yet none of them have used it for the purpose for which it is so universally fitted. As our Saviour shows (Matt. xxii. 32) the Promises to the Fathers imply the resurrection, they never having been given possession of the Land whilst they lived. Even a small portion of it for a burying-place Abraham had to obtain by purchase; yet after they were all dead, God calls Himself "the God of Abraham, of Isaac, and of Jacob," intimating that He would be true to the promises made to these men, and which He could only be as raising them from the dead; "for He is not the God of the dead but of the living." Preparatory to this full and permanent possession of the Land great revolutions were to occur therein; previously to which Israel, as intimated by MOSES, were to be moved off from it, and hidden among the nations till the calamities were overpast; after which they were to be manifested, collected, and led back (Deut. xxxiii.)

This recovery of Israel, their clear enjoyment of the gospel but doubtful belief of the prophecies, together with their previous state as being sown in these countries after their dispersion, and previous to that again in the partial possession of the Land of Israel after the conquest thereof, under Joshua down to the first coming of Christ, even BALAAM their enemy, who was hired by the King of Moab to curse them, declared as plainly as their leader Moses had foretold their sin and its punishment, which have been so long and so strikingly apparent.

BALAAM delivered four several prophecies, the first of which seems to refer to Israel's *latter end;* when, after their hiding and dispersion among the nations in the north, they were to come up in the promised power to the Land of their fathers. This prophecy was delivered in Kirjath-huzoth—*i.e., the city of streets*—and from the high places of Baal, that thence he might see "the *utmost* of the people" (Num. xxii.–xxiv.)

"And he took up his parable, and said, Balak, the King of Moab, hath brought me from Aram, out of the mountains of the east, saying, Come, curse me Jacob; and come, defy me Israel. How shall I curse whom God hath not cursed, and how shall I defy whom God hath not defied?" And, as if catching a glimpse of the people in their long hiding in the north country, when they were to be lost to the view of the world, he exclaims, *"For from the top of the rocks I see him, and from the hills I behold him."* Notwithstanding all their scattering, and being to appearance lost among the Gentiles, after all, *"Lo, the people shall dwell alone, and shall not be reckoned among the nations!*" And now is fulfilled the promise made to Abraham, and written in his name, "*Who can count the dust of Jacob,*"—who have supplanted the nations,—"*and the number of the fourth part of Israel?*" referring to the house of Judah. And beholding the rising of the saints, and their gathering together unto Christ, to reign with Him in His Millennial Kingdom, he concludes, "*Let me die the death of the righteous, and let*"—or, so that—"*my last end be like his!*"

The *second* prophecy (Num. xxiii. 18-24) seems not to reach so far as the first, but rather to *Israel's state and prospects in the place of their hiding*, before the truth of the prophecy would have become fully apparent, and while men were in doubt as to whether God would indeed accomplish the promises.

> "Rise up, Balak, and hear;
> Hearken unto me, thou son of Zippor:
> God is not a man, that He should lie,
> Neither the son of man, that He should repent:
> Hath He said, and shall He not do?
> Or hath He spoken, and shall He not make it good?
> Behold I have received to bless;
> And He hath blessed, and I cannot reverse it,"—

notwithstanding all the temptation of the wages of iniquity. Then, referring to the justification of Israel through the blood of their Redeemer—

> "He hath not beheld iniquity in Jacob,
> Neither hath He seen perverseness in Israel
> The Lord his God is with him (or Imm-nu-l),
> And the shout of a King among them."

True, Israel is still comparatively in bondage to the kingdoms of the world, and in the place spiritually called Egypt, but

> "God brought them out of Egypt:
> He hath, as it were, the strength of an unicorn."

Every effort has been made to divide and lessen that strength, but

> "Surely there is no enchantment against Jacob,
> Neither divination against Israel.
> According to this time it shall be said of Jacob and Israel,
> What hath God wrought!
> Behold the people (עַם *Am*) shall rise up as a great lion,
> And lift up himself as a young lion :
> He shall not lie down till he eat the prey,
> And drink the blood of the slain."—(See Ezek. xxxviii.-xxxix.)

Balaam pronounces his *third* prophecy (Num. xxiv. 2-9) with his face toward the Wilderness, and seems to regard *Israel's flight into the north*, when they were sown along the rivers and coasts of Europe, according to the wise appointment of the God of Providence—

"And Balaam lifted up his eyes, and saw Israel abiding in tents according to their tribes, and the Spirit of God came upon him. And he took up his parable, and said—

"'*Balaam, the son of Beor, hath said, and the man who had his eyes shut, but now opened, hath said.*'"

It seems to be in allusion to the time of deafness and blindness prophesied of by Isaiah, in chapter vi. 10, that Balaam thus enlarges upon his qualifications—

"Make the heart of this people fat, and make their ears heavy, and shut their eyes, lest they see with their eyes and hear with their ears. Until the cities be wasted without inhabitant, and the houses without man, and the land be utterly desolate, and the Lord have removed man far away, and a great forsaking in the midst of the land."

> "He hath said which heard the words of God,
> And saw the vision of the Almighty, falling, but having his
>   eyes open :
> How goodly are thy tents, O Jacob,
> Thy tabernacles, O Israel !"

Even in the land of their captivity, and the place of their hiding, they are given favour and blessing—

"As the valleys are they spread forth, as gardens by the river's side,"—(such as those of the Rhine and the Danube)—

"As the trees of lign aloes which the Lord hath planted,
As cedar-trees beside the waters.
He shall pour water out of his buckets,
And his seed in many waters;
And his king shall be higher than Agag,
And his kingdom shall be exalted."

Then, pointing to an example of the power whereby the kingdom can be raised out of that comparatively low estate, he continues—

"God brought him forth out of Egypt;
He hath, as it were, the strength of an unicorn;
He shall eat up the nations, his enemies,
And shall break their bones,
And pierce them through with his arrows."

This he hath done in the destruction of the oppressive Romans, and other foes of Israel: "He couched, he lay down as a lion, and as a great lion," so that men knew not his place of hiding. "Who shall stir him up?" They perished in the attempt.

"BLESSED IS HE THAT BLESSETH THEE, AND CURSED IS HE THAT CURSETH THEE."

Balaam's *fourth* prophecy seems to refer to *the condition of Israel previous to their being entirely cast out of their own land*, as the *third* does to that *after* their dispersion, the *second* to the time *approaching* the close of their wilderness state, and the *first* to the period of their glorious *return*. Like the third, it refers to a period when Israel's eyes were closed; and accordingly he begins, as before—

"Balaam, the son of Beor, hath said, and the man who had his eyes shut;

> He hath said which heard the words of God, and knew the knowledge of the Most High,
> Saw the vision of the Almighty, falling, but having his eyes open."

(This period includes the first appearing of the Lord Jesus Christ, the Redeemer of Israel.)

> " I shall see him, but not now;
> I shall behold him, but not nigh:
> There shall come a Star out of Jacob,
>
> " And a Sceptre shall rise out of Israel,
> And shall smite through the princes of Moab,
> And destroy all the children of Sheth.
>
> " And Edom shall be a possession;
> Seir also shall be a possession for his enemies,
> And Israel shall do valiantly."

These seem to be the conquests of David, the distinguished type of the King of Israel, with regard to whom it is said—

> " Out of Jacob shall come he that shall have the dominion,
> And shall destroy him that remaineth of the city."

"And when he looked on Amalek"—whose name seems to have been given with reference to their being a kingly people—"he took up his parable, and said, Amalek, the first of nations; but his latter end that he perish for ever" (which has long since been accomplished).

"And he looked on the Kenites," whose name means *nest*, "and he took up his parable, and said, Strong is thy dwelling-place, and thou puttest thy nest in a rock. Nevertheless, the Kenite shall be wasted, until Asshur shall carry him away captive."

"And he took up his parable, and said, Alas! who shall live when God doeth this?" Even the house of Israel would then to appearance be made to cease. Yet would the Lord be mindful of them, and recompense vengeance to their enemies, whilst more fully removing them from off the Land. The first of the "fishers" who were sent to "fish" them are then alluded to (Jer. xvi. 16). "And ships shall come from Chittim, and shall afflict Asshur, and shall afflict Eber, and he also shall perish for ever," supposed to refer to the Greek expedition under Alexander the Great. See Lecture ii.

And every other power shall perish for ever that has afflicted Israel. "Thou shalt seek them, and shalt not find them, *even* them that contended with thee : they that war against thee shall be as nothing, and as a thing of nought." (Isa. xli. 12). "But Israel shall be saved in the Lord with an everlasting salvation : ye shall not be ashamed nor confounded world without end" (Isa. xlv. 17).

Having been duly prepared in the Wilderness, Israel are at length brought forward into the LAND, which is granted them according as required, and as they have a heart to take possession. Moses and Joshua are dead, but JEHOVAH their King liveth, and is Almighty. They lie exposed to their enemies, who surround them on every side, and give them continual occasion for the vigorous exercise of their minds in defence, and in the wise management of their national relations. Their enemies have no power, except when Israel themselves give it, by rebellion against their heavenly King. They are taught to depend upon the Almighty, who will infallibly protect them in the right, and punish them in the wrong. Their Judges are His officers raised up for the occasion. To them the nation must not look, but to that God who hath appointed them. If they look to man, they are disappointed and broken.

Now more especially the Lord is training them to go alone. Each individual is in a great measure made to think and act for himself. A more powerful or better consolidated government than that of the Judges might have given to the body of the people more strength; but it would not so much have braced their individual character, and the Lord was training them with regard to this much more than for the purpose of giving them present ease as a nation. It was to make them "a nation of kings and priests unto God" (Exod. xix. 5, 6; 1 Peter ii. 10; Rev. v. 10) that He had delivered them from their Egyptian task-masters; not that they should become useful instruments of one man, as under an absolute monarchy.

But they did not "consider their latter end," for which He was preparing them. They grew impatient of this state of things, and "required a king like the nations around them." He warned them of the evils into which they were plunging; but they were importunate, and "He gave them a king in His anger, and took him away in His wrath." They are again taught the folly of trusting in man. The king, who was to combine their scattered energies, and lead them forth successfully to battle, left them in the hands of the enemy.

But the Lord has another bright course of training for them, for which the concentrated form of a kingly commonwealth is better adapted, and David is raised up to execute this purpose of God. It would be difficult to name a single faculty of the human mind, affective or intellectual, which was not remarkably manifested in David, who from feeding his father's flock was taken to feed the flock of God, the people of Israel (Ps. lxxviii. 71).

His genius with regard to Music and Poetry was especially remarkable. To the beautiful appointments in the service of God addressed to the *eye*, chiefly ministered by Moses, he added those which were addressed to the *ear*, and no less necessary and instructive; and the songs of rejoicing are sung which anticipate the glory of Messiah's Kingdom, when the song of salvation shall resound throughout the world.

The character of David's powerful mind appears to have been indelibly impressed upon the nation. He was indeed an eminent type of the King of Sion, both in his sufferings and in his triumphs. DAVID, whose name means *beloved*, seems to have been eminently distinguished for reigning in the affections of his people. When this throne was taken from him, as by Absalom stealing away their hearts, he refused to remain on his throne in Jerusalem, and withheld himself therefrom until the people voluntarily called the king back (2 Sam. xix. 15). And the Redeemer will be given the throne of His father David in both respects: His people "shall be willing in the day of His power," when He shall "send the rod of His strength out of Sion" (Ps. cx. 3).

But the Kingdom of Messiah is to be eminently a Kingdom of Peace, and "Wisdom and Knowledge" will be the stability of His times (Isa. xxxiii. 6). The sapphire—heaven-assimilated—throne in which the King will reign over the earth is seated upon a body of brightness, like to the terrible crystal (Ezek. i., &c.) As if to represent this peaceful light, the true support of powerful love, Solomon, the peaceful prince and wisest of mortals, is raised up, to give the widest range to the observing, and the deepest tone to the reflective, faculties. He gives a grand example of the Temple of Knowledge to be filled with the glory of the Lord; and he is permitted to rear the TEMPLE at Jerusalem, that wondrous type, holding forth the great mystery of godliness, and embracing so many lessons of love and holiness.

Yet, as if to teach the utter folly of leaning upon an

arm of flesh, or of putting implicit confidence in any man in the things of God, this greatest king of Israel and wisest among men was allowed to fall into the very dregs of folly, and lead the way in the spiritual adultery of the nation. Also, by elevating the monarchy, he seems to have lowered the people as to their standing in the commonwealth, to have oppressed the nation he was appointed to protect, and whose capital he was gilding with foolish magnificence; thereby making it only a more tempting prize for the enemy.

Thus also was his father, "the man after God's heart," allowed to fall into the basest and most revolting crimes. Thus was Moses, "the meekest of men," guilty of the greatest impatience. Thus also do we find righteous and benevolent Joseph, the preserver of nations, guilty of one of the greatest public wrongs and most sweeping calamities—leading one of the most highly improved nations into a state of even personal slavery, and putting them into such a position as that any political change would be esteemed by them a gain. Thus was Jacob, so generally without guile, guilty of the grossest deception. Thus was pious and affectionate Isaac guilty of an attempt to frustrate the purpose of God, occasioning thereby the greatest domestic confusion and bereavement. Thus did faithful Abraham so little trust his God as even deliberately to deny his bosom companion. Thus was righteous Lot found halting, after being so signally delivered from Sodom. And thus was Noah also an object of shame to his own children, after resisting such a world of ungodliness, and being so wonderfully preserved from that destruction which overwhelmed it. How instructive is the history of the Patriarchs of Israel, and indeed of the world! How incessant in commanding us to "cease from man, whose breath is in his nostrils!" "Trust ye in the Lord for ever; for in the Lord Jehovah is everlasting strength!" and "Let him that thinketh he standeth, take heed lest he fall."

The Kingdom of Israel had been rapidly attaining to an elevated position among the nations, and had matters so progressed, it might have been supposed that now was come the expected glory. Men might have been in danger of mistaking the type for the thing typified. But it is only too plain that the purposes of God with regard to Israel were not at all accomplished or consummated whilst they were under the Kings.

The religious state of the people had greatly degenerated before the death of Solomon; and this being the case, their political prosperity could not long continue. Immediately after Solomon's death the kingdom was divided (1 Kings xi. 25-38). That house of which Christ, the One Promised Seed, was to come (Gen. xlix. 10), retained its attachment to the family of David; whilst the house of Ephraim, of which the multitudinous seed was to come (Gen. xlviii. 19), erected a new kingdom for themselves under Jeroboam. An ignoble termination was thus made to so glorious a beginning, plainly intimating that Israel had not yet arrived at the point for which they had been so long under training.

EPHRAIM was separated from Judah not only in a political, but also in a religious sense (1 Kings xii. 28). During the reigns of their respective kings, both houses were taught many severe lessons as to the unprofitableness of departing from God, although He was dealing with them in kindness, and preparing them for their different destinies. The "Jews," who were not designed to be a maritime people, but a kind of universal medium of communication among mankind by land, were given an entirely inland position; while ISRAEL, who were still more extensively to be a band of union to the human race, and were to be spread out unto the most distant "isles," were in the most careful manner taught maritime affairs, even from the time they entered Canaan; not only as possessing the small sea of Galilee, but also by their being placed along the eastern border of the Great or Mediterranean Sea, in connection with such perfect masters of those matters as were the inhabitants of Tyre and Sidon, by whom also already their architectural taste had been considerably improved (1 Kings vii. 13).

The keeping of cotemporary chronicles of their own and other nations, the art of war, the power of making expeditions by sea, of planting colonies, and of keeping up an extensive correspondence with distant parts of the world, were especially necessary. And all this was, in the kind providence of God, prepared for them before the final breaking up of their nation, when, for the misimprovement of their many great privileges, they were cast out, and left to become "wanderers among the nations" (Hos. ix. 17). They had been instructed in all that they could receive at home, and had now to go forth on their travels to learn in foreign countries that which they would not be taught at home. Let us not forget that they were thus to suffer for the good of others also. Their casting away was to be "the riches of the Gentiles," and their restoration "like life from the dead" (Rom. xi. 25).

> "He will have compassion upon us,
> He will subdue our iniquities,
> And Thou wilt cast all their sins into the depths of the sea.
> Thou wilt perform the truth to Jacob,
> The mercy to Abraham,
> Which Thou hast sworn unto our fathers from the days of old."
> —(Mic. vii. 19, 20.)

The most superficial view of the known history of ISRAEL may convince us, therefore, that they cannot be found an inferior, or even a stationary, people. They were ever in a state of transition, passing on from one lesson to a higher in the school of their Great Teacher. In them eminently was the saying to be fulfilled, "Train up a child in the way he should go, and when he is old he will not depart from it." See Deut. xxxii., xxxiii. Their symbols are the cedar, the olive, and the palm-tree, which all bring forth fruit in old age. "They shall be fat and flourishing, to show that the Lord is upright, my Rock, and no unrighteousness in Him" (Ps. xcii.)

"This people have I formed for myself,
They shall show forth my praise."

They were "vessels of mercy afore prepared unto glory" (Rom. ix. 23), and, as such, were subsequently to be "called," in order that they might be fully fashioned and used according to the good purpose of God, which was to be accomplished not only with regard to a portion of those who, under the name of "Jews," remained in the Land, but also more particularly as to the house of Israel, who were "lost" that they might become "the riches of the Gentiles;" and who were cast away for "the reconciling of the world" (Rom. xi. 12-15).

THE TRAINING OF ISRAEL—in the Fathers, in Egypt, in the Wilderness, under the Judges, and under the Kings, more especially before the separation of Ephraim from Judah, and also afterwards under the Prophets—all seems to indicate a peculiar interest taken in this people by the infinitely wise God, who has claimed them as His children, and has avowed His purpose to make of them a Royal Priesthood (Exod. xix. 5, 6; Isa. lxi. 6; 1 Peter ii. 5-9).

In Education two things require to be attended to. One of these is the INFORMATION OF THE MIND; the other, and perhaps most important, is the TRAINING OF THE INTELLECT AND MORAL POWERS, so as to enable the person or community to think rightly and act efficiently. In the former case the rules are made known; in the second they are put in practice, in some instances, perhaps, without the scholar being able to tell the rules according to which he has been taught to act. The form in which they are received by the mind may be forgotten; or, on the other hand, they may be retained in word, and lost in substance. Judah appears to have made most proficiency in regard to the letter; and the men of Ephraim, let us hope, profited more in respect to the law being written in their hearts. The last act recorded of them, previous to their removal from the Land, is full of hope as regards their ultimate destiny when cast out among the nations, and left to be confounded with the common Gentiles.

The fact referred to is recorded in 2 Chron. xxviii. 8–15; and seems to be most kindly remembered by our Lord in the parable of the Good Samaritan. See "WATCHMEN OF EPHRAIM," i. 146. "When the Son of man sitteth upon the throne of His glory, and before Him are assembled all nations," conduct like that of these men of Ephraim will be found characterising the nations which shall be placed at the King's right hand. They fed the hungry, clothed the naked, released the prisoners, and conducted them back in safety to their own borders (Matt. xxv. 31; Luke x. 30).

When these four men of Ephraim "expressed by name" restored the captive Jews to their brethren, they were themselves near their "end" (B.C. 741). But surely "there is hope" in such an "end," that *their* "children shall return again to their own border" (Jer. xxxi. 16, 17). It might be expected that the Assyrian yoke would be speedily removed from their own necks, even as they had accomplished deliverance for their brethren of the House of Judah.

Priests and Levites had been appointed in Israel to attend to the temporal and spiritual wants of their own people, and of the strangers among them: but these Samaritans "expressed by name" applied the word of the Lord to their own case, and to that of the poor strangers, so that their wants, weaknesses, and wounds should be attended to, and that they should be conveyed to "their own border."

The Friend of strangers, who, in regard to His manhood, was of Judah, reckoned those acts of kindness as done to Himself. We may be sure He did not forget them when the children of those men of Samaria became "wanderers" in the northern wilderness. He would not the less fulfil to them the promises made unto their fathers, even that they should be entrusted with His ministration of Blessing to the nations according to the stewardship which God in His great goodness has bestowed upon our people in the New as well as in the Old World.

VII.

ISRAEL AND JUDAH.

> Israel called All Israel, or the Whole House of Israel—Different purposes the Two Houses were intended to serve—Captivity of Israel—Time of their Resurrection Foretold at the time of their Political Death—Completeness of the Captivity—Its Continuance—Places to which they were carried; Assyria and Media—Design of the Assyrian, and that of the God of Israel, very different—Importance of the Lost House of Israel—Who are Jews—The more valuable portion of the Jews became mixed with Gentiles—The Jew hath inherited the Curse of both Canaan and Edom; yet still the Promise is to the Jew, and it cannot be less to Israel—Prophecy specially points to the Return of Israel's Captivity, and then will Christ be rejoiced in by the Jew, as having become also his Salvation.

WE should always try to discriminate clearly between the two Houses of Israel, the one of which is generally called in the Scriptures by the names EPHRAIM (Hosea v. 9–13), ALL ISRAEL (1 Kings xii. 16), THE HOUSE OF ISAAC (Amos vii. 16), for the Ten Tribes; and "Judah" (2 Kings xvii. 18) or "the Jews" (2 Kings xviii. 26), for that portion that remained with the family of David. Sometimes, indeed, the latter is also called "the House of Israel" (as in Ezek. xi. 15, xxxvii. 11, 16, and in various other parts of the same Prophecy), and then the Ten Tribes are called ALL ISRAEL, or THE WHOLE HOUSE OF ISRAEL.

This distinction between the two Houses seems to have been made very early; for David reigned six years and a half in Hebron, "over the House of Judah," before he reigned "thirty-three years in Jerusalem over Israel and Judah" (2 Sam. v. 5). His son Solomon reigned forty years. For seventy-three years, therefore, the House of Israel remained entire, when another and more permanent separation took place—a breach which hath not hitherto been healed.

Upon the death of Solomon, when the Tribes met at Shechem for the acknowledgment of his Son Rehoboam as king, they presented a Bill of Rights, requesting that their burdens should be lessened. This he ultimately refused, threatening them with still heavier oppression, and a more severe rule than they had been visited with by his father (1 Kings xii. 16)—"So when ALL ISRAEL saw that the king hearkened not unto them, the people answered the king, saying,

> 'What portion have we in David?
> Neither have we inheritance in the son of Jesse.
> To your tents, O Israel!
> Now see to thine own house, David.'

"So ISRAEL departed unto their tents: but as for the Children of Israel which dwelt in the cities of Judah, Rehoboam reigned over them." He afterwards attempted to raise tribute from ALL ISRAEL without their consent; but they stoned Adoram, who was over the tribute, and Rehoboam himself was glad to get up into his chariot and flee to Jerusalem. "So ISRAEL rebelled against the House of David unto this day." We find it then recorded (ver. 20) that ALL ISRAEL called Jeroboam the son of Nebat unto the congregation, and made him king over ALL ISRAEL. "None remained to the House of David but the Tribe of Judah only." It is probable, however, that ultimately a portion of each of the tribes was joined to either House of Israel. Certain it is that "the Levites left their suburbs, and such as set their hearts to seek the Lord God of Israel, came to Jerusalem to sacrifice unto the Lord God of their fathers" (2 Chron. xi. 12-17, xxx. 11).

About three times as long as they had been united under the House of David did Israel and Judah remain together in the land, separated as to government, and much also as to religion. During this time many changes took place in the House of Ephraim. They seem to have been in continual movement; but like the unseemly heavings of the chaotic mass before beauty covered the face of this fair creation, the spirit of change wrought rather darkly. Amid these revolutions many went over to the House of David or kingdom of Judah, which was more stationary, and continued to cherish the vision of their departed glory, and the hope of its return to abide for ever.

The two Houses seem to have been intended to fulfil different purposes in God's economy of grace to the world. Of Judah was to come the One promised Seed, the Heir of all things; of EPHRAIM the multitudinous Seed, so much promised to the fathers—"the many brethren," who are also called the Lord's "first-born" (Jer. xxxi. 9, 10). Judah has been a standing witness to the prophetic word; whilst ISRAEL, long to appearance lost, is to come forth in the latter time with overwhelming witness to the truth (Isa. xliii. 9, 10). Of Judah were "the first-fruits" gathered in the apostolic age; but ISRAEL is "the harvest" to be gathered at the Lord's return. Judah was privileged to carry out the gospel to the north and northwest, to the "many nations" that have come of Jacob; while ISRAEL has been employed in carrying it out thence unto "all the ends of the earth" (Zech. ix. 12-16). Judah and his brethren were to be preserved alive in the midst of famine; but this was to be accomplished by their unknown brother JOSEPH, who had been sent before them, and given a headship over the heathen. JUDAH seems to be given no home but that of his fathers; whilst blessings unto "the utmost bound of the everlasting hills" are promised to come "upon the head of JOSEPH, upon the crown of the head of him that was separated from his brethren" (Gen. xlix. 26). Their cities are to be "spread abroad" (Zech. i. 17); they are to be such an "innumerable multitude," that although the Land of Israel will be their common centre, they will at the same time be possessors of sea and land unto "the ends of the earth" (Ps. lix. 13; Isa. xli. 9). But then indeed Israel and Judah will have become one. They will be "one nation upon the mountains of Israel for ever" (Ezek. xxxvii. 22).

Israel had been solemnly warned (Lev. xxvi. 18, 21, 24, 28) that if they refused to be reformed by the four sore judgments—War, Famine, Pestilence, and the Beasts of the Earth—with which they were to be visited in the land, God would then proceed to punish them "Seven Times for their iniquity." He would cause them to be lost among the Gentiles "till Seven Times should pass over them." These "Seven Times" do not refer so much to the Jews as to ISRAEL (Hosea i. 6, 7). The "Jews" were to have mercy shown to them, but ISRAEL was not. The "Jews" were still to retain their name, and were to be known as the children of those unto whom the promises were made: not so ISRAEL, who were to be made "Lo-ammi" (Hosea i. 9). They were to be so lost among the Gentiles as not to be known as the Lord's people (Hosea i. 10; 1 Peter ii. 9, 10).

The TIME having come for the removal of ISRAEL unto their place of hiding, or rather their destined position as the administrators of blessing to the nations whom the Lord intended to bring into His inheritance, He prepared fit instruments for the purpose, who seem to have spared neither labour nor cost that the work should be fully accomplished.

The first grand instrument was the King of ASSYRIA, the "rod" of the Lord's anger for the correction of Israel (Isa. x. 5). In 2 Kings xv. 29, we read that, "In the days of Pekah, king of Israel, came Tiglath-Pileser, king of Assyria, and took Ijon, and Abel-beth-maachah, and Janoah, and Kedesh, and Hazor, and Gilead, and Galilee, all the land of Naphtali, and carried them captive to Assyria." Assyria lay northward of the Holy Land, approaching the Caspian and Euxine Seas. This captivity of the north-eastern portion of Israel is supposed to have happened B.C. 740.

This first captivity is also adverted to in 1 Chron. v. 26. After having remarked that Israel had transgressed against the God of their fathers, and gone a-whoring after the gods of the people of the land, whom God destroyed from before them, it is said, "And the God of Israel stirred up the spirit of Pul, king of Assyria, and the spirit of Tilgath-Pilneser, king of Assyria, and he carried them away, even the Reubenites, and the Gadites, and the half tribe of Manasseh; and brought them unto Halah, and Habor, and Hara, and to the river Gozan, unto this day." [There is still in that quarter a country called *Zozan*, and the river *Kuzal Ozan*, running into the Caspian.] (2 Kings xviii. 9–12.)

About nineteen years after this partial captivity, another and a more complete removal of Israel took place, with regard to which it is said (2 Kings xvii. 6), "In the ninth year of Hoshea, the king of Assyria took Samaria (the capital of the kingdom of Israel), and carried Israel away captive into Assyria, and placed them in Halah, and in Habor, by the river of Gozan, and in the cities of the Medes." This second captivity is said to have occurred B.C. 721—that is, about one hundred and twenty years before the captivity of Judah to Babylon under Nebuchadnezzar.

We are now past the middle of the Third Thousand years since the political death of that people which is so frequently called in Scripture ALL ISRAEL; but as "one day is with the Lord as a thousand years, and a thousand years as one day;" and even as the Lord, who condescended to fulfil in Himself many things which are accomplished in His people, on the third day arose from the dead to ascend into glory, so is ISRAEL given to say, as in Hosea vi. 2, 3—

"After two days will He revive us;
In the third day He will raise us up;
And we shall live in His sight:
Then shall we know,
. . . We follow on to know the Lord :
His going forth is prepared as the morning;
And He shall come unto us as the rain,
As the latter and former rain unto the earth."

So much as to the Time of the Captivity; and now as to the COMPLETENESS thereof. It has been objected, that the difficulty of transporting such a multitude of people to any great distance was so great as to make it altogether improbable that anything like the whole nation was carried away as described. It may, perhaps, be also said, that only the more useful and noble part of the inhabitants were taken, the common people being left to cultivate the

Land. This hypothesis, however, is not borne out by either the language of Scripture or the facts of the case.

But it is expressly mentioned with regard to the captivity of *Judah* (which took place long afterwards), that the "poor of the people" were left (2 Kings xxv. 12, &c.), which may have been to obviate the very evils incurred in the case of ISRAEL'S captivity, which was so complete that the wild beasts multiplied in the Land, and greatly annoyed the new Gentile inhabitants; so much, that they felt obliged, as they thought, to propitiate the God of the Land by uniting the worship of the God of Israel with that of their other gods; and for this purpose they were under the necessity of sending to the King of Assyria for an Israelitish priest (2 Kings xvii. 25–29). No such supply of new inhabitants and no such multiplying of wild beasts do we read of in the case of Judah's captivity, which yet we know was very great.

Let us also consider, that when the captivity of ISRAEL is mentioned, it is uniformly spoken of as being national, and not merely in part. Before the captivity took place, Amos declared, "Israel shall surely go into captivity, *forth* of his land" (ch. vii. 17). And immediately before it took place, Isaiah very graphically described the desolation which would ensue. In 2 Kings xvii. 23, it is thus depicted:—"The Lord removed ISRAEL out of His sight, as He had said by all His servants the prophets: so was Israel carried out of their own land to Assyria unto this day." Thus COMPLETE was the captivity.

Now let us inquire as to its CONTINUANCE. Were the children of ISRAEL ever restored to their own Land, like the House of Judah after the Babylonian captivity? In the Book of Kings, which brings down the history of the

Jews to the year B.C. 562 (about one hundred and sixty years after the captivity of Israel, and long after the breaking up of the Assyrian Empire), as we have just seen, it is expressly said that *the captivity of Israel had not then been restored* (2 Kings xvii. 23).

And upon the release of the Jews from their seventy years' captivity in Babylon, we have no evidence whatever that ISRAEL returned with them. The two Houses had become greatly alienated. After the return of "the Jews" to build Jerusalem, Samaria still remained in possession of the Gentiles; and so far from interchange of favours, as is foretold respecting the return of ISRAEL to their own mountain of Samaria (Jer. xxxi. 22, 23 ; Micah v. 3), we find "the Jews" cursing the Samaritans, and refusing to have any dealings with them.

Galilee, north of Samaria, afterwards came into union with Judah, but not as being peopled by returning ISRAEL. It was only a Jewish colony, intermingled with Gentiles. The conviction of "the Jews" themselves is that they have never yet been joined to the Ten Tribes, for whom they pray as still in dispersion ; which assertion they have little temptation to make, seeing that their prospect of a happy settlement can never be realised until they are fully reunited unto Ephraim, "the first-born." From their own Scriptures the Jews may most clearly know that without EPHRAIM they cannot be blessed; even as clearly as that when the two nations are made one, Messiah's glorious Kingdom will be established in the earth.

Many, overlooking the case of ISRAEL, have fixed their eye exclusively upon the people called "Jews;" as if all that is said in Scripture about Israel was to be fulfilled in "the Jews;" and as if "the return of the Jews" from Babylon was the grand fulfilment of those glorious descriptions given in the prophets respecting the perfectly peaceable and permanent resettlement in the Land of ALL THE HOUSE OF ISRAEL, "after their old estates," when the Lord is to do even better for them than at their beginnings (Ezek. xxxvi. 11). Even the restoration of the Jews from Babylon was only partial, and but a pledge of what is hereafter to take place with regard to both Judah and ISRAEL. The great body of the people seem to have remained in the land of the enemy.[1]

It certainly could not be of that time that the Lord hath said, as in Ezek. xxxix. 28, 29—

> "I have gathered them unto their own land,
> And have left none of them any more there,
> Neither will I hide my face any more from them:
> For I have poured out my spirit upon the House of Israel,
> Saith the Lord God."

It was not from thenceforth that Jerusalem was "safely inhabited," and that no stranger passed through her any more (Zech. xiv. 11). The very contrary of all these things in a remarkable degree took place, as if to urge our view forward to the grand truth of prophecy, the full redemption of Israel.

But now let us speak for a little with those who seem to take a more rational view of the subject, and look upon

---

[1] Josephus says (chap. v. book 11), "When Esdras (Ezra) had read this epistle (from Xerxes) he was very joyful, and began to worship God, and confessed that He had been the cause of the king's great favour to him, . . . and sent a copy of it to all those of his own nation in Media; and when those Jews had understood what piety the king had towards God, and what kindness he had for Esdras, they were all greatly pleased. Nay, many of them took their effects with them and came to Babylon, as very desirous of going down to Jerusalem; but then the entire body of the people of Israel remained in that country. Wherefore there are but two tribes in Asia and Europe subject to the Romans, while *the ten tribes are beyond the Euphrates till now* (A.D. 93), and are an immense multitude, and not to be estimated by numbers."

the promises as still future, to be accomplished in the people called "Jews," the recognised children of the fathers unto whom and to whose seed the promises were made. Let *them* remember that very many of "the Jews" who were dispersed in the East at the time of the Babylonian captivity became mingled among the nations, and their descendants are not now known as "Jews." They may have much tended to improve some of those tribes that border upon India and Persia, which are said to considerably resemble "the Jews," and are generally Mohammedans. Many of the Jews in other parts also embraced the religion of Mahomet, whose descendants are not now known to be Jews.

A much more pleasing dispersion of them took place in the apostolic age, when "multitudes of even the priests (of the tribe of Levi) were obedient to the faith" (Acts vi. 7). Doubtless the more favoured portion of the Jewish nation embraced the gospel, and comprised the true heirs of the promises (Rom. i. 28); and we may be certain, that if there were peculiar blessings in store for the natural seed of Abraham in the line of Isaac and Jacob, *those promised blessings were not forfeited by their acceptance of Christianity.* The children of these early Christian converts doubtless initiated their children into the faith of their Christian fathers, gathering up others also with them into the same family of God. And because they did so, are their children to be disinherited?

But what were the people called "Jews" doing in the meantime? Why, in their own way, the very same thing. Thus we read that, about B.C. 129, a whole nation was introduced into the Jewish Church; and that nation was the very people against whom, as Malachi, the last Old Testament prophet, declares (chap. i. 4), "the Lord hath indignation for ever." John Hyrcanus having conquered the Edomites or Idumeans, reduced them to this necessity: either to embrace the Jewish religion, or to leave the country and seek new dwellings elsewhere. They chose to leave their idolatry rather than the Land of Israel, and all became proselytes to the Jewish religion. (See Josephus, B. xiii. c. ix. § 1, and "Prideaux Connection," vol. iii. p. 413.) And when they had thus taken on them the religion of the Jews, they continued united with them ever after; till at length the name of Edomites was lost in that of "Jews," and both people became so consolidated into one and the same nation, that at the time the true "King of the Jews" was born, Herod, an Idumean, swayed the sceptre of Judea, and was the great restorer of the Temple to that magnificence for which it was admired by our Lord's disciples before its destruction by the Romans (Mark xiii. 1).[1]

Now, the children of Edom were cursed (Obad. 1-16), and have not escaped that curse by nominally becoming "Jews." Nay, Edom must have increased the unhappiness of his position by thirsting after the blood of Christ as soon as He was born unto the world, and by afterwards joining in the cry "His blood be upon us and upon our children" (Matt. xxvii. 25).

But more than this: It would seem that even the Canaanites themselves, who were emphatically the children of the curse (Gen. ix. 25), were gradually, and at length fully, amalgamated with "the Jews," so as to become one people with them, in even Jerusalem, the capital of the kingdom, where were the Throne and the Temple, and which (immediately before these were placed there) was inhabited by Jebusites, whose king had been

---

[1] Several cities in Spain are named after Dukes or cities of Edom, which might account for the bitter hostility there manifested to true religion.

the leader among the Amorites, one of the most accursed nations of Canaan (Deut. xx. 17, 18). We are expressly told that the tribe of Judah could not put out these Jebusites, nor did the tribe of Benjamin put them out; but they remained among the children of Judah and the children of Benjamin until the time of David, when they were built up in the very midst of "the Jews," retaining even possession of the land—as in the case of Araunah, the Jebusite, over whose threshing-floor the angel stayed his hand, when cutting down the people because of the sin of David, their king (2 Sam. xxiv. 18). That was literally true which the Lord said by Ezekiel (xvi. 3), and which those should not gainsay who plead for the literal interpretation of Scripture—

> "Thus saith the Lord God to Jerusalem,
> Thy birth and nativity is of the land of Canaan;
> Thy father was an Amorite,
> And thy mother a Hittite."

The very first mothers of "the Jews" were Canaanites of the children of Heth: Shuah, the mother of Judah's first three children, and also Tamar, the mother of Phares and Zara. But was that tribe or that city therefore excluded from the inheritance of Israel? No. Of that very tribe, in this very line, came Christ the Saviour, the promised Son of David and rightful King of Israel, although Rahab of Jericho, another Canaanitess, and Ruth the Moabitess were brought into His ancestry. This very city He made one of the principal scenes of His ministry. Here He commanded His apostles to commence theirs after His resurrection. Here the Holy Ghost descended in power on the day of Pentecost; and hence was the glad sound of salvation in the name of Jesus sent forth unto "the ends of the earth."

Do we bring forward these historical truths to disparage the Jew? Far from it. Only to illustrate the truth respecting ISRAEL; and to show that ISRAEL, who were taken out of the land, cannot be more lost among the heathen than were the people called "Jews" who remained in it. If one people were cursed above another, it was Edom, of the children of Abraham, and Canaan among the more immediate descendants of Noah; and with both of these "the Jews" have become most signally mingled, so as to become one people with them, and inherit the curse of both. As Ham, the father of Canaan, exposed Noah, the saviour of his family, to shame, so, as being the inhabitants of Jerusalem, have his children exposed to shame the Saviour of the world upon "the accursed tree;" and as Edom pursued his brother Jacob, so have his descendants among the Jews pursued with unceasing hatred not only Christ, the Head, but also His followers, so long as they had the power. But are they to be excluded? No. Even although the Canaanites dwelling along the sea-coasts were also ultimately taken up into Judah, yet—even granting that with them are Askelon, Ashdod, and Ekron—we have the word of prophecy (Zech. ix. 7)—

> "He that remaineth, even he, for our God;
> And he shall be as a governor in Judah;
> And Ekron as a Jebusite."

Even Ekron shall be as that portion of the Canaanites who were built up in the very midst of His people. And if God will deal thus kindly with "the Jews," who are so unequivocally *one* with the children of the curse, we may surely expect that He will at least equally deal according to promise with that other house, which so comprehends the body of the people as to be called ALL ISRAEL; and which, however mingled among the Gentiles, cannot be more so than "the Jews," about whose case, as the subject of prophecy, so little doubt has been generally entertained.

When the great RESTORATION OF ISRAEL is referred to in prophecy, let it be again remembered that it is ISRAEL or EPHRAIM, which had been accounted lost, which is ever brought to remembrance. "Jerusalem and her daughters" are not to return until they return in the midst of "Samaria and her daughters," and also, it would seem, amid the children of Lot (Ezek. xvi. 46). Not by her own covenant will Judah be given possession of the land; but in the right of the One Seed, Christ, the true First-born, their crucified Messiah. At length they will acknowledge that God has been indeed "a Father to ISRAEL," and that EPHRAIM is His first-born, in whose religious privileges as well as temporal blessings they will be glad to participate. Then will "the children of Judah walk with the House of Israel, and they shall come together out of the land of the north, to the Land" that the Lord, in the name of the promised Messiah, hath given to the fathers. This grand gathering together will take place in the north, and chiefly in the north-west (Jer. iii. 18). But not here alone, where Antichrist hath his seat, and where Christ hath so much been for "a stone of stumbling and rock of offence to both Houses of Israel," will the lost sheep be recovered. The "remnant" left in all the countries around will be brought back unto their Father's house. The prophet Isaiah, besides mentioning in the preceding part of chap. xi. the great release from "the Wicked" here in the north-west in verse 11 makes quite a circuit of the land, mentioning "Egypt and Pathros" in the south, "Cush and Elam" in the east, "Shinar and Hamath" northward, and "the Islands of the Sea" in the west.

It was not of Judah alone, whose captivity was in a measure restored from Babylon and who was not, like ISRAEL, taken captive by the Assyrians at the time Isaiah prophesied, but of ALL ISRAEL that he foretold as follows [1] (Isa. xi. 11-16)—

"And it shall come to pass in that day,
The Lord shall set His hand again the second time,
To recover the remnant of His people,
Which shall be left from Assyria,
And from Egypt, and from Pathros,
And from Cush, and from Elam,
And from Shinar, and from Hamath,
And from the Islands of the Sea.

"And He shall set up an Ensign for the Nations,
And shall assemble the Outcasts of Israel;
And gather together the Dispersed of Judah,
From the four corners of the earth.

"The envy also of Ephraim shall depart,
And the adversaries of Judah shall be cut off:
EPHRAIM shall not envy JUDAH,
And Judah shall not vex Ephraim.

"But they shall fly upon the shoulders of the Philistines toward the west;
They shall spoil them of the east together;
They shall lay their hand upon Edom and Moab;
And the children of Ammon shall obey them.

"And the Lord shall utterly destroy the tongue of the Egyptian sea;
And with His mighty wind shall He shake His hand over the river,
And shall smite it in the seven streams,
And make men go over dry shod.

"And there shall be a highway for the remnant of His people,
Which shall be left from Assyria;
Like as it was to Israel,
In the day that he came up out of the land of Egypt."

---

[1] The studious reader is referred also to The Parallel Histories of Judah and Israel, by the Rev. Maximilian Geneste. Bagster & Sons, 1843.

VIII.

CERTAINTY OF THE RECOVERY OF ISRAEL.

Objections Answered—Israel have become Mingled among the Gentiles—What is to become of the latter—The Literal and Spiritual Israel—Abraham's Three Families, correspondent to the Three Sons of Noah—Ishmael and Ham—Children of Keturah and Shem—Jacob and Japhet—Prophecy points Northward, to the Places whither Israel had gone, and whence they are yet to be brought—The Great Prophetic Line of Empires running North-West—Antichrist, the Consummation of the Tyrant Empires in the North-West (Isa. xi. 1-10)—Four Songs, of fourteen lines each (Isa. ix. 8-21; x. 1-4), describing the progress of Israel's Punishment—Our Saviour's Ministry went out Northward—That of the Apostles proceeded North-Westward—The Epistles all sent to Places in the same Direction—The Apocalypse carries our View onward to our own part of the World—Conclusion of the Argument: Here are to be found the Sheep of God's Pasture.

NOTWITHSTANDING the clearness of the Prophetic word respecting the recovery of Israel in the latter time, like the birth of a son to Sarah, their very existence has to many appeared all but impossible. But just so surely as Isaac was born will all the Nations that were to come of Jacob be forthcoming. The Prophets expatiate greatly upon this, and the New Testament has explicit information. But for a moment let us turn aside to hear what man has to say on the matter, that so we may better be prepared to appreciate the evidence which has been provided in the kind providence of God to remove our objections, and confirm us in the truth of God's most Holy Word.

THE RECOVERY OF ISRAEL.

Some have supposed that "*Israel, if not lost, are yet at least so blended with the Gentiles that they cannot be restored.*" And it is indeed true, that "Ephraim hath mingled himself among the people;" that the Lord hath "sown" Israel to Himself in the earth; and that, like seed sown in the earth, he was for a while to all appearance lost. But it was also to be true that—

> "He shall cause them that come of Jacob to take root;
> Israel shall blossom and bud,
> And fill the face of the world with fruit."—(Isa. xxvii. 6.)

"Jezreel," the seed of God (Hosea i. 4), was therefore not in reality to be lost. God's design with regard to the people will most assuredly be accomplished. To the same purpose we read in Isa. lxi. 9–11, "Their SEED shall be known among the Gentiles, and their offspring among the people; all that see them shall acknowledge them that they are the SEED the Lord hath blessed." The people that have come of ISRAEL ARE TO BE DISTINGUISHED AMONG THE GENTILES, and their superiority is to be acknowledged by all impartial witnesses. They are also to be found, as a people, eminently blessed by divine grace as well as by nature and providence. Theirs are "the garments of salvation," "the robe of righteousness." And here, again, the beautiful emblem of seed sown in the earth is used to illustrate the case of a people whose growth is naturally progressive, and yet such as may well astonish the world, that through their instrumentality "righteousness and praise" may "spring forth and spread abroad in the sight of all people." Such was the design of God with regard to Israel from the beginning; and He will do all His pleasure.

Others, perhaps, have run into the contrary extreme, and have supposed that something very remarkable is to distinguish the children of Israel, so as to make them shine out individually as the favourites of heaven, to the exclusion, as it were, of other people; that "*they are and will remain altogether distinct.*" Such seem to forget all that is said in Scripture about the intermarriage of Israel with other nations, and overlook what has been constantly occurring in the world all down from the times of the Apostles, who left their children among so-called Gentile Christians. But is it true that the Gentiles are so to be excluded? Is it not rather that Israel has been, and will be, exalted for the purpose of communicating blessing to the Gentiles? What saith the prophet of the stranger, who, upon finding God's wonderful manifestation of love to the children of Israel throughout all generations, might be apt to murmur, "the Lord hath utterly separated me from His people?" (Isa. lvi. 6–8.)

> "Also the sons of the stranger,
> That join themselves to the Lord,
> To serve Him,
> And to love the name of the Lord,
> To be His servants,
> Every one that keepeth the Sabbath from polluting it,
> And taketh hold of my covenant;
> Even them will I bring to my holy mountain,
> And make them joyful in my house of prayer:
> Their burnt-offerings, and their sacrifices,
> Accepted upon mine altar;
> For mine house shall be called
> An house of prayer for all people.
>
> "The Lord God which gathereth the outcasts of Israel saith,
> Yet will I gather others to him,
> Besides those that are gathered unto him."

Yes, thus it is written, even with regard to their great and final settlement in the land (Ezek. xlvii. 21–23)—

> "So shall ye divide this land unto you,
> According to the tribes of Israel.
>
> "And it sha'l come to pass,
> Ye shall divide it by lot for an inheritance unto you,
> And to the strangers that sojourn among you,
> Which shall beget children among you:
>
> "And they shall be unto you as born in the country,
> Among the children of Israel;
> They shall have inheritance with you,
> Among the tribes of Israel.
>
> "And it shall come to pass,
> In what tribe the stranger sojourneth,
> There shall ye give him his inheritance,
> Saith the Lord God."

An opinion was once prevalent that "*the prophecies respecting Israel refer to these Christian nations as being the spiritual, or surrogate, Israel; and consequently we are not to look to the literal Israel as the people in whom the Scriptures are to be fulfilled.*" Now it is indeed true that the prophecies do apply to these Christian nations, but not to the exclusion of the literal Israel, which not only contain the main body of the spiritual Israel, but are also, as we shall see, *literally* that people.

On the other hand, the idea has lately been scouted by some of applying these prophecies to nations called "Gentile;" "for," it is said, "*the prophecies refer exclusively to the literal Israel.*" And it is quite true that the prophecies do indeed apply to the literal Israel; but for that very reason they apply to the modern nations of Europe, and especially to the English nation, lineally descended from the lost son Ephraim.

Thus the opposing parties of prophetic students, having each attempted to magnify a portion into the whole of truth, have come into direct contradiction to and wide separation from each other. But here is common ground upon which they may meet and embrace as brethren both in flesh and spirit; forgetting their disputes, as lost in admiration at the wonderful kindness of the God of their fathers towards them, and as feeling the responsibility under which they are placed, as the depositaries of the divine bounty, to minister the manifold wisdom of God to the Jew on the one hand, and to the Gentile on the other.

Such being the importance of the subject, let us earnestly apply our minds to a patient investigation of the truth respecting it. And first let us look at the indications afforded us of the PLACES of Israel's sojourn, as these may be discovered by the course of God's Providence and the leadings of His Word.

There is a symmetry in all God's working; and here it may be well to revert to the case of Abraham, to whom the Promises were first and so emphatically made. He may be said to have had three families, which seem to have been designed to leaven the three families of Noah, as already adverted to, p. 19. ISHMAEL, his first son, was by Hagar the Egyptian, and received his portion in Arabia, where he has multiplied and spread abroad as promised. The greater part of Africa may also be said to be leavened by his posterity. The Arabs have extended their conquests along the southern bank of the Mediterranean even as far as the Atlantic; and had not the Gothic race come into Europe, probably they would also have taken possession of it likewise. But here a barrier was placed, which they could never entirely remove. The prophecy delivered to Hagar has been amply fulfilled in her son Ishmael (Gen. xvi. 10-12)—

> "I will multiply thy seed exceedingly,
> That it shall not be numbered for multitude.
> Behold, thou art with child,
> And shalt bear a son,
> And shalt call his name Ishmael;
> Because the Lord hath heard thy affliction.
> And he will be a wild man;
> His hand will be against every man,
> And every man's hand against him;
> And he shall dwell in the presence of all his brethren."

ISAAC, the child of Sarah, was Abraham's second son; and in him was the Promised Seed to be "called" (Gen. xxi. 12).

Abraham's third family was by Keturah, of whom it is said (Gen. xxv. 2, 5, 6), "She bare him Zimran, and Jokshan, and Medan, and Midian, and Ishbak, and Shuah." "And Abraham gave all that he had unto Isaac. But unto the sons of the concubines, which Abraham had, Abraham gave gifts, and sent them away from Isaac his son (while he yet lived), eastward, unto the east country." Proceeding eastward, it is supposed some of the children of Abraham by Keturah reached India, where their descendants are still called BRAHMINS, who have certainly a moral and intellectual constitution superior to that of the Hindoos generally, and manifest the extreme firmness of purpose, with mildness, which we may suppose to have characterised Abraham in his declining years, after all his trials and exercises of faith; just as in Ishmael we see reflected the roving and vigorous character of his earlier years. As Ishmael seems to have been mainly given the south, or Africa—the dwelling of Ham—so in the East the children of KETURAH have spread among the descendants of SHEM. Learning and science have been chiefly possessed by them; and throughout the various changes of rule in India they have generally kept a powerful hold on the public mind. True, their religion has become greatly corrupted; but such has also been the case with regard to Christianity, the types and parables of which have been in most cases as little understood as are those of the Brahmins. The time, however, is near when the rubbish will be removed, and the pure gold of sacred truth appear in all its native brightness.

As regards these children of Abraham in the East, ISHMAEL has been dwelling "in the sight of his brethren" (Gen. xvi. 12). Arabia, the eastern dwelling of Ishmael, being over against India, where the Brahmins have spread. It may thus be observed that two of the families of Noah having come into most intimate connection with two of the families of Abraham—Ishmael with Ham, and the children of Keturah with SHEM—it remains that Abraham's other son, ISAAC, the child of promise, be given his portion. For him there remains the north, and especially the north-west; in the sight of which Ishmael has been dwelling, as being spread along the south border of the Mediterranean Sea over against Europe. Here, among the isles anciently possessed by the children of JAPHET, do we find a Semitic people eminently favoured by nature and providence, and pre-eminently by divine grace; correspondent to the many great and precious promises which were so surely made to the seed of Abraham in the line of Isaac, Jacob, Joseph, and Ephraim.

But that we may be still more sure as to the PLACES in which "the lost sheep of the House of Israel" (Matt. xv. 24) are to be found, let us again look into the prophetic Word, to see if we can discern its leadings in this respect;

and we shall find that it as certainly points northward as does the mysterious needle whereby the people of the North have been in safety and with certainty guided in all directions over the wide waste of waters. Thus, when a message is sent after captive Israel, it goes forth to "the north country" (Jer. iii. 12-19). Thence are both "treacherous Judah and backsliding Israel" to return (ver. 18; xvi. 14; xxiii. 7, 8; xxxi.)[1]

As if relenting over "backsliding Israel," the Lord gives command to the prophet, saying (Jer. iii. 12)—

> "Go and proclaim these words toward the NORTH,
> And say, Return, thou backsliding Israel, saith the Lord,
> And I will not cause mine anger to fall upon you:
> For I am merciful, saith the Lord,
> And I will not keep anger for ever."

> "In those days, the House of Judah shall walk with the House of Israel,
> And they shall come together OUT OF THE LAND OF THE NORTH,
> To the land that I have given for an inheritance to your fathers," ver. 18.

It is not only clear that Israel, as distinguished from Judah, was in the NORTH when the prophet spoke, but also that even after Judah would have wandered into the NORTH, Israel would be still found there; and that out of it they are to be brought when the Lord makes Jerusalem His throne, and the heads of the people from all the cities and families of Israel are to be gathered together. The same return from "the north country" is again and again intimated throughout Jeremiah's prophecies, as in chap. xxiii. 7, 8—

> "Behold, the days come, saith the Lord,
> That they shall no more say, The Lord liveth,
> Which brought up the children of Israel out of the land of Egypt:
> But, the Lord liveth, which brought up and which led

---

[1] See also Title-Deeds of the Holy Land.

> The seed of the House of Israel OUT OF THE NORTH COUNTRY,
> And from all countries whither I had driven them;
> And they shall dwell in their own land."

Thus it is plainly declared that when Israel shall be given to enjoy the blessedness of Messiah's reign, it will be as having been brought up from "THE NORTH COUNTRY," where they had been wonderfully sustained and delivered. The same thing is again stated in chap. xxxi. 8—

> "Behold, I will bring them from the NORTH COUNTRY,
> And gather them from the coasts of the earth."

That we may be at no loss to ascertain the truth as to what people are here spoken of, it is added, ver. 9—

> "For I am a Father to Israel,
> And Ephraim is my first-born."

Those Empires which in Nebuchadnezzar's dream (Dan. ii.) are represented as the several parts of one Great Image, are so distinguished in prophecy on account of their connection with the cause and people of God; and the whole image is frequently called after Babylon, the head, at the destruction of which God will grant deliverance to Israel.

By looking along this line of Empires, and seeing to what countries and to what people they lead, we may expect to have some light reflected upon our path, when in search of "the lost sheep of the House of Israel." How then does this line lead us?[1]

BABYLON, "the head of gold," lay north-eastward of the land of Israel. The MEDO-PERSIAN Empire, "the breast and arms of silver," arose still more northward, and extended itself westward as far as the utmost extremity of

---

[1] Watchmen of Ephraim, vol. i. p. 438.

Asia Minor, and indeed spread also far eastward. The GREEK EMPIRE, represented by the "brass," arose still farther north and westward in Europe. The ROMAN EMPIRE, "the legs of iron," arose still farther north-west. And, lastly, there are "the feet, partly iron and partly clay,"— THE ROMAN EMPIRE IN ITS GERMANIC FORM, in which "the children of God" were to mingle themselves with the seed of men, but would not cleave one to another, "even as iron is not mixed with miry clay." It is this part of the image that "the Stone" is to strike, when the "manifestation of the sons of God" takes place; when "strangers shall no more serve themselves of Israel, but they shall serve the Lord their God, and David their King," whom I (saith Jehovah) "will raise up unto them." Christ is that Stone, upon which the Jews fell and were "broken;" and also that Stone with regard to which it is said, "Upon whomsoever it shall fall, it will grind him to powder" (Matt. xxi. 44; Gen. xlix. 24).

In Dan. vii., the same Empires are represented as Great Beasts.[1] They are the Wild Beasts that have been ravening on the mountains of Israel. Here BABYLON is represented as a Lion; the MEDO-PERSIAN as a Bear, with three ribs of the torn carcase of Israel "between its teeth." Then there is the GREEK EMPIRE, represented by "a Leopard with four heads," in allusion to the four kingdoms into which Alexander's Empire was parted. Then we have "the fourth Beast, with great iron teeth," the Devourer—the Breaker in Pieces—the ROMAN EMPIRE. And lastly, the ANTICHRISTIAN dominion is described, synchronising with "the feet of iron and clay," or the Germanic Empire. This fifth power is represented in Rev. xiii. as a Beast, having on his heads "the name of blasphemy." He

[1] See Watchmen of Ephraim, vol. ii. p. 29.

has the characteristics of all the Great Empires that have preceded him, and which are mentioned in the order in which they lie from the north-west. Thus, this Beast is "like a Leopard," by which GREECE had been represented; "his feet were as those of a Bear," the MEDO-PERSIAN Empire; "and his mouth as the mouth of a Lion," or boastful BABYLON. As regards the fourth Empire, it is expressly said, "the Dragon"—"the Dreadful Beast"—"the Devourer"—"the Breaker in pieces"—gave him his "seat, and power, and great authority." Messiah's destruction of this "Wicked," with "the rod of His mouth," at His glorious appearing, is much the subject of prophecy in both the Old and the New Testaments; as, for example, in Isa. xi. 1-5—

> "And there shall come forth a rod out of the stem of Jesse,
> And a Branch shall grow out of his roots:
> And the Spirit of the Lord shall rest upon him,
>
> "The spirit of wisdom and understanding,
> The spirit of counsel and might,
> The spirit of knowledge and of the fear of the Lord;
>
> "And shall make him of quick understanding in the fear of the Lord.
> And he shall not judge after the sight of his eyes,
> Neither reprove after the hearing of his ears:
>
> "But with righteousness shall he judge the poor,
> And reprove with equity for the meek of the earth:
> And he shall smite the earth with the rod of his mouth,
>
> "And with the breath of his lips shall he slay the Wicked;
> And righteousness shall be the girdle of his loins,
> And faithfulness the girdle of his reins."

What, then, results with regard to the kingdoms of this world? Even that which had been described in Dan. vii., where it is said, "Their dominion is taken away, but their lives are prolonged for a season and a time." The Wild Beasts that had been ravening upon the mountains of

Israel are deprived of their evil power, and are made to associate quietly with the children of peace. Here they are each mentioned, and again in the same order as they lie from our dwelling in the north-west. The fourth Beast hath its terribleness removed, and is simply spoken of as "the Wolf," whereby ROME was ordinarily represented; after which we have the "Leopard," "Bear," and "Lion" —their evil natures being taken away by the knowledge of the Lord (Isa. xi. 6–10).[1]

The prophet had been speaking of the glorious appearing of Messiah to exercise His beneficent reign, when the poor in spirit shall have the promised "kingdom of heaven," and when "the meek shall inherit the earth." Preparatory to this, "He shall smite the earth with the rod of His mouth, and with the breath of His lips shall He slay 'THE WICKED,'" who is also spoken of in Ps. l. 16–23; which compare with 2 Thess. ii. 8: look also at Dan. vii. 8–12, and compare with what is here said, Isa. xi. 9. All these passages speak of the same grand consummation of tyranny, that concentration of iniquity and personification of wickedness in which the Great Empires terminate, which have lorded over the land and people of Israel. The bond of wickedness is then broken, and those who had been as Wild Beasts preying upon the mountains of Israel—the ROMAN Wolf, the GRECIAN Leopard, the MEDIAN Bear, and the BABYLONIAN Lion—are separated from each other, and associated with those whose influence is holiness and peace. The knowledge of the Lord destroys their evil influence. They no longer seek to ravage the Holy Mountain, but flow thereto for lessons of love, and to become more largely possessed of the true riches. This destruction of Antichrist takes place in the north-west,

[1] See Lecture I.

whence the prophetic line of Empires stretches back eastward along the north border of the land.[1]

Thus backward and forward along this north-western line are we constantly led by the Prophetic Word, from the Assyrian captivity, when Isaiah prophesied, and as pointing forward to the time when Shiloh shall come, unto whom was to be "the gathering of the peoples" (Gen. xlix. 10).

In Isa. ix. 8–21 ; x. 1–4, there is a very striking series of paragraphs each ending with

> "For all this His anger is not turned away,
> But His hand is stretched out still."

Upon more minute examination, it will be found that each consists of fourteen lines, and they may thus be considered as regular sonnets. They refer to the House of ISRAEL, which, at the time the words were spoken, was being taken away captive by the Assyrians. In a very animated manner they describe the several degrees of the punishment of Ephraim, and seem to give clear indications of the place of ISRAEL's sojourn.

The first of these sonnets (ver. 8–12) describes the punishment of ISRAEL immediately before being removed out of the land.

The second (ver. 13–17) describes their being cut off entirely from the land, and also to the view of the world, by the Assyrian captivity.

The third (ver. 18–21) describes them, when out of the land, as at war one portion with another, and as being all against Judah, which supposes them to be grown into a number of hostile nations, and in the same countries with "the Jews."

The fourth (chap. x. 1–4) seems to describe a dreadful

---

[1] See Watchmen of Ephraim, vol. i. p. 516.

course of trial which would precede their great deliverance, and for which they would probably be unprepared.

The first points expressly to ISRAEL or EPHRAIM (ix. 8-12)—

> " The Lord sent a word into Jacob,
> And it hath lighted upon Israel.
> And all the people shall know—(Ephraim, and the inhabitants
>   of Samaria),
> That say, in the pride and stoutness of heart,
>
> " The bricks are fallen down,
> But we will build with hewn stones:
> The sycamores are cut down,
> But we will change them into cedars.
>
> " Therefore the Lord shall set up the foes of Rezin against him,
> And join his enemies together.
> The Syrians before, and the Philistines behind,
> And they shall devour Israel with open mouth.
>
> " For all this His anger is not turned away,
> But His hand is stretched out still."

Thus was Ephraim to be so surrounded with thorns and briers as that a removal from the land would be rather accepted as a boon by many. Others, however, would be loth to leave the land of their fathers. At the same time they would not leave their sins, and for such the more severe judgment was prepared of casting the whole people forth, and the entire extinction of their glory as a nation; and so the second proceeds (ver. 13-17)—

> " For the people turneth not unto him that smiteth them,
> Neither do they seek the Lord of Hosts.
> Therefore the Lord will cut off from Israel,
> Head and tail, branch and rush, in one day.
>
> " The ancient and honourable, he is the head;
> And the prophet that teacheth lies, he is the tail.
> For the leaders of the people cause them to err,
> And they that are led of them are destroyed.

> "Therefore the Lord shall have no joy in their young men,
> Neither shall have mercy on their fatherless and widows :
> For every one is an hypocrite and an evil-doer,
> And every mouth speaketh folly.
>
> "For all this His anger is not turned away,
> But His hand is stretched out still."

The entire removal of Israel having thus taken place, and they having been brought out into the Northern Wilderness, we are next presented with a view of their condition there as still undergoing punishment (ver. 18-21):—

> " For wickedness burneth as the fire ;
> It shall devour the briers and thorns,
> And shall kindle in the thickets of the forest,
> And they shall mount up like the lifting up of smoke
>
> " Through the wrath of the Lord of Hosts is the Land darkened ;
> And the people shall be as the fuel of fire :
> No man shall spare his brother.
> And he shall snatch on the right hand, and be hungry ;
>
> " And he shall eat on the left hand, and they shall not be satisfied :
> And they shall eat every man the flesh of his own arm,
> Manasseh, Ephraim ; and Ephraim, Manasseh ;
> And they, together, shall be against Judah.
>
> " For all this His anger is not turned away,
> But His hand is stretched out still."

This strikingly describes the condition of the northern nations at the time of their being driven in upon the Roman Empire. The slaughter and rapine which resulted were prodigious, during which the different nations of Europe were dreadfully racked by wars with each other. But, however opposed among themselves, they all united in persecuting " the Jews," their power of doing which is here plainly intimated.

The next and last Sonnet carries us forward to a more settled state of things to outward appearance, when wrong would be perpetrated, not so much by outward violence as by force of law and unjust legislation, to the injury of the rights of the poor and needy; depriving the poor of bread, or preventing their free enjoyment of the Word of Life. Glory and triumph are spoken of, but in language full of warning, and upon which we have no pleasure in dilating. It may be that this Sonnet (chap. x. 1-4) synchronises with "the third woe, which cometh quickly," referred to in Rev. xi. 14 :—

> " Woe unto them that decree unrighteous decrees,
> And that write grievousness which they have prescribed :
> To turn aside the needy from judgment,
> And to take away the right from the poor of my people,
>
> " That widows may be their prey,
> And that they may rob the fatherless !
> And what will ye do in the day of visitation,
> And in the desolation which shall come from far ?
>
> " To whom will ye flee for help ?
> And where will ye leave your glory ?
> Without me they shall bow down under the prisoners,
> And they shall fall under the slain.
>
> " For all this His anger is not turned away,
> But His hand is stretched out still."

Thus are we by this very interesting line of prophecy led directly to our own part of the world as to the PLACE OF ISRAEL'S SOJOURN.

Let it be again remarked, that the prophecy cannot apply to ISRAEL as being in some corner of the earth shut out entirely from other people, where they could have no opportunity of manifesting hatred to their brethren, "the Jews." Nor can the words be fulfilled in them as being under some mighty empire; such, for example, as that of China, where they would be without the power of warring with each other, or of letting Judah feel their strength. To no people does this series of songs so well point as to the nations of Europe. Yes, although ISRAEL seemed to be cut off from hearing the Word of God, it hath, after all, "lighted upon Israel."

The prediction that the Word of the Lord should light upon ISRAEL or EPHRAIM, and that they should know that Word, is most consistent with God's purpose respecting ISRAEL, as having been designed to become its administrator to the nations. We may, therefore, not expect to find them out of the course of that Word, but, as it were, in the highway thereof. If we glance at Mimpriss's maps of our Saviour's Life and Ministry, and of the Acts of the Apostles (not originally prepared to illustrate our particular subject), we shall see at once that these journeys all went out northward; and although the greater part of the tribeship of Judah lay south of Jerusalem, we do not find one of our Saviour's journeys in that direction recorded, after the flight into Egypt in His infancy. NORTHWARD, through Samaria, we trace them; and round about the coasts of Galilee, the most northern part of the Land, He went preaching the glad tidings of the kingdom, and "healing all manner of sickness and disease among the people;" and it was when in His farthest journey in that direction, on the coasts of Syro-Phœnicia, that He pronounced the important word, "I am not sent but to the Lost Sheep of the House of Israel." After the "sheep" who had wandered into "the north country" were drawn ever and again to the feet of their Good Shepherd who "came to seek and to save that which was lost," His mission to the nations promised to come of ISRAEL in "the north country" was more fully carried out by His apostles (Ezek. xxxiv.; Luke xv.; John x.)

Look at the great extent of Africa to the south, and of

Asia to the east, where anciently existed mighty empires, and such myriads of human beings : look north-west at Europe, this comparatively small quarter of the globe : and then look at Mimpriss's map describing the journeys of the Apostles, as recorded in the Book of their Acts, and see again how they all came out towards our own part of the world. Journeys were doubtless made in other directions where scattered portions of ISRAEL were located ; but the Inspired Record, as it were, leaves the world behind, and closes in our attention to this part of the globe, whence the Word of God was ultimately to spread abroad to every land, as having reached the Nations that have come of Jacob. Every successive journey was a further development of the gospel NORTH-WESTWARD. It was to Samaria, to Damascus, to Antioch, and to the cities of Asia-Minor. In this course the Apostle of the Gentiles was divinely inspired to proceed still farther, being constrained as well as invited to pass over into Europe (Acts xvi. 9), and then on through the cities of Greece. In short, "from Jerusalem round about unto Illyricum" was it that he could say "I have fully preached the gospel of Christ." The providence of God led him farther still in the same direction to Rome itself. But even this was not to end his journeys hitherward, his purpose being to proceed as far west as Spain (Rom. xv. 24). Some have hazarded the conjecture that he even preached the gospel in Britain ; but the Divine Record does not carry us at this time so far.[1]

It may perhaps be said, that Paul was influenced to proceed in this course because in the West was Rome, the capital of the Empire into connection with which the Jews

---

[1] It is remarkable that Eubulus, Rufus, Pudens, Linus, and Claudia, mentioned in 2 Timothy, were all members of the family of Caractacus, the British King, then in Rome.

had then come. But, independently of the supernatural influence in the case, which is plainly avowed, we find that when Paul expressed his purpose in the matter, it was not so much to make Rome the special object of his journey as SPAIN, the much farther point; and he intended calling at Rome, as being on the way to the more western country, anciently called Tarshish. We thus find that Paul and his fellow-disciples who ministered the Word of God which was to "light upon Israel," all followed out the course indicated by the Great Shepherd, and directs our attention to our own part of the world as the place where the lost sheep of Israel were to be found (Rom. xv. 24).

Thus far as to the spoken word. But now as to the Scriptures. Although no journeys of the Apostles are recorded to the other extensive and populous portions of the globe, it might be expected that at least some of their epistles would be sent into those quarters. But if we look at PAUL'S EPISTLES, we find them all directed in the same course as his journeys—to places lying between us and the Land of Israel—to this part of the world, in which the grand doctrine of free and full justification by faith through the blood of Jesus, advocated by this Apostle, has been so clearly brought out and proclaimed to the world.

The EPISTLE OF JAMES is expressly sent to ISRAEL: "To the Twelve Tribes which are scattered abroad." If this hath not come to the places where the Twelve Tribes are to be found, and if ISRAEL be not among the people on whom "hath lighted" this Word of God, it has missed its direction. It does not address a people who have not heard the Word of God, but those who are making a great profession of faith; stronger in doctrine than in practice, and requiring to be aroused out of Antinomian sluggishness into a fuller and more consistent practice of Christian virtue; especially into the brighter exhibition of that spirit of love which becometh the gospel. It recognises a state of society more like our own than such as may be found in any other part of the world.

The EPISTLES OF PETER, which are sent to the same royal "priesthood," to "the holy people" now scattered abroad, expressly point NORTHWARD, being addressed "To the strangers in the dispersion throughout Pontus, Galatia, Cappadocia, Asia, and Bithynia," all places in our direction from the Land of Israel. The EPISTLES OF JOHN and of JUDE are equally applicable as to their contents, although no names are given. It is in England more especially that these, with all other parts of Scripture, have been read, translated, and spread abroad. True, as yet we know but little of the Bible; yet more than any other people we have made it our own; and the things which it saith, whether with regard to the law or the gospel, it saith to them that are under its hearing.

To sum up all, we have our attention turned in the same direction by the APOCALYPSE, which closes the volume of inspiration; where we find the Good Shepherd by His voice from heaven amply confirming the indications of His personal ministry, and still expressing a peculiar interest in the north-west. In Asia-Minor, over against Greece, were the Seven Churches to which were first directed the Seven Epistles in the commencement of this wonderful book. And by the most esteemed commentators, it is supposed to proceed more and more in the same direction, until it closes the detail of judgment in our own part of the world, when the grand "mystery" of God is disclosed, and the great events of which all the prophets witness are about speedily to ensue. There is then the rending of the veil which hath been spread over all people (Isa. xxv. 7).

The Book of REVELATION fills up the gap of prophecy between the times immediately succeeding the First, and preceding the Second, coming of Christ. Where it ends the line of judgment, there most certainly may ISRAEL be found: the Second Appearing of Christ being so intimately connected with the discovery of God's grand purposes respecting ISRAEL, whom He will then have made ready to receive Him with songs of everlasting joy; as in Rev. xv. 2-4:—

> "And I saw as it were a sea of glass mingled with fire;
> And them that had gotten the victory
> Over the beast, and over his image,
> And over his mark,
> —Over the number of his name,
> Stand on the sea of glass,
> Having the harps of God.
>
> "And they sing the song of Moses,
> The servant of God,
> And the Song of the Lamb, saying,
>
> "Great and marvellous—Thy works!—
> Lord God Almighty!
> Just and true—Thy ways!—
> Thou King of saints (or *Nations*)!
> Who shall not fear Thee, O Lord,
> And glorify Thy name?
> For—only—holy!
> For all nations shall come
> And worship before Thee;
> For Thy judgments are made manifest."

Concisely to recapitulate:

If there be proportion between the seed of Abraham and the other nations of the earth, as is specially avowed with reference to Israel (Deut. xxxii. 8), then are we led to look for the LOST CHILDREN OF JACOB AMONG JAPHET'S POSTERITY (although not of them), IN THE NORTHERN PORTION OF THE GLOBE.

Again: It is assumed that the Restoration of ISRAEL will be one of the grand consummations of those prophecies whose tenor has reference to a beneficial change of the very face of nature, and which affect universal mankind. "The whole creation groaneth and travaileth together until now, waiting for the manifestation of the sons of God" (Rom. viii. 19, 22); when, "in the place where it was said unto them, 'Ye are *Lo-ammi*' (not My people — Gentiles), it shall be said unto them, 'The sons of the Living God!'" when the children of Israel and the children of Judah will be gathered together under One Head, and "great shall be the day of the seed of God" (Hosea i. 10, 11). If so, then are we led to look for the Lost House of Israel, and especially for Joseph's posterity, here in the north-west; for the plain indications of Old Testament prophecy, and the whole course of its descriptions all POINT NORTH-WESTWARD; while the intimations presented by the New Testament history of the personal ministry of Christ, the "Good Shepherd," who "came to seek and to save the Lost Sheep of the House of Israel," extended by "the heart's desire" of those who carried out from Jerusalem the ministration of Christ's gospel, as expressed fervently in the whole course of their recorded preaching, and in their epistolary communications, under the immediate direction of the Spirit of God—all corroborate the inferences to be drawn from the language of the older Revelation.

If, therefore, the Word of God, as contained in both the Old and the New Testaments, be intended to throw light upon this momentous subject (which, from its uniformity, we may justly infer it is designed to do), *then* are we of necessity led to look for the Lost Sheep of the House of Israel in the NORTH-WEST—in our own part of the world, whither the Word of God hath ever followed them, and where the whole course of Providence testifies to this truth of the Word of Prophecy.

"He that scattered Israel" promised to "gather them, and keep them as a Shepherd doth his flock."[1] And he hath indeed proved a Shepherd to Israel. He hath led "Joseph like a flock;" and upon Him may we now in truth call—

> "Turn us again, O God,
> And cause Thy face to shine,
> And we shall be saved."

---

[1] Dr Abbadie, the Huguenot refugee and Dean of Kilaloe in Ireland, a well-known writer and antagonist of Bossuet, whose works were published at Amsterdam in 1723, thus writes: "Unless the Ten Tribes have flown into the air, or been plunged to the earth's centre, they must be sought in that part of the north which, in the time of Constantine, was converted to the Christian faith—namely, among the Iberians, Armenians, and Scythians, for that was the place of their dispersion, the wilderness where God caused them to dwell in tents, as when they came out of the land of Egypt. Perhaps (he adds) were the subject carefully examined, it would be found that the nations who, in the fifth age, made irruption into the Roman Empire, and whom Procopius reduces to ten in number (he wrote De Bello Gothico, and died about A.D. 500), were in fact the Ten Tribes, who, kept in a state of separation up to that time, then quitted the Euxine and Caspian, the place of their exile, because the country could no longer contain them. Everything fortifies this conjecture, as the extraordinary multiplication of this people, marked so precisely by the prophets, the number of the tribes, the custom of those nations to dwell in tents, according to the oracle (see Pocock): Hosea xii. 9, and many other usages of the Scythians, similar to those of the children of Israel." He concludes that the Ten Tribes, separated or not from other people, could not fail, in their circumstances, to multiply exceedingly, and that they found God again in their dispersion. (This writer's conjecture was not known by Mr W. till A.D. 1800.)

IX.

THE ESCAPED OF ISRAEL.

The Tribe of Dan—Whither went the Escaped of Israel—What became of those that Fled into Egypt—Surprising Growth of Free Commonwealths in the West after the Assyrian Captivity—The Twelve Kings in Egypt—Twelve Ionian Cities—Simeon and Levi—Twelve Etrurian *Lucumonin*—Asher—The Danes and Jutes—Picts and Welsh—Israel, the Lord's Measuring Line enclosed Jerusalem, and took the Jebusites into the Portion of the Lord, in the time of David: Samaria in the time of our Saviour's Personal Ministry—Analogy between this and the Ministry of His Church, in the same Direction, down into Europe, as into the Place within the Veil.

THE blessing of DAN by Jacob (Gen. xlix.) is—

"DAN shall JUDGE his people as one of the tribes of Israel.
DAN shall be a serpent by the way, an adder in the path,
That biteth the horse heels so that his rider shall fall backward."

Moses also prophesied (Deut. xxxiii).—

"DAN is a lion's whelp: he shall leap (זנק *snk*) from Bashan."

—a corner of which the tribe conquered afterwards—(Judges xviii. 27).

This word paraphrased "leap" is not again used in Scripture. The passage might be more clearly translated—*Dan is a lion's whelp that shall not easily be caught. He shall never pass Bashan, and so shall elude the grasp of his Assyrian conquerors.* At Laish or DAN, Jeroboam set up the worship of the golden calf (1 Kings xii. 28, 29).

[The Jews have a tradition that in Jeroboam's time the tribe of Dan, being unwilling to shed their brethren's blood and to fight against them, took a resolution of leaving their country, and going into Ethiopia, where they made a sort of alliance with the inhabitants of the place, who became their tributaries. In the roll of 1 Chron. iv, DAN is omitted; while in chap. vi., Levitical cities are mentioned as belonging to Ephraim, which in Joshua xxi. are spoken of as being in the tribeship of DAN.]

Having lost neither name nor independence, DAN perhaps did not require to have a portion "sealed" out of it, like the others which were "scattered abroad;" and thus it may be that his name is omitted from the list of those tribes out of each of which 12,000 were sealed in apostolic times (Rev. vii.)

[At a very early period Deborah asked (Judges v. 17)—"Why did DAN remain in ships?" and there is no lack of evidence that he had used his nautical skill and association with his Phœnician neighbours to some purpose in preparing the way for those who were able to "escape of Jacob" (Isa. x. 20). His ports were on the same coast, he spoke the same language, and 2 Chron. ii. 14 supplies evidence of other intimate relationships. It need not be surprising then that the countries with which the Phœnicians traded should retain traces of both peoples. Ancient Irish story asserts that the Gadhelians (Heb. גדול, *gadōl*, "great ones" (Gen. xii. 2; xxiv. 35; xlviii. 19, &c., were in general called "Scots," because they came out of Southin (the land of the sojourners); that they continued in Gothland on the Euxine 150 years after leaving their own country, and went by Spain to Ireland. Eber Scot, the name of their most renowned leader, means literally *Hebrew wanderer*. Deborah's question was asked 77 years before their reputed first appearance in Ireland, and 550 years before the Assyrian captivity.

Traces of DAN are to be found in the history and topography of nearly all the coasts and islands of Europe, and even in connection with America hundreds of years before the days of Columbus. In Ezek. xxvii. 16, 17, he is mentioned as trading with Javan or Greece. In several languages (such as the Spanish) his name is synonymous with lord, ruler, master, or judge; thus proving that in these countries he had obtained the supremacy. Greek writers allude frequently to the *Danai;* while Irish and Scandinavian history are full of a people called *Danuans*, evidently of superior capability and attainments. The *Vetus Chronicon Holsatiæ* (p. 54) states that "the Danes and Jutes are Jews (?) of the tribe of Dan." " The Swedes anciently worshipped a brazen bull."—*Geijer's Sweden.*

The tribe of DAN was among the first to learn the idolatry of the Phœnicians, with whom they were associated in secular affairs; and which, as might be expected, has since been a hindrance to their identification as the people of the God of Abraham. But all this was clearly foretold (Deut. xxxii. 17, &c.) In some countries, such as Italy, Spain, and France, the powers of darkness seem to have at times been allowed almost an entire triumph over the witnesses for God. Especially was this the case in Spain —"Tarshish" of old time. At the period of the Reformation, in one single night 800 persons were hurried off to the prisons of Seville; Don Carlos, the heir-apparent, was beheaded secretly at the instigation of his own father; and in ten short years the prosperity of Spain was burnt out. But signs of spiritual life have begun to re-appear in all parts of the Spanish Peninsula. In 1824 Wesleyans began to realise that Gibraltar must have been given to England in mercy to Spaniards, and used it for their evangelisation; and in 1848 believing friends in Scotland began to pray for her in earnest; since which, by degrees, a remarkable influence has seemed to act upon the people. They begin to yearn for they know not what; try the Bible, and agree that freedom of conscience and liberty of worship must be maintained. In 1875, for the first time in history, Protestantism or Evangelical Christianity is recognised by the State; and in six years it is found that 40,000 have enrolled themselves as Protestants.

The first look of many Spaniards on hearing the glad tidings of free salvation is of wonder. When they have more fully realised the "good news," they not unfrequently begin to weep; after which joy finds expression in rapturous song. The Word has been prophesied over the "dry bones" (Ezek. xxxvii.), and prayer has been made to "the wind or Spirit" to "breathe upon these slain that they may live." Shall we wonder at the result? So far back as 1859, the Bishop of Cadiz (the oldest city in Europe) issued the following charge :—" The enemy of mankind desists not from his infernal task of sowing tares in the field of the Great Husbandman; and to us it belongs, AS SENTINELS OF THE ADVANCED POST OF THE HOUSE OF ISRAEL, to sound the alarm, lest his frauds and machinations should prevail," &c.]

The **DANES** who have retained the name of their father, were among the last of these nations to receive the gospel; and "in the way" of Zebulon, "going out" from all these northern seas, they were remarkable for their piracies. There they lay in their long keels called "snakes," lurking for their prey, ready to seize it whether on land or water (Gen. xlix. 17). "The white horse" was the standard of the Saxons, and still is of at least one of the royal houses of Saxony, apparently derived from the " strong ass " of Issachar. Truly, as " an adder in the path that biteth the horse heels," were the DANES; and the " white horse," then the ensign of those who were to be the Lord's " arrows," or messengers to the nations (Zech. ix. 14; Rev. vi. 2), was for a time impeded in his course.

[The tribe of Dan is the first mentioned in the re-settlement of the Tribes (Ezek. xlviii.) Danes also were the first to plant modern missions in India.]

The port of Joppa, in the tribeship of DAN, was nearest to Judah, and may have afforded to some of that tribe also the means of transporting themselves westward. From thence Jonah took ship to flee to Tarshish, in which direction we know the Phœnicians traded for amber and tin.

Long before the Assyrian captivity of Israel we find JOEL (B.C. 800) prophesying respecting a portion of JUDAH which had been taken into slavery westward, chiefly through the instrumentality of Tyre and Sidon, who had " sold the children of Judah and the children of Jerusalem to the sons of the Grecians, that they might be removed far from their border" (chap. iii. 4–8). The Lord there promises to raise up these Jews who had been thus enslaved, to bring them against Tyre, and threatens to give the Tyrians into their hands.

The following communication has not perhaps been generally observed in Josephus (B. XII. iv. 10; XIII. v. 8) and 1 Macc. xii :—" AREUS, KING OF THE LACEDEMONIANS, TO ONIAS SENDETH GREETING. We have met with a certain writing, whereby we have discovered that both the Jews and the Lacedemonians are of one stock, and are derived from the kindred of Abraham. It is but just, therefore, that you, who are our brethren, should send to us about any of your concerns as you please. We will also do the same thing, and esteem your concerns as our own, and will look upon our concerns as in common with yours. Demotoles, who brings you this letter, will bring your answer back to us. This letter is four square; and the seal is an eagle with a dragon in his claws."—(The ensign of Dan ?) The Jews acknowledged this claim, and long after directed their ambassadors to Rome to make a friendly call on their brethren at Sparta.

The LACEDEMONIANS were remarkable for the wisdom of their political arrangements, having much the same mixed form of government as that of the English. They were also uncommonly brave in war, but when Alexander the Great resolved upon his Persian expedition, they were the only people of Greece who refused to be led by him against the East. Refusal, however, seems to have been out of the question after his successful expedition to the Danube and cruel destruction of the Thebans; and thus were these brethren of the Jews raised up and led contrary to their wish against Tyre, to execute upon it the judgment written. For the Tyrians having refused to admit Alexander as a master, he wholly demolished old Tyre on the continent, to make a causeway whereby to reach new Tyre, which was previously an island. Having effected his purpose, he burned it to the ground, and destroyed or enslaved all the inhabitants. In sacking the town he slew 8000; 2000 were crucified; and 30,000 were sold as slaves. It is no extravagant idea to suppose that the Lacedemonians had been Jewish slaves, who by some means had obtained their freedom. The 2000 Tyrians who were crucified had sentence executed upon them under the pretext that they were descended of slaves, who, having conspired against their masters, murdered them all in one night, and by marrying their mistresses had continued in possession of the town.

It is intimated (Isa. x. 20) that a considerable number had fled from the land rather than remain to be led away at the will of the Assyrians, which was the more likely, as those dwelling along the coast of the Great Sea had warning given them nineteen years before the great captivity, by the forcible removal of those who lived eastward of the Jordan. Many doubtless escaped between these two captivities;[1] and it may have been partly to prevent the greater withdrawal of Israel from under their yoke, that the Assyrians came up and so entirely swept away the remnant. Westward down the Mediterranean Sea or into Egypt was the way of escape. Every other door of hope seemed to be closed against them.

[On the walls of a rock temple, about twenty miles from Bombay, a Hebraic inscription has been discovered in ancient Pali (secret) characters. The facsimile will be found in Bird's "Historical Researches on the Origin and Principles of the Bauddha and Jaina Religions." It concludes thus :—

(6) "And his (Saka's) mouth enkindling them, brought the *Scrim* together of the race of *Harari* (2 Sam. xxiii. 11, 33).

(7) My mouth also hastened the rupture, and as one obeying my hand thou didst sing praise.

O unclean one, his religious decree is his bow.

(8) He who complains of the presence of the inflicted equality turns aside. My gift is freedom to him who is fettered, the freedom of the polluted is penitence.

(9) As to DAN, his unloosing was destruction, oppression, and strife ; He turned stoutly away, he departed twice.

---

[1] Sailman, in his "Researches in the East" (1818), cites the statement of "Eldad," who sent to the Spanish Jews his memoirs of the Ten Tribes, that many of the people did not go into captivity, but evaded "the calamity," going off with their flocks and turning nomads, and that the chief or prince whom they appointed could muster 120,000 horse and 100,000 foot.

(10) The predetermined thought is a hand prepared. The redeemed of Kasha (Isaac) wandered about like the (il ck) overdriven (Ezek. xxxiv.)

(11) The prepared was the ready; yea, GOTHA, that watched for the presence of DAN, afforded concealment to the tribe whose vexations became his triumphs; and SAKA also being re-invigorated by the calamity, purified the East, the vices of which he branded."— *Moore's "Lost Tribes," p. v.*]

By the Prophet HOSEA it had been said (chap. ix. 8, 9), "Ephraim shall return to Egypt;" and "Egypt shall gather them up, Memphis shall bury them." Memphis, it may be remarked, is that city of Egypt in the neighbourhood of which are the Pyramids and other remarkable burying-places. By the language of this prophecy it would appear that "the dispersed of Israel" would be prized in Egypt, and honoured in their burial. It is, perhaps, worthy of notice that, shortly after the Assyrian captivity, the influence of Israel really seems to have been felt in Egypt.

Herodotus says (Euterpe, cxlvii.), upon the death of the king who reigned over Egypt in the time of Sennacherib, King of Assyria, "the Egyptians recovered their freedom, and chose twelve kings, among whom they divided the different districts of Egypt." Thus, immediately after the Assyrian captivity, an elective government was established in Egypt, consisting of twelve communes, during the very lifetime of the refugees belonging to the twelve tribes of Israel. However rapidly liberty might spring up, Egypt does not seem to have been the soil in which it could then firmly take root.

These twelve kings built the celebrated labyrinth, near the lake Moeris, to which Herodotus says even the Pyramids were inferior. It was composed of twelve covered courts, six towards the north and six towards the south; and three thousand apartments, fifteen hundred under ground, and fifteen hundred above, of incredible grandeur and beauty. They are now supposed to be covered by the sand. *Savary* supposes the re-opening of them may throw considerable light upon the past history of man; and possibly our own subject would profit thereby as much as any.

But although a portion of Israel doubtless did find thus an asylum and occupation in Egypt, they were neither to continue nor to take root there. It is said of Ephraim (Hosea xi. 5), "He shall not return into the land of Egypt." No more would they find there that rest which they sought to obtain as forgetting their Maker, building temples, and choosing altars to sin. The Egyptian commonwealth was speedily dissolved, and one of the twelve chiefs, named Psammiticus, obtained the supreme command. From that time Egypt appears to have been thrown open to strangers; and doubtless then, also, many of the freedom-seeking Egyptians removed to other countries, in which the Israelitish refugees would be foremost.[1]

[1] Bunting, in his "Ancient Music of Ireland," says (pp. 47, 50), "The instrument submitted to the reader from the other monument above referred to (a sculptured cross at Ullard Church), is evidently of a much older date. The musical inquirer and general antiquary cannot fail to regard it with interest; *for it is the first specimen of the harp without a fore-pillar that has hitherto been discovered out of Egypt;* and but for the recent confirmation of Bruce's testimony with regard to its Egyptian prototypes, might be received with equal incredulity. For, to the original difficulty of supposing such an instrument capable of supporting the tension of its strings, is now added the startling presumption that the Irish had their harp out of Egypt. . . . .

"Should these grounds appear sufficient for the surmise that the harp is really a variety of the *cithara* or *testudo*, derived through an Egyptian channel, the importance of our Bardic tradition of the progress of the early colonists of Ireland from Egypt through Scythia will at once be ap-

On the opposite side of the Mediterranean, in the western extremity of Asia-Minor, and extending to the islands nearest the coast, we find afterwards springing up the IONIAN Commonwealth, consisting of twelve tribes or states, and a limited monarchy resembling the Israelitish Government. It is clearly inferred from *Herodotus* that their having a commonwealth of just twelve states was rather a matter of choice than of chance.

Their principal city was Miletus, whence there was such migration westward in ancient times. They were remarkable for their personal beauty, mental vigour, and love of liberty. Their connection with the Egyptians was most intimate; and they are said to have been the first among the Greeks who undertook long voyages. They had been in rather a wandering state previous to their settlement in IONIA, where at length, as in a second Eden, they had taken up their abode. But this was not to be their rest, and they appear to have been given this position in order that they might be still more extensively sown over the earth; as if to give the fullest scope to the execution pronounced by Jacob: "SIMEON AND LEVI are brethren; I will divide them in Jacob, and scatter them in Israel" (Gen. xlix. 5, 6). Three several times were they reduced by the Persians, and by them sown over the earth. Some of them were carried even as far as Ampe, a city

parent. There can be no question of the fact, that at a very early period a strong tide of civilisation flowed into the east of Europe from the Nile, and thence spread northward and westward; and there are many grounds, extrinsic to this inquiry, on which it appears that a strong *argument* may be raised for intimate international relations between the original inhabitants of these islands and the ancient occupants of the east of Europe."

The Harp became the national standard of Ireland only from the time of Henry VIII., when he was elected King of Ireland by common consent of the Irish princes. Previous to that they had the LION.

near where the Erythrean Sea (or Persian Gulf) receives the waters of the Tigris.

And it is worthy of observation, that this dispersion took place about the same time that the Jews returned from Babylon, in consequence of a revolt occasioned by their fear of being replaced in the Land of Israel, which they had voluntarily abandoned as "a land that devoureth its inhabitants," and had found a happy home abroad. They had become alienated from both the throne of David and the Temple at Jerusalem; so that what was a joy to the Jews was naturally a terror to them.

The term "brethren," so emphatically applied to Simeon and Levi, appears to have been much in use in this neighbourhood, such as "Philadelphia"—*i.e., loving brethren*, and a very remarkable and exceedingly rich temple called "Didymus," or *Twins*. Nor is it of small importance that to this quarter our attention is particularly directed, not only by the preaching and epistles of Paul, but also by the Book of Revelation, chap. i. Here were the Seven Churches, symbolised by the seven candlesticks in the Sanctuary, the epistles to which so often conclude with an apparently special allusion to the name "Simeon" —*i.e., hearing:* "If any man have an ear to HEAR, let him HEAR WHAT THE SPIRIT SAITH to the churches."

Many of the greatest lights of antiquity arose in this neighbourhood; but as tyranny prevailed, mental vigour declined, or rather travelled farther west into Greece, and afterwards still more and more into Europe and onwards. This important office of "the dispersed of Israel," as instructors of the Greeks, appears to have been understood by the Jews in the time of our Saviour's sojourn among them. When He threatened (John vii. 35) to leave them, and go where they could not find Him, they said,

"Whither will He go that we shall not find Him? Will He go to the dispersed among the Greeks, and teach the Greeks?" (So it is in the original.) This clearly enough indicates that they thought some at least of "the dispersed" had gone among the Greeks, and communicated to them much knowledge, of which the Jews were so selfishly proud, and of which the Greeks do not seem to have made the very best use. That knowledge had indeed become greatly corrupted before the Assyrian captivity; and by his nearness to Egypt and Philistia, SIMEON had been peculiarly exposed to such corruption.

The words of the Jews seem to imply that, at the time they were spoken, "the dispersed among the Greeks" had ceased to be recognised as of Israel. It was as much as to say, "Let Him go from us; it will be His own loss, as it has been that of the portion of our people who departed from us, and especially of those sent to Javan or Greece, who, so far from manifesting the God of Israel there, have themselves been lost." Our Saviour's view of the matter was different when told that certain Greeks who had come up to the feast desired to see Him, and seems to have recognised them as being of ISRAEL, who had to human eye been lost like seed sown in the earth. As promised in the prophecy of Hosea, 780 years before, they had been sown to the Lord among the nations, and were now beginning to spring up and ripen unto the harvest (chap. ii. 23). Frequently, as here, the same things are said of both the One Seed, Christ, to come of Judah, and the multitudinous seed to come of the other House of Israel.

It may be remarked that the very names, order, and number of the Greek letters give evidence of their having been learnt from the Hebrews. Thus from the *Hebrew* Aleph we have the *Greek* Alpha; *Heb.* Beth, *Gr.* Beta;

Heb. Gimel, *Gr.* Gamma, &c.; and their letters, so essential to the existence of their literature, speak plainly of the quarter whence the Greeks had derived much of which they were most disposed to boast. Their sacrifices, oracles, and free government all tell of the influence of the Israelitish refugees who had so early encircled their coasts. They would doubtless be called Phœnicians, as coming from the coast of Phœnicia; or as coming directly from the tribeship of SIMEON, on the borders of Egypt, or even from Egypt itself, they would be confounded with the Egyptians. Nor would they, in the circumstances, be likely to boast of their true origin. It was not until sufficient time had elapsed after the Assyrian captivity that the "seed" thus sown along the coasts of Greece ripened, as in Athens, into that intellectual fruitfulness for which it was in after ages so distinguished.

Proceeding farther down the Mediterranean, we find in the north-west of Italy another commonwealth, consisting of twelve states or *lucumonin*—a word doubtless from the same Hebrew root as that from which we have "county," or *comte*. This country was anciently called Tyrsenia, or second Tyre.[1]

This state seems to have been at first only a Tyrian colony; but at an early period it appears to have undergone a considerable revolution, after which it generally bore the name of ETRURIA. The inhabitants were then formed into a commonwealth of twelve states; each *lucumo*, or state, being in some measure independent, and having its own prince; but all, like the tribes of Israel, under one

---

[1] The word *senia* is from the same Hebrew root, שנה, *shanah* or *sunna*, to repeat or do again, from which we have *sen* or *son*, attached to so many northern names, as in Sacsonia, &c.

king. These changes we may well believe took place in consequence of extensive immigrations of Israelites, especially of ASHER, in whose tribeship was Tyre. They are said to have first formed themselves into twelve states on the west of the Apennines, and afterwards to have established a similar commonwealth on the east side, thus possessing themselves of both passes into Italy.

The language of the Etrurians is said to have been the same with the Hebrew or Phœnician; and anciently they believed in one Supreme Being, whom they called Jave or Jove—Jehovah, the peculiar name of the God of Israel. They considered Him to be what the very word imports—the Principle of life and motion, as well as the Great Governor of the universe. They also looked forward to a future state of rewards and punishments. Their sacrifices; eagerness to have the knowledge of future events communicated to them from a supernatural source; and even their real prophecies regarding the Messiah, which Virgil, the great Roman poet, learned from them, and has paraphrased, all bespeak their Hebrew origin.

From the ETRURIANS, the Romans received almost everything they possessed of any value, whether in arts, arms, or civil polity or religious rites and ceremonies. The Roman nobility were in the habit of going to Etruria to learn "the secrets" of their religion, or the truth contained under the veil of their various ceremonies, called the Etruscan art or discipline, just as they were sent into Greece to learn philosophy. By the Romans, however, the Etruscans were at length subdued, and made greatly subsidiary to their political importance. The Romans served themselves of them, even as the Persians did of the Ionians, and the Macedonians of the Spartans and Athenians. They had yielded themselves to be the slaves of idols, and so were allowed to become the servants of men. They became such proficients in wickedness as to teach the wicked ones their ways; and so "that Wicked" was allowed to lord it over them. Of this tribe Moses said (Deut. xxxiii. 25)—

> "Asher—Blessed with children;
> Let him be acceptable to his brethren,
> And let him dip his foot in oil.[1]
> Thy shoes—iron and brass;
> And as thy days so shall thy strength be."

The word translated here "children," may better be rendered *sons*. Now this part of Italy has been remarkably prolific in "sons," or men of manly intellectual power; and hence colonies were early sent out to many other parts of the world. The power of Genoa on the one hand, and of Venice on the other, was great by sea long ago, when the rest of Europe was immersed in a kind of midnight gloom. Here have been produced some of the most beautiful creations of Art and most masterly performances in Literature. And degraded as Italy has been, this northern part has wonderfully preserved its ancient dignity, character, and productions.

Etruria had been subdued by the Roman Empire, and incorporated with it previous to its attacks upon the other Tribes of Israel, who, therefore, at a distance, very naturally confounded the one with the other. The prophecy not merely intimates alienation of heart between Asher and his brethren, of which there were early indications (Judges v.), but also describes what till recently was the actual position of the parties; nearly the whole north of Italy being in the grasp of the Germanic race, who are supposed not to have shown much favour, and scarcely even equity, in their government of this interesting country. And, therefore,

---

[1] So remarkably is Etruria an oil country, that the people have a common saying, "If a man would leave an inheritance to his children, let him plant an olive."

the parental admonition is not without its meaning, even as to those of Israel who are under the same degrading superstition which has so long oppressed Italy. How much more so with regard to those tribes lying still farther north, which, as being alienated also on account of religion, have been too apt to give up ETRURIA as being lost, without using the means necessary for securing ASHER's " blessedness " in the gospel!

It may be observed that, notwithstanding all the pride of Macedonia and Rome, represented in the Great Image by the " belly and thighs of BRASS" and the "legs of IRON," they both became as highways, or *under* the shoes to ASHER, whereby to traverse the then known parts of the earth. Early and bright have been "the days" of ETRURIA. When all Europe was immersed in comparative gloom, Etruria was shining forth in beauty. When Rome was as yet but a pitiful den of robbers preying upon the borders of Israel, ETRURIA was in peaceful order; and again when Rome was writhing from the wounds received from the remains of nations butchered in her very wantonness of power, the genius of ETRURIA arose as if from an oppressive incubus, and ushered in that better day for Europe, the brightness of which, however, as being so near Rome, she has not been allowed to enjoy till very recently. The manly strength of ETRURIA still remains, and may yet be fully manifested in the cause of truth and goodness, preparatory to the great day of the Lord.

[This has been actually the case; and since the foregoing was written a great change for the better has taken place, of which Florence is the centre. With a free Evangelical Church in united and represented Italy, a free press, and a Bible-reading population, great national strides may be taken with unobserved rapidity. Our latest intelligence is worthy of note. The date is " 20th May 1875." "To-day the Lord Provost of Florence, who is also Member of Parliament for the city, presided at the annual examination of the Free Christian Schools, in the beautiful old church and premises secured two years ago through British liberality. The Florentine Town Council gives annually £40 to these schools—the first instance of municipal support in Italy being extended to anything distinctly evangelical. This week has been printed here the first No. of a little Italian monthly on 'Revival, Consecration, and Holiness,' of which 5000 copies are to be sent regularly and gratuitously to the evangelists and church members of all the evangelical churches in Italy."] See also Rev. J. A. Wylie's "Dawn in Italy."

Moses says—

"Rejoice, ZEBULON, in thy going out,
And ISSACHAR in thy tents."

The reason is given in the end of the next verse, " For they shall suck of the abundance of the seas, and of treasures hid in the sand." In a double sense the DUTCH have sucked of the abundance of the sea; and in old times were accustomed to make much gain by trading in the amber which is found in great quantities "hid in the sand" along the borders of the Baltic. In the time of David it is given as a characteristic of the children of Issachar that they had understanding of the times to know what Israel ought to do; "and all their brethren were at the commandment of two hundred leaders."

Jacob in blessing the tribes says (Gen. xlix. 13), " Zebulon shall dwell at the HAVEN of the sea ; and be for an HAVEN of ships : and his border unto Zidon." [1] Zebu-

---

[1] The Hebrew word *Hôf*, here translated "haven," seems to be the same from which our word *hope* or *hove* is derived.

lon had been long waiting to obtain the object here presented to his *hope*, having in his fatherland rather an inland position. At one point his border is supposed to have reached towards the sea, but not where there could be any great "haven of ships." In the west, however, we have a coast so remarkably adapted for being a haven of ships that it has been called "the great storehouse of Europe." It is defended by the British Isles from the rage of the rough Atlantic, and is wonderfully indented with bays and inland seas, which are further assisted by broad rivers and numerous canals. The district more properly commences at Boulogne (which, indeed, may possibly be a contraction of ZEBULON, the first syllable being, as usual in such cases, omitted). It reaches down to Zuyder-Zee, and is chiefly inhabited by the Dutch, Belgians, and Normans, who are, perhaps, the most enterprising and prudent people on the face of the earth, over many parts of which, like the Zidonians, they have extended their commerce and spread their colonies. The invention of printing has been claimed by the Dutch; and they still are much distinguished for " handling or drawing with the pen of the ready writer," which is particularly remarked of Zebulon in the song of Deborah (Judges v. 14).

Our Saviour's ministry was in embryo that which has been accomplishing ever since. As Samaria, occupied by the Gentiles, lay between Judea and Galilee, the two portions of the Jews, of which the latter was the great scene of His preaching and "doing good;" so, between the Land of Israel and this goodly heritage of the host of nations, here in the north-west interposed a tract of country mainly possessed by the Gentiles, through which the gospel had to pass; and here, as in Galilee in the north-west portion of the Land, has been the greatest display of the goodness and manifestation of the unwearied care of the Shepherd of Israel.

All along this line in which the gospel has travelled westward were placed portions of the people who had been prepared for the name of Jehovah, to transmit it from one part to another until it reached these "isles afar off," whence it was to be declared unto "all the ends of the earth," as being encompassed by Israel—"the cord, or lot, or measuring-line" of the Lord's inheritance.

The great body of the people had been either led into the north or had fled into the west. They had encircled the western coast of Asia Minor, and that was taken into the Lord's inheritance: there was the great preaching of the gospel and planting of churches in apostolic times. Israel had encompassed Greece. They were to the north, south, and west of Macedonia; and that became thence a carefully-laboured portion of the vineyard. Israel had also proceeded to the north-west of Italy. They had, as it were, enclosed Rome; and it also became blessed with the preaching; and thereto was sent one of the most valuable epistles of the Apostle Paul. But not only have *portions* of "the escaped of Israel" come into the west: "the fulness of nations," promised to Ephraim, have also been brought forth, and have come into possession of the extreme north and west. They had, like the palm-tree, been long in proving worthy of their name Ephraim, that is, *fruitful;* but at length the time came that they should be blessed, and be the means of blessing all the nations of the earth. And, accordingly, the light travels onward; the sap progresses in "the Branch" of the Lord's planting (Isa. lx. 21). The ALBIGENSES, or Paulicians, who had migrated from Armenia to Thrace, appear in the north of Italy to testify to the truth of God's Word in opposition to the superstition which was then covering the earth. On the north-east of the Alps the witnesses thereafter appear as WALDENSES, whose ancient Confession of Faith declares their Israelitish origin thus : "The Scriptures teach that Christ was promised to our forefathers, who received the law, to the end that, knowing their sin by the law, and their unrighteousness and insufficiency, they might desire the coming of Christ, to the end that He might satisfy for their sins, and accomplish the law by Himself."

The same doctrines are afterwards proclaimed in England by Wickliffe, still farther west, and his voice reaches back to BOHEMIA. In the north of Germany the bold Luther stands forth among the SAXONS, denouncing in the strongest terms "the man of sin," who, having defiled "the Temple of God" (2 Thess. ii. 4), shall be destroyed; "for the Temple of God is holy, which Temple ye are," said Paul to some of the first-reached of the European population. HERE is "the place within the veil" which shall be cleansed. "The idols He will utterly abolish ;" and "the Lord alone shall be exalted in that day." And now was declared in its fulness the doctrine of free justification by the blood of Jesus.

> "For through Him
> We both have access by One Spirit
> Unto the Father.
>
> Now therefore ye are no more strangers and foreigners,
> But fellow-citizens with the saints,
> And of the household of God.
>
> And are built upon the Foundation of the apostles and prophets,
> Jesus Christ Himself being the Chief Corner—
> In whom all the building, fitly framed together,
> Groweth unto an holy temple
> In the Lord.
>
> In whom ye also are builded together
> For an habitation of God
> Through the Spirit."— Eph. ii. 18-22.)

X.

THE EARLY CONNECTION OF BRITAIN WITH EASTERN LANDS.

Mara Zion and Market Jew—Tin-mines of Cornwall—Paran Zabuloe—Origin of the Name Britain—King Brute, Beyrout, and the Brettii—Ramifications thereof Westward—Important Notes on Baal-worship, the Silence of the Druids and Buddhists, Introduction of Christianity, Cassi-terides, &c.—Half-tribe of Manasseh—Jacob's Pillow—Irish—The Royal Standard in the North of India—Welsh related to both the Picts and Israel—Early British Christians in Rome—King Arthur and Chivalry—Culdees, Kelts, Caledonians, Galatians, &c., &c.

ENGLAND had intercourse with the coast of Palestine ages before the Anglo-Saxons found their way hither. The Hebrew word translated "sold" in Joel iii. 6, is that from which our word "market" is supposed to be derived; and one of the most likely places to which "the children of Judah and the children of Jerusalem" were brought to market is still called "Mara Zion," and a part of it "Market Jew." It is worthy of note that both Judah and Jerusalem, or Zion, are mentioned (B.C. 800) by the prophet Joel; and also that two such remarkable names are still given to the same place in the British Isles, which were by the prophets spoken of as "The isles afar off" (Isa. lxvi. 19, &c.)

At a very early period Palestine had much trade with Cornwall on account of its tin-mines. The labours of these expatriated Jews would be valuable to those who had charge of their working and the preparation of the metals for the merchants of the coast of Palestine. Most likely at "Market Jew" no more acceptable exchange could be offered than a sufficient supply of slave labour for the mines and smelting furnaces of Cornwall.

If Naomi, as having been left alone in the land of Moab, whither she had voluntarily removed, could say "Call me not Naomi (*my pleasantness*), but call me Marah (*bitterness*), for the Almighty hath dealt bitterly with me," how much more might these poor Jews, cruelly removed "from their own border," which they loved, be disposed to call the place where they were sold "Mara Zion?" Looking forward to the remainder of their days, as having to be passed in the mines of Cornwall, they would doubtless "weep bitterly" when they remembered "Zion;" and with Naomi be ready to say "The Almighty hath dealt *bitterly* with me."

God may, however, in these poor outcasts, have been taking possession so far of this land, covenanted to Messiah in Ps. ii. 8: "Ask of Me, and I will give Thee the nations Thine inheritance, and the uttermost parts of the earth Thy possession."

Some, who have been better acquainted with heathen mythology than with their Bibles, have supposed that the Jew could have nothing to do with Cornwall at the early period "Market Jew" received its name, and that it cannot have been *Jew* that was meant, but Jovis; because Mara Zion had a market upon Thursday, the day devoted to Jove. But such should have considered that to hold a market on Thursday was far from being peculiar to "Market Jew;" and also that such a derivation of that name would leave "Mara Zion" unexplained. Whereas, correctly viewed, the two names explain and account for each other, and are thoroughly consistent with the facts of the case.

Diodorus Siculus relates that the inhabitants near the promontory of Bilerium (Land's End), after forming the tin into cubical blocks, conveyed it in waggons to an island named Ictis, since at low tides the space between that island and Britain became dry. At Ictis the tin was purchased by merchants who carried it across to Gaul.

The name of another place in Cornwall "Paran Zabuloe," or *beautiful dwelling*, is very suggestive, when we recollect that Paran was the quarter into which Israel moved when coming up out of the Wilderness of Sinai, and where they were "dwelling" when they sent forth spies to report upon the land of their future possession. In our own day, an ecclesiastical building, "Paran Zabuloe," has been dug up out of the sand, by which it had been covered up from ancient times.

Our island also very early obtained somehow the name of "Britain." Various derivations have been ascribed to it. Certain it is, however, that in Hebrew it means simply "the land of the covenant," as if it had been specially referred to in the promise or covenant to the Son.[1]

---

[1] It is curious to observe that the title "Son," given to Messiah after this promise (ver. 12), although in our translation the same as used in the earlier part of the Psalm, is different in the original Hebrew, and consists of the first two letters of the name "Britain." "Kiss the Son," בר, the *pure one*. Names in Scripture often most remarkably approximate, not only to the subject of discourse, but also to objects simply adverted to therein. And true it is, that from Britain was to go forth the universal invitation to be reconciled unto the Father through the Son of His love—the declaration that "Blessed are all they that put their trust in Him." The "fulness of the nations," promised to come of Ephraim, and dwelling in "the ends of the earth," spoken of in covenant to the

There was at one time a vague tradition that Britain had its name from one King Brute or Brutus.[1] It is not likely that such a person ever ruled in Britain; but it is quite possible that *Beyrout* was really the name of the power which at the first colonisation of Britain held sway here, or at least ruled over that part of it which, on account of its commercial advantages, was held possession of by a Phœnician community.

Of the three Phœnician cities, Tyre, Sidon, and Beyrout, which seem to have had extensive ramifications both east and west, Beyrout was the most northern, and most directly in the route, through Damascus, from the East.

There was among the Phœnicians a fabulous god, "Baal Berith," or *Lord of the Covenant;* but that which was only fabled among them was real in regard to the children of Israel. In fulfilment of an ancient covenant, Beyrout and Britain were thus most likely related very intimately in the times of old.

On account of its semi-insular position, Cornwall could

Son, having been brought in or reconciled,—the Father having kissed His returning prodigal,—he is in Christ, "the Son, who truly abideth ever," made the happy instrument of conveying the kiss of peace to all mankind, and those that bless Him are blessed. We have examples of the use of Bar for son in "*Bar-jona,*" &c.

"And if still clearer light should evince that our name, ברית, Brit (the title of Christ as the Covenant Sacrifice, Isa. xlii. 6; xlix. 8) was conferred upon us in the unsearchable wisdom and by the controlling providence of Jehovah-Jireh, as that *hidden name* of Christ which time should reveal as the name of His chosen people, and the name also of His appointed possession at the ends of the earth (Ps. ii. 8), it will then follow that the highly distinguished name of ברית, Brit, being put upon us as a people or church, is the same thing as to write upon us *Beloved*, and fully harmonises with those parts of Scripture which represent the true church as a people bearing the hidden name of their Redeemer (Isa. xxviii. 15–17; lxvi. 19, 20." *Wedgwood,* A.D. 1814.

[1] Cymru was said to be one of his three sons.

be more easily retained by a strong maritime power, as in this comparatively small space was principally stored up the mineral on account of which the Phœnicians had come from far. And as, over a territory so circumscribed and compact, they could more easily exercise an oversight, so as to prevent the dispersion of those employed by them, they were the less likely to spread rapidly over the island, and more likely to be jealous of their business here being interfered with by others, such as the Romans, who had other ends to serve, and who for its own sake, and not merely in the interests of commerce, both sought and fought for the extension of territory; their object being to bring the nations generally under the influence of the'r government and law.

Berytus or *Beyrout* was a place remarkable for the teaching of law, especially as applied to mercantile affairs, in which we might expect the Canaanites (or merchants) to be most interested. A writer in the *Quarterly* for October 1846, says, "Elsewhere the ordinary course of academic training closed on a student's attaining his twentieth year; but it was not supposed that any one could have imbibed all the learning of Berytus till five years more had supervened. This same Berytus, the metropolis of ancient law, was only a provincial town, and so far subordinate to Tyre, the capital of the district of Phœnicia. It abounded, not only in law, but also in merchandise, as innumerable traders were attracted thither by the fame and plenty of Tyrian purple. Still more ominously, it had been the favourite scene of gladiatorial shows. Constantine[1] (A.D. 306) desired to soften the

---

[1] His mother was the British Princess Helena, "the fair," who did so much with her great British army for the localisation of the Holy Places. He was born at York, and is said to have rebuilt the White Tower of London.

legal heart, even from its cradle; and hence his celebrated edict against such cruel exhibitions," was first promulgated at Berytus.

"Berytus may have been interested in this decree, not so much from being itself remarkable for gladiatorial shows, as for being a principal mart of slaves—a place where men were procured to be disposed of in the most arbitrary way, and who before being sold may have been there tested as to their fighting qualities. And yet laws with regard to them it was most needful the nations concerned in the trade should both have and carefully observe." Accordingly we are informed by an old writer "that learned practitioners were drafted from thence as assessors to the governors of the foreign settlements of the Empire, and that *Berytus* was the copious source whence all these rills of law were derived." And he goes on to show the encouragement held out to teachers by granting immunities to every class of engineers, surveyors, builders, and mechanics. As aspiring to eminence in the arts of peace, Berytus may the more have escaped unhurt amid the revolutions of empires, and have retained the influence of her schools down till the formal establishment of Christianity in the Empire under Constantine, when the law with regard to traffic in human beings became so greatly ameliorated.

Berytus or *Beyrout* appears to have had extensive connections westward. Sicily, Calabria, Spain, &c., are pointed out as quarters to which the coin of the *Brettii* extended. The head upon this is not unlike that of an Englishman; and curiously enough, at the back of the head we have the *Trident* which figures upon the English penny,[1] and the

---

[1] The same has been found on ancient Buddhist coins belonging to Affghanistan.—See *Prinsep's Historical Results.*

head of the *Bull*, the ensign of Ephraim, just as "John Bull" is now the generic term for Englishmen.

The medal of Severus, also, has Britannia with the same *Bull's* head on a shield at her left. In her left hand is a spear surmounted by the Cap of Liberty, and in her right hand a sceptre with two horns on the end.[1]

---

[1] The Rev. W. D. Waddilove, of Hexham, in his Lamp in the Wilderness (A.D. 1847), supposes that the figure on the coin of the *Brettii* may have a reference to the blessing of Joseph (Deut. xxxiii. 17). It is possible, however, that the two figures—the Trident and the Bull's head —may refer to Commerce and Agriculture, for the promotion of which the confederation of the *Brettii* may have been primarily founded, calling their centre of unity Berytus or *Beyrout*, Brit, or Bret, in commemoration of, or as witness to, the league or *covenant* into which they had entered; and the laws of which covenant it seems to have been a prime object of the schools at *Beyrout* to teach.

"There is no doubt that Tyre, who is noted in Scripture for 'sealing up the sum, full of wisdom and perfect in beauty' (Ezek. xxviii. 12), knew where Land's End was. The Tyro-Samaritan traders, who have left the most indubitable traces of their early visits and connection with this island, must have been well acquainted with Isaiah's prophecy, and the faithful among them were doubtless warned to flee to Land's End and Kittim (or sealed) on or before the destruction of the kingdom of Samaria and the siege of Tyre; and their observance of those repeated commands to 'keep silence' (Isa. xli. 1), to 'be still'—to hide till the indignation be over and past—(Isa. xxvi. 20), may sufficiently account for the Druids, who were called Sarronidæ, not so much from their oaks, or from their astronomy, as from SARRA; צוֹר, Tyre, their mother city, being so strict in forbidding writing to their students, by which means, in a few generations, their origin was buried in all that obscurity which they wished. The kindred they claimed to Tyre is further supported by the emblems on the coin of Antoninus, as naval dominions descended from the rock, which צוֹר means, and on which the emblem of Britain sits and holds, as in the coins of Berytus, also a daughter of Tyre."—*Wedgwood.*

"Old *Sarum*, or *Saron*, is so named from a king of that name, who is said to have been the first who founded public schools among the Britons." —*Lewis's British History*, pp. 6 and 25.

A remarkable allusion in Amos (B.C. 787) is to the circumstance that "silence" shall mark the necessity of the time predicted: "THERE-

It does not appear that the Jews had any home in Beyrout. It is not once mentioned in the Acts of the Apostles, although Damascus on the east, and Antioch to the north of it are. It may be that the Jews were known in Berytus chiefly as merchandise; and that law for them was the denial of all law, and such as for a long time also prevailed in Britain.

If this be so, Britain, the great coloniser of the world, was itself once a wilderness, belonging to a small Phœnician colony, in the market of which our brethren of the House of Judah were sold into painful servitude.[1]

Part of the half-tribeship of MANASSEH—in which were both Carmel and Samaria—reaching down to the Mediterranean Sea, opportunity was afforded to many for sharing the fortunes of those who "escaped" rather than those of the "remnant" who were taken captive. From Jacob's words (Gen. xlviii. 15–20) we might reasonably expect

---

fore the prudent shall keep 'silence' in THAT time, for it shall be an evil time" (v. 13). The word in relation to "silence" is the same from which we derive our word *dumb*, and the Buddhists that of *Damma*.—*Moore's Lost Tribes*, p. 337, A.D. 1861].

[1] Baal-worship seems to have been introduced by a maritime power from the East. The general scheme, and the very name of the great object of worship—Baal, Bel, Bol, or Vol—plainly give it a Phœnician origin. At Torbolton, in Ayrshire, on the evening preceding the June fair, a piece of fuel is demanded at each house, and is invariably given by the poorest inhabitant. The fuel so collected is carried to a particular part of the hill, and placed upon an altar or circular fire-place of turf about three feet high. A huge bonfire is kindled, and many of the inhabitants, old and young, men and women, assemble on the hill, and remain for hours, apparently occupied with observing a feat performed by the youths, who are to be seen leaping with indefatigable zeal upon the altar or turf wall enclosing the ashes of former fires and supporting the present one. From 1 Kings xviii. 26, it appears that much of the worship of Baal consisted in leaping upon his altar. Though our translators have written the name of the false god so worshipped as BAAL, it is "Bol;" so that the town at Baal's Mount is called Tor-Bol-Ton (Hosea ii. 16).

that MANASSEH would henceforth be found spreading out widely towards the extremities of the earth, mingling among other peoples. There is a remarkable tradition among the western SCOTCH, that their ancestors came from the East, and were the descendants of an Egyptian Princess—which would be the case, as being children of JOSEPH.[1]

Moses invokes upon this tribe "the good-will of Him who dwelt in the Bush" (Deut. xxxiii. 16; Exod. iii. 2–4), and the official seal of the General Assembly of the Church of Scotland is the Bush burning but not consumed. The UNICORN also, mentioned in ver. 17, is, along with the LION of Judah, upon the national coat of arms. The cautious, adventurous foresight of JOSEPH seems still to characterise many of his children. They are continually going forth in search of new possessions, and are seldom a loss to the countries in which they settle. The solving of riddles and dreams, for which he was so remarkable, used to be a favourite amusement among them, and their great regard to "second-sight" may have had a similar origin.

That branch of the people which early came into Ireland by way of Spain, as the Tuatha or Tribe de *Danaan, Scuite, Scots, Wanderers*, &c.,[2] and thence passed over into Scotland, have especially been "separated from their brethren;" being eminently distinguished by the faculty of firmness,

---

[1] In corroboration of such ancestral traditions, it is remarkable that the form of the SCOTCH head should be so extremely like that of most of the skulls of the Egyptian mummies I have seen, only, of course, an improvement upon them. Its resemblance to that of the BOHEMIAN also was observed by Mr Combe while visiting that country. By some the many coloured tartan worn by the Scotch is considered to remind of "Joseph's coat" of many colours.

[2] Colonel Gawler has also ably followed out the Scythians in the *Hebrew Christian Witness* for June 1875.

which gives much efficiency to the other powers, and enables one to triumph over many natural disadvantages, unless hindered by idolatry, upon which the curse was threatened. The penetrating "unicorn" forehead not inaptly describes their mental power; they *have* "pushed the people together to the ends of the earth," in all parts of the world, so that in the corners only of the lands which they chiefly inhabit are the remains of inferior races to be found.

They boast of theirs being the crown of Israel, and the stone of Jacob as having been that upon which their kings were crowned. It is now in the Chapel of Edward the Confessor in Westminster Abbey.[1]

---

[1] The conjectures, researches, and discoveries of Rev. F. R. A. Glover on this subject have a most fascinating charm of congruity and fitness, as well as of probability; especially when we consider that Jeremiah was given a commission with regard to the Jewish remnant, "to root up and to plant," including of course the royal family. Indeed, he had special charge of the king's daughters, chap. xli. 2, 3.

Of those *conjectures* this is the sum, viz.:—

"1. That England is the possessor and *rightful* owner of the Stone of Jacob, called Jacob's Pillow, now used as the coronation throne: the 'Pillar of Witness,' consecrated by the Patriarch some 3600 years since.

2. That England is, in her royal family, of the stem of Jesse; and therefore is, as the hereditary holder of the Perpetual Sceptre, and inheritor of the Standard of Judah, the fostered remnant of Judah.

3. That *Angle*-land, in her origin and descent, is the reality of Joseph in her own position, and the Ephraim of Jacob, *i.e.*, the Israel of Ephraim, in that of her colonies.

4. That in this COMBINATION of the TWO FAMILIES (Jer. xxxiii. 24) has COMMENCED the fulfilment of the prophecy which foretells the union of these two elements of the world's approaching future (Isa. xi. 13)—the prediction that Judah shall not vex Ephraim, nor Ephraim envy Judah; by which COMBINATION, also, England is qualified to be standard-bearer of all Israel:—and that,

5. Herein is involved the responsibility of action, which is clearly pointed out as the privilege of the Israel of Blessing in Isa. xix.; that pleasant instrument of a happy future to *Egypt* (the Mohammedan), God's "*My*

A very interesting work has been written by Sir William

People," "and Assyria (the Hindu, Brahmin, and Buddhist), *the work of My hands;*" and as THE THIRD of sanctification to the other TWO-THIRDS, and the incipient development of the accomplished promises of God to "*Israel mine Inheritance,*" viz., ENGLAND—the now living reality and representative of Abraham, Isaac, and Jacob.

The Stone of DESTINY (called Lia Phail, from פליא, *Phelia,* wonderful, or פלא, *secret*—Ps. cxviii. 22, 23; Isa. xxviii. 29) of Ireland, called Hebraically after it the Isle of DESTINY, is "the Jacob's Pillow" of England, on which was once crowned (B.C. 587), on the hill of TARA (תורה, *Torah,* "the Law of the Two Tables"), in Ireland, TAMAR (or Teamair), the KING'S DAUGHTER of JUDAH, wife of Eochaid, under the STANDARD of JUDAH, by the עולם פולה, *Ollam Fola,* or Prophet of Destiny, of Ireland. Jeremiah, Jehovah's "Prophet to the Nations" (Jer. i. 5), who there set up the TORAH, or Law of God (in place of the previous Baal-worship), instituted the office of the JODHAN MORAN, the REACTAIRE of Tara, and founded the Mar-OLLAM-Ham, or School of the Prophets, to teach the Law at the place which was from that time called TARA.

It is very evident that an Eastern beast (the lion), never indigenous to these countries, was once the standard of Ireland, or of the reigning family of Ireland, which goes to establish the fact of a connection of that family with the East; and further, that this figure of a lion rampant is the ensign of the Hebrew tribe of Judah, which concurrence tends much to show the likelihood of a *Hebrew* connection between Ireland and the East. Certainly, whatever be the ancient facts of the case, this Irish connection has been the means of introducing and maintaining, in constant display on the national keep of royalty, over the anointed head of this united Empire, the blazon *identical* with the standard of the tribe of Judah. This *may* indicate what has been suggested, or it may mean nothing. It may be accident, and *not* Providence. It certainly ties Ireland to the East, to those of the East who had a lion rampant for their standard. The son of Jesse had a lion rampant for his standard; and if there be any reason to imagine that Jeremiah (B.C. 587), in the exercise of his office and mission "to plant and to build" the kingdom of Judah for the perpetuation of the sceptre thereof, and the continuation of the throne of David, set up any mark of Jewish nationality and descent, what badge would he have brought and left as the mark and sign of that monarchy but the old, well-known, and prophetically-inspired standard of the race he represented? A people interested in "the king's daughters," and ready to receive the Ollam Folla, must have been there previously; and the Romans perhaps were not far wrong in calling the land after Heber.—*England the Remnant of Judah,* Rev. F. R. A. Glover.

Betham, the distinguished antiquary, to prove that the

> In the able and learned work by Dr Wood, entitled An Inquiry Concerning the Primitive Inhabitants of Ireland, Cork, 1821, we have the following:—
>
> "The distracted state of Ireland before and during the first century may be ascribed to ignorance of the arts, independence of Celtic tribes from each other, and the consequent want of unanimity which always distinguished the Celtic from other nations. These causes probably enabled the Armorican settlers to subdue and lay them under tribute. The subsequent interruption of tranquillity was caused by the restless and plundering disposition of the Belgæ or Fir-bolg, who obtained an ascendant power over the Celtic inhabitants about the third century, which they continued to uphold till the eighth or ninth,[*] when they themselves found a new enemy in one branch of their own family, called Danes and Norwegians; and, in the twelfth century, one still more formidable in another denominated Saxons or English.
>
> "Their shifting pastoral life and law of equality prevented improvement; and their practice of pillage not only prevented it among their neighbours, but caused a general neglect of agriculture, and consequent want of the common necessaries of life."
>
> "All foreign writers from the third to the fifteenth century call the Irish 'Scots,' an appellation which insinuates that they were Goths, or a people of Gothic descent. The bards take little notice of the Belgæ or Damnonii under these names, and even limit their duration in Ireland from thirty to eighty years. The native writers never imagined that the posterity of the Cauci, Menapii, Iblearni, &c., who used the Celtic language, could have been distinct tribes from their neighbours the Brigantes, with whom they were at war for centuries. Nevertheless, Irish history unknowingly traces the Belgic conquests into every province in Ireland, in which their descendants divided themselves into septs, toparchs, and clans, seizing upon large tracts of land and occupying them. Like the Romans d Britons, who considered the Picts a savage people distinct from themselves, the Irish, ignorant even of their own history, never conceived that the manners and customs of Germany were the predominant manners and customs of Ireland. Yet all the Irish bards were aware of the dominion of a Gothic or Scythian family in Erin; but, ignorant of the tribes by which it had been effected, they have preposterously ascribed it to the arms and transferred it to the family of the Celtic Brigantes.
>
> "The Belgæ (in Kymric meaning "War-men," the same as Germans and

---

[*] See *Eginhartus*, A D 790, and A D. 812, according to *Hermannus Contractus* and the *Annales Fuldensis Monasterii*, also in A.D. 815, according to the *Ogygia*, p. 433.

Welsh are related to the Picts or Pechts, who were of
German race; and some hints were thrown out by Abdiel,

Allemanni) seem to have plotted the subjugation of the Celtæ between
the second and third century, and succeeded at length in seizing upon
their possessions. Another branch of the same family, called *Saxons*,
reduced the Celtæ of Britain in about four centuries after the Roman
conquest, when its population was thinned by the emigration of its youth,
and by frequent skirmishes with the plundering Picts and Scots. The
Belgic or Scottish tribes of Ireland, after the reduction of the Celtæ, continuing a life of rapine, preyed upon each other, and reduced their population so
considerably, that in the twelfth century a small army of adventurers, composed of Saxon and Norman descendants, conquered a large portion of
these Belgic septs, and obtained possessions in this country.

"Thus the Belgæ and Saxons, two branches of the same family, differing
in language, manners, and customs, then occupied the soil of Ireland.
Jealousy, nurtured by prejudice and pride, opposed itself to inconsiderateness, folly, and power, from the twelfth to the seventeenth century, during
which time these causes prevented the bonds of consanguinity from uniting
the Irish and British people in fellowship; they prevented the principle of
mutual interest from producing unanimity and happiness. Yet both were
descendants of the Goths, and consequently one family, connected by the
tie of kindred to a long line of British monarchs, descended from a race
common to both—a *tie* strengthened by allegiance, and still connecting,
through German origin, the subjects of Great Britain and Ireland to their
present gracious sovereign.

"Different modes of education have caused different manners and
customs: these constitute discriminating traits of character; but, though
they differ in these respects, both are, as regards family, of the same race;
and as to relative rank, the Irish are equally brave, benevolent, generous,
and susceptible of education."

"A Christian Church existed in Ireland even before the time of St
Patrick (A.D. 430), its great Bible teacher. No country effected more for
humanity (in the same time) than Ireland in its pre-papal days, affording
a refuge and a school in which the sacred lamp of revelation was kept
vigilantly burning. Students in thousands resorted to her immense colleges of Armagh, Clonard, Mungrit, and Clonmacnoise. Far more than
Italian teachers, Scoti of Erin were the early Christian educators of Europe
for some 700 years."

[Alas for England's share in her subjection to Rome under Henry II.
and her unfaithfulness in our own day!]

"Amongst the emblems seen on the coins of Buddhist kings, the

a very able writer in the *Jewish Expositor* for 1828, intimating that the Welsh are of Israel.[1]

In many respects they have shown themselves superior

---

trident has been mentioned. This is now peculiar to English coins; but the *shield* of Britannia and the *lion* at her feet are also Buddhist and ancient Saxon symbols. Our banner of union, with the Cross of St George on it, may be seen engraved on the gates of the large tope at Sanchi or Sachi: it is remarkable that the star banner is also there. The lion and unicorn may be seen crouching in peace at the feet of Buddha, as he sits on his marble throne at the entrance of the vast rock-temple of Ajanta. The creature we vulgarly (? commonly) call a unicorn is more naturally portrayed there; for the people who chiselled out that cavernous cathedral knew its nature better than to present but one horn, though they well knew, as we know from Assyrian monuments, that it was often conventionally so represented. Our unicorn is a strange anoma'y, a bizarre, un-English beast, and yet not a mere heraldic invention: it combines somewhat of the figure of a horse with the foot and leg of an antelope; and in fact, it originated in the desire to combine two creatures in one, the antelope and the horse. These were both emblems of the Saxon race, and are found separate in the Buddhistic monuments of India. The original of the unicorn is probably the *Hippelaphus* of Aristotle, which is the *Equi-cervus* or horse-stag of Cuvier (*Règne Animal*, ii. 2, §§ 3, 4).

"Being usually sculptured in profile on bas-reliefs, its two erect horns of course appear as one. Ignorant sculptors would suppose this its characteristic, and represent it in all positions as one-horned. Hence the traditional heraldic emblem—a unicorn. There is, however, a large Tibetan goat, the horns of which grow so closely as to be almost united, and even recent travellers in the neighbourhood of Tibet have assured us that they have seen a live unicorn. However we may explain the symbol, we here see the origin of our Royal Arms, together with the source of the flag that for more than 2000 years has braved the battle and the breeze."—*Moore's Lost Tribes*, p. 224.

[1] Welsh traditions tell of their migration to the White Island of the West from the Summer Land of the Crimea, which the old book Varaha states was in possession of the Sacs from an early period, who called it Saxsen (As. Res. xi. 61), under Hu Gadarn, or the Mighty, who also mnemonically systematised for them the wisdom of their ancestors in the justly celebrated triads. But their designation as Cymbri we shall hereafter see tells of their idolatrous Omni organisation, worship, and priesthood, rather than of their relation to Gomer, as generally supposed (Hosea i. 3). The standard of Hu Gadarn was an ox.

to the other portions of the ancient inhabitants of Britain, and their institutions and language give undoubted evidence of a very close connection with Israel. Cumberland and the south-west of Scotland were early inhabited by the same race, and the whole island was in old time claimed by them.[1]

---

[1] Recent researches have shown the connection of Druidism with Buddhism, by which Baal-worship was superseded, and prepared the way for purer light. When Druidism merged into Christianity, its rites, festivals, and canonicals became those of the Christian Church. Little variation exists between the modern ceremonials of religion, as witnessed in a Roman Catholic cathedral, and those of Druidic Britain 2000 years since. Some of these observances are common to Judaism and Druidism, others are to be found in Druidism alone. A tenth of the land was appropriated among the Britons for the support of the Druidical priesthood.—*Morgan's British Kymry*, p. 56.

"Consistent with this was the early introduction of the Gospel, 'the way of God,' as it was called, by some of the disciples who were scattered everywhere at the death of Stephen, being invited hither by Bràn, the father of Caractacus, and other eminent British Druids, who had been converted at Rome under Paul's preaching. It is recorded that he brought back with him as teachers three Israelite Christians, Illtyd, Cyndaf, and Arwystli (the Welsh for Aristobulus), to whose friends or household Paul sends salutation (Rom. xvi. 10). Gildas gives the introduction of Christianity to Britain before the defeat of Boadicea, A.D. 61.

"Patrick is said to have been abbot of the monastery of Bangor Illtyd, in Glamorgan, which, under Illtyd himself, contained more than 2000 students and holy men, among whom were the sons of kings and nobles. The course of instruction there embraced not only a clerical education, but likewise included husbandry and other useful arts."—*Williams' Ecclesiastical Antiquities of the Cymri*.

It is said, however, that the first edifice for British Christian worship was built at Glastonbury, in Somersetshire. The names of the apostle Philip and Joseph of Arimathæa have floated down the stream of time in connection therewith; and before an acre of Britain was *incorporated* with Pagan Rome, Britons had not only received the Gospel, but had also been the blessed instrumentality of its propagation to nations on the Continent.

Admiral Fishbourne writes in *The Missing Link Magazine* for 1873, "Among the many things of interest in Rome, not the least

The south-west of Scotland, between England and the Firth of Clyde, like the north of England, called Cumberland and North Cumberland, appears to have been possessed by the Welsh or Cymri. Two small islands in the Clyde, which probably were on the frontiers of their possessions in that direction, are still called the Cumraes;

interesting to English visitors is the house of Aulus Rufus Pudens, to whom Claudia, grand-daughter of Brân, was married. These are the Rufus Pudens and Claudia of Rom. xvi. 13, and 2 Tim. iv. 21, &c."— *Stillingfleet's Antiquities of British Churches.*

"The Britons are said to have been always famous for three things—handsome women, brave warriors, and eminent bards. Martial, lib. i. Ep. 32, and lib. iii. Ep. 20, says—

'For mountains, bridges, rivers, churches, fair
Women, and wool, England is past compare.'

"The word 'bard' originally implied among them a prophet, musician, poet, philosopher, teacher, and herald. His dress was of sky-blue, as an emblem of truth and of his sacred character; not unlike the primitive priesthood; for the Lord commanded Moses, 'And thou shalt make the robe of the Ephod all of blue' (Exod. xxviii. 31; xxxix. 22; Lev. xix. 27, 28. The Scythians had also their poets or warlike singers, whom they called *Singbardos*; and their chiefs that delighted in music *Abbardos*, *Dagobardos*, and *Realtbardos* (Holinshed's 'History of Britain,' vol. i. p. 29). *Gwrgon*, the Bushy Beard, flourished about B.C. 375. He first built the city of Cambridge, and called it after his own name, *Caer-Gwrgant*, or the *city of Gwrgant* (Heb. Kir.) The *Dacians* refused to pay him a tribute which had been usually paid to his father, *Beli*; in consequence of which he mustered a strong army, set sail for Denmark, and conquered that kingdom. On his return home, he met at sea a fleet of ships, with a colony which came from Spain to seek a new place of habitation; and they requested of him to grant them some vacant country to inhabit as his subjects; on which he sent them to Ireland, at that time depopulated by a plague. And probably *Gwrgon* sent his son *Gwdlelin* as chieftain over them; for the Welsh call the Irish *Gwyddelod* to this day."—*Lewis's History of Britain*, p. 52.

"Cambria Formosa, B.C. 373, the Fair Oracle, was a daughter of *Belinus*, and niece of Brennus. She greatly promoted the building of cities and castles. She taught the women to sow flax and hemp, and weave it into cloth; was a priestess as well as princess, and made the laws for the

and Dumbarton, or Dumbreton, appears to have been their stronghold in that direction. Some of the principal names of rivers, &c., have been evidently given them by the Welsh, resembling the names of similar objects in Wales, though smaller.

The history of the kingdom of Strathclyde is, however,

Sycambrians. Her grandfather, Dyfnwal Moel-Meod (B.C. 430), is said to be the first King of Britain who wore a crown of gold. He gave privileges to temples, cities, ploughs, and highways leading to the same, that whosoever had need thereof might repair thither and be safe.

King Arthur, the father of chivalry, was a descendant of Constantine, and was crowned King of Britain A.D. 516. For his conquests of Norway, see Hakluyt's Account of Navigation, vol. i. He gave the charter to the University of Cambridge in A.D. 531, in accordance with the decree of King Lucius. In A.D. 528, he took the title of "*Patricius Arturius Britanniæ, Galliæ, Germaniæ, Daciæ Imperator.*" See Ashmole's Order of the Garter, p. 184.

An intelligent Jew tells the following anecdote. He was on board a steamer far at sea. It was a dark night. Approaching the prow of the vessel as she was ploughing the waves, he heard a solemn Hebrew tune sung or crooned by a muffled figure in the attitude in which when alone the Jews chant the Psalms. He waited to the end, and then went up to salute, as he thought, a brother Jew, when he was answered in Gaelic by a Scotch Highlander. The Hebrew tune had come down to this man from his forefathers, and the Jew and the Highlander had inherited it from some common ancient source. "Cruiskeen Lawn" is also Hebrew.

Irenæus, Bishop of Lyons, very early in the second century mentions the existence of Christian churches among the Keltoi, and says the apostles planted them. Tertullian, writing rather later, speaks of "those localities of the Britons, hitherto inaccessible to the Romans, which had become subject to Christ." M'Crie's Annals of English Presbytery give interesting information concerning the early churches of Christ among the Kelts or Cymri, who mainly peopled Europe before the Saxons appeared on the stage of our history, though at the beginning of the Christian era they existed as distinct nationalities, chiefly in Ireland, Scotland, and Wales. Neander and others are of opinion that especially in Scotland and Ireland the Christian missionaries were from the East (testified by the presence of so many names of holy places associated with the words "mar," a saint, and "kirk," house of the Lord). D'Aubigné says

very obscure. We can neither tell when it began nor when it ended, nor what were the fortunes of its sovereign and people. This part of the island had been possessed by the Romans. Here Christianity was early propagated, and from this part of Scotland proceeded St Patrick.

When the south part of our island came into possession of the Angles and Saxons, it seems to have to a great extent followed the fortunes of England; and, accordingly, the principal proprietors are of English or Saxon descent, such as the various families of Cunningham in Ayrshire (Könning-ham).

The dialect of the English most generally spoken along the east coast, and, indeed, generally throughout the country, is much the same with that prevailing along the

---

Columba *found* Culdees in Iona in the sixth century, who had found there a refuge from the dissensions of the Picts and Scots. Toland quotes from an early Irish MSS. that the word is derived from Ceiledé (or in Welsh, Coel y Duw), *The separated or espoused of God.* The earliest Latin form is "Kaledei," *worshippers of God*, which comes very near to "Kaldai" or "Kaldani"—(is this the origin of the name Caledonia?)—the name by which the Remnant of Exiled Israel, or Nestorians, still call themselves in Mesopotamia, as well as "Nusrany Syriany." They came from Babylon, whence Peter dates his Epistle, which recognises them as "strangers" passing through Pontus, Galatia, Cappadocia, Asia Minor, and Bithynia, bringing them into actual intercourse with the Gaels and Kelts of apostolic days.

The Galatians were the Gauls or Kelts of that era, a restless wandering, patriarchal people, who from B.C. 300 had been making incursions on their Western neighbours. They afterwards overran Asia Minor, in the centre of which a colony of villages settled. Though unstable enough soon to depart from Paul's teaching, they welcomed him as an angel of God. Peter beseeches his brethren who were "strangers and pilgrims" on their way to Europe to "abstain from fleshly lusts," "and to have their conversation honest *among the Gentiles.*" He addresses them as "a chosen generation, a royal priesthood, an holy nation, a peculiar people," who are to "show forth the praises of Him who hath called them out of darkness into marvellous light" (Ex. xix. 5). And lest we should lose sight of the fact, in 1 Pet. ii. 10, he points back to their description in

north-eastern coast of England. The inhabitants of the Highlands and Islands are not all of Keltic origin. Many of the principal families are of Norman descent. In early times the Danes and other Northmen made plundering expeditions all round the east and north coast, and throughout the Western Isles. In many of these they made conquests; but being few in number, as compared with the original inhabitants, the language of the latter prevailed. In other respects, also, they became much assimilated to those among whom they had settled, and by whom their power was to be sustained as either maintaining their ground or making further conquests. And just as many of the English who first settled in Ireland became more Irish than the Irish themselves, so many of

---

Hosea i.: "Which in times past were not a people (Lo-ammi), but are now the people of God (Ammi); which had not obtained mercy (Loruhamah), but now have obtained mercy."

Dr Lorimer says, "The early Culdean Church was a missionary Church in a sense peculiarly its own. The spirit of missions was the creative life-force which gave law and order to all its arrangements. It had an Episcopate, a Presbyterate, and a Monastic order, but all these in a different form from later Churches. Its bishops were without dioceses, without jurisdiction, and without exclusive powers of ordination; its presbyters were preachers and dispensers of the sacraments, but rarely pastors; and its monks took neither of the three vows of poverty, chastity, or obedience; they might have vows, they might have private property, and they were free to leave their monasteries at any time; the explanation of all these peculiarities being found in the fact that it was before everything a missionary Church and not a parochial one—a Church of Evangelists, not of pastors—a Church of motion, not of settlement and rest; and such a Church it was when it did its best work." Professor Ebrard of Erlangen tells of the labours of the Culdees in France and Germany, and how all their presbyters and bishops were reduced to external conformity with Rome. Montalembert in his Monks of the West gives exact references to all the original authorities.

Jerome puts the German extraction of the Galatians beyond doubt, by telling us, from personal knowledge, that their speech was the same with that of the Treveeri in Germany, where he studied.

these Northmen became more Keltic than the Kelts in the Highlands and Islands of Scotland; and to them doubtless much that has distinguished the Highlanders is to be attributed. The heads of the clans having greater vigour than the body of the people, they naturally possess superior influence when living in the midst of their vassals, than they could expect to enjoy among their equals in intellectual capacity and moral power.

And it is to be observed that by the same route as Sharon Turner brings the Anglo-Saxons to the north of Europe, does Pinkerton in his "Early History of Scotland" bring the Pechts or Picts, and other tribes, at an earlier period into the north of Britain.

And if "the escaped of Israel" have thus been strewn along the coasts of the very countries into which the tribes carried captive were about to come: if those who fled westward have come into the very quarter into which those who were taken away north-eastward in bonds have ultimately been brought, where the two long-separated streams have commingled in the bonds of the gospel, thence to spread their fructifying influence all over the globe; so far also has that prophecy been fulfilled, which at the time it was given seemed most difficult (Micah ii. 12, 13).

> "I will surely assemble,
>   O Jacob, ALL of thee;
> I will surely gather
>   The remnant of Israel;
> I will put them together
>   As the sheep of Bozrah,
> As the flock in the midst of their fold;
> They shall make great noise
>   By reason of men.
>
> The Breaker is come up before them:
> They have broken up;

> And have passed through the gate;
> And are gone out by it;
> And their King shall pass before them,
> And the Lord on the head of them."

They have been gathered together into one place, and the Lord hath there kept them as a shepherd doth his sheep. "The Breaker"—"the Dreadful Beast and strong exceedingly"—the Fourth Empire (Dan. vii.), "that breaketh in pieces the whole earth," came up before them. They were obliged to associate more closely together, and break up the Roman Empire which aimed at their utter destruction. They obtained possession of "the gate of their enemies," and have gone out by it.

Israel have thus been indeed the Lord's "measuring line" from the very time of their calling and being placed in the Promised Land. They have been enclosing one portion after another of the human race, until now in a manner they embrace the world. We have already adverted to the fact of Jerusalem having been retained as a Canaanitish city until the time of David. It was enclosed within the bounds of Israel, who were dwelling on all sides of it, and at length was taken up into the Lord's inheritance, being chosen above all places by the God of Israel to place His name, and where His congregation should be established before Him. (See p. 109.)

Afterwards by the Assyrians the body of the people were removed farther back into the north. Their place in Samaria was left to be filled with a first-fruits of a variety of other nations, who were enclosed within the remaining portion of the Lord's people; the Jews dwelling in Judea and Galilee having these Gentiles inhabiting Samaria in their centre. "The Lord must needs go through Samaria" in going down from Judea into Galilee. His apostles followed in the same course; and thus the Samaritans came into participation of the blessings of the gospel, as being in the way in which the Lord went, and in which He sent His messengers forth for the blessing of His chosen people, "the cord or *cable* of His inheritance" (Deut. xxxii. 9).

XI.

HISTORICAL CONNECTION OF THE LANGUAGES OF EUROPE.

Purposes of the Assyrian opposed to those of the God of Israel—Khumri Israelites—Why so called ?—Time of the Horn of Israel Budding Forth —Language no Criterion of Race — Words in Twelve Western Languages compared with the same in Persian, Syrian, and Sanskrit—Hebrew the Basis of the English and other North-Western Tongues—Shibboleth and Sibboleth—Most Probable Origin of the Aryan Languages—Media the Common Centre of the Indo-Germanic Languages ; whence came also our Anglo-Saxon Ancestors.

WE should never forget that the portion of ISRAEL, taken captive or otherwise dispersed by the Assyrians, was that which, in both the historical and prophetical parts of Scripture, was called THE WHOLE HOUSE OF ISRAEL, or ALL ISRAEL, at the time they separated from Judah (1 Kings xii.), and also after their captivity (Ezek. xi. 15, 16). They are not merely as "one piece of money" of the Lord's "peculiar treasure" (Exod. xix. 5 ; Luke xv. 8), but the greater part of His royal diadem (Isa. lxii. 3). Of the "sheep" of the Lord's pasture, they are not merely as *one* of the hundred, but the whole "ninety and nine" who had wandered into the wilderness (Ezek. xxxiv. 10–16 ; John x. 4). Of the family of our Father in heaven—the God of Abraham—they are not merely "the younger son," but also the Lord's "first-born ;" for thus He hath said, " I

AM A FATHER TO ISRAEL, AND EPHRAIM IS MY FIRST-BORN" (Jer. xxxi. 9 ; Luke xv. 12).

Although the proud Assyrian had laboured so diligently in the removal of Israel from his own land into the north country, his purpose was very much opposed to that of the God of Israel. He thought to interweave the several parts of his empire together, so as to make them more entirely one. Thus proudly did he boast (Isa. x. 13, 14)—

> "By the strength of my hand I have done it,
>   And by my wisdom, for I am prudent.
> And I have removed the bounds of the people,
>   And have robbed their treasures,
> And I have put down the inhabitants, like a valiant one,
> And my hand hath found, as a nest, the riches of the people.
> And as one gathereth eggs left, have I gathered all the earth :
> And there was none that moved the wing, or opened the mouth, or peeped."

But thus did the Lord answer (ver. 15-23)—

> "Shall the axe boast itself against him that heweth therewith ?
>   Shall the saw magnify itself against him that shaketh it ?
>   As if the rod should shake against them that lift it up ;
>   As if the staff should lift up *as if it were* no wood.
> Therefore shall the Lord, the Lord of hosts, send among his fat ones leanness,
> And under His glory He shall kindle a burning, like the burning of a fire,
>   And the Light of Israel shall be for a fire,
>   And His Holy One for a flame ;
> And it shall burn and devour his thorns and his briers in one day ;
>   And shall consume the glory of his forest,
>   And of his fruitful field,
>   Both soul and body :
>   And they shall be as when a standard-bearer fainteth,
> And the rest of the trees of his forest shall be few, that a child may write them.
>
> "And it shall come to pass in that day, the REMNANT OF ISRAEL,
>   And such as are ESCAPED OF THE HOUSE OF JACOB,
>   Shall no more again stay upon him that smote them,
>   But shall stay upon the Lord, the Holy One of Israel, in truth.

The Remnant shall return, the Remnant of Jacob, unto the mighty God,
 For though Thy people Israel be as the sand of the sea,
  A Remnant of them shall return :
 The consumption decreed shall overflow with righteousness,
 For the Lord God of hosts shall make a consumption,
 Even that determined, in the midst of the land."

He had been used as an "axe" or "saw" in the hand of the Lord for cutting off "the branches" of Joseph, and therewith "the whole House of Israel." He had also been as a "rod" or "staff" for the correction of Judah. He thought that by his own wisdom and strength he had been enabled to do all this; but it was threatened that when the work was accomplished for which he had been raised up, he should be foiled in his further efforts. In the ruins of his own splendid palaces he was left buried till our own day, when they have been laid bare, contemporary with the discovery of the glorious destiny of the people he was the means of removing far from their own border.[1]

 " The King who built the Palace of Khorsabad, excavated by the French, is named *Sargina* (סרגון, *Sargon* of Isaiah). In the first year of his reign he came up against the city of Samaria (called *Samarina*, and answering to the Hebrew ישמרון) and the tribes of the country of *Buth-'Omri* (עמרי) or 'Omri, being the name of the founder of Samaria, 1 Kings xvi. 24 ; xviii. 16; Micah vi. 16). He carried off into captivity in Assyria 27,280 families, and settled in their places colonists brought from Babylonia, appointing prefects to administer the country, and imposing the same tribute which had been paid to former kings. The only tablet at Khorsabad which exhibits this conquest in any detail is unfortunately much mutilated. Should M. de Saulcy, however, whom the French are now sending to Assyria, find a duplicate of Shalmaneser's annals in good preservation, I think it probable that the name of the king of Israel may yet be recovered."—*Colonel (now Sir Henry) Rawlinson* in the *Athenæum*, August 23, 1851.

 " Now the Israelites of Samaria were often called Khumri ; and some writers, such as Parkhurst, have hinted that it was because of their idolatrous priests, called "Chemarim." But is it not more likely they were so named from their being *after the order of Omri?* (Micah vi. 16).

It is generally supposed that one of the principal means of arriving at the truth on the subject of Ethnology is the study of Language; not that the use of any particular form of speech by a people would prove that it was originally spoken by them. For example, the Jews, when they were in Babylon, learned to speak Chaldee, and it is said afterwards used its written character in preference to their own. WOULD IT, THEREFORE, ON THAT ACCOUNT, BE FAIR

The Kimbri, Cymry, or Kumri, are always mentioned by Tacitus (s. xxxvii.) as forming part of the great Germanic race. As Scythians (Skuthoi or nomads), they have occupied Denmark, a small part of the north of Germany, and Great Britain, where the Cambrian Scythians and Cumry are called Welsh. Herodotus says (B. iv. s. 11), that "the Cimmerians came from the region called Kimmerion" (or the Crimea), the land of the Khumri Israelites. The Kimbri swore by a brazen bull which they carried with them.

"The Hebrew word 'Chemarim' occurs only three times in the Bible: Zeph. i. 4; 2 Kings xxiii. 5; and Hosea x. 5. The final letter *m* being merely part of the masc. plural, the word stands in English letters KMRY—כְּמָרֵי.

"It may be observed that many of the names of tribes among the Scythians follow the same rule of derivation from the Hebrew, when read from left to right.

"JUDAH, as well as ISRAEL, were concerned in the idolatrous worship, of which the "Chemarim" were the leading teachers. This word is only found three times in the Old Testament. In Zeph. i. 4, in relation to JUDAH, and of which 2 Kings xxiii. 5 (see marginal reading) is the historical fulfilment.

"The passage relating to ISRAEL is in Hosea x. 5, of which we, 'upon whom the ends of the age are come, find the historical fulfilment attested by the disinterred monuments of Nineveh, concerning that long-buried people whose graves the Lord promised to open (Ezek. xxxvii. 11 16; and the promise of whose national recovery and manifestation yet remains to be fulfilled, with the forgiveness of their iniquity as a people: "The iniquity of Ephraim is bound up; his sin is hid. . . . I will ransom them from the power of the grave; I will redeem them from death," &c. (Hosea xiii. 12 14).

"To return to the inscription on the Nineveh tablet, and the natural deduction suggested by it as to the increase of the people, whose multiplicity is so often and so distinctly foretold in the Scriptures, even to the

TO ARGUE THAT THE JEWS THEMSELVES WERE OF CHALDEE ORIGIN?

Their ancestors had come out of Ur of the Chaldees; but that does not account for their speaking and writing the language of Babylon on their return after the seventy years' captivity. It happened so, simply because they had been located among a Chaldee-speaking people, and had occasion to speak the language of the country.

hour of their final triumph and restoration: "*And they shall increase even as they have increased*" (Zech. x. 7, 8). Let us distinguish between these solemn predictions and those concerning the disobedient and unbelieving portion of Israel (actually fulfilled in the Christ-rejecting part of the House of Judah): "And *ye shall be left few in number*, BECAUSE THOU WOULDST NOT OBEY THE VOICE OF THE LORD THY GOD" (Deut. xxviii. 62). "That Prophet" (Deut. xiii. 3). "This is my Beloved Son in whom I am well pleased: Hear ye Him" (Matt. xvii. 5.)

"If 'Sargon carried away 27,280 families' of Israel, and we allow the usual average of five to a family, the actual number of persons taken captive would be 136,400. The date of this captivity from Samaria, as given in our Bibles, is B.C. 721; and a remarkable passage in the prophecy of Ezekiel affords interesting data respecting the time of their regaining their independence, which coincides with the account given by Herodotus of the various disturbances in the cities of the Medes, whither Israel had been deported by the Assyrian monarchs. The marginal date for the prophecy to which we refer (Ezek. xxix. 17) is B.C. 572, the year of the invasion of Egypt and its spoliation by Nebuchadnezzar. Respecting that time, it is there written, "In that day will I cause *the horn of the House of Israel to bud forth*, and I will give thee the opening of the mouth in the midst of them," &c.

"Now between the date of Sargon's raid on Israel, and that of Ezekiel's prophecy, there is an interval of one hundred and forty-nine years; and allowing another year for its actual accomplishment, one hundred and fifty years would have run their course, during which period—at a rate of increase far below that recorded during their sojourn in Egypt—these 136,400 captives, doubling their numbers every twenty-five years, would have increased to above 8,000,000.

"What wonder, then, that their 'horn,' or power, should have begun to bud forth at the very time when that of their brethren of the House of Judah, captives in Babylon or refugees in Egypt, and doomed to destruction there, was at its lowest ebb!"

Also, the Jews throughout Russia use a dialect of the German, picked up by them, during the middle ages, in the cities of Germany; and although it is neither their original tongue, nor that of the people among whom they now sojourn, it is there used as their vernacular. THE USE OF GERMAN BY THE RUSSIAN JEWS DOES NOT PROVE THAT THEY ARE OF THE SAME RACE AS THE GERMANS; IT MERELY INDICATES THEIR PREVIOUS SOJOURN IN GERMANY.

So also the use of the Spanish language by what are called the Spanish Jews, merely shows that another portion of the same people have formerly resided in Spain; from which, as we also know, they were long expelled.

In like manner, the NORTHMEN, having settled in that part of France which, after them, was called NORMANDY, came over to this country, speaking French; but originally they spoke Norse, a language akin to that of the Danes, from whose neighbourhood they had proceeded to France, where they adopted the French language, which, in the eleventh century, they brought into England, imposing it upon the English court and lawyers.

And so, the fact that we speak a dialect of the Indo-Germanic, is merely consistent with Sharon Turner's idea that our ancestors once inhabited a region bordering upon Persia and Armenia, the district lying between these two countries being that which was called "Media," the common centre of the Indo-Germanic languages. At first he scouted this idea; but in the fifth edition of his "History of the Anglo-Saxons," he says, vol. ii. p. 470: "Since I printed the fourth edition of this work, the probable derivation of the Saxon race from the region near the Caspian led me to examine what affinities existed between the Asiatic languages in these parts and the Anglo-Saxon. The Hon. Mr Keppel calls the country where the ancients placed the

Sacæ and Sacasani, and which he visited, 'the beautiful province of Karabaugh.' It lies between the Aras and the Kur, which are the ancient Araxes and Cyrnus, near the northern parts of Persia. His travels induced me to compare the Anglo-Saxon with the Persian, and afterwards with the Zend, the earliest speech that is known to have been used in Persia; and also with the Pehlevi, which succeeded it there. The result of this was, that I found 162 words in the modern Persian, 57 in the Zend, and 43 in the Pehlevi, so similar in sound and meaning to as many in the Anglo-Saxon, as to confirm the deduction of the progenitors of our ancestors from the regions of ancient Asia."

Long ago, a writer in the "Encyclopædia Britannica" came to the following conclusions :—" It plainly appears that Pehlevi was the ancient language of Persia; and, second, that the ancient Persian was a cognate dialect of the Chaldean, Hebrew, Arabic, and Phœnician; and M. Anquetil has annexed to his translation of the Zend-Avesta two vocabularies in Zend and Pehlevi, which he found in an approved collection of Rawayah, or traditional pieces, in modern Persian.

" His vocabulary of the Pehlevi strongly confirms the opinion concerning the Chaldean origin of that language; but, with regard to the Zend, it abounded with vast numbers of pure Sanskrit words, to such a degree, that six or seven words in ten belonged to that language.

" From this deduction, it would appear that the oldest languages of Persia were Chaldaic and Sanskrit, and that, when they ceased to be vernacular, the Pehlevi and the Zend were deduced from them respectively, and the Parsi either from the Zend, or immediately from the dialect of the Brahmins; but all had perhaps a mixture of Tartarian. The best lexicographers assert that numberless words in ancient Persian are taken from the Cimmerian. With regard to the last of these, we cannot help being of opinion that colonies of people from the neighbourhood of Persia (say of Media) did transport themselves into Crim Tartary, and perhaps into Europe. These colonists brought along with them those vocables which still occur in their dialect. Emigrants from those quarters must have found their way into Scandinavia, since numberless Persian words are still current in these regions. Perhaps Odin and his followers emigrated from the neighbourhood of Media and Persia, and brought with them the dialect of the nations from whose country they had taken their departure."[1]

That our forefathers had not merely stray words from the PERSIAN, but actually learned the language of the MEDES, in the same way that the Russian Jews learned German, will plainly appear hereafter. Meanwhile, let us for example take four words expressive of family relationship, and show that while these words are used by us in common with other European nations speaking different dialects of the Indo-Germanic, we have not received our pronunciation of them from any intermediate source, but immediately from the quarter whence the Saxons are said to have come into Europe.

English	Father	Mother	Daughter	Son	Brother
Anglo-Saxon	Feeder	Moder	Dochter		Bruder
Persian	Phader	Mader	Dochter	Sunna	Broder
Gothic	Fadrein	Mœla	Dauhtar		Brothar
German	Vater	Mutter	Tochter	Sohn	Bruder
Belgic	Water	Moeder	Dochter		Broeder
Danish	Feder	Moder	Dotter		Broder
Swedish	Fadder	Moder	Dotter (?)		Broder
Greek	Πατηρ	Μητηρ	Θυγατηρ		φρατηρ

---

[1] "The fact that we have six or seven hundred words in our language of Persian origin agrees with our own origin amongst the Persians, but not (as) of them."—*Dr Moore's Lost Tribes*, p. 91 (1861).

Latin	Pater	Mater		Frater
Italian	Padre	Madre		Fratello
Spanish	Padre	Madre		Frayle
French	Père	Mère		Frère
Syriac		Maddra	Dochtera	
Sanskrit	Pita	Matu	Dugida	Brader *Armenian* Breuzr
Hebrew				Senah

The words are somewhat varied in spelling or sound in the different languages, but it will scarcely be questioned that

    Fœder, in Anglo-Saxon, is the same as
    Phader, in Persian; and that
    Moder, in Anglo-Saxon, is the same as
    Mader, in Persian; and that
    Dochter, in Anglo-Saxon, is the same as
    Dochter, in Persian; and that
    Broder, in Anglo-Saxon, is the same as
    Broder, in Persian, &c.

    F of Fœder, or Father, may be Ph in the Persian; or
    V in the German—Vater; or
    W in the Belgic—Water; or
    Π in the Greek—Πατηρ; or
    P in the Latin—Pater.[1]

The *d* of the Anglo-Saxon and Persian has become *th* in the modern English. It is simply *t* in Belgic and German; also in Greek, Latin, and Sanskrit. Like the Anglo-Saxon, it is *d* in the Danish, *Fœder*; and double *dd* in the Swedish, *Fadder*. But there cannot be a doubt that it is the same word throughout; only slightly modified in form, according to the character of the dialect in which the word is used.

Thus, Father, Mother, Brother, have all *der* for their

---

[1] "There are numerous words in the Persian language which are, in sound and signification, precisely the same in the old English; we will instance one—Witten-a-gemote, which, in both tongues, literally means a national assembly (of wise men). *Huet* says the German language bears a greater affinity to the Persian."—*Penine's Historical Drama*, 530.

termination, in both Anglo-Saxon and Persian; whereas the Gothic seems to have all the endings different—*drein, da, tar, thar.*

The Greek has τηρ throughout; and the Latin *ter* in the three words *Pater, Mater, Frater,* which, it may easily be observed, are not so near the Persian as *Father, Mother,* and *Brother.* The Latin has no word correspondent in sound to the Persian *Dochter:* the Greek has Θυγατηρ, which, although evidently the same word as the Persian, is not nearly so like as the Anglo-Saxon, *Dochter*—identical with the Persian,[1] and not far from the Syriac, *Dochtera.*

The French language, it may be observed, omits the *t* in all the other three—*Père, Mère, Frère;* while the Spanish and Italian give evidence of a nearer relationship to the Gothic than to the Latin, in their *Padre* and *Madre.* From a comparison of these words, as pronounced in the several languages, it may be seen that we are not dependent upon France, or even Germany, nor upon the Latin, nor the Greek, for evidence of our intimate connection by language with the East.

The English language has a closer affinity to the Persian than either the French, German, Latin, or Greek; and in such a way as can best be accounted for by our later and most intimate relationship to the Persians. In resemblance to the Persian, our own and the Scandinavian tongues generally seem to have the advantage. When words occur

---

[1] "To the Himalaya mountains we trace home the streams of the Gothic and Saxon nations, who all call their heaven by the Oriental name. Thus in Mœso-Gothic (A.D 400) heaven is *Himin*; in Allemanic (A.D. 720), *Himele*; in Frankic (A.D. 900), *Himile*; in old German (A.D. 1300), *Humele*; in recent German, *Himmel*. The most remarkable word for heaven, however, is that of the Old Saxon (A.D. 900), viz., *Himil-arikea*, a combination of the Sanskrit *Himil* and the Hebrew word signifying the expanse."—*More's Lost Tribes.*

in English which we know to have branches in French, German, Latin, or Greek, we should not at once take it for granted that we have thence *derived* the words. We may have to look farther east for what has been really the root of the word as we have it.

It is indeed true, that through our former ecclesiastical relations with Rome, and making so much use of Latin literature in education and the three learned professions, we have transferred much of that language to our own, independently of the adulterated LATIN received through a French medium, and relating to matters connected with the court, war, dress, and fashionable life generally.

From the GREEK we have long been in the habit of taking scientific terms for various inventions, as well as for the expression of our ideas respecting the mental powers, philosophy, art, &c.

The Holy Scriptures having been so long, and everywhere, before the eyes of our people, and constantly sounded in our ears, have not only stereotyped the common English, but also introduced into it a great many HEBREW names and other words, besides an immense number of beautiful and expressive phrases and allusions, the value of which it would be difficult for a stranger to estimate. There must have been something in the mental constitution of the Anglo-Saxon which enabled him thus to avail himself of these. It has been observed that the Hebrew Scriptures can most easily be translated into English, the idiom of the two languages being so much alike.

Indeed, the basis of the English language may to a remarkable extent be found in the HEBREW. Many of our most common words and names of familiar objects are almost pure Hebrew. I have observed this particularly with regard to the Lowland Scotch. *Pirie, Parkhurst, Lowth,*

Gorett, Tomlin, &c., have all pointed out many English words of Hebrew derivation. We seem not to have been altogether strangers to the Hebrew Scriptures previous to our conversion to Christianity, but rather to have been thereby engrafted into our own olive-tree again, more especially at and after the Reformation, when the Latin veil which had been cast over the Scriptures was rent asunder, and we came into immediate contact with them. (*Watchmen of Ephraim*, vols. i. ii. and iii.)

This connection of our English language with the Hebrew is said to characterise the North-Western tongues generally. It is also acknowledged that it has been poured into them through a Gothic medium.[1]

---

[1] Dr ANDREW, in his "Hebrew Dictionary and Grammar," said (A.D. 1823), "The dispersion and incorporation of the Ten Tribes of Israel amongst the Assyrian and other northern nations, accounts most satisfactorily for the numerous traces of the Hebrew language that still remain amongst the languages of Europe," &c.

And in A.D. 1866 the Rev. JACOB TOMLIN, in his "Comparative Vocabulary of 48 Languages" (Liverpool: Arthur Newling), says, "By inspection of the Table of Affinities, it is apparent that the Anglo-Saxon and Gothic family of languages stands in close relationship to the Hebrew— the Syriac and Arabic alone, of the whole forty-eight languages compared, taking precedence of them. The Saxon stands first in this class, rising to No. 34 in the scale of affinity with the Hebrew, being two degrees above the Gothic. The English and German also rise to an honourable position, being nearly upon an equality at Nos. 32 and 31. From this scale it also appears that about one-fourth part of the words in our own Saxon tongue bears an affinity with the Hebrew in a primary or secondary degree. . . . Not only in words does this close affinity exist between our original mother-tongue and the Hebrew; but in the arrangement of ideas, and the simple structure of sentences, it has also a near agreement; and for this reason it is comparatively easy to translate the Hebrew Scriptures into English. This similarity between the two languages was noticed by Tyndal, the first translator of the Hebrew Bible and Greek New Testament into English. He said, 'The Greke tongue agreeth more with the Englyshe than with the Latyne; and the properties of the Hebrew tongue agree a thousand tymes more with yᵉ Englyshe than with yᵉ Latyne.' . . .

It is evident that we have not derived our Hebrew from the Jews, nor from the Israelites who dwelt east of the Jordan; for the hissing sound whereby the men of Ephraim were detected by the Gileadites at the fords of the Jordan (Judges xii. 5, 6) characterises our pronunciation of words derived from the Hebrew, while the Jews retain a predilection for the broad sound of the ש—*sh*.

The Gileadite, like the Jews, said "Shibboleth;" the Ephraimite, "Sibboleth."

"The English language has also a remarkable affinity with the Persian. In the Table of Affinities, the latter, it will be observed, ranks No. 28 in its relation to the English, and No. 17 to the Hebrew. The Hindostani also, which is the Hindo-Persian spoken in Upper India, comes pretty near it, being No. 26. Many words in these two languages are almost the same as in English, and particularly those relating to family kindred: as, *Fader, Modar* or *Mudar, Brudar*. I have noticed some English words and phrases which are evidently from the Persian; for instance, *Reynard* signifies *fox* in Persian, and *quack* (an irregular medical practitioner) is an appellative for *doctor* in Persian.

"Many national customs, laws, manners, &c., of the Persians seem to assimilate them with ourselves," &c., &c.

"The Mœso-Gothic of Ulphilas' New Testament, written in the fourth century, contains Hebrew, Greek, Sanskrit, and Tartar words."—*Moore's Lost Tribes*, 1861.

Professor or Canon Rawlinson, in his edition of *Herodotus* (i. 663), says, "It may reasonably be conjectured, as has been already remarked, that the scene of the original development of the Indo-European dialect, or at any rate of the first large increase of the races speaking this language, was the mountain district of Armenia. It is from this point that the various tribes constituting the Indo-European family may with most probability be regarded as diverging. As Cymry, Gaels, Pelasgi, Teutons, Arians, Sclaves (?), &c., they poured forth from their original (?) country, spreading, as we have said, northward, eastward, and westward."

Sir H. Rawlinson has shown that the language of the ancient Medes and Persians resembled the parent stock of the Indo-Germanic races—the sons of Japhet—and, like them (unlike the Semitic languages), is read from left to right, which might account for so many Hebrew names being found among them reversed.

So the Jew has שאל, shaul—to ask, desire, &c.; and we have *soul*, and in the north *saul*, for the desires of man.

So, for שאון—*soon*, noise, we have *sound*.

From שאיר, *sair*—to leave, comes *soar*.

" שאר, *soor*—leaven, or that which is left; and from this our English word *sour*, the taste of leaven.

To the Hebrew שבע—shavan, our word *seven* is most likely related.

From Shaver—to break or tear—we have Sever.
	Shabath—to rest	"	Sabbath.
	Shad—desolation, &c.,	"	Sad.
	Shacath—destruction	"	Scathe.
	Shatap—to drown	"	Steep.
	Shalak—to lay	"	Slake.
	Shaman—fat	"	Saim — fat of swine.
	Shanah—a repetition	"	Son.
	Saul—hollow of the hand	"	Sole of the foot.
	Shafat—to judge	"	Sift.
	Shpak—to pour out	"	Speak.
	Shakah—to water, or give drink	"	Soak, suck, sack.

" Shakat—quiet—we have "Scot and lot"—dues paid on account of peace and war.

" Shakal—to weigh—we have Scale.

" Shekel — A shilling or skilling is about half a *shekel*.

" Skap—to look—we have Scope.

" Shathal—to plan   "   Settle.

In some words the hissing sound is used by us both, thus—

שטן—the adversary	*Satan.*
Sich—to complain	*Sigh.*
Sakel	*Skill.*
Saar	*Sore.*
Sack	*Sack.*
Sar—prince	*Sir and Sire.*
Sarad—to remain	*Shred.*
Satah—drunkard	*Sot.*
Satath—to set	*Sit, Site, Seat.*
Dash—thrashing	*Dash.*
Is	*Is.*
Yasper	*Jasper.*
Rackas—getting, or,	*Riches and Cash.*

It is curious to observe how Hebrew derivation accounts even for the seeming inconsistency of pronunciation in some of our common words with their spelling. For example, the word spelt *l a u g h*, and so pronounced in the north, in the south is sounded as if it were written *l a u p h*. Now, there are two words in Hebrew which are very similar in form, sound, and meaning, from which the Scottish "*laugh*" and English "*lauph*" seem to have been respectively taken. The first is in 2 Chron. xxx. 10. It is used with regard to Ephraim, Manasseh, &c. A little before their final deportation, when Hezekiah, King of Judah, sent them an invitation to turn to the Lord, and come up to Jerusalem to keep the Passover, "they *laughed* them (the messengers) to scorn, and MOCKED them."

The word here translated *mocked* appears to be that from which we have our word "laugh," and is so translated in Job ix. 23, Ps. lxxx. 6; while the other word, translated *laughed* in the description of the reception of

Hezekiah's messengers by the Ephraimites, is the same from which we have the name ISAAC.

The Hebrew word from which our southern pronunciation of *laugh* is derived seems to have been only once used in the Scriptures, and then in describing the conduct of the Jews as being similar to that of their brethren, who had "mocked" the messengers sent by Hezekiah to rescue them from impending destruction, 2 Chron. xxxvi. 15, 16 —"The Lord God of their fathers sent to them by His messengers, rising up betimes, and sending; because He had compassion on His people and on His dwelling-place: but they MOCKED the messengers of God."

The principal difference between the two words is that the first terminates with a guttural and the second in a labial, as in *laugh* and *lauph*. We might be tempted to suppose that a ב had been written for a ג in the one instance in which the second word occurs, were it not that the Chaldee Targums frequently use לעב in the same sense.

We have now seen that our language, even from a slight comparison in relation to one letter, shows an intimate connection of our ancestors, not only with Media, but also with a Hebrew-speaking people, yet pronouncing the Hebrew more after the manner of Ephraim than of the other tribes.[1]

---

[1] Respecting the foregoing, *Professor Piazzi Smyth* says, "This is, without doubt, a very capital point; because—as clearly as linguistic connections can make them so, and agreeably with all the principles of language applied to ethnological science, and which, indeed, seldom has such broad and ample foundations to work upon in its ordinary discussions and conclusions—the Anglo-Saxons are shown to be compounded of the very Israelite people of old; in fact, they are the representatives of those Israelites, or may be said to be themselves of Israelite descent, and, therefore, heirs of whatever portions of Hebraism were retained when the more particular religious rites of Mosaicism were abolished and superseded under King Jeroboam."—*Life and Work at the Great Pyramid*, vol. iii. p. 581, &c.

THE LANGUAGES OF EUROPE. 195

We are said to have much from the Coptic, the ancient language of Egypt; much from the Arabic; while the grammatical structure of our language is the same with the Sanskrit and the German. These derivations indicate our early connection with Egypt, Arabia, Palestine, and the cities of the Medes. From not considering this, much needless mystification has been allowed to take the place of sound knowledge. For example, the first great act of husbandry in Egypt was the preparation of the ground by irrigation. It was flooded by the waters of the Nile, after which they "cast their bread upon the waters," expecting to "find it after many days" in an abundant harvest, springing from the opened and softened ground, into which had been pressed the seed-corn by the feet of the ox and the ass, or whatever means they found most convenient for the purpose.

Now the word which is made use of to express that whereby this commencement of tillage was produced—this opening of the ground to receive the seed—was denominated אר in Hebrew. This is the word which is used in Amos viii. 8, where the Lord is speaking of such a clearing change in "the land" as accompanies the commencement of agricultural operations, "Shall not the land tremble for this, and every one mourn that dwelleth therein? and it shall rise up wholly as a flood; and it shall be cast out and drowned as by the flood of Egypt."

The word which is translated "flood" in the first of these instances is אר, "*Ar*," and seems to denominate the stream or canal which was led off from the Nile, or from one of the reservoirs it supplied at the time of its overflowing. The Nile itself, in its overflowing, appears to be referred to in another form of the same word, יאור.

The overflowing of the Nile in Egypt, whereby the

ground was opened and prepared for receiving the seed, was analogous to our *ploughing*, the old English word for which commencing act of tillage is "EARE." This seems to be the case with regard to the languages spoken by nations likely to have been much influenced by Egypt in regard to tillage. The Greeks have their αραειν, "to plough," and the Romans their *arare*, from which many other languages in the West have derived words from the same root relating to agriculture, such as "arable," &c. I should not have thought of introducing this word into the evidence for our Israelitish origin, but that so much has been made of it lately by philologists for other purposes. Nevertheless, it is quite true that the Saxon "*aryan*," and our English words "*earing*" and "*eare*," as applied to preparing the ground for receiving the seed, most clearly indicate our ancient agricultural connection with Egypt.

In language we have also, of course, something in common with the Servian or Sclavonian race left behind us in the north-east; and it may be that we have taken something from, as well as imparted something to, the Celtic-speaking tribes among whom we have come.

The result of our researches is, that our forefathers came out of that part of the Persian empire anciently called MEDIA, which is said to be the common centre of the Indo-Germanic languages; that our speaking a dialect of the Indo-Germanic, or any intervening language, does not prove it to have been our original language; the greater probability being that we previously spoke Hebrew, a great many of our simplest, most familiar, and even vulgar words being derived therefrom, and pronounced in the same way as we know they were by the people who built Samaria, who were "wholly" carried away captive from their own land by the Assyrians, and located in "the cities of the

Medes" and neighbouring countries, whence our ancestors came.[1]

---

[1] The tune now known as "Yankee Doodle" is not of American birth, but has several claimants for its paternity. "In England the air has been traced back to the time of Charles I.; and it appears that the doggrel verses that are sung to it can claim nearly as respectable an antiquity. This, however, is not all. The song is said to be identical with one sung by the agricultural labourers in the Netherlands. Kossuth and his fellow-Hungarians, when in America, are said to have recognised it as one of the old national airs of their native land. And recently Mr Buckingham Smith, our then Secretary of Legation at Madrid, has asserted that it is the ancient sword-dance of the Biscayans."—*Blackwood.* [The name seems to be a Hebraic nursery epithet of endearment, and it would be interesting to trace the history of the tune, still more remotely.]

XII.

BREAKING UP OF THE ASSYRIAN EMPIRE.

Progress of captive Israel northward—Assyria—Media—The Kuzal Ozan, or Gozan—Causes which may have led to the breaking up of the Assyrian Empire—Revolt first in the Median provinces wherein captive Israel had been located — Median monarchy formed under Deioces, previously a judge, B.C. 710—Another disturbance in B.C. 635 — Scythians overrun Media and the countries between it and Egypt—Some settle on the east of the Jordan—Siege of Nineveh by the kings of Media and Babylon, B.C. 626—Finally destroyed by Nebuchadnezzar and Cyaxares, B.C. 583—Speed's origin of the name "Saxons"—Notes on the Magi, &c.

In tracing the progress of *captive* Israel north-westward, Assyria and Media are among the places most easily identified. Assyria lay north-east of the Holy Land, and Media still farther in the same direction; but in maps it is usually made to include the southern border of the Caspian Sea as far west as the river Araxes. This north-western portion, however, seems to have been somewhat independent of Media Proper, and was perhaps claimed by the Medes rather than actually at all times possessed by them. If this was the quarter to which Ephraim was carried captive, or of which he took possession, it was less likely to be so. The river running into the Caspian Sea, south-east of the river Araxes, is now called Kuzal Ozan, and is the "Gozan" mentioned as that on the banks of which some of Israel were located (2 Kings xvii. 6).

We now come to inquire whether, within the secular historic period, there was a convenient opportunity for Israel to leave MEDIA, when things were in such confusion that it was scarcely possible any record could be made thereof; and also more particularly respecting the people who were placed in Media *previous* to these opportunities of escape therefrom. Were they a people likely to make use of such opportunities of escape? Were they a people whose parentage, expectations, previous history, and long and various training, warrant us to suppose they would be impatient of the Assyrian yoke, and be ready to rise in revolt? Would they have the skill to devise, the vigour and prudence to carry into execution, a scheme of combined action in regard to an exodus into the north country? The children of Israel had long been living under Judges of very limited authority, "every man doing that which was right in his own eyes." Even after choosing to live under a monarchy, they had no scruple in overturning the divinely-established throne of David, and in taking for their king whomsoever they would. Their monarchy was what may be called constitutional; the crown was refused to him who would not engage to rule according to the constitution. People of this spirit were not likely to let the Assyrian have it all his own way. As soon as they found themselves in a position to avenge their national defeat and degradation, they would doubtless awake from their stupor, and engage with energy in a war of independence, and, possibly, of revenge. We are not, therefore, surprised to hear that this part of the Assyrian dominions, into which had been deported the restless tribes of Israel, was the first to shake off the Assyrian yoke.

B.C. 444, *Herodotus* says, "The Assyrians had been in possession of Upper Asia for a period of five hundred and twenty years. The Medes first of all revolted from their authority, and contended with such obstinate bravery against their masters, that they were ultimately successful, and exchanged servitude for freedom." But liberty degenerating into licentiousness, and their government not being well established, they fell into a kind of anarchy worse than their previous subjection. Injustice, violence, and rapine prevailed everywhere, because there was nobody that had either power enough to restrain them, or sufficient authority to punish offenders.

In such circumstances, when private wrongs were left unredressed, movements in which considerable numbers were able to act in concert were not likely to be prevented. Moreover, separation from such a condition of society would be deemed desirable by those who liked to enjoy their own in quietness. Many, especially of those dwelling in cities, which are generally dependent for their prosperity upon a settled state of society, would be inclined to take counsel, "and get them up out of the land." The disorders prevailing among the Medes, as living in a state of mere voluntary association, every man doing that which was right in his own eyes, led to much the same result as it had done in Israel—the establishment of a monarchical government, which again ended in despotism, and then in imbecility.

The formation of the Median monarchy is supposed to have taken place about the year B.C. 710. That is also said to be the year when the proud king of Assyria "came up against all the defenced cities of Judah, and took them," and about thirty years after their brethren of the house of Israel had begun to be deported into the cities of the Medes.

The Assyrian monarch might now be expected to return

from his Syrian campaign resolved effectually to quiet the troubles of Media, and cause the rebellious north again to own his conquering sway. To prepare for resisting such an attempt, it was needful that a strong government should now be established by the revolted Medes.

Deioces, who had long been much occupied as a judge, having been, by the Medes, chosen king, resolved to have his dignity attended with all the marks that could inspire awe and respect for his person. He obliged his subjects to build a magnificent palace in the place he appointed, which he strongly fortified, and chose out from among his people such persons as he judged fittest to be his guards. After providing for his own security, he applied himself to polishing and civilising his subjects, who, having been accustomed to live in the country and in villages almost without laws and without polity, had contracted the disposition and manners of savages.

We suppose the Israelites to have been introduced into Media about thirty years previous to the election of Deioces, and to have passed out of it previous to the discomfiture of the Assyrian host before the walls of Jerusalem.

They may have despaired of an opportunity being given them of returning to their own land. Looking to mere human power, they may have expected to hear of their ravisher returning loaded with the spoil of their brethren, the Jews, and as having at length leisure and abundance of means to punish them for their impatience under his yoke. So, in place of seeking their strength in quiet confidence, and waiting upon the God of their fathers for an opportunity of returning to their own land, they seemed to have said, "Our hope is lost, we are cut off for our parts;" and, taking counsel with despair, they left to the Jews the name and expectations of Israel, and passed out into the northern wilderness, with a resolution to seek out a resting-place for themselves, more free from the danger of becoming the prey of marauding tribes or of imperial despots.

ISRAEL had been accustomed to live in cities and towns as well as in the country; and their position among the nations, and training under David and Solomon, must have made them very different from the people recognised by *Herodotus* as inhabiting Media immediately before they resolved upon having Deioces for their king. The Israelites may be said to have been the representatives of Egyptian, Phœnician, and Aramean civilisation. They had by the Assyrians been placed in the Cities of the Medes; but of neither the Cities of the Medes, nor of such a people inhabiting them, do we find any account. The probability is that they had previously left that district.

The Medes, generally, were a rude agricultural people, dwelling in scattered villages; while the supposed immigrants from the Land of Israel had by the Assyrians been placed in *cities*, to which, of course, the surrounding country would be subject. If those who, by their ability, natural and acquired, were qualified to act as magistrates and police among the Medes, and in whose hands had been placed the governmental and administrative power, were combinedly to leave their appointed posts, then the country would, as a matter of course, be left in the condition in which it seems to have been when the light of secular history is first let in upon it.

We are to suppose that, according to the system pursued by the Assyrians in such cases, a people had been violently torn from their homes, transported from one extremity of the empire to another, and placed amongst strangers, perhaps newly-conquered; or in cities which, like Samaria, had been robbed of their inhabitants. These cities would be expected to hold the surrounding country in subjection to their captors. Assyria lay between these outcasts of Israel and their former homes, barring their return thither. All to the north was an unknown wilderness, cold and uninviting; wandering into which, they would, to appearance, be altogether cut off from their native land. Such a movement would not be expected, and no provision may have been made against it. But supposing the Cities of Media to have once become so deserted, then we can see some reason why at least the capital of the new kingdom should be defended, not only from attack, but also from sudden desertion by its own inhabitants.

We can have little difficulty in believing that the Israelites deported to the Cities of the Medes and other places on the northern frontier of the Assyrian empire, may have been more desirous of securing their own liberty, than of riveting the chains of their conqueror upon the ruder tribes *among* and *over* whom they may have been placed. After accomplishing the revolt, it is likely they went whither they would. And now it was felt necessary to supply their place, and to commence civilisation anew, by building a city upon another plan than had been followed in those deserted by the Israelitish immigrants.

To this end Deioces commanded them to build a city, himself marking out the place, and the circumference of the walls. This city was compassed about with seven distinct walls, all disposed in such a manner that the outermost did not hinder the parapet of the second from being seen, nor the second that of the third, and so of the rest.

The situation of the place was extremely favourable to such a design, for it was a regular hill, whose ascent was equal on every side. Within the last and smallest enclosure stood the king's palace, with all his treasures; in the sixth, which was next to that, were apartments for lodging the officers of his household; the intermediate spaces between the other walls were appointed for the habitations of the people, and the first and largest enclosure was about the size of Athens. The name of this new city was Ecbatana. It was magnificent and beautiful; for beside the arrangement of the walls, which formed a kind of amphitheatre, the different colours wherewith the several parapets were painted formed a delightful variety.

After the city was finished, Deioces was so wholly taken up in humanising and softening the manners of his people, and in making laws for their good government, that he never engaged in any enterprise against his neighbours, though his reign is said to have lasted from B.C. 710 to B.C. 657—more than eighty years after Israel had begun to be carried captive.

Phraortes, the son of Deioces, reigned twenty-two years. Being of a warlike temper, and not contented with the kingdom of Media left by his father, he attacked the Persians, and, having defeated them in a decisive battle, he brought them under subjection to his empire. Then, strengthened by the accession of their troops, he attacked the neighbouring nations, one after another, till he made himself master of almost all the Upper Asia, which comprehended all that lies north of Mount Taurus, from Media as far as the river Halys. He thus possessed a wide extent of territory east and west.

He then turned his arms against the Assyrians, at that time indeed weakened through the revolt of several nations, but yet in themselves very powerful. A great battle ensued, which proved fatal to Phraortes. He was defeated, his cavalry fled, his chariots were overturned, and put into disorder, and his enemy, Nebuchodonosor, gained a complete victory. Taking advantage of the defeat and confusion of the Medes, the enemy entered their country, took their cities, pushed on his conquests even to Ecbatana, forced the towers and the walls by storm, and gave the city to be pillaged by his soldiers, who plundered and stripped it of all its ornaments. Phraortes having been cruelly put to death, the Assyrian returned to Nineveh with all his army, which was still very numerous, and for four months together did nothing but feast and divert himself with those that had accompanied him in this expedition.

Here was another confusion in the Median commonwealth, amid the distractions of which those bordering upon the Caucasus could, if they chose, have ample opportunity to escape.

Cyaxares,[1] the son of Phraortes, having regained the throne of his father, and settled matters at home, reconquered all Upper Asia, and then set himself with all his might to attack Nineveh, intending to avenge the death of his father by the destruction of that great city. The Assyrians came out to meet him, but were driven back. The besieged city was about falling inevitably into his hands when it was relieved in the following remarkable manner, which afforded a third and still greater opportunity for those who chose to withdraw from Media in a northern direction.

A formidable army of Scythians, from the neighbourhood of the Palus Mæotis, had driven the Cimmerians out

---

[1] "The Nebuchadnezzar who took Jerusalem (B.C. 607) married the daughter of this Cyaxares of Media."—Dr Angus' Bible Handbook.

of Europe, and was still marching under the conduct of King Madyes in pursuit of them. The Cimmerians had found means to escape from the Scythians, who had advanced as far as Media. Cyaxares, hearing of this irruption, raised the siege from before Nineveh, and marched with all his forces against that mighty army, which, like an impetuous torrent, was going to overrun all Asia. The two armies engaged, and the Medes were vanquished. The Barbarians, finding no other obstacle in their way, overspread not only Media but almost all Asia. After that they marched towards Egypt, from whence Psammeticus diverted their course by presents. They then returned into Palestine, where some of them plundered the Temple of Venus at Ascalon, the most ancient of the temples dedicated to that goddess, after which they were seized with a mysterious sickness. Some of the Scythians settled at Bethshan, a city in the tribeship of Manasseh, on this (the east) side Jordan, which from them was afterwards called "Scythopolis." The Scythians, for the space of twenty-eight years, were masters of Upper Asia—namely, the two Armenias, Cappadocia, Pontus, Colchis, and Iberia—during which time they spread desolation wherever they came. The Medes had no way of getting rid of them, but by a dangerous stratagem. Under pretence of cultivating and strengthening the alliance they had made, they invited the greatest part of them to a general feast, which was made in every family. Each master of the feast made his guests drunk, and in that condition were the Scythians massacred. The Medes then repossessed themselves of the provinces they had lost, and once more extended their empire to the banks of the Halys, which was their ancient boundary westward.

In B.C. 626, Cyaxares, as soon as he found himself again

in peace, resumed the siege of Nineveh, which the irruption of the Scythians had obliged him to raise. Nabopolassar, King of Babylon, with whom he had lately contracted a particular alliance, joined with him in a league against the Assyrians. Having therefore united their forces, they besieged Nineveh, took it, killed Saracus, the king, and utterly destroyed that mighty city. The two armies enriched themselves with the spoils of Nineveh, and Cyaxares, prosecuting his victories, made himself master of all the cities of the kingdom of Assyria except Babylon and Chaldea, which belonged to Nabopolassar. After this expedition Cyaxares died, and left his dominions to his son Astyages.

Astyages reigned thirty-five years. This prince is called in Scripture *Ahasuerus*. Though his reign was very long, yet have we no particulars recorded of it in history. He had two children, whose names are famous, namely, Cyaxares, by his wife Aryenis, and Mandane, by a former marriage. In his father's lifetime he married Mandane to Cambyses, the son of Achimenes, King of Persia; from this marriage sprung Cyrus, who was born but one year after his uncle Cyaxares. The latter succeeded his father in the kingdom of the Medes. CYAXARES II. is the prince whom the Scripture calls DARIUS THE MEDE.

Cyrus having, in conjunction with his uncle Darius, or Cyaxares, taken Babylon, left it under his government, after whose death, and that of his father Cambyses, he united the kingdom of the Medes and that of the Persians. He was, it need scarcely be said, one of the most famous princes, whether in profane or sacred history.

This brief view of the circumstances of the Median kingdom or commonwealth, from just before the close of the eighth century, and during the greater part of the seventh, before Christ, may convince us that ample opportunity was given once, and again, and a third time, for the discontented Israelites to leave Media, especially as passing off northward into the quarter whence came the Scythians into Asia, and whence also subsequently came our Anglo-Saxon ancestors into the north-west of Europe.

One of the most learned, earnest, honest, and successful of our English antiquaries, Speed, who wrote towards the close of the seventeenth century, elaborately discusses the origin of the name Saxon, and examines several of the theories that have been advanced as to the country from which they originally came. He refers, among other authors, to Albinus, the friend of Bede, who lived in the eighth century. *Albinus*, he says, believes the Saxons to have been descended from the Sacæ, a people in Asia, and that afterwards, in process of time, they came to be called Saxons, as if it were written Sax-sones, *i.e.*, the sons of the Sacæ. "To this opinion," says Speed, "Master Henry Ferrers, a gentleman of ancient descent, great reading, and a judicious antiquary, agreeth, whose judgment for any particular I have always honoured, and from his 'Progeny of the English Monarchs' I have taken my principal proceedings in these Saxon successors."

The old English chronicler proceeds—"As touching the ancient place of their abode, *Ptolemy*, the Alexandrian, placeth the people Sasones in the inner Scythia, betwixt the mountains Alani and Tapuri; and Amianus Marcellinus citeth the Sacæ (no doubt the very same), a fierce and savage nation, who inhabited overgrown places, commodious only for cattle, at the foot of the mountains Ascanimia and Comedus, near unto which the city Alexandria, Tribatra, and Drepsa were adjoining, and are so set by Ptolemy. Neither is it less probable that our Saxons descended from the SACÆ in Asia, than the GERMANS from those Germans in Persia of whom *Herodotus* writeth. . . . Of the Sacæ, *Strabo* writeth that they made invasious into countries afar off, as namely, Armenia, where they left the memory of their success in a part of that country by calling it Sacacena, after their own name. From these parts of Asia, as Scythia and the rest, one band of them, consisting chiefly of their youth, proceeded by degrees into Europe, and passed the Ness or Foreland, which the Romans called Cimbrica Chersonesus, being at this day the continent part of the kingdom of Denmark, in which place they were first known by the name of Saxons, and here, also, they, among themselves, began first to be distinguished into other tribes, but more properly, we may say into Saxons, Angles, and Jutes. From hence, afterwards, they departed, and passing over the river Elbe, divided themselves into two companies, whereof the one taking into the upper parts of Germany, by little and little obtruded themselves into the ancient seat of the Suevians, which now of them is called Westphalia, and Saxony; and the other encroached upon Friesland and Holland (then called Batavia), with the rest of those countries that lie along the German seas. . . . Most certain it is, by *Eutropius* and *Bede*, that before the year 300, when Diocletian swayed the Roman sceptre, the Saxons out of Cimbrica Chersonesus sore offended the coasts of Britain and France with their many piracies, and were fearful even to the Romans themselves. These multiplied in number and strength, seated in the maritime tract of Jutland, Sleswick, Alsatia, Ditmarse, Breme, Oldenburgh, all Friesland and Holland; and indeed, according to the testimony of *Fabius Quæstor*, ' wholly all the sea-coasts, from the river Rhine unto the city Donia, which now is commonly called the Denmarc.' And whither *Henry of Erfurd* affirmeth Saxon-land to stretch from the river Albis unto the Rhine: 'the bounds of no one people of all the Germans extending any way so far,' saith he." He adds, "These Getæ (no doubt the Jute) Ptolemy likewise placeth in the Island Scandia, lying very near the coasts of Germany, upon whose uttermost promontory—as said an ancient MS.— the Jutes did for certain inhabit, which unto this day of the Danes is called Juteland. These Jutes, Gutes, Getes, Goths, or, as *Bede* calls them, Vites, gave names to those parts of Britain which they inhabited. . . . This may suffice for the originals of these three people; who, as *Cisner* affirmeth, retained still the same manners after they were settled in Europe as they had formerly done in Asia."—Speed's Chronicles, 1660.

Amidst all his gropings he has entirely overlooked the real and very simple origin of the name "Saxon," upon which origin of the name he thus writes. There was a name which it might be expected Israel would retain, for by it the promised seed of Abraham were to be called; and that is the name of his son Isaac. By this name the house of Israel was being called a little time before their captivity: 'Now therefore hear thou the word of the Lord; thou sayest, Prophesy not against Israel, and drop not thy word against the house of ISAAC' (Amos vii. 16). The name of Isaac means 'he shall laugh.' Sarah said at his birth, the Lord hath made me to laugh, so that all people shall laugh with me. But the name may also be taken in an evil sense; and in this it seems to have been deserved by the Ephraimites, when bitter weeping was about to be their portion. They laughed to scorn, and mocked the messengers which King Hezekiah sent to call them to repentance. Of two kinds of laughter the Jewish remnant were warned to beware: 'Now, therefore, be ye not mockers' (Isa. xxvii. 22). It is as rejoicing in God's salvation, and as making known that joy to others, that we were to bear the name of Isaac. The first syllable of that name, it may be noticed, is no original part of the Hebrew word 'to laugh,' and would naturally be dropped when compounded with the word 'son,' or 'sen,' meaning a repetition or copy of his father. 'Isaac's son' naturally becomes Isaac-son or Saxon." (See p. 187.) [1]

---

[1] The name Sakai was applied to them first as simply *the Tribes*, perhaps adopted by themselves, but ultimately it came to signify Bowmen, because they, like the Ephraimites and English, were so famous for the use of the bow. *Sak* is simply part of the Hebrew word for "bow" reversed (Gen. xlix. 24).

Xenophon, in his retreat (B.C. 400) with the 10,000 Greeks, passed over the Chebar on his way from Bactria to the plains of Zacko or Sacho. It must have been in these plains that the sons of Isaac mostly dwelt during their captivity, and here Ezekiel conferred with their elders, chap. iii. 15. If we would discover relics of exiled Israel, let us dig among these ruins on the banks of the Chebar. "The mounds and ruins of Bhutan are numerous, and would doubtless repay a Layard for any amount of exploration."—Moore's Lost Tribes, 1861.

The first Buddha is said to have been born B.C. 618, and to have died B.C. 543, not *very* old certainly, only seventy-five. He is called Maga (a Magian) by the Burmese (Asiatic Researches, ix. 20), and the sacred language of Buddhism is called that of the Mags or Magi in Burmah, Arracan, Ceylon, and Siam. The priests of the Persians, Bactrians, Charasmians, Arians, and Sakai are equally called Magi, and these are described as so many tribes descended from the Sacas. Query, were not "the Magi or Wise Men" of lost Israel, who "came from the East" to worship Immanuel? They brought just such offerings as would come from India; and if Roman coins of the same period have been found among Buddhist relics, is it improbable that the land of Israel, so much nearer, was unknown? Parthians and Medes were among the devout Israelites at Jerusalem on the day of Pentecost.

XIII.

THE PROGRESS OF ISRAEL WESTWARD.

The Beni-Israel near Bombay—Their manner of burial—Hebraic rock temple inscription near Bombay—Ossetes in the Pass of Dariel—Israelitish tombs northward of the Caucasus, and on all the shores of the Bosphorus—The Karaim of the Crimea—Buddhist monuments in Aberdeenshire.

I HAVE seen several accounts from India of a people numbering about 7000, who are supposed to be a remnant of the Ten Tribes. They are called Beni-Israel, and are said to be the descendants of seven men and seven women who about 1600 years ago were saved from shipwreck on the coast near Bombay, from which they have been scattered over the country. They profess to be of the Tribe of Reuben, and consistently therewith call more of their children by that name than by any other. If the facts be so, the prayer of Moses seems to have been signally answered—" Let Reuben live, and not die." At the same time they seem to fulfil the words of Jacob, " Unstable as water, thou shalt not excel" (Gen. xlix. 4). They are in the middle rank of society. When they enter the army, they are valued as musicians, and generally attain to the rank of native officers; but none of them appear to rise to great eminence in any respect. Except as influenced by surrounding society, they seem as a people to have been remarkably stationary.[1]

Among them have been signally preserved some of those customs belonging to ancient Israel, with which it is important to our present inquiry that we should be acquainted. Those which regard the interment of the dead shall first engage our attention. And, indeed, it is a curious coincidence that, upon proceeding northward from Assyria and Media (as we have been directed in search of Israel after their political death and burial), the first remarkable objects that strike our attention are tombs, which by their construction plainly tell that at some period Israel must have passed that way. The funeral ceremonies of the Beni-Israel are thus reported:—When one of them dies, "they wash the body and clothe it with white linen, laying it on a plank and carrying it to the burying-ground. They sing alternately all the way as they go, 'Hear, O Israel,' &c., and continue the same till the body is committed to its original dust. On the fourth day some of the relations visit the grave and perform the following ceremony:—

"They raise up the grave a foot high with sand, and afterwards cover it over with a piece of white linen; then they take a little fire in a vessel or pot, and place it at the head, eastward; they then burn incense, during which time they collect in another vessel a quantity of different kinds of grain, with cocoa-nuts made into small pieces, and flowers of all kinds mixed together, and sprinkle them over the grave, while covered with the linen cloth; then they remove the linen cloth which covers it, and sprinkle over

[1] A religious awakening has been going forward, however, among this people within the last few years, resulting from the voluntary labours of some native preachers, taught many years ago by the late A. N. Groves and others, who went out to Persia in 1829 at their own expense.—1875.

the grave a little *chunnam* mixed with water, which they have previously prepared, and then disperse.

"On the seventh day they again visit the grave, but use no ceremony with the exception of a prayer, which is offered up for the soul of the deceased, if there be any person present able to perform the duty, which is seldom the case, owing to their extreme ignorance. They then go to it no more."

Were they to repeat their visits and leave what they thus place upon the grave, as was probably the case in more ancient times, then would there be over it alternate layers of earth and vegetable matter. Covering the grave, however, seems now to have degenerated into a mere ceremony.

Let us recollect that Israel did not so much bury in the earth as in a cave, either built of stones or dug in the rock. A stone lay upon the grave's mouth, which was eastward. The grave seems to have been covered by alternate layers of earth or sand and vegetable matter, the sand being first laid on, which manner of covering their dead may have been adopted the better to preserve the interior of the tomb from damp. Over the grave, in distinguished cases, they were accustomed to raise high heaps, perhaps to serve as monuments, as well as preserve the tomb from spoliation (Joshua vii. 26; viii. 29; 2 Sam. xviii. 17).[1]

---

[1] The Beni-Israel of Malabar have a history, clearly written, well preserved, and continued to the present time, in which it is recorded that the Ten Tribes, with the exception of colonies in Spain and India, migrated towards the Caspian Sea, some on the borders of Media and Persia, and others in the direction of Chinese Tartary. The tribes of Simeon, Ephraim, and Manasseh are represented to have settled on the north-east of the Caspian Sea, the country of the Chozar Tartars, in a region named in the record *Makhe*. Thus we have evidence sufficient to prove that a people who were connected with the country of the Sacæ, and under

It is remarkable also that, since we have been in some measure prepared to account for the fact, a people should be found in the PASS OF DARIEL identified, on the one hand, by their domestic and agricultural implements, with the Germans; and on the other, with ancient Israel, by their traditions and religious observances. In his "Trans-Caucasia," Baron Haxthausen relates that he made a short expedition to a village of the OSSETES, one of the Caucasian tribes, which lies between the northern Georgian frontier and Ingusches, in the line which runs from Teflis to Mozdok on the Terek by the famous PASS OF DARIEL. They are remarkable for the similarity of their manners in many respects to those of the Germans. Their plough resembles the Mecklenburg hoeing plough. Of all the Circassians they alone brew beer from barley, and give it the same name that it bears in Germany and England. A similar correspondence exists in their cradles and bedsteads (which latter are frequently placed in a niche, as in Germany), and in their churns and three-legged tables, neither of which useful articles are found among the other Caucasian tribes.

They prepare a kind of cake, composed of cheese, butter, dough, and onions, which is said to be common among the Thuringian peasantry (the country of Luther). For light, they use a burning piece of pine-wood stuck in the wall, or a wick in a little bowl of melted tallow, both of which practices, although common to Western Europe, are unknown to their neighbours.

Hebrew rulers, held dominion over Central India and Afghanistan previous to the Mohammedan invasion. Mr Forster points out ("Primeval Language") as a curious confirmation of the Malabar record of the Beni-Israel, that Ptolemy places the *Tos Manassa* ("the far-banished Manasseh") in the land of the *Gomeri* (Chomari or Cymri), and to the north of them a people called *Macha-geni,* or people of Maacha (the grandson of Joseph).

Their religion is a strange mixture. Their guardian and patron is the prophet Elijah, whose cave is said to be situated in a grove. No strife nor rapine dare disturb the calm of these holy precincts. Once in the year the eldest descendant of a family, in which the service is hereditary, ascends the sacred rock, and entering the cave alone, offers a mystic sacrifice.

In the centre of the cave, the interior of which is composed of emerald, stands an altar of rock, on which is a golden goblet filled with beer. By the aid of this the priest divines the events of the coming year, which he communicates the next day to a solemn assemblage of the neighbourhood at a great banquet.

Both on the first day of the week, which they call *Chatzawiben* (Lord's day), and on the seventh, *Shabate* (Sabbath), they go with the head bare, but do not distinguish those days by any other special observances. The part of the population in the neighbourhood of the Georgian frontier are nominally Christians of the Greek Church, while those of the Circassian border are often Mohammedans. They are, however, semi-pagans, and retain traces of an elemental religion in the common practice of offering sacrifices of flesh, fish, and bread in caves and groves. In fact, the eating or the abstinence from pork is the practical test with them of Christianity or Islamism.

One of their superstitions is very curious, and will remind the classical scholar of parallels both in Greece and Italy. Persons struck by lightning are considered sacred. The victim of the thunderbolt in Ossetia is regarded as taken by the prophet Elijah to himself, and is interred amid universal rejoicing and shouts of " *O Elijah, El der Tschoppe!*"—" O Elijah, lord of the rocky mountain!"— and his grave, distinguished by a black goat-skin hung beside it, becomes a resort of pilgrims from that time forward.[1]

Among whom might be expected so remarkable a remembrance of Elijah in connection with caves, as among that people with regard to whose national destiny the scene at Horeb had such an important bearing? (1 Kings xix. 8).[2]

Now let us, with Dr Clarke, visit the country on the shores of the Black Sea beyond the Caucasian mountains, and directly north-west from the places to which Israel were carried by the Assyrians. Here are immense plains, producing the most beautiful herbage, and apparently capable, with cultivation, of sustaining immense multitudes, though now chiefly remarkable as a place of graves.

"By much the most frequent objects were the tumuli; and, from their great numbers, I should have been inclined to suppose they were occasionally raised as *marks of guidance* across these immense plains during winter, when the ground is covered by snow; but whenever any one

---

[1] The blood-feud prevails among the Ossetes, with one curious characteristic. Relationship on the mother's side is not recognised. A man is bound to revenge the death of his cousin, who bears his name, a hundred times removed, but to that of his maternal brother he is quite indifferent. On the other hand, the notions of clansmanship are as conventional as they are strict. Every child born in marriage is considered as a legitimate offspring: and to such an extent is this idea carried, that if a husband dies without male issue, and has no brother, or even father, surviving him, whose duty it would be in that case to continue the succession by marrying the widow, it is not uncommon for her to live with another man, and any children which may result from such a connection are considered as the legitimate offspring of the first marriage.

[2] That a large body of Hebrews had proceeded northward from Armenia, and were resident in the neighbourhood of the Caspian Sea, appears probable, as already stated, from the circumstance that after the Jews were permitted to return to Palestine, Ezra sent to "Iddo, the chief of the place Casiphia," for ministers (Ezra viii. 17).

has been laid open, the appearance of a sepulchre puts the question of their origin beyond dispute, and the traveller is left to wonder and perplex himself in conjectures concerning the population which supplied the labour for raising these numerous vestiges of interment, as well as the bodies they served to contain. The number greatly increased as we drew near to the Kuban; and in the last stage, before we reached the river, I counted ninety-one, all at once in view.

"No trace of any ancient work afterwards appeared, excepting tumuli, until we came to the Bay of Taman. Then, on the shore, immediately above some very high cliffs, we observed the remains of a very large fortress and town, entirely surrounded with tombs and broken mounds of earth, indicating evident vestiges of human labour. The geography of these coasts is so exceedingly obscure, that a little prolixity in noticing every appearance of this kind may perhaps be tolerated. We soon reached the posthouse of Sienna, actually scooped in the cavity of an ancient tomb. In the neighbourhood of this place we found remains of much greater importance. Its environs were entirely covered with tumuli, of a size and shape that could not fail at once to excite a traveller's wonder, and stimulate his research. The commandant of engineers at Taman, General Vanderweyde, had already employed the soldiers of the garrison in opening the largest. It was quite a mountain. They began the work, very ignorantly, at the summit, and for a long time laboured to no purpose. At last, by changing the direction of their excavation, and opening the eastern side, they discovered the entrance to a large arched vault, of the most admirable masonry. I had the pleasure to descend into this remarkable sepulchre. Its mouth was half filled with earth, yet, after passing the entrance, there was sufficient space for a person to stand upright. Farther, towards the interior, the area was clear, and the work perfectly entire. The material of which the masonry consisted was a white crumbling limestone, such as the country now affords, filled with fragments of minute shells. Whether it was the work of Milesians, or other colonies of Greece, the skill used in its construction is very evident. The stones of the sides are all square, perfect in their form, and put together without any cement. The roof exhibits the finest turned arches imaginable, having the whiteness of the purest marble. An interior vaulted chamber is separated from the outer, by means of two pilasters, swelling out wide towards their bases, and placed, one on each side, at the entrance. The inner chamber is the larger of the two.

"Concerning everything found in this tomb, it is perhaps impossible to obtain information. One article alone, that was shown to me by General Vanderweyde at Taman, may give an idea of the rank of the person originally interred there. It was a zone for the leg, or bracelet for the arm, of the purest massive gold.[1] The soldiers employed in the undertaking stole whatever they deemed of value, and were able to conceal, and destroyed other things which did not appear to them to merit preservation. Among these were a number of vases of black earthenware, adorned with white ornaments. The bracelet was reserved by General Vanderweyde, to be sent to St Petersburg for the Emperor's cabinet; but . . . a more particular description of it may be necessary. Its weight equalled three-quarters of a pound. It represented the body of a serpent, curved

---

[1] The same may be seen on the Great Tope of Sachi. See Major Cunningham's Bhilsa Topes, p. 189.

in the form of an ellipse, having two heads, which, meeting at opposite points, made the opening for the wrist or ankle. These serpents' heads were studded with rubies, so as to imitate eyes, and to ornament the back part of each head with two distinct rows of gems. The rest of the bracelet was also adorned by rude graved work. It possessed no elasticity, but on account of the ductility of pure gold, might with sufficient force be expanded so as to admit the wrist or ankle of the person who was to wear it; and probably, when once adapted to the form, remained during the life-time of the owner. I could not but view it as the most ancient specimen of art which perhaps exists in the world; and which, while it shows the progress then made in metallurgy, and in the art of setting precious stones, at the same time offers a type of the mythology of the age in which it was made; the binding of the serpent round the leg or arm, as a talisman, being one of the superstitions common to almost every nation in an early period of civilisation.

Immediately above the stone-work constructed for the vault of the sepulchre appeared first a covering of earth, and then a layer of sea-weed, compressed by another superincumbent stratum of earth to the thickness of about two inches. This layer of sea-weed was as white as snow, and when taken in the hand separated into thin flakes, and fell into pieces. What the use of this vegetable covering could be is very uncertain, but it is found in all the tombs of this country. *Pallas* observed it placed in regular layers, with coarse earthenware vases, of rude workmanship and unglazed, which were filled with a mixture of earth and charcoal. It is said that a large marble soros or sarcophagus, the top of which now serves for a cistern, near the fortress of Yenikale in the Crimea, was taken from this tomb.

The appearance of the entrance, however, in its present state contradicts the story, as the opening has never yet been made sufficiently wide for its removal, even had it been so discovered.[1]

"Similar tombs are found on all the shores of the Bosphorus. Close by that which I have discovered are many others, and some nearly of equal size. *Pallas*, in his journey over this country, mentions the frequent recurrence of such appearances all round the Bay of Taman. Indeed, it would be vain to ask where they are not observed. The size, grandeur, and riches of those on the European and Asiatic sides of the Cimmerian Straits excite astonishing ideas of the wealth and power of the people by whom they were constructed; and in the view of labour so prodigious, as well as of expenditure so enormous, for the purpose of inhuming a single body, customs and superstitions are manifest which illustrate the origin of the Pyramids of Egypt,[2] the caverns of Elephanta, and the first temples of the ancient world."

I was somewhat at a loss to ascertain the connection with our subject of this golden serpent, the only remarkable object found in the tomb seen by Dr Clarke; but I observe that the Beni-Israel in India are accused of having each in their secret chambers a silver serpent, to which they burn incense twice a day, throw a little flour before it, and sing, accompanied with a small tomtom beating during the ceremony. Nor is this strange, as, even in the

---

[1] From the "Ynglyngasaga" we learn that in Sweden Odin established the same laws which had been observed by the Asæ. . . . In memory of distinguished men, sepulchral mounds, now called by the people *Kin-barrows*—(ätte högar)—were to be erected; and memorial stones (bauta stenar) besides, to every man who had shown himself valiant.—*Geijer*.

[2] But, see Our Inheritance in the Great Pyramid, 2nd edition, 1874.

house of Judah, the same superstition appears to have long continued. It was not until after the Ten Tribes had been carried away that Hezekiah arose, as recorded 2 Kings xviii. 4, and "brake in pieces the brazen serpent that Moses had made; for unto those days the children of Israel did burn incense to it. And he called it Nehushtan;" *i.e.*, a piece of brass.

The tombs referred to commence north of the river Kuban, which empties itself into the Euxine near Taman, in the neighbourhood of which there are other places whose names argue a Hebrew origin. They stretch from the Kuban northward, to an immense distance, and the direction they take seems clearly to indicate that the people who there deposited their dead proceeded, not eastward towards Siberia along the back of the Caspian Sea, but, with the usual tide of emigration, westward along the back of the Euxine.[1]

In the CRIMEA, also, there is a remarkable community calling themselves "Karaim," who say they originally came here in the time of Shalmaneser, being part of those who were carried away captive by that monarch in the reign of Hoshea, King of Israel, B.C. 721, as mentioned in 2 Kings xvii. They have always been a people of importance under the various dynasties that have held sway in the Crimea. The present rabbi and his father seem to have "entertained doubts;" *i.e.*, they have been really convinced that Jesus of Nazareth is the true Messiah.

The following is a translation of a Hebrew document of

---

[1] The Russian Archæological Society, of which Prince Woronzow, Governor-General of Odessa, is President, has brought to light many interesting relics found in this region, many hundreds of epitaphs from tombs, &c., some of which go back to pre-Christian times, and date from the "year of our exile." They are chiefly Rabbis of the Karaim.

great antiquity belonging to the Karaim. "I, Jehudi, the son of Moses, the son of Juhadah the mighty;[1] a man of Naphtali, of the family of Shilmi, who was carried captive in the captivity of Hoshea, King of Israel, with the tribe of Simeon, together with other tribes of Israel, who were carried away captive by the prince Shalmaneser from Samaria. They were carried to Halah, to Habor (which is Cabool) to Gozan (which is Gozna), and to Khorsonesus. Khorson was built by the father of Cyrus, and afterwards destroyed, and again rebuilt, and called Krim, and 'the rock of the Jews' (Tchoufut-Kaleh) in Krim is a fortification."[2] Oliphant, in his "Russian Shores of the Black Sea," &c. says, p. 277, "It must be a great comfort to the Tartar ladies that their religion obliges them to remain veiled in public; for I have little doubt that they would be fairly eclipsed by the lovely Jewesses (?), whose graceful costume in the group before us contrasted favourably with that of their waddling companions. There is nothing 'Israelitish' [query, *Jewish*] about these Karaite maidens. The Grecian nose and fiery nostril, the short proud upper lip and exquisitely turned mouth seem almost to belie their Hebrew origin; while those large eyes, so deeply set, require no white fereedgee to give additional effect to their lustre.

"The Karaites hold simply to the letter of Scripture,

---

[1] Query, is this the same "Hu the Mighty" held in such honour among the Welsh Cymri?

[2] According to *Demetrius*, some of the ten tribes were carried from Samaria in February, B.C. 695, which agrees with the date preserved by the Karaim, as witnessed by several tombstones found at Tchoufut Kale, which have been carried up to the library of the Academy of St Petersburg. Facsimiles of three of these tombstones are in the Preface to "Messiah the Prince" (Longmans). (But as it is not likely that they would have migrated to the Crimea the same year as their captivity, the Scripture chronology is most likely the more correct.)

without admitting the authority of the Talmud, or the interpretations of the Rabbis. The Talmudists accuse the Karaites of retaining the errors of the Sadducees. This is not entitled to much weight, coming from so hostile a quarter. There is, however, no doubt that the two sects differ in many material points from one another, as for instance in the different degrees of relationship forbidden in marriage, in their rules controlling the succession of inheritance, and more especially in the entire recognition of polygamy. Like all 'Jews' they display extraordinary care in the education of their children, who are publicly instructed in the Synagogue.

"About 5000 Karaites are resident in Poland, who acknowledge the old Rabbi of Tchoufut Kale as their principal chief. They are said to have emigrated originally from the Crimea. But it is not by the difference which exists upon points of doctrine or civil discipline that the stranger can at once distinguish the Karaite from the Talmudist, but by the strange contrast which is invariably presented in the members of these opposing sects. The Karaite merchant enjoys everywhere so high a reputation for probity, that throughout the Crimea his word is considered equal to his bond.

"As almost all the Karaites are engaged in trade or manufacture, and as they observe the most scrupulous honesty in their dealings, it has naturally followed that they are a prosperous and thriving community; while, as if an exception had been made in favour of this portion of that interesting people whose unhappy destiny has been so wonderfully accomplished, probably the only settlement exclusively Jewish (?), which still exists, is the fortress of Tchoufut Kale, the summit of one of the highest crags in the Crimea. The population of Eupatoria is composed mainly of Karaites, nearly two thousand of whom are now residents there, and some of these are wealthy merchants."[1]

[And here allusion may be made to the results of Dr Moore's investigations respecting the Newton stone in Aberdeenshire, the first inscription on which is such as may be seen on the coinage used by the propagandists of Buddhism in north-western India, before and after the invasion of Alexander the Great. Conjoined with words in this so-called Arian character are other words, or rather a monogram, belonging to the most ancient form of Sanscrit, or Pali[2] writing; thus affording ocular demonstration of the former presence in Aberdeenshire of Buddhist missionaries from the east. There is historic evidence that such missionaries were always chosen and appointed to go where there were people who spoke their own language at the time of their own conversion. And Dr Moore therefore infers that a Hebrew-speaking company of Buddhists visited and lived in Aberdeenshire amongst another people, who also were familiar with Hebrew, but who used the Oghams in writing, which they had probably been taught by the *Tuatha de Danaan*, or Scots from Ireland.[3]

The Buddhistic symbols sculptured on so many stones, and even becoming ultimately mixed with what are considered Christian symbols on memorials of the dead, prove that Buddhism must have prevailed to some large extent in the north-east of Scotland. As that religion originated in Northern India, it must have found *some* means of extending itself thence to Britain, carrying with it the ideas

---

[1] See *Jewish Intelligence* for March 1875.
[2] The Hebrew word "Pali" means *secret*; as in Judges xiii. 18.
[3] Ancient Pillar-Stones of Scotland, &c. Edmonston & Douglas.

of the far east, and, as we have seen, also the written characters wherewith to express them. When rendered into our modern Hebrew letters, they are found to have been inscribed by a Hebrew-speaking people; and it becomes us to inquire what connection there can have been between these two far separated countries.

In the first place, according to the testimony of learned men who have had opportunities of considering the matter, it appears that the language now spoken by the great body of people in Afghanistan—the ancient Aria—is merely a corruption of a language which was originally Hebraic. Dr Moore thinks the people of Aria were those whom the Persians called *Sakai* (the Tribes, or Bowmen), and designated by Ptolemy "The Aristophyloi," or *Noble Tribes* (another name for Israelites, *i.e.*, princes of God). The Sakai or Sacæ were, to a large extent, converted to Buddhism during the life of its first teacher. They are also supposed to have previously had the primary elements of Buddhism among themselves. Care must be taken not to confound these Sakai with the Scythians, with whom they were on friendly terms.[1]

The gradual progress of the Sacæ westward from Aria, Media, or Afghanistan is traced; the fact is noted that the deported tribes of Israel were placed in a district of Media, which, in 1 Chron. v. 26, is expressly called Hara (הרא) and evidence is educed from the Nineveh marbles, that an Arian people,[2] called Esaksha, had rebelled against the Assyrians about the year B.C. 670, or nearly a hundred years after the captive Israelites had been placed there,

---

[1] בדים, *Bedim*, in Hebrew signifies the detached or separated branches of people—Ezek. xvii. 6 and xix. 14; Hos. xi. 6.

[2] Their central land was called *Magadha* or *Noble*.

who, in their own country, had called themselves *Beth-Isaac* (Amos vii. 9–16).

Dr Moore ascribes the agglomeration of those mysterious Kjokkenmödding, which have been found in Norway, Denmark, and the north-east of Scotland (similar to those we have been considering), to the work of the Buddhists; and considers that the old Druidical Hymn in praise of Lludd the Great—which also is pronounced, by modern critics, to have been composed in corrupt Hebrew—throws light upon their originally intended signification. In that hymn there is an invocation to Saka, the Indian name of the last Buddha, which shows that it must have been composed subsequently to the year B.C. 545. The devotees, in chanting it, signified that they had covenanted with death, in a Buddhistic sense; and that the witness of that covenant was supposed to dwell in the heap by which the covenant was symbolised, and hence called "a dwelling of strength" (Isa. xxviii. 18).

Students of ancient history do not require to be told that two thousand years ago, communication between the East and the West was quite as easy, if not more so, than now, as regular caravans were established, and no passports were then required. It will also be in the remembrance of some of our readers, that, a few years ago, two men were taken, footsore and *weary*, to the Asiatics' Home in London, for whose language there was much difficulty to find an interpreter. At last it was discovered that they were Nestorians, from Persia, and that they had walked nearly all the way from Ooromiah, knowing only two English words, one of which was "London;" their object being to represent to the English people their own down-trodden state. And there is good reason for believing that experimental travelling and knowledge were much more general and extensive formerly than we have been accustomed to think.

Dr Moore infers that from the connection of the tribe of Dan with the Sidonians, it is likely that the *Tuatha de Danaan*, who appeared in Ireland, are some of the tribe of Dan who escaped by the sea when Palestine was invaded by the Assyrians, and for which they had ample opportunity. He observes, very justly, that in all endeavours to find traces of the lost tribes, we should bear in mind, that it is useless to look for them as retaining any very distinct remains of the Mosaic ritual. They had joined themselves to idols (Hos. iv. 17), and were, as a punishment for their sins, to be allowed to have their own way in becoming so like heathen that they would be called "Gentiles" (Hos. viii. 8).]

XIV.

"*SET THEE UP WAYMARKS.*"

The names of rivers between the Don and the Danube indicate Israel's sojourn there—Mœsia—The Getæ, or Goths; attacked Darius, Alexander, and the Romans—Dacia—The Goths precipitated upon the Romans by Attila and his Huns; regain possession of Mœsia; war with the Romans—The storm passes over to Africa; leaves the Gothic race in possession of Europe—Their important position; traditional prophecies, as in "Voluspa," consistent with their Israelitish descent, and supposed to be handed down from the days of Elijah, who had ministered the Word of God chiefly in this House of Israel.

IN addition to the "high heaps" noticed in our last, we have sufficiently legible "waymarks" of Israel's wanderings towards the north-west (Jer. xxxi. 21). Thus, the names of all the great rivers north-west of the Black Sea seem to refer to the JORDAN (which has its rise near DAN, or Laish), as being the original seat of some people who, before the great migration of nations westward, inhabited the country north of the Euxine between the Don and the Danube. Proceeding westward from the Don, we have the Danez flowing into the Don itself; farther, in the same direction, is the Danieper, contractedly Dnieper. Still farther westward we meet with the Daniester, or Dniester; southward from thence, and flowing from the far West, we have the Danube, or Danau, which I have heard that the Germans understand to mean the river of Noah; as if the people who gave it this name had expected, after bearing much tossing and great affliction, to find here "*rest*," comfort, and salvation.

Much of this district is now thinly populated, although it appears to have been anciently well inhabited. So entirely has it been left in obscurity, that, before the truth on this subject was presented to my mind, I thought if there was one portion of the globe of less importance than another it was this. Nothing of any interest seemed to have been transacted in it; and yet, out of Palestine, there is scarcely any spot that would now be more interesting, or more likely to reward a careful examination. Though now comparatively empty, this, and not the barren north, appears to have been the great storehouse of nations, into which it was emptied in consequence of the dreadful incursions of the barbarous tribes from the East, who have since mainly possessed it as pasture-ground. These barbarians were assisted in this work of destruction by the great empires that have been called civilised, who, by their murderous inroads previously, had inclined the inhabitants to seek refuge in the inhospitable north, whence they rebounded upon their destroyers, and have possessed themselves of their possessions. Rather than inhabit a fertile land subject to barbarian sway, they carried with them civilisation, free institutions, superior intellectual capacity, and moral constitution, even into the frozen regions of Iceland.

The quarter in which we can obtain the most distinct view of this people in very ancient times is perhaps on their southern frontier, nearest Greece. Here, along the south bank of the Danube, between this river and the mountains of Hæmus, the country was anciently called Mœsia; and the description given of the ruling race inhabiting this district corresponds with the idea of their being disciples of Moses. In describing the progress of Darius northward, in his wanton invasion of the *Getæ* (who were afterwards called GOTHS), Herodotus says ("Melpomene," xciii. 4): "Before he arrived at the Ister, he first of all subdued the *Getæ*, a people who pretended to immortality. The Thracians of Salmydessus, and they who live above Apollonia, and the city of Messambria, with those who are called Cyrmianians, and Nypsæans, submitted themselves to Darius without resistance. The *Getæ* obstinately defended themselves, but were soon reduced; these, of all the Thracians, are the bravest and most upright.

"They believe themselves to be immortal; and whenever any one dies, they are of opinion that he is removed to the presence of their god Zamolxis, whom some believe to be the same with Gebeleizes. Once in every five years they choose one by lot, who is to be despatched as a messenger to Zamolxis, to make known to him their several wants. And they seriously believe that there is no other deity."

Evidently there is much fable mixed up with this account of the *Getæ*, but it is clear that they were distinguished from surrounding peoples by their religion. They were called "Immortals," because of their confident belief in a future state. While they seem to have been highly improved in arts of peace, they were also distinguished for their moral rectitude. They cultivated grain for exportation as well as for their own consumption, while the Scythians around them were chiefly pastoral. But apparently that for which they were most remarkable was their being followers of Zamoxis, or Zamolxis, or Zalmoxis, after whom the country seems to have been called. This Zamoxis is said to have left to these *Getæ* the institutions of their religion in books, the loss of which is much lamented by the learned, but which most probably we have in the first books of our Bible.[1] There seems to be some confusion as to the name of their great teacher, and whether he should be reckoned the object of their worship, or merely their religious instructor. This is not remarkable among the heathen, having been abundantly manifested in their accounts of the Jews. In the present instance there was the greater liability to error, from the likeness between the sound of the words, Za-El-Moses—"The God of Moses;" and Za Moses—Zamoxes—simply, "That Moses."

It may be remarked that from this quarter, including Thrace, came the principal earliest poets and musicians (such as Orpheus), who are said to have so assisted in charming the previously rude inhabitants of Greece into the mildness of civilised life. In later times they were still remarkable for musical talent; so that the Greeks were in the habit of hiring men from this quarter to mourn at their funerals. In other respects, such as gardening and architecture, they seem to have been of very great service to the Greeks.

Macedonia, the original inheritance of Alexander the Great, lies between Mœsia and Greece; and we are told that, previous to turning himself to fully settle matters in Greece and passing over to make his conquests in the east, he went northward and subdued the country as far as the Danube. However willing many of the inhabitants of this country may have been to labour individually for hire, they were too proud to submit to national servitude, and

---

[1] The reader will remember a similar tradition among the Karens of Birmah. See Watchmen of Ephraim, vol. ii. 320.

accordingly passed over the Danube towards the north; choosing rather to enjoy their beloved freedom in a colder clime than retain their former homes under the Macedonian yoke. Those who remained being the dregs of the people, and perhaps the mere aborigines, may have caused the name of "Thracian" and "Mœsian" to sink ultimately into disrespect. A principal portion of those who withdrew beyond the Danube were called "Getæ," most likely of the tribe of Gad, and are identified with the GOTHS, who were thus early made again to wander forth in search of another resting-place.

North of the Danube was a powerful and extensive republic, anciently called Dacia, and the people Davi, afterwards Dacians. But when comfortably seated in this more northern abode, they were attacked by the Romans, the next great masters of the world, who not only made Mœsia a Roman province, but also drove the people still farther into the northern wilderness. After a most violent struggle, which lasted for several years, Dacia was at length nominally subdued, and multitudes of the brave captives were condemned to suffer cruel deaths in the amphitheatre for the amusement of the Romans. No wonder they hated the rule of such conquerors. Rather than bow his neck to the Roman yoke, like many of the Jews at the destruction of Jerusalem, their king destroyed himself. After a time many of the inhabitants who had withdrawn northward returned, and made the retention of the province so troublesome to the Romans that ultimately these resigned their conquests north of the Danube, when a considerable number it is presumed resettled in the land. Partly from internal troubles, however, and partly from external assaults, they were not long allowed to enjoy quietness; and the people among them that sought peace seem principally to have settled farther north, where they planted commonwealths much after the Israelitish pattern, as in Germany, Sweden, and along the western coasts of Europe.

The banks of the Danube, on which Israel appear to have been previously given rest after the tossing of their captivity, was also the place from which Israel was appointed to spread into power, so as to possess the gates of their enemies, and merit eminently the title of Jacob or "supplanter," at the moment of their greatest extremity. When released in Dacia from the Roman yoke, Attila and his Huns came pouring down upon them from the wilds of Tartary, and swept them from off the face of that whole land, where afterwards they remained only in corners. The Servians, a more slavish race, came into their possessions, under the shadow of rude barbarian power, which however soon passed away "like a rolling thing before the whirlwind." This "blast of the terrible ones" (Isa. xxv. 24), was most severe while it lasted, and was indeed like "a storm" against the Roman "wall;" upon which it precipitated the Goths to such a degree, that they were glad to beg for shelter from that people by whom the bones of their brethren had been heretofore scattered at the grave's mouth, as "when one cutteth and cleaveth wood upon the earth" (Ps. cxli. 7).

What greatly conduced to the flight of the beautiful Goths was the horrific appearance of the Huns. They lacked not courage to meet a foe of their own kind, but appear to have doubted the propriety of having much intercourse with such monsters in human shape, whose polluting habits also they may have been glad to shun. They begged a shelter within the bounds of the Roman empire, and with seeming generosity their request was granted. The Goths were required to deliver up their arms. It was also stipulated that their children should be given to the Romans, and dispersed throughout the provinces of Asia. These were hard terms for a people so brave and affectionate to their offspring as the Goths, who must have been reduced to the utmost extremity ere they could submit to them. They seem, however, to have been faithfully observed, until perfidy appeared on the part of the Romans. The children of the nobility were separated from the multitude without delay, and conducted to the distant places assigned for their residences.

The emigrants spread themselves over the uncultivated plains between the ridges of Mount Hœmus and the Danube, in the same country from which they had been driven by the early conquests of Alexander the Great. Here, in the land of their fathers, they seem to have been offered little but a grave, into which it was threatened they would fall by hunger. When they accepted the hard conditions alluded to, they were promised provisions for their immediate supply which came far short of the demand. They had to expend all to purchase food, and at length, in order to preserve a miserable existence, many of them had to sell themselves as *slaves*. If it could be at all mended, was such a state of things to be endured? At length insult was added to injury: they became exasperated, and in their exasperation began to concert desperate measures. These Western or Visi-Goths at length procured assistance from their brethren the Ostro-Goths, who, not having been admitted within the Roman Empire, had of course retained their arms. War was resolved on. They fought and overcame.

In the meantime, the Gothic youth dispersed over the Asiatic provinces were slaughtered by order of the Roman Government. We are accustomed to talk of the barbarism of the Goths, and of the ruthless hands they laid upon the Roman Empire. But was not vengeance to be looked for in return for such cowardly cruelty as these strangers received from the masters of the world? And accordingly Alaric, king of the Visi-Goths, was raised up for the correction of the Romans. To this office he reckoned himself specially appointed, calling himself "the Fire of God" and the "Scourge of Rome," which he abundantly was, weakening it in various parts; especially ravaging Greece, and thus punishing in their children the ancient dispossessors of his fathers when Alexander led his conquering arms into Mœsia. At length Alaric marched upon Rome itself; and after twice sparing it, and repeatedly meeting with treachery and insult, he sacked and plundered the city, carrying away an immensity of treasure. The barbarians whom Alaric had joined to his army ran into great excesses, the blame of which the Goths have in a great measure borne, although it is said they behaved themselves with much mildness and humanity.[1]

[It is remarkable that the first book supposed to have been printed, is the translation of the gospels and other parts of the New Testament, made by Bishop Ulphilas for the Mœso-Goths about A.D. 360, the language of which is essentially the same with the Anglo-Saxon. It is even said to be one of the very best books in which the latter may be studied.]

The barbarians who had caused the emigration of the Gothic nations rolled meanwhile over the Roman Empire, sweeping away many "mingled people." Some passed over to Africa, which they conquered, or rather ravaged;

---

[1] See Gibbon's Decline and Fall of the Roman Empire, and Kingsley's Roman and the Teuton.

whence returning under Genseric, their prince, Rome again suffered still more severely. Even the Capitol was uncovered for the sake of its gilded brass; and the sacred vessels belonging to the Temple at Jerusalem, brought to Rome by Titus (which Alaric refused to touch on account of their holiness), were among his trophies. A storm, however, deposited them at the bottom of the Great Sea, and at length this barbarous power, which at one time threatened to erect an empire embracing both sides of the Mediterranean, melted away, and can no more be found.

Such has been the fate of all the nations which came like a furious "whirlwind" to drive Israel into endless ruin. They have passed away like a night vision. All their mighty conquests are now but as a troublous dream. Even the Roman eagle, which under her wide-spreading wings in such mockery of hospitality and truth proffered a refuge to Israel, is now as nothing; whilst the poor and needy have indeed, as promised, taken root, spread, and flourished.

GERMANY was speedily peopled by various tribes of the ALLEMANI. The North of SPAIN, as well as a considerable portion of ITALY, came into the possession of the GOTHS. Gaul was laid hold of by the FRANKS, other branches of the same great family, and from them has been called FRANCE. The largest and most valuable part of Britain came into possession of the ANGLO-SAXONS, and from them has been called ENGLAND. In the course of the revolutions we have briefly sketched, the Gothic nations were chiefly driven in towards the north, where they erected free commonwealths in what was anciently called CIMBRIA and SCANDINAVIA, which they civilised and rendered comparatively fruitful, but from which many of them rebounded back by sea upon the more fertile countries of Europe, making not only great depredations, but also large conquests in some cases, as in that of NORMANDY. By one means or another, and mostly as if from necessity, EUROPE has fallen almost entirely into their possession; whence they have spread themselves over a great part of the globe.

The great *supplanting* has been ever going forward. This people have indeed been "Jacob" from the beginning, particularly since their settlement within the bounds of the Roman Empire. But it is especially north of that where they have displayed the most mental power, which, as we have seen, has been in training from the earliest period in order that they might be prepared for acting under the other name of Jacob—that of ISRAEL, or *Prince of God*. They are to be made "princes in all the earth," according to the order of the kingdom of heaven, the greatest of all being as the servant of all; even like "the Prince of the kings of the earth," "who came not to be ministered unto, but to minister, and to give His life a ransom for many." God is already laying liberally to their hand, not for either self-glorification or luxurious ease, but that they may enjoy the high dignity of being dispensers of His bounty to mankind. May they soon fulfil their destiny, and be given to rule in judgment under the King of Righteousness; justifying the prediction:—"The people which shall be created shall praise the Lord!"

Only look for a moment at the important position occupied by this people, whose name but lately was synonymous with barbarism! They possess the most improved portion of our globe, the greater part of which was but a wilderness when they took possession. There is scarcely any place of much importance in any part of the world that they do not now occupy; except indeed their own Land of Israel and those laid hold upon by their great rival in the north-east, and who, as grasping at the whole, is yet to act so important a part at the close of the present dispensation. They have colonised or are colonising all the New World; a great part of Asia is in their possession; whilst Africa is in a manner surrounded by them. Either directly by power, or indirectly by diplomatic agency, they can control almost all the nations of the earth. All the facilities of good are being rapidly provided. True, there is a deadness unworthy of this position, and as it were the silent waiting for the powerful word of the living, life-giving God: "Come from the four winds, O breath, and breathe upon these slain that they may live!"

Now may Mahommedan delusion depart, and Ishmael associate with Isaac in his efforts to raise the long-oppressed children of Africa to the full dignity of man! Now may the younger children of Abraham in the east—the Brahmins—behold the truth of their perverted allegories, and become efficient missionaries to all the families of Shem so densely crowded into that part of the world! Now may the Jews, spread everywhere, knowing all countries, languages, customs, and engagements of mankind, turn their penetrating minds unto "the truth as it is in Jesus," and labour to bestow upon all the true riches! Now may Judah walk with Israel, and may they also "come together out of the north country in the name of the Lord to Jerusalem," and thence go forth like lightning to the utmost corners of the earth, as vessels of honour fit for the Master's use, to carry out blessings unto the ends of the earth, and preach the gospel of the kingdom in all the world for a witness unto all nations before the end come!

But it may be objected that, if these things be so, there must surely be some traditional remains among this people tending to prove their Israelitish origin. With regard to the Scriptures, of which it is most desirable we should find them in possession, we have the parallel case of Judah, where in the reign of Josiah they were so scarce that when a copy was found it was as if some remarkable discovery had been made (2 Kings xxii. 8–20). It plainly appears also that upon the return of the Jews from Babylon they had up to that time been remarkably wanting as to Scripture knowledge (Ezra ix.). Now, if this was the case with regard to "the Jews," who retained Jerusalem, the place of rule and the place of worship, who had the best opportunities of being instructed in what God had done for His people in the days of old, and what He had appointed them to observe as the symbols of allegiance to Himself the Lord of Hosts, the Great Governor among the nations, scarcely *less* forgetfulness could be expected of the fugitive HOUSE OF ISRAEL, who were ever in a state of change, and had separated from the worship of God long previous to their removal from the Land.

Although they are not known to have had the books of Scripture actually in their possession, yet it might be expected they should have traditions of another kind, more especially as Elijah and Elisha chiefly prophesied in ISRAEL; and their prophecies would more naturally regard the people among whom they ministered, rather than Judah, to whom they did not minister, and who have no record of these prophecies.

However adulterated by heathenish admixture, something might be expected to remain among these northern nations of the traditions of their fathers to attest the truth we have been advocating, and such is remarkably the case.

"SET THEE UP WAYMARKS."

The oldest poem these people are known to have possessed appears to have been produced with the special design of collecting the traditions of their fathers. It is called VOLUSPA, *i.e.*, the spae or prophecy of Vola (*Baal* or the Lord, Hos. i. 16.) The Edda is a comparatively modern commentary upon Voluspa. It commences thus,—

> "Be silent, I pray, all holy creatures,
> Greater or small, sons of Heimdallar!
> I will tell of the devices of Valfodar,
> The ancient discourses of men,
> The earliest I know;"

and proceeds to describe the raising of this creation out of chaos, the separation of light from darkness, and the appointment of times and seasons. Then there follows much in very enigmatic language, adverting occasionally to incidents recorded in Scripture, such as the case of Judah and Tamar, until it comes to what may have been specially derived from the prophesying of Elijah when the language becomes comparatively clear, and the meaning more apparent. Thus it then proceeds,—

> [Captive Israel cast out into the northern wilds.—]
> "She saw the bound one,
> Lying under the Grove of the Huns.
> The perfidious funeral,—
> One, like Lok,
> There sat, as Sigynia,
> Never dear to her husband.
> Know you more? What is it?"

Having been brought out into the north country, into the vast plains northward of the Caucasian mountains, and been given there an apparently peaceable settlement, there is then the rushing of "many waters," of the fierce barbarians from the east that inundate these plains, and sweep the people to which the prophecy applies in towards the north, and thus, accordingly, the poem proceeds:—

"A river flows from the east,
  Over poisoned vales,
  Carrying mud and turf;
  It is called Slidur."

[Promise of a refuge in the north.—]

"There stands towards the north,
  In Nidafiollum,
  A golden palace, named Sindra;
  But another exists in Okolni:
  The ale-cellar of the Jotun,
  Which is called, Brimir."

[Disappointed as to the obtaining the promised refuge in the north.—]

"She saw a palace stand far from the sun,
  In Nastrondum;
  It looks at the doors of the north.
  The building is twisted from the spines of serpents,
  Poisoned torrents
  Flow through its windows."

[Dreadful state of society, as mingled among the northern barbarians: whilst the Roman Wolf was busy in his work of destruction.—]

"There she saw, amid the dreadful streams,
  The perjured and the murderers,
  And those that pull the ears
  Of another's wife.
  There Nidhoggur
  Tore the flesh from the corpses.
  The fierce Wolf devoured the men
  Know you more? It is thus."

After much more to the same purpose, the poem then goes on to describe the fulfilment of the words of Isaiah ix. 18-21; to which allusion was made in p. 128:—

"Brethren will fight and slay each other;
  Kindred will spurn their consanguinity;
  Hard will be the world;
  Many the adulteries.
  A bearded age, an age of swords:
  Shields will be cloven.
  An age of wind, an age of wolves,
  Till the world shall perish,
  There will not be one that will spare another."

Further on, we have an account of those dreadful convulsions of the material creation which will precede the full establishment of peace and bestowment of blessing There is still a mingling of heathen fable with the truth of prophecy, but which through it may all the while be discerned:—

> "The sun darkens;
> The earth is immerged in the sea;
> The serene stars are withdrawn from heaven;
> Fire rages in the ancient world;
> The lofty colour reaches to heaven itself.
> Garmur barks from the cave of Guipa:
> The chains are broken,
> Trees rush out."

> "She sees at last, emerging from the ocean,
> An earth, in every part flourishing.
> The cataracts flow down;
> The eagle flies aloft,
> And hunts the fishes in the mountains."

Then there is an evolving of the mysteries of Providence as to the past, and an easy divining of the future as in the days of old:—

> "The Asœ met in Ida Valle,
> And talked of the world's great calamities;
> And of the ancient runœ of Fimbultyr.
> These things done, the wonderful dice,
> Are found gilt in the grass,
> Which those of former days possessed."

Then the earth yields her increase; and want and woe are felt no more:—

> "There were fields without sowing,
> All adverse things became prosperous."

> "The Asœ will dwell without evils,
> Do you yet understand?"

Then the two brothers being reconciled, choose for themselves one Head, and are given the promised headship over the heathen:—

> "Then Heimar shares the power of choosing Vidar,
> And the sons of the two brothers
> Inhabit the vast mansion of the winds.
> Do you know more?"

Then there is the promised glory: Israel and Judah have walked "together out of the north country" to Mount Zion, the glory from which shall cover the earth:—

> "A hall stands, brighter than the sun,
> Covered with gold in Gimle,
> There virtuous people will dwell,
> And for ages enjoy every good."

The millennial ages having run their course, there is the loosing of the serpent (Rev. xx. 7-10,) and so the poem concludes:—

> "Then will come the obscene dragon flying,
> The serpent from Nidar fiolli,
> He carries the corpses in his wings,
> He flies over the ground;
> —The infernal serpent, Nidhogghur;
> Now the earth gapes for him."

So clearly indeed have the traditions of the north been related to the contents of our Bible, that at one time it was supposed our ancestors had become acquainted with them through the medium of Christianity; but such a supposition is now abandoned, and they remain as incontestable evidence of the truth of the Israelitish origin of the people who possess them.

Well may this outcast house of Israel, who had seemed to be "no more dear to her Husband," but to be given a bill of divorce and sent away, be addressed as in Isa. liv. 1-8. The address is evidently made to a people who had previously been in the Lord's favour, and yet not to the Jews (Gal. iv. 27). The words are thus confined to Israel as cast out among the Gentiles, preparatory to her Husband's manifesting Himself more fully as her "Redeemer," and at the same time as "the God of the whole earth:"—

"Sing, O barren,
   Thou—didst not bear;
Break forth into singing, and cry aloud,
Thou—didst not travail with child:
For more—the children of the desolate
Than the children of the married wife, saith the Lord.

"Enlarge the place of thy tent,
And let them stretch forth the curtains of thine habitations:
Spare not, lengthen thy cords,
And strengthen thy stakes;

"For thou shalt break forth on the right hand and on the left;
And thy seed shall inherit the Gentiles,
And make the desolate cities to be inhabited.
Fear not; for thou shalt not be ashamed;
Neither be thou confounded; for thou shalt not be put to shame;
For thou shalt forget the shame of thy youth,
And shalt not remember the reproach of thy widowhood any more.

"For thy Maker—thine Husband;
The Lord of hosts His name;
And thy Redeemer, the Holy One of Israel:
The God of the whole earth shall He be called.

"For the Lord hath called thee as a woman forsaken and grieved in spirit,
And a wife of youth, when thou wast refused, saith thy God.
For a small moment have I forsaken thee;
But with great mercies will I gather thee.

"In a little wrath I hid my face from thee for a moment;
But with everlasting kindness will I have mercy on thee,
   Saith the Lord thy Redeemer."

XV.

THE STATE OF EUROPE SUBSEQUENT TO THE NORTHERN INVASIONS OF ROME.

Israel brought out into these Maritime countries—Consternation of the former Inhabitants—Complete supplanting of the Enemies of Israel, and the powerful Instrumentality clearly foretold, as in Isa. xli. 1–16—Great Whirlwind among the Nations (Jer. xxv. 15–33), sweeping Israel out of her Place of Hiding into the Foreground of Europe—State of Europe consequent upon the Whirlwind described by History—Theories as to the Increase of the Northern Nations—They are the Seed the Lord hath blessed—Mixed form of Government and happy Constitution of Society—Cossacks of the Ural—Feudalism—Provision for the Clergy—Chivalry—Commercial Leagues and Corporations—Freemasonry—Heraldry—Crusades—Language, Music and Poetry—Introduction of Christianity—Religious and Temporal Blessings—All consistent with the Idea of their being the Line of the Lord's Inheritance—Four Objections.

THE bringing of Israel forth from the east into Europe and these islands where the people were to "renew strength," and were to be given power over those who had usurped the dominion of the world, appear to have been all clearly foretold in the prophetic word, as, for example, in Isaiah xli.:—

> "Keep silence before me, O islands,
> And let the people renew strength;
> Let them come near,—then let them speak:
> Let us come near together to judgment.
> Who raised up the righteous from the east,

> Called him to his foot,
> Gave the nations before him,
> And made—rule over kings?
> He gave—as the dust to his sword,
> As driven stubble to his bow,
> He pursued them,—passed safely;
> By the way he had not gone with his feet.
> Who hath wrought and done—calling the generations from the beginning?
> I, Jehovah, the First, and with the last; I am He.

God "hath not seen iniquity in Jacob, neither perverseness in Israel," not that there was none, but in His grace He hath clothed him with the robe of righteousness. He hath beheld him in the Righteous One—the multitudinous seed in the One Seed Christ.

In the succeeding verses (5–9) is described the consternation of these countries, and their vain superstitious recourse to images, which then began to multiply in the churches called Christian; but from which the spirit of Christianity seems to have almost entirely vanished at the time the Gothic race broke in upon Western Europe. This people who had, as was prophesied, lost their name of Israel, are repeatedly pointed to their origin, and have also their "end," or the purpose of God with regard to them, declared. Like Israel in Canaan, however, too many of them have learnt the way of the heathen, whom the Lord cast out before them:—

> "The Isles saw, and feared;
> The ends of the earth were afraid, drew near, and came.
> They helped every one his neighbour;
> And said to his brother, Be of good courage.
> So the carpenter encouraged the goldsmith,
> He that smootheth with the hammer, him that smote the anvil,
> Saying, It is ready for the soldering;
> And he fastened it with nails,—it should not be moved.
> But thou Israel,—My servant,
> Jacob whom I have chosen, the seed of Abraham, My friend,

> —Whom I have taken from the ends of the earth,
> And called thee from the chief men thereof,
> And said unto thee, Thou My servant;
> I have chosen thee, and not cast thee away."

Israel is here pointed forward to his higher destiny than the being a servant of idols. He is chosen to be the servant of the living God. And he is one between whom and God none may interpose. He is chosen of God and delighted in by him, as the seed of Abraham His friend, with whom He condescended to have familiar intercourse, and who in opposition to all human unbelief here emphatically declares, "*I have not cast thee away.*"

The complete supplanting of the enemy, of whose gates he had been given possession, is then described (ver. 10-12):—

> "Fear thou not; for I am with thee:
> Be not dismayed; for I am thy God:
> I will strengthen thee,
> Yea, I will help thee,
> Yea, I will uphold thee with the right hand of My righteousness.
>
> "Behold, all they that were incensed against thee,
> Shall be ashamed and confounded:
> They shall be as nothing;
> And they that strive with thee shall perish.
>
> "Thou shalt seek them,
> And shalt not find them,
> Them that contended with thee:
> They that war against thee shall be as nothing,
> And as a thing of nought."

The powerful instrumentality, whereby this great supplanting would be effected, is next pointed out. All difficulties would be removed and swept away, and Israel would take root and flourish as promised (ver. 13-16):—

> "For I the Lord thy God will hold thy right hand,
> Saying unto thee, Fear not; I will help thee.

THE STATE OF EUROPE.

> Fear not, thou worm Jacob, ye men of Israel ;
> I will help thee, saith the Lord,
> And thy Redeemer, the Holy One of Israel.

> "Behold, I will make thee a new sharp threshing instrument, having teeth ;
> Thou shalt thresh the mountains,
>   And beat *them* small,
> And shalt make the hills as chaff.
>   Thou shalt fan them,
> And the wind shall carry them away,
> And the Whirlwind shall scatter them ;
> And thou shalt rejoice in the Lord,
> Shalt glory in the Holy One of Israel."

The truth of the foregoing prophecy may perhaps best be illustrated by the following account of the attack of the Romans upon what were called "the barbarous nations in the north of Europe," and next of the ample revenge which the latter took of "that great beast, and strong exceedingly, that brake in pieces the whole earth," Dan. vii. 7. This account of one of the Roman invasions is partly by the Emperor himself under whose conduct it took place.

After the assassination of Alexander Severus, the ferocious Maximin assumed the contaminated purple, and announced his accession to the north of Germany, in a course of victorious slaughters and unrelenting devastations. So irresistible was the tempest, that unless, says the historian, the Germans had escaped by their rivers, marshes, and woods, he would have reduced all Germany into subjection. His haughty letters to the senate display the exultation and ferocity of his mind. "We cannot relate to you," says he, "how much we have done. For the space of four hundred miles we have burnt the German towns; we have brought away their flocks, enslaved their inhabitants, and slain the armed. We should have assailed their woods, if the depth of their marshes had permitted us to pass."

This destructive invasion, like many other evils, generated, by the greatness of the necessity, a proportionate benefit. A modern writer has very happily ascribed to it the "formation of that important confederation, which under the name of Franks, withstood the Roman army, and preserved the liberties of Germany."[1]

The Breaker thus came up before Israel; nor was it long before they passed through the gate, and went out by it, to the encompassing, as they now do, of the world.

The irruption of the northern, or rather north-eastern, nations into the south and west of Europe, and of the settlement herein of the Gothic and Saxon race is given in the words of the distinguished historian, *Robertson*, a writer of great authority. Still, we must make allowance for mistakes, occasioned by the writer being anxious to assign a cause for every thing, without being acquainted with the true theory according to which the phenomena might be rightly explained.

"When the fierce barbarians in the north of Europe, and of Asia, fell upon the Roman Empire, wherever they marched their route was marked with blood. They ravaged or destroyed all around them. They made no distinction between what was sacred and what was profane. They respected no age, or sex, or rank. What escaped the fury of the first inundation, perished in those which followed it. The most fertile and populous provinces were converted into deserts, in which were scattered the ruins of villages and cities, that afforded shelter to a few miserable inhabitants whom chance had preserved, or the sword of the enemy, wearied with destroying, had spared. The conquerors who first settled in the countries which they had wasted, were expelled or exterminated by new invaders, who, coming from regions

---

[1] Turner's Anglo-Saxons, vol. i. p. 138, fifth edition.

farther removed from the civilised parts of the world, were still more fierce and rapacious. This brought fresh calamities upon mankind, which did not cease, until the north, by pouring forth successive swarms, was drained of people, and could no longer furnish instruments of destruction. Famine, and pestilence, which always march in the train of war, when it ravages with such inconsiderate cruelty, raged in every part of Europe, and completed its sufferings. If a man were called on to fix upon the period in the history of the world, during which the condition of the human race was most calamitous and afflicted, he would without hesitation, name that which elapsed from the death of Theodosius the Great, to the establishment of the Lombards in Italy. The contemporary authors, who beheld that scene of desolation, labour, and are at a loss, for expressions to describe the horror of it. *The Scourge of God, the Destroyer of Nations*, are the dreadful epithets by which they distinguish the most noted of the barbarous leaders; and they compare the ruin they had brought on the world, to the havoc occasioned by earthquakes, conflagrations, or deluges,—the most formidable calamities which the imagination of man can conceive.

"But no expressions can convey so perfect an idea of the destructive progress of the barbarians, as that which must strike an attentive observer, when he contemplates the total change which he will discover in the state of Europe, after it began to recover some degree of tranquillity, towards the close of the sixth century. The Saxons were, by that time, masters of the southern and most fertile provinces of Britain; the Franks, of Gaul; the Huns, of Pannonia; the Goths, of Spain; the Goths and Lombards, of Italy and the adjacent provinces. Very faint vestiges of the Roman policy, jurisprudence, arts, or literature, remained. New forms of government, new dresses, new languages, new names of men and countries, were everywhere introduced.

"To make a great or sudden alteration with respect to any of these, unless where the ancient inhabitants of a country have been almost exterminated, has proved an undertaking beyond the power of the greatest conquerors. The great change which the settlement of 'the barbarous nations' occasioned in the state of Europe, may therefore be considered as a more decisive proof than even the testimony of contemporary historians, of the destructive violence with which these invaders carried on their conquests, and of the havoc which they had made from one extremity of this quarter of the globe to the other."[1]

The immense increase of these northern nations has been acknowledged on all hands. Different theories have been formed to account for it; and also for how they could have been contained in the north from which they seemed to issue in such myriads. If in truth they had been produced and sustained solely there, this would have been no less a miracle than the feeding of their fathers in the wilderness of Sinai previous to their being given possession of the Land of Canaan. But there is no necessity for pleading such a miracle, when we allow them the position we have pointed out in the east of Europe immediately behind that great wall of empires by which the way of Israel was so long hedged up that she could not "find her paths."

Sir William Temple supposes these nations had increased by an indiscriminate commerce of the sexes, or by a plurality of wives; whilst directly the contrary of all this was the case; these people being remarkable for chastity

[1] View of the State of Europe, Sec. I.

in their homes: and as regards polygamy we may see from the case of the Turks, that it rather tends to *decrease* the population. He supposes that men will increase faster as barbarians than as being civilised, which facts seem abundantly to disprove.

For example, look to the case of the red and white races in America. Whether they be at war with each other or living at peace, the former are melting away before the latter. It may be said that the American Indians are busy destroying each other if not at war with the whites; but so also were the northern nations, and yet they continued to increase. It may be said also, that the North Americans are destroyed by an excessive use of ardent spirits; but this also existed among these northern nations in Europe, so that "a drunken Dane" came to be a common expression; and yet they continued to increase and overflow all around them. Nor have they ceased to do so. Their increase is indeed more peaceable, but still it is onward, and even much greater than before; only now they do not require to break through the bounds of others to obtain room for themselves. Having reached these maritime parts, they spread abroad in every direction, plant themselves on every shore, and colonise the globe. Their case cannot be accounted for, either before taking possession of the foreground of Europe or since, except upon the supposition, that the Lord " had a favour for them," and that they are " the seed which the Lord hath blessed."

That they are indeed the very people we are in search of, will still farther appear, if we consider the aspect of society in Europe after the Roman Empire had been entirely subverted, and when the genius of this new people had full time to develope. Let us see whether the character of those great changes which then came over the face of society be fully consistent with the idea that the people who produced them were the children of those fathers whose training we have traced in Lectures IV. and V. We shall now briefly advert to a few of the more general outlines, and afterwards exemplify the truth of our proposition more minutely in the case of the ENGLISH nation.

We have seen that Israel were not allowed to rest in the Patriarchal form of government. As soon as their circumstances allowed, they were accustomed first to ARISTOCRATIC rule, or government by a few natural leaders of the people. Thereafter they had the DEMOCRATIC principle introduced among them, the people delegating their power to men who acted in their name for either counsel or judgment.

Now one of the grand changes which took place upon the dissolution of the Roman Empire was the universal establishment of this same mixed form of government. Sir William Temple observes :—

"Wherever they seated themselves they left a constitution, which has since been called in most European languages 'the States,' consisting of three orders—noble, ecclesiastic, and popular, under the limited principality of one person, with the style of king, prince, duke, or count. The remainder at least, or traces hereof, appear still in all the principalities founded by these people in Italy, France, and Spain, and were of a piece with the present constitutions in most of the great dominions on the other side of the Rhine."

It may be remarked that the Northerns claim for their CIVIL INSTITUTIONS an origin in the most remote antiquity, and some of them even an Israelitish origin. Their Governments were almost all representative or constitutional, a form peculiar to Israel and the nations of Europe. Their laws were strict, and were generally administered in each nation by twelve judges having appointed circuits, as we find recorded in the Book of Samuel. The kingship was generally hereditary in particular families, but the individual was often determined upon by popular election. Their KINGS were the principal agents in getting the law carried into effect, and in conducting the defence of the commonwealth, rather than arbitrary monarchs making everything minister to their private gratification. The PEOPLE themselves, by their minute subdivision into Hundreds and Tythings, and by their mutual subordination and oversight—exactly analogous to what was the case with regard to ancient Israel—greatly assisted in the preservation of social order; so that their home condition was often strongly in contrast to the buccaneering or piratical excursions of the more restless, who went forth to be avenged on Rome, their great adversary, and to take possession of the colonies of that empire, which had been so continually driving them in upon the inhospitable north. Whether migrating or abiding at home, their form of society seems to have had a most germinating power. Every little band formed a community, with such rules and partition of duty as might enable them either to maintain their present position, or expand into a powerful State, as occasion might require or circumstances allow. This subdivision of the people, and the association of these little communities for more general purposes into tribes or kingdoms, prepared the way for that association of comparatively independent States, as in the German Empire, or still more largely, in the great European family of nations.[1]

[1] "The Cossacks of the Ural are in a very peculiar position, forming an

And as to PROPERTY, the change was equally characteristic of Israel, among whom, although land was heritable, still individuals had not absolute possession thereof. It seems to have been reckoned a kind of public property. Those who held it owed certain duties to the State, and were liable to be called out in its defence. They were thus supported in order that they might support the commonwealth. Civil offices might be paid for in the same way as

almost perfect community. All the land is owned by the community as a body, and there is not an inch which belongs to private persons, though they may hold buildings and the land of which they have the use. In the same way the fisheries and the meadows form common property, under very strict regulations, from which no one dares to deviate. The majority of this population of about 90,000 men does not belong to the Russian Orthodox Church, but is composed of Dissenters, probably not more than 100 of them being orthodox. Between the ages of 19 and 41 every male Cossack is considered to be in the military service, either within or without the boundaries of the district, though probably for a good part of this time he is really on furlough, so that out of 10,000 men who should be with the colours, there are seldom more than 3000 or 4000 actually serving at one time. The peculiarities of this position, where the Cossack is obliged to pass the greater part of his life in the military service, have given rise to some customs which have been found practically convenient. A Cossack who is married young, and has a family, suddenly finds himself called upon to throw aside his farm, leaving it in the hands of people who are unable to manage it, and on his return, after a few years' service, discovers that his property has gone to destruction, and that his wife and children are almost beggars. Rather than attempt to renew his fortunes by agriculture, or fishing, he prefers to go off on another expedition, perhaps this time taking his family with him. On the other hand, many who have been settled quietly at home do not like to throw up everything and expose themselves to the risk of war, or of service, and it has therefore become quite the habit, as only a certain number of men out of the 10,000 are wanted, to hire substitutes to fill their places. A substitute for two years' service in Tashkent would probably bring in about three hundred roubles. Thus, if the number of Cossacks fit for the field were 6000, and 600 men were wanted for service in Turkestan, every ten men would club together to pay the expenses of the one man who was going as their substitute."

military services. The people were thus less liable to taxation. From the lowest to the highest they might all feel that they were members of one whole, and that each had duties to perform for the good of the whole.

Such was, and is again to be, the case in the land of Israel, even with regard to the prince. Ezek. xlv. 8—" In the land shall be his possession, and my princes shall no more oppress my people." It need not be remarked how naturally this accounts for the FEUDAL SYSTEM, over the origin of which among these nations so much mystery has hung; which also prevailed equally among those that were farther removed from the Romans. The principle among all was this, that land was public property, for which services were due to the State—to the king, as the representative of the State—by the great landholders in the first instance, and then by the subordinate holders through them, each rendering his service to him who was immediately above him, until it reached the throne, which itself was supposed to be held "by the grace of God," as expressed in the voice of the people. There was wisdom in the contrivance beyond what could be expected to originate in "barbarism" or mere chance. The system was doubtless abused; and the great holders now retain the property without the trouble of rendering the State any considerable recompense for that with which they were originally entrusted for the public good. Among some of these people, as, for example, in Norway, the right of redemption remained, as in Israel.

A like provision was made in Israel for the MINISTERS OF RELIGION. The Levites had their own possessions in land throughout the tribes, besides the free-will offerings presented to them by the people (Lect. xxiii.) They had also much to do in the teaching and administration of the

R

law. Correspondent to this is the change noticed by Sir William Temple to have taken place in the state and provision of the clergy in Europe, after the embrace of Christianity by the northern nations.

Like Israel in the time of the Judges, when these nations were only in a manner holding military possession of Europe, and had not fully established their civil institutions, they had an order of men assisting in the administration of justice, who could only be looked for among a people whose moral feelings had been cultivated to a remarkable degree. I advert to THE ORDER OF CHIVALRY (initiated by King Arthur of Britain, A.D. 510), to an order of men, who, sacrificing personal ease, and all expectation of private gain, went forth in search of opportunities of avenging wrong and relieving the oppressed; combining in their character, besides this remarkable display of conscientiousness and benevolence, the most courteous and chaste regard for women, and reverence for religion. With them the sword was consecrated by religion to be wielded by the most punctilious honour in support of morality. Doubtless chivalry degenerated much into empty parade and other abuses; but withal it had immense influence in improving the civil condition and social intercourse of these nations after the confusion that accompanied their first settlement in Western Europe.

The TEUTONIC ORDER OF KNIGHTHOOD was not more remarkable than the TEUTONIC LEAGUE for the furtherance and protection of commerce. The vast extension of the HANSEATIC LEAGUE, spreading its ramifications throughout Europe, and bringing together the productions of India, the manufactures of Italy, and the bulky, though not less useful commodities of the North; the wisdom with which the measures of the League were planned in their general assemblies, and the vigour and regard to principle with which they were conducted towards a successful termination, until they cleared the rivers and all other great thoroughfares of the predatory bands which had infested them, and made their alliance to be courted and their power dreaded by the greatest monarchs, all argue an intellectual and moral capacity inconsistent with the idea that these people were mere "barbarians." Not among the remains of the Latin race, but among the new inhabitants of Europe, all this took place.

In its degree the same thing happened in the several towns and cities of these people, where those following the same craft or occupation generally associated together for their mutual assistance and protection, as in GUILDS, which were combined in burgh corporations, in which, again, the representative principle was at work, and men were in training for more extensive public employment.

By FREEMASONRY, the ancient architecture of the days of Solomon, and the mystic meaning of the ancient symbols which were used by this art in the more important buildings, such as cathedrals, are supposed to have been preserved. If our theory be correct, as doubtless it is, there may not be so much vain pretension in "the Craft" as many have rashly supposed. Their origin may then, at least, be truly referred to the days of "Solomon, King of Israel, and Hiram, King of Tyre," and a better account may be given of our peculiar style of architecture, and its narrow lights, than has hitherto been proposed. The rites of Freemasonry also indicate such a connection with Egypt as the Children of Israel had anciently.

HERALDRY, or the science of ensigns and symbols, as connected with the history of nations or lesser societies, or of distinguished families or individuals, or as designating office, the origin and use of which has been so lost in obscurity, seems to have had the same source as the institutions already referred to. Some faint indications of it may perhaps be found previously in Europe; but the great blaze of its glory is only to be seen after the settlement here of these nations during the Crusades. This use of such variety of ensigns, and of the language of colours, and precious stones and metals, may best be accounted for by the variety of standards existing among the Tribes of Israel, and by the symbolical use which was made amongst them of these very matters, even in things the most sacred, and to which we should be glad more particularly to direct attention than we have now an opportunity of doing.

The CRUSADES themselves (first initiated by a British Princess, Helena, the mother of Constantine, A.D. 300), are highly consistent with the truth of our view. It has been observed that this was the only enterprise in which the European nations all engaged with equal ardour. To say the least, this is somewhat singular. It may help to account for the frenzy which then so generally seized the minds of men in this matter, if we suppose that there were still some lingering recollections existing among them of the value of the Land of their Fathers, and some remaining hope of a happy return to the scenes of their early, and also their prophesied, glory, which, mingling with the views and prospects of Christianity as they had received it, became so blended therewith as that the former was lost in the latter; and the yearning they had for their "mother dear, Jerusalem," and the place of their fathers' sepulchres, took the form of a zeal for the defence of the Holy City and the place of the Holy Sepulchre from infidel cruelty, rapacity, and pollution.

Thus the "Whirlwind" went round, and the West was precipitated back upon the East. Like Israel coming up from the Wilderness, they made a wilful attempt to take possession of the land ; in which they were put to shame, and made to turn back from before their enemies into the northern wilderness of the people, until they had been so schooled and trained as that (consistently with their true good) it could be given them in permanent possession.

From that time the course of this people has been ever progressive. God has been enriching them by His providence, and unfolding to them still more clearly and largely the treasures of His grace. Discovery and invention have gone hand in hand, and opportunities of consecrating these to the good of man and the glory of God have correspondingly abounded. EQUALLY WITH THE PLAIN DECLARATIONS OF HIS WORD, THE PROVIDENCE OF GOD MOST DISTINCTLY TESTIFIES TO THE TRUTH OF OUR ISRAELITISH ORIGIN.

The TIME OF THE FORMAL INTRODUCTION OF CHRISTIANITY among the Anglo-Saxons is rather remarkable. It was just when Christianity was fading away into mere formalism or superstition in all other parts of the world, and when throughout the East it was being so engulfed by Mohammedanism as to be threatened with entire extinction in all its original seats. Contrary to the case of all other people with regard to religion, their course has been progressive, as it has been with regard to everything else ; and thenceforward did this become emphatically "Christendom."[1]

---

[1] Lucius, the grandson of Claudia, in A.D. 155, at a national council at Winchester, had established Christianity as the national religion instead of Druidism, when the Christian ministry were inducted into all the rights

It need scarcely be remarked that both POETRY and MUSIC were greatly cultivated in Israel. These were accomplishments which it might be expected would be eminently possessed by a people who were to be peculiarly devoted to the worship of "the Most High over all the earth," and accordingly these nations have been remarkable for musical talent and genius, which appears to be very much like that of the Jews.[1] (See p. 173.)

These nations have been equally remarkable with regard to POETRY in all its varieties. In the cities of Germany, even among the operatives, it was greatly cultivated. And in Italy, after the genius of the Gothic race began to develop itself in verse, one of the most important changes that we observe is the production of the sonnet or song of fourteen lines, in which so much was written by Petrarch. In the same age, *Antonio a Tempo*, a civilian at Padua who wrote on Poetry, distinguishes sixteen different kinds of sonnet. Now the like variety of this kind of composition prevails to an immense extent in the Scriptures; but it will scarcely be said that these people learned to write sonnets from their perusal of the Scriptures as conveyed to them through a Christian medium; for, so far as I know, these sonnets have lain unobserved in the Scriptures from the time the Bible was first circulated in Europe. This kind of composition, along with many others, amounting to

---

of the Druidic hierarchy, *tithes* included. The usages of Britain required the consent of the whole nation to any innovation in religion.—Morgan's Briti h Kymry.

[1] King Alfred, in his commonplace-book, noted that in the preceding century Aldhelm, a pious monk, used to take his stand in some public place, and sing psalms or pious songs in the Saxon tongue, to the delight and instruction of the crowd that never failed to gather round him.

above a hundred, seems to have been preserved among the people of Israel during all their wanderings, although they do not appear to have recognised it in their own Sacred Writings, when these were restored to them through the medium of Christianity.[1]—Sir W. Temple's Miscellanea.

These northern peoples have already been blessed with the choicest intellectual and spiritual blessings. When darkness overspread the earth, "and gross darkness the people," on them the light dawned at the Reformation. Towards their part of the world came the preaching and epistles of the apostles at the beginning of the Christian dispensation. They have shown the greatest adaptation of mind for the study of the Scriptures, which they have also translated into almost every tongue, previous to distributing them all over the globe. They are besides most in the position of waiting for the return of their Lord, and the promised outpouring of the Spirit. Though much less so than they ought to be, still they are most in the position commanded and promised to Israel.

Many also are the temporal blessings which have been conferred upon this race, the numberless discoveries and improvements which have sprung up among them, and by

[1] By some it is said that Christianity has caused all the difference in the nations of Europe. Granted: it is this which causes the difference between their present and their former state. Christianity clears the perceptions, and gives full exercise to the powers of the understanding, while it sanctifies and elevates the affections. But there is power and utility in the working of God's providence upon the natural capacity and character. All God's working with regard to Israel was to form a people for Himself—to prepare a people for His name (Isa. xliii. 21). Let us honestly look around us in the world, and see whether Christianity *alone* has produced the differences which we see in European character.

them distributed over the globe. Among the first of these was PAPER, the very fine substance of which books are now made, allowing what would formerly have been a rather extensive library to be condensed into a volume that may without inconvenience be carried in the pocket. That this may more effectually be accomplished, and copies multiplied at comparatively little labour and expense, they have been given PRINTING.

By STEAM POWER, the process of printing has been still further facilitated to an immense extent, and the publications rapidly spread all over the globe, with almost unvarying certainty of reaching their destination at the appointed time. By the application of Steam Power, also, and the Electric Telegraph, the city has been spread all over the country, and the country brought, as it were, into the city; remote corners of the earth have been brought into conjunction, whilst human labour is lightened, and the conveniences of life multiplied to an amazing extent.

Nor could these advantages have been enjoyed but for the previous discovery of the MARINER'S COMPASS, by the aid of which the great waste of waters can so easily be traversed; and GUNPOWDER, by which all obstructions can be so rapidly removed, in "exalting the valleys, and making low every mountain," that "highways" may be "cast up" for the rapid conveyance of men and the means of blessing them.

How rapidly of late has EDUCATION proceeded! SCIENCE has been searched out, ARTS have been improved, ANTIQUITIES ransacked, and INVENTIONS multiplied. The Lord hath indeed been hastening His work in these our times. He hath been putting most liberally into our hands. He hath also been opening the eyes of many here and there to see wondrous things out of His Law. May the beauty of His Word be indeed made to appear, and may its power be felt! And for this may the Spirit be poured upon us from on high; may our people indeed see their position and their privileges, and be thoroughly persuaded to live, not unto themselves, but "unto Him who died for them, and rose again," reckoning nothing that they may have as their own, but as entrusted to their care for the good of all as they have opportunity!

I know not of any objection to the supposition of the Anglo-Saxons especially being of Israel which has not been anticipated by the Spirit of Prophecy, and which is not to the advantage of our argument. Thus:—

Had they, like the Prodigal Son, wandered into a far country among fields of swine? Were they found eating things that are ceremonially unclean? Such was foretold of Israel. Was it not prophesied by Hosea, chap. ix. 3, that he would "eat unclean things in the land of Assyria?" Had they corrupted their religion, so as even to become worshippers of wood and stone, and of "new gods which had newly come up?" Such also was plainly foretold of Israel (Deut. xxxii. 17). Had they lost even the name of Israel, so as not to be known as the peculiar people of God? This also was foretold in Hosea i. 9, 10. "The Prodigal Son" was not only to be lost to his father and to his brother, but even to himself (Luke xv.) But the lost son, Ephraim, was at length to "come to himself," and he has already, even when afar off, been found of his Father.

"Doubtless Thou our Father,
  Though Abraham be ignorant of us,
  And Israel acknowledge us not:
  Thou, O Lord, our Father,
  Our Redeemer:—
  Thy Name from everlasting.

O Lord, why hast Thou made us to err from Thy ways,
—Hardened our heart from Thy fear?
Return, for Thy servants' sake,
THE TRIBES OF THINE INHERITANCE.

The people of Thy holiness have possessed but a little while:
Our adversaries have trodden down Thy sanctuary.
       We are — :
Thou never bearest rule over them;
They were not called by Thy Name."—ISA. lxiii. 16-19.

XVI.

ISRAEL'S GRAVE THE SAXON'S BIRTHPLACE.

Lombard Laws—Allemani—Gothic-Scythian Race—Ancient Sakai and Modern Saxon branch—Reach the North-West of Europe, and betake themselves to sea—Come to the assistance of the Inhabitants of South Britain against those of the North—Their Beauty, Justice, and Truth—Independence—Interest in Public Affairs, and Tendency to Improvement—Benevolence: its possession befits the design of God with regard to Israel, and the present position of the English People, for which they have been also intellectually gifted—Promises to Israel as acting worthy of her destiny.

HAVING previously shown that the Scriptures lead us to expect to find "Ephraim and all the tribes of Israel, his companions" under blessing, more especially in the north-west, and that the whole scheme of Providence with regard to the administration of the Word of God corresponds thereto, we then proceeded to inquire what other branches of evidence favour our view, and have seen that History, Language, Waymarks, High-heaps, and the Traditions of the North all really require it, in order that much which is otherwise inexplicable may be cleared up.

By the sixth century after Christ, when "the Whirlwind" of nations, described in our last Lecture, had abated, and the atmosphere had been so cleared that a distinct view could be had of how matters were settled, everything, as far as we looked at it, gave unequivocal indications that Israel had been given *possession*, to the exclusion of both the Romans and barbarians, who had sought their destruction, and had robbed them of the homes they previously had between the Don and the Danube, the neighbouring districts of the northern Wilderness.[1]

[1] Respecting the LOMBARD Laws, Rev. Charles Kingsley says, "They are valuable to you, as giving you a fair specimen of the laws of an old Teutonic people. You may profitably compare them with the old Gothic, Franco-Salic, Burgundian, Anglo-Saxon, and Scandinavian laws, all formed on the same primeval model, agreeing often in minute details, and betokening one primeval origin of awful antiquity. By studying them you may gain some notion of that primeval liberty and self-government common at first to all the race, but preserved alone by England. . . .

"These laws were collected and published in writing by King Rothar, A.D. 643, seventy-six years after Alboin came into Italy. The cause, he says, was the continual wearying of the poor, and the superfluous exactions, and even violence, of the strong against those who were weak. They are the 'laws of our fathers, as far as we have learnt them from ancient men, and are published with the counsel and consent of our princes, judges, and all our most prosperous army,' *i.e.*, the barons and freemen capable of bearing arms, and are confirmed, according to the custom of our nation, by *garat hinx*; that is, as far as I can ascertain from Grimm's German Law, by giving an *earnest, garant*, or *warrant* of the bargain."

"Sixteen kings," says the preface, "had reigned from Agilmund *to Rothar*; and seven times had the royal race been changed, though all descended from Woden. The British Constitution is represented as a clumsy and artificial arrangement of the year 1688. 1688 after Christ? 1688 before Christ would be nearer the mark. It is as old in all its essentials as the time when not only all the Teutons formed one tribe, but when Teutons and Scandinavians were still united, and when that was, who dare say? We at least brought the British Constitution with us out of the bogs and moors of Jutland, along with our smock-frocks and leather gaiters, brown bills and stone axes; and it has done us good service, and will do, till we have carried it right round the world.

"And if our English law, our English ideas of justice and mercy, have retained, more than most European codes, the freedom, the truthfulness, the kindliness of the old Teutonic laws, we owe it to the fact that England escaped, more than any other land, the taint of effete Roman civilisation; that she, therefore, first of the lands in the twelfth century, rebelled against, and first of them in the sixteenth century, threw off the Ultramontane yoke."

Our English words "all" and "whole" seem to have been derived from the Hebrew word *Kol,* כל (see *Gesenius*), the same in sense, and a name whereby all Israel was denominated, Mal. iv. 4; 1 Kings xii. 1, 3, 12, 16, 17, 20; xviii. 19, 20, 30, 39; Isa. xxix. 11; xlv. 22; Ezek. xi. 15; xx. 40; xxxvii. 16, &c. In the historical Scriptures, and also in some of the prophets, as Ezekiel and Isaiah, "all" is a usual prefix to Israel when "Ephraim and his companions" are spoken of as distinct from the Jews.

It is indeed worthy of note that, in addition to the abundant evidence already adduced for our Israelitish origin, our German brethren should have retained the very name of *All*—Allemani, the name whereby these tribes were pleased to call themselves, meaning All the men, or *All the numbered.* The Hebrew word *Mâna* means *to distribute in classes, number, rank,* or *proper place.* In its Chaldee form it was the first word in the handwriting upon the wall at Belshazzar's feast, and was interpreted by Daniel as meaning *numbered and finished.* Although not in the sense in which Belshazzar's kingdom was numbered, a MAN (which, by the way, was the standard of Reuben) was one of the numbered. True, a man was only one of the MANY; but he was also a person of consideration, a recognised member of the commonwealth. He had his appointed place in society, and a voice at least by delegation in its management. Those unable, or not having a right, to bear arms were left out of account.

To be one of the numbered was to be A MAN. True, the very word is not used in Num. i. 2, where we find the phrases so frequently repeated, "All that were numbered," "All that were able to go forth to war;" but here we have the very idea connected with the term *All. He-mani,* "the numbered," is likely to have been familiarly used to express more briefly that which it was necessary to mention so frequently—the condition of being enrolled in the armies of the commonwealth, and of being one of the many who constituted the body and power of the State.

The word, as signifying "numbered," or a recognised part of the great whole, was thus discriminative of much more than sex. It had a meaning which is still sometimes attached to it; as, when speaking of one who betrays a mean or cowardly spirit, we say "He is no man," or of another who takes his place in society, and maintains it bravely, and altogether as becomes him, "He is every inch a man." In common *parlance*, to put one in a good and honourable position in society, and enable him to keep it, is to "make a man of him."

It may also be noticed that the other name whereby the Allemani are generally denominated is "Germans," which means WAR-MEN, or Men of War, and that "All that were able to go forth to war" is the expression given by Moses, equivalent to "All that were numbered." (*Fir-bolg* in Kymric, and *Belgæ* in Latin, mean the same.)

We are, however, to look for the descendants of All-Israel, not only among the Germans and their Anglo-Saxon offspring, but also in Italy, and especially in France and Switzerland. The Goths, some of whom passed northward into SCANDINAVIA; the Ostrogoths, who turned southward into sunny ITALY, and the Visigoths into Spain; the FRANKS (or Free Men), after whom Gaul is now called FRANCE; as well as the Saxons, Angles, Jutes, Danes, and Northmen who came into Britain, were all branches of the same people. Some, violently broken off, and seemingly cast away, having since been planted in many a goodly soil, have been made to spread abroad and fill the face of the world with fruit.

Herder says, "By them all the modern kingdoms of Europe were founded, their distinctions of rank were introduced, and the elements of their jurisprudence were inculcated. More than once they attacked, took, and plundered Rome. Several times they besieged, and even made themselves masters of, Constantinople. At Jerusalem they founded a Christian monarchy; and in the present day, partly by the princes whom they have seated upon every throne in Europe, and partly by the kingdoms they have founded, they exercise more or less dominion, either as possessors, or by their manufactures and trade, over all the four quarters of the globe."—Philosophy of Man, b. xvi. c. iii.

"The arts which other nations have brought to perfection, the Germans for the most part first attempted. They repaired to foreign lands in numbers, and were the instructors in various mechanical inventions of many nations, east, west, and south. Amid all the disorders of the dark ages, the inextinguishable fidelity and probity of the German character remain evident.

"The women of Germany were nowise inferior to the men: domestic activity, chastity, fidelity, and honour, were the distinguishing features of the females in all the Germanic nations and tribes."

We have seen that "All" is a term applied to Israel as distinct from the Jews. It was in All-Israel, and not among the Jews, that Elijah prophesied. It was for the turning back the "heart" of All-Israel that Elijah prayed (1 Kings xviii.) What he so much desired was not granted him during his former sojourn upon earth; rather their perversity was such that he made supplication against them. It was, nevertheless, the purpose of God to answer his prayer in their behalf, although perhaps not at the time, nor perhaps in the manner, expected by the prophet.

We have contemplated the remarkable scene at Horeb (Mission of Elijah, p. 35), when Elijah received a commission to separate Israel from the national covenant which had been there mediated by Moses. We have seen (Lect. xiii.) how on the Caucasus a people have been left to point with one hand back to Elijah the prophet of All-Israel, and forward to the Allemani as brethren, being themselves evidently descended from the people unto whom Elijah ministered.

Let us pray for the salvation of the Allemani. Among them that Reformation commenced in the blessings of which we have so richly shared, and Germans have been among our most successful associates in spreading the gospel among the heathen.[1] But many of them, as in Austria, remain devotees of Romish superstition; many are so occupied in neologian speculations, as to have little time and less inclination to attend to the truth of divine revelation; many are indifferent; and multitudes of them, as

---

[1] Germany has also led the way in modern home and foreign philanthropic effort. Let us never forget the honoured names and labours of Muller of Bristol, Van Meter of New York and Rome, John Falk, Immanuel Wichern, Theodore Fliedner, Gossner, Gobat, Louis Harms, Basedow, Pestalozzi, Oberlin, Swartz, the Moravian Brethren, and the Basle Mission, from whose consecrated, gifted, and devoted lives England has received so much blessed instruction, and example and help in the art of fulfilling her destiny of blessing to the nations. And let us remember, that while England has been comparatively so slow to believe the teaching of Prophecy and Providence, Germany, according to her means and ability, in her own quiet way, has far outstripped us in successful colonisation and cultivation of the Holy Land. The scientific, poetic, plodding, "praying-and-working" yearners for the good of all men are indeed making "the waste and ruined cities" ready for habitation.

well as among ourselves, are ignorant of the gospel of the grace of God.

If the Allemani are what we have supposed them to be, a great change must take place in them before the restoration of All-Israel can be effected. But it is not greater than the Power which is to accomplish it, and that Power is to be called forth by prayer. "The effectual fervent prayer of a righteous man (of a man walking in the truth) availeth much. Elias was a man subject to like passions as we are, and he prayed earnestly that it might not rain; and it rained not on the earth by the space of three years and six months. And he prayed again, and the heaven gave rain, and the earth brought forth her fruit" (James v. 16-18). Long enough have we proved the negative power of prayer. Now let us with heart and life devotion unitedly pray for the accomplishment of Elijah's mission in answer to his prayer—

> "Hear me, O LORD, hear me,
> That this people may know that Thou art the LORD God,
> And *that* Thou hast turned their heart back again."
> —1 Kings xviii. 37.

We now enter still more minutely into this latter part of our subject, and as a specimen of this grand family of nations, propose to take the ANGLO-SAXON branch. This, of course, is not to the exclusion of the others; but it happens to be the first that arrested the lecturer's attention, and with regard to which it is of most importance some of us should be resolved.[1] To this class of evidence also we have the most easy access. It surrounds us on every side; and hereafter one of the most remarkable facts connected

---

[1] Let us ever remember that it was in Isaac, or as sons of Isaac, that Abraham's seed was to be "called" or celebrated (Gen. xxi. 12).

S

with this subject will be, that such multifarious and obtrusive evidence should have been so long disregarded.

We propose taking a view of the ANGLO-SAXONS chiefly anterior to their embrace of Christianity, at a time when their manners and political or religious institutions were uninfluenced by the Bible as received through that medium. If at that time their physical appearance, mental and moral character, conduct in the private and public relations of life, civil institutions, religious opinions, rites and ceremonies, and all else respecting them be such as might reasonably be expected of Israel: if there be no incongruity but every correspondence in their case, surely we may say that the truth has been arrived at on this important and hitherto most perplexing point, and proceed to ascertain what should be its practical influence. If a young man had gone astray—and this is the "lost son"—what else could be done? His Father has pointed out the marks by which his son may be identified, and has clearly enough indicated the direction in which he wandered. Let us endeavour to make ourselves familiar with these various marks; for we may rest assured that the people to whom they all apply are the very children of promise, "the nations" that were to come of Jacob, the seed of Abraham according to the flesh, as well as the greater part of those who are also his children by faith.

We have already seen that Scripture history leaves captive Israel in the Cities of the Medes and other places in the northern possessions of Assyria. And it is a very important fact that in his valuable history Sharon Turner has traced the ANGLO-SAXONS to this very quarter. WHERE ISRAEL WERE LOST, THENCE CAME THE ANGLO-SAXONS.

These two puzzling difficulties have been long enough before the historian: What became of ISRAEL, the most important people as to the promises and purposes of Jehovah? Whence sprang the Anglo-Saxons, the most distinguished in the providence of God of all the families of mankind, and especially as to the benefits which He hath bestowed upon them, and enabled them to bestow upon others?

But why should we continue needlessly to create difficulties, so as to make the Most High appear to work contradictively, and produce miracles without a cause? Why cut off the people to whom the Promises were made, whom He said He would not utterly destroy, although He might seem to do so (Jer. xxx. 11), and out of the same place raise up another people, from an origin altogether unknown, answering in every respect to the character which for ages He had been giving to Israel, and in the most minute particulars fulfil to them *their* long-promised destiny? Is this at all consistent with the wisdom, truth, and faithfulness of God? Certainly not; and having nothing either in or out of Scripture to support it, should at once be rejected.

Speaking of the second stock of the European population, *Sharon Turner* observes (vol. i. 94)—" It is peculiarly interesting to us, because from its branches not only our own immediate ancestors, but also those of the most celebrated nations of modern Europe, have unquestionably descended. The Anglo-Saxons, Lowland Scotch, Normans, Danes, Norwegians, Swedes, Germans, Dutch, Belgians, Lombards, and Franks, have all sprung from that great fountain of the human race, which we have distinguished by the terms Scythian, German, or Gothic. . . . The first appearance of the Scythian tribes in Europe may be placed, according to *Strabo* and *Homer*, about the eighth, or, according to *Herodotus*, in the seventh century, before the Christian era." [Even the former of these dates, it may be observed, is the same with that of the Assyrian captivity.] "The first scenes of their civil existence, and of their progressive power, were in Asia, to the east of the Araxes." [The very district into which Israel had been brought by those whose purpose with regard to them was so different from that of God.] "Here they multiplied, and extended their territorial limits, for some centuries, unknown to Europe."

The account of *Diodorus* is, that "the Scythians, formerly inconsiderable and few, possessed a narrow region on the Araxes; but by degrees they became more powerful in numbers and in courage. They extended their boundaries on all sides; till at last they raised their nation to great empire and glory. One of their kings becoming valiant and skilful in the art of war, they added to their territory the mountainous regions about Caucasus; also the plains towards the ocean, and the Palus Mœotis, with the other regions near the Tanais" [the very quarter in which are to be found the Israelitish burying-places before pointed out (Lect. XIII.)]

"In the course of time they subdued many nations between the Caspian and Mœotis, and beyond the Tanais, or Don. . . . In the time of *Herodotus* they had gained an important footing in Europe. They seem to have spread into it from the Tanais to the Danube, and to have then taken a *westerly* direction; but their kindred colonies in Thrace had also extended to the south. They have best been known to us in recent periods under the name of Getæ, or Goths, the most celebrated of their branches."

With regard to the SAXONS in particular, *Sharon Turner* observes (vol. i., p. 100)—"They were a German or Teutonic, that is, a Gothic or Scythian tribe; and of the various Scythian nations which have been recorded, the

Sakai, or Sacæ, are the people from whom the descent of the Saxons may be inferred with the least violation of probability. They were so celebrated, that the Persians called all the Scythians by the name of Sakai. They seized Bactriana, and the most fertile part of Armenia, which from them derived the name of Sakasina. They defeated Cyrus, and they reached the Cappadoces on the Euxine. That some of the divisions of this people were really called Sakasuna (from which we have our word Saxon, or Sacson) is obvious from *Pliny* (bk. vi., c. 19); for he says that the Sakai who settled in Armenia were named Sacassani, which is but Saka-suna spelt by a person who was unacquainted with the meaning of the combined words; and the name Sacasena, which they gave to the part of Armenia they occupied, is nearly the same sound as Saxonia. It is also important to remark, that *Ptolemy* mentions a Scythian people sprung from the Sakai, by the name of Saxones."[1]

Many opinions have been given as to the origin of this name Saxon. We may mention one, which has not the less

---

[1] Dr Moore, in his "Lost Tribes," p. 172, says—"The Chinese Buddhists say (Fo-kwe-ki, cxvii. note 17) the name Saki signifies 'repose or silence.' As Hebrew, it will admit of that meaning, but only in the sense of ceasing to resist, as in Num. xvii. 5. It is especially interesting to discover that the invocation of *Sak* was known in Britain at a very early period; for this fact connects the first arrival of the Saki or Saxons in Britain with Buddhism as known by the Saki of India, thus proving the similarity of their origin. My authority for this statement is found in that singular and very ancient Druidical hymn known as Gwawd Lludd y Mawr, or 'The Praise of Lludd the Great.' It is quoted from 'Welsh Archæology' (p. 74), by Rev. E. Davies, in his work on 'The Mythology of the British Druids' (App. 12). Four short lines are given in this poem as the prayer of 500 men who came in five ships. The words of this prayer were suspected by Mr D. to be Hebrew, in consequence of Taliesin, the Bard (A.D. 600), having declared that his lore had been delivered to him

probability of truth from the fact that every former one has proved unsatisfactory. As we have already seen, it may have been derived from "Isaac," by which this house of Israel had begun to denominate itself just before the captivity (Amos vii. 16). It was usual to contract the

in Hebrew or Hebraic. Mr D. therefore transcribed the passage in Hebrew letters,—

וברִיתִי בְּרִית עִי   And I have covenanted a covenant, a heap (Job xxx. 24,
נוּ עֵץ נוּ הֲדִי   A home of wood is a home : my guide (witness)
בְּרִיתִי בְּרִית אֲנִי   I have covenanted a covenant, O ship,—
שַׂךְ הֲדִי הֲדִי רֵעִי   *Sak* is my guide, he is my Friend (or Shepherd).

"Query, is this last word not the French word 'Roi?'

"In the time of Cæsar's invasion (B.C. 56) we find a people bearing a name precisely similar to that adopted by the Buddhists in the most ancient period of record—the *Cassi* or *Kashi* (or *Sak* reversed); and from Druidical record we know that a people using Hebraic language did visit Britain when Druidism was the dominant religion, proving their connection with the Sacæ and the Buddhists of the East, alike by their language and their religion. That the *Cassi*, who inhabited the *Cassiterides*, mentioned by Cæsar (Comm. bk. v. c. 20) were not natives of Britain, but warlike and powerful invaders, is indicated by him. They were also called *India-bŏnĕ* in the middle ages. *Endia* is evidently *India*, and *bŏnĕ* a Hebrew word for *sons*—the earliest German denomination of the people ultimately known only by their generic title of SAXONS, who always boasted of their *As-Khan* or Asian prince. An old Vatican MS. states that they came from *Esco* or *Visico* (Isaac), *Armenius* (Armenia), and *Ingo* or *India*." *Ibid.* p. 354.

A correspondent writes—"After reading Wilson's 'Israelitish Origin of the Saxons,' who are supposed to be derived from the Sacæ, I thought I would refer to *Pliny* to see what he says respecting them, where I found the following remarkable passage (bk. vi. c. 17)—'*Ultra sunt Scytharum populi. Persæ illos Sacas in universum appallavere a proxime gente ; antiqui Aramœos. Celeberrimi eorum Sacæ,*' &c ('Beyond are the people of Scythia. The Persians called them all together Sakai, from a neighbouring nation; the ancients more frequently called them Aramei, the most celebrated of them Sakai.') I must observe that אֲרָם, *Aram*, is the Hebrew name for Syria. Some parts are called *Aramnaharaim*, or '*Aram of the rivers*,' answering to the Greek name Mesopotamia, because situated between the two rivers the Tigris and the Euphrates. All Syria on this side of the Euphrates is proved by Dr Keith to be a part of the grant made to Abraham,

commencement of the name, especially when combined with any other word, or when applied in a familiar manner. Saxon is literally, or when fully expressed, *the son of Isaac.* But our argument stands not in *need* of etymology.

although it was seldom possessed by Israel. David, however, 'went to recover his border at the river Euphrates' (2 Sam. viii. 3) ; and 'Solomon went to Hamath Zobah, and prevailed against it' (2 Chron. viii. 3). But in general the territory which Israel possessed extended no farther northward than Dan, which was 139 miles from Beersheba, less than half the distance.

"The Land of Israel might be considered as Syria by foreigners; and Syria proper, having Jews mixed with them, as 'Galilee of the nations,' might cause that when the Ten Tribes were carried away captive they were called indiscriminately 'Syrians.' The people of Syria were to go into captivity unto Kir (Amos i. 5) ; and to this day there is a river called *Kur*, a country called *Kurdistan*, and a people called *Kurds*.

"The following considerations might justify any one in calling Israel 'Syrians.'—1. Isaac married 'Rebekah, the daughter of Bethuel the Syrian (Gen. xxv. 20) of Padan-Aram (Syria), sister to Laban the Syrian,' whose daughters Jacob also married, and most of his children were born there ; so that by foreigners who had not a distinct acquaintance with them, Israel might well be considered as Syrians or Aramites. 2. Every Israelite was commanded to say when he brought his firstfruits (Deut. xxvi. 5), 'A Syrian (Arami) ready to perish was my father,' referring to Jacob, who resided there for twenty years. By *Diodorus Siculus* Hebrews are called 'Syrians ;' and *Pliny* says that the Scythæ were called Sakai by the Persians, but originally 'Aramei ;' showing that they must have been a people transplanted from Syria. It is generally allowed that the Saxons were Sacæ who are often mentioned by *Xenophon* in his history of Cyrus, coupled with the Cadusii, which word is easily derived from קדוש, *Kadosh* or *Cadūs*—i.e., 'Holy'—so nicknamed perhaps by their enemies, as God's people in after-ages have been called 'Puritans' in England. *Homer* calls the Scythians δικαιοτατοι ανθρωπων, *the most just of men*, and well they might be, if descended from Israel ; 'for what nation is there so great that hath statutes and judgments so righteous as all this law ?' &c."

The White Island, England, Sacam or Saxam, as pronounced by our Saxon ancestors (as well as certain adjacent parts of the continent such as Saxony), is stated in the Puránás (or very old writings) named "Varada and Matsya' to have been in possession of the Sacs, who conquered it, at a very early period.—"Asiatic Researches," xi. 54, 61.

The Saxons having reached the Cimbric Chersonesus, now called Jutland, and having spread out to the three smaller islands, North Straudt, Busen, and Heligoland, betook themselves much to a seafaring life, and gave considerable trouble to the Romans by their skilful and courageous attacks upon the western provinces of the empire. They early made descents on Britain; so that even while the Romans held possession of this island, an officer had to be appointed to guard the eastern coast from their attacks, which began now to get the name of "the Saxon shore." When what were called "the Barbarians"[1] began in earnest to avenge themselves on Rome and the Romans, these were obliged to withdraw their forces from the more remote provinces of the empire, in order to defend those nearer to the centre and more valuable, and left the so-called Britons to manage matters for themselves, who, through disuse, it is said, had become incapacitated for either counsel or war. When left by the Romans, who had previously kept everything, as it were, in their own hands, they felt themselves quite unable single-handed to meet the dangers that surrounded them.

The whole east coast of Scotland north of Edinburgh, now inhabited by a people speaking that dialect of the Gothic which has been called "Lowland Scotch," and is akin to the English, was anciently possessed by a people called Picts, or Pechts, who are supposed to have come over from Vitland, now Jutland, about two or three hundred years before the Christian era. They had previously come out of modern Prussia, whence, under the name of "Peukini," &c., they extended back eastward to the bor-

---

[1] See Kingsley's "Roman and the Teuton," and Gibbon's "Decline and Fall."

ders of the Black Sea. By much the same route as *Pinkerton* thus traces the passage of the Picts into North Britain, does *Sharon Turner* trace the after-passage of the Saxons into the southern portion of the island. Uniting with the Scots, or Scyths, another branch of the same people, who as coming from Ireland had settled on the west coast, they came pouring in upon the enervated Britons from the north, while the SAXONS renewed their descent upon the eastern coast. The idea seems to have struck "the Britons" of playing off these enemies one against the other, in which they were so far successful.

The SAXONS came into the pay of "the Britons." Some say it was at the earnest request of the Britons that the Saxons now visited South Britain, to defend it against their brethren of the PICTISH line. However this may be, certain it is that they came, and fought successfully for the Britons. They were given the Isle of Thanet, and afterwards obtained the county of Kent. Onward they proceeded, until the greater part of the island came into their possession. By one means and another the original inhabitants were subdued, so that Saxon laws, religion, and language gained the ascendancy.

These people came over in companies, at different times, and planted a number of independent states, generally called the Heptarchy, which gradually merged into one kingdom. Meanwhile they adopted the profession of Christianity, but were fast degenerating into monkish sloth and superstition, when they were fearfully aroused by the rude incursions of the DANES (Lect. IX.), who bore sway for some time in the island, and at length became one nation with them, apparently throwing them back into partial barbarism, but really invigorating the English stock, and therefore fitting this people the more for future greatness.

After a time came the NORMANS, and produced another revolution in England, and another renewal of the northern blood, they being a colony of the same people who had settled in that part of France which after them was called NORMANDY. These three great immigrations into England having been all obviously from the same great source, we might take either the ANGLO-SAXONS, the DANES, or the NORMANS as the particular subject of our inquiry. But, independently of other considerations, the ANGLO-SAXONS seem now to claim our principal attention.

In considering the case of ancient Israel (Lect. IV.), our attention was early drawn to the personal beauty of the mothers of the race, and especially of JOSEPH, whose posterity we seek now to identify. Many of the modern Jews are very dark complexioned, chiefly, perhaps, as having become so intimately blended with the children of Ham; but much is said of the fairness of ancient Israel (Lam. iv. 7, 8).

Correspondent to this is the description of the Anglo-Saxons upon their coming into Britain. They are described as being "fair of complexion, cheerful of countenance, very comely of stature, and their limbs to their bodies well proportioned." Two most remarkable events in the history of this people are connected with their beauty: these are, their early settlement in the country, and their conversion to Christianity. As to the former, we read that the kinswoman of Hengist, one of their first leaders, so won the heart of the British monarch that he delivered himself over to her counsels, and so left the greatest and most valuable part of the island to be possessed by her countrymen, whilst he retired and began to build for himself in Wales.[1]

It may be gathered from Scripture, that among the Israelites considerable attention was paid to dressing the hair. Now fine and well-dressed hair is not readily found among a rude people, but rather indicates that the race possessing it has been very long under mental training. And among the ANGLO-SAXONS and DANES fine hair was considered one of the greatest ornaments, and they were at no little pains to set it off to the best advantage.

Another thing which struck me in this inquiry, and exceedingly puzzling before I knew how to solve the problem, was the great similarity of Jewish heads to those of the English. "If these be of two different sons of Noah," thought I, "the one of Japhet and the other of Shem, how is it that they are *both* reckoned to be of the most improved branch of the Caucasian family?" Those who have looked at and diligently compared the heads of the other different races, and seen them to be in general so strongly in contrast to the European head—which is far superior in beauty and power—will readily acknowledge

---

[1] There are examples at that period of English youths being preserved from execution because of their beauty, even after they had been sentenced to death. We are also told that when, after the settlement in Britain, some of their youths were exposed as slaves in the markets at Rome, they so attracted the attention of Gregory, afterwards Pope, that he stopped to ascertain what they were, and whence they had come; and upon being told they were Angles, he said they were rightly called angels. "It suits them well," said he, "they have angel faces, and ought to be co-heirs of the angels in heaven." So powerfully did the sight of these youths impress his imagination, that he ceased not until he procured a mission from Rome, consisting of Austin and other monks, for the conversion of their countrymen.

that this is no minor matter. The educated Jewish and English heads are of the same general form; and what is far from being the case among the several branches of the Caucasian family, they are the very largest possessing any pretension to beauty. The heads are high, and have an ample anterior development. Being by no means deficient in the domestic propensities behind, they are elongated rather than round, and the sides are perpendicular rather than sloping.

The size and form of the heads serve to identify a race much more accurately than complexion. Correspondent as it is to the difference of character pointed out in Scripture between the two families of Israel, even the difference that does exist between the form of the English and that of the Jewish head serves to corroborate our view. (Lect. IX.)

One of the principal things in which Israel were educated, strict attention to which was interwoven with all their private and national concerns, and ought therefore to be expected to distinguish the race, was *a regard to justice and truth*, as averred in the presence of the heart-searching God. Their laws were not merely put upon public record, but were also made familiar to the understandings of the people from infancy (Lects. IV. V.)

And such was the case as to the ancestors of the English, of whom it is written, that "their laws were severe, and vices not laughed at; and good customs were of greater authority with them than elsewhere were good laws; no temporising for favour, nor usury for gain." It need not be remarked, with regard to their descendants, that their probity is depended upon all over the world. It may not, of course, have in every instance been so complete as is desirable; but still it is distinguished, and has greatly conduced to procure them influence, both individually and nationally. True, the Jews are represented as not being always so strict in their observance of truth as might be expected from the training they enjoyed. Supposing the accusation to be correct, something must be allowed for the deteriorating circumstances in which, as an oppressed people, they have long been placed; whilst their brethren of the house of Israel have been rather enjoying a kind of supremacy over others. But even at an early period the two houses were distinguished by different names, correspondent to this difference of character, the one being called *treacherous* Judah, and the other *backsliding* Israel (Jer. iii. 11).

A wayward, independent spirit, a stiff-neckedness of disposition, an abuse of the tendency to exercise rule, is very much complained of in Scripture as belonging to Israel; and the same self-esteem and firmness are no less remarkable among many of their English descendants. Their independent spirit in respect to government has been such as to procure them, more than a century ago, the following character from Defoe:—

> "No Government could ever please them long,
> Could tie their hands, or rectify their tongue;
> In this to ancient Israel well compared,
> Eternal murmurs are among them heard."

This murmuring, however, seems to have arisen in a great measure, not merely from their self-will, but also from that *Prospectiveness* so long cultivated in ancient Israel; not only by the prophets, but also by the whole tendency of their institutions. These looked forward at least as much as backward; not merely serving as a chronicle or record of the Lord's past kindness to them, but also as indications of the far greater goodness He would yet bestow. Accustomed to occupy their minds upon future national events, and to form an opinion of what ought to be, they have been more ready to find fault with the measures of Government, which, of course, have not always corresponded with their individual anticipations. They may have been the more induced to take habitually an interest in national concerns from the fact of its having been continually impressed upon them that they were dealt with by Providence not merely as individuals, but as a nation; that the people were as responsible for the conduct of the rulers as the rulers were for that of the people. Their interests were one, and the oversight was therefore mutual.

ISRAEL, we have said, were ever taught to *look forward*. They were ever in a course of instruction; and a spirit of change was produced in them which has continued down throughout all their wanderings to these their remote posterity, in whom a restless spirit of improvement is most remarkable, and of itself distinguishes their Anglo-Saxon descendants, and their European brethren and American children generally, from all other people. The history of their constitution, religion, sciences, arts, literature, and of all connected with them, almost without exception, is an exemplification of this most important law of their nature. Everything is progressive, and at the same time wonderfully continuous; all which is most consistent with both their origin and the training they received in their fathers, as well as with God's expressed design of making them the instructors of the world.

Benevolence—a hearty interest in the welfare of strangers as well as of kindred—was especially needful for them, as occupying this important relation to the other branches of the human family. They were educated to consider each other, and to contribute systematically to the relief of the poor. When they looked up to the Most High, they were taught to look compassionately upon the meanest around them, and to express their thankfulness to God the Giver of all Good by liberality to the poor and needy. They were trained to see the claims their kindred had upon them, and they were also made to know the heart of a stranger" (Exod. xxiii. 9).

And so, with regard to the ANGLO-SAXONS, it is said that they even received all comers into their houses, and entertained them in the best manner their circumstances would allow. This hospitality was doubtless abused when they became intermingled with strangers, and restrictions were necessarily adopted. Although not so extravagant, the modern English are still remarkable for their good-will. They are perhaps the most genuinely benevolent people on the face of the globe. Their own poor they support systematically, and the poor of other countries they have frequently assisted in the most liberal manner. Not seldom have they a good deal embroiled themselves in the quarrels of their neighbours, as taking a hearty interest in their welfare, and as being desirous of putting them to rights. Their benevolence has latterly been most delightfully exercised in earnest endeavours to benefit the whole human race with the riches of Divine Truth, which have been entrusted to their distribution. They have at the same time been endeavouring to break every bond, as in the case of the previously-enslaved negroes; and they have done much to confer upon the nations the blessings of an enlightened education, and a free constitution. We do not speak thus of every individual of the English nation; but benevolence—a generous interest in the welfare of others—is undoubtedly a national characteristic, no less than the tendencies that dispose, and in some measure qualify, for the exercise of rule.

This race has manifested that cultivation of the *Reasoning Powers* so carefully bestowed upon Israel, that tendency to look to causes and effects, necessary for the investigation of the natural laws in the furtherance of science, and in the application of knowledge thus acquired to the production of useful inventions, the improvement of the arts, for lessening the evils, increasing the comforts, or gratifying the intellectual tastes of man. In no other branch of the human family may we find the pleasing and useful so agreeably combined. They are well qualified to be the grand producers of good to man, as well as its most liberal distributors.

It need scarcely be observed that the other intellectual faculties more particularly cultivated in Israel—such as the power of measuring distances or estimating proportions, of drawing analogies and contrasts, of readily judging and clearly illustrating, necessary to a people who were to bear an important relation to universal man as instructors and administrators of the manifold wisdom of God,—were and still are the characteristics of the Anglo-Saxon race, equally with those we have already indicated. And their natural taste for symmetry, extreme regard for order, and capacity for enjoying "the double" (Job xi. 6; Isa. lxi. 7; Zech. ix. 12), will yet receive abundant gratification from that Word of God, the "Bread of Life," which they have now in truth begun to deal out to the nations.

It is when she thus acts in her true character, that her true name will be given to Israel; for thus of old it was said unto her, just as the darkness was beginning to thicken around her, prospectively to her being given her present most important position amongst the nations (Isa. lviii)—

¶ "Is not this the fast that I have chosen,
  To loose the bands of wickedness;
  To undo the heavy burdens,
  And to let the oppressed go free,
  And that ye break every yoke?

§ "Is it not to deal thy bread to the hungry,
  And that thou bring the poor that are cast out to thy house:
  When thou seest the naked that thou cover him,
  And that thou hide not thyself from thine own flesh?

∥ "Then shall thy light break forth as the morning,
  And thine health shall spring forth speedily;
  And thy righteousness shall go before thee,
  And the glory of the Lord shall be thy rereward:
  Then shalt thou call, and the Lord shall answer;
  Thou shalt cry, and he shall say here—I."

¶ "If thou take away from the midst of thee the yoke,
  The putting forth of the finger, and speaking vanity.

§ "And thou draw out thy soul to the hungry,
  And satisfy the afflicted soul.

∥ "Then shall thy light rise in obscurity;
  And thy darkness shall be as the noonday.
  And the Lord shall guide thee continually,
  And satisfy thy soul in drought,
  And make fat thy bones;
  And thou shalt be like a watered garden;
  And like a spring of water whose waters fail not.
  And—of thee shall build the old waste places;
  Thou shalt raise up the foundations of many generations;
  And thou shalt be called the Repairer of the breach—
  The Restorer of paths to dwell in."

And as charity is to accompany piety, so a religious regard to the Day and the Word of God is to accompany the exercise of benevolence. The thoughts which the LORD hath spoken are not to be treated as if they were *mere* words. Let us earnestly seek to enjoy them for ourselves, and to deal them out to others in all their richness of meaning. "The liberal soul shall be made fat; and he that watereth others shall be watered also himself."

XVII.

SOCIAL AND POLITICAL RELATIONS OF THE ANGLO-SAXONS.

Ferocity of the ancient Saxons and Danes accounted for—Analogous Case of the Cossacks, inhabiting the same Country from which the Saxons came, and apparently of the same Race—Saxons' Respect for Woman—Their Marriage Ceremonies derived from Israel—Relation of Parent and Child—Avenging of Blood—Voluntary Associations—Institution, by Moses, of Elective Government—Correspondent arrangement among the Anglo-Saxons—Israelitish Character of their Constitution, by two old Authors—Common Law—National Chronicles—Conclusion :—Their Social Institutions, equally with their Personal Character, witness to the truth of their Israelitish Origin.

To the representations made in our last lecture respecting the natural benevolence of the ANGLO-SAXON race, it may, perhaps, be objected that considerable ferocity of disposition was manifested in their early history. But this can be accounted for otherwise than by supposing them to possess a predominant propensity to cruelty. Previous to coming into Britain their very best feelings were turned to evil. They were taught to believe that their admission into the Hall of Odin, Woden, Bodhen, or Godama, the father of slaughter and god of fire and desolation, depended upon the violence of their own death, and the number of enemies they had slain in battle. This belief inspired them with a contempt of life, fondness for a violent death, and a thirst for blood, which happily are now unknown.

Thus that association of the warlike propensities with the religious sentiments still existed, but in a depraved state, correspondent with the change in their object of worship, which had been produced in their national youth, when, under the guidance of the Lord of Hosts, they went forth to execute the sentence of extermination upon the wicked nations of Canaan, and which was also afterwards manifested in the wars of David. In many instances even their sense of justice had much to do with their deeds of violence. They had been robbed of their lands by the Romans, and obliged to take refuge in the inhospitable north, where they were crowded together without the possibility of maintaining their existence, except as turning back upon the Roman provinces and serving themselves therefrom as they best could. The pusillanimous people who supported the proud oppressor might expect to suffer as well as himself; and the habit of committing violence having been acquired, it was easily transferred to other objects in regard to which there was not the same excuse.

That their *courage* was more of principle than of mere animal ferocity, is evident from the fact of their so soon after their conversion to Christianity settling down into a state of peace. With an enthusiasm equal to that with which they had devoted themselves to war, they then poured the energies of their minds into the more tranquil exercises of religion, and attempted conquests of another kind, many of them becoming most active and efficient missionaries among other nations, especially in the north of Europe. It was at the instigation also of Alcuin— an Anglo-Saxon—that Charlemagne established so many facilities for learning and science on the Continent, and especially in Germany, which have produced such a powerful influence upon the human mind ever since.

The condition of the ANGLO-SAXONS at this period of their history may be illustrated by that of the Cossacks, who inhabit the same country as we suppose Israel to have dwelt in during the earlier part of their sojourn in the north country, and from which the Saxons came; that is, near the mouth of the Don, and along the back of the Black Sea. These people have had the credit of being wild and savage. They certainly are dangerous enemies, and do not brook oppression. So much is this their character, that even under the despotism of Russia they long formed among themselves a kind of republic, and had much the same free and liberal institutions as the English. These seem to be natural to the Saxon race generally; and we shall see that the most important of them they possess in common with ancient Israel.

"Nothing has contributed more to augment the colony of Don-Cossacks than the freedom they enjoy. Surrounded by systems of slavery, they offer the singular spectacle of an increasing republic; like a nucleus, putting forth its roots and ramifications to all parts of an immense despotic empire, which considers it a wise policy to promote their increase, and to guarantee their privileges."

"Some of the public edifices in Tscherchaskoy (their capital) are as follow:—

"The Chancery, in which the administration of justice, and all other public business, is carried on. One room in it is appropriated to their assembly for public debates, which much resembles our House of Commons. When a general assembly is convened, it consists of a president, with all the generals, colonels, and staff-officers, who hold councils, not merely of war, but of all affairs relating to the public welfare.

"Another court of justice, called Selvesnesut, which signifies justice by word. The assemblies here answer to our quarter-sessions. Parties who have any disagreement meet, with their witnesses, and state their grievances. Each receives a hearing, and afterwards justice is decided.

"The Public Academy, in which their youth receive instruction in geometry, mechanics, physic, geography, history, arithmetic, &c.

"The Apothecaries' Hall.

"The Town Hall, of the eleven stanitzas into which the town is divided."—*Clarke's Travels.*

In personal appearance, and even in customs of a very minute kind, as well as with regard to the general framework of their society, there is also a striking resemblance; and possibly there is some connection in even the name, the latter part of the name Cos-sack being the same with the first part of the name Sac-son. It is the same name, the former having a prefix, the latter an affix. Possibly from *Goi*, "a people," or "nation," *Izak;* thus, *Goi-zak*, dropping the initial letter, according to the oriental idiom.

These people are supposed to have come from the West, whence some parties, as from Poland, have joined them. But that intelligent traveller, Dr Clarke, is clearly of opinion that their own account of themselves, and that of ancient history, are correct, which both give them rather an Eastern origin.

They are a remnant of the Saxon or Gothic race, left in that neighbourhood when the great body of the people were driven westward, and appear to be busy leavening the surrounding apparently heterogeneous masses, such as the beautiful Circassians on the one hand (who call themselves Cossacks), and the horrible Calmucks on the other, together with Tartars, Poles, Greeks, Armenians, Russians, and Turks. From the whole an improved people is being produced, speaking indeed the Russian language, but having the mind and manners of the Cossack.

Now, what *is* the Don-Cossack, who at a distance has appeared to us only as a wild freebooter, and who certainly has not been placed in circumstances the most favourable to morality?

"The Cossacks are justified in acting towards the Russians as they have uniformly done, that is, in withdrawing as much as possible from all communion with a race of men whose associations might corrupt, but never advance their society." Dr Clarke observes—"The people of the house in which we had been so comfortably lodged positively refused to accept payment for all the trouble we had given them. No entreaty could prevail upon any of them to allow us further satisfaction by any remuneration. 'Cossacks,' said they, 'do not sell their hospitality.'"

In describing an entertainment given to him by the Commander-in-Chief of the Cossack army, he says—

"The morning after our return to Oxai we received a message from General Vassili Petrovich Orlof, Commander-in-Chief of the Cossack army, stating that he expected us to dine with him at his country seat upon the Don. We set out, accompanied by our friend Colonel Papof, and a Greek officer in the Cossack service, whose name was Mamonof. The general had sent his carriage, with six fine Cossack horses, and several Cossacks mounted, with lances, to escort us. We passed along the steppes, and occasionally through vineyards, planted with cucumbers, cabbages, Indian wheat, apple, pear, peach, and plum trees, and melons, for about ten miles, till we arrived at his house, which stood upon the European side of the river, opposite the town of Tscherchaskoy, and distant from it about five miles. Here we found elegant and accomplished women assembled round a pianoforte, and afterwards sat down to as magnificent a dinner as any English gentleman might afford, the whole of which was served upon plate. The company consisted of about twenty persons. The general presented us with mead thirty years old, which tasted like fine Madeira. He wished very much for English beer, having often drunk it in Poland. A number of very expensive wines were brought round, many of them foreign; but the wine of the Don seemed superior to any of them. As we sat banqueting in this sumptuous manner, I called to mind the erroneous notions we had once entertained of the inhabitants of this country, and which the Russians still continue to propagate concerning the Cossack territory. Perhaps few in England, casting their eyes upon a map of this remote corner of Europe, have pictured in their imagination a wealthy and polished people, enjoying not only the refinements, but even the luxuries of the most civilised nations. The conversation had that enlightened and agreeable cast which characterises well-educated military men. Some peculiarities, which distinguished the manners of our ancestors, and are still retained in the ceremonial feasts of ancient corporate bodies, might be observed. The practice of drinking toasts, and rising to pledge the security of the cupbearer, was a remarkable instance. Another very ancient custom, still more prevalent, is that of bowing and congratulating any one who happens to sneeze. The Cossacks of the Don always did this. When we took leave of the general, he said if we preferred returning by water, for the sake of variety, we might use his barge, which was prepared, and waiting to convey us. Being conducted to it, we found it manned by ten rowers, and decorated in a most costly manner. It was covered with fine scarlet cloth, and Persian carpets were spread beneath a canopy of silk."

The character of a people may be very much ascertained by their manner of treating women. The estimation in which they were held by ancient Israel appears to have been remarkable. We find them eminently influential for both good and evil; as in the cases of Deborah among the Judges, and of Jezebel among the queens, after the separation of the nation into the two kingdoms of Israel and Judah; among whom were prophetesses and witches, as well as true and false prophets. Sometimes their counsels prevailed in the most important public affairs, and under their guidance the arms of the nation were occasionally wielded with the greatest success. Not until after the separation of the two kingdoms do the men and women seem to have been separated in public worship, by the latter being given an outer court in the Temple. Even so early as at the passage of the Red Sea, we find Miriam, the sister of Moses and Aaron, taking a timbrel, and leading forth the women with timbrels and dances in the public rejoicing, saying—

> "Sing ye to the Lord,
> For He hath triumphed gloriously;
> The horse and his rider hath He thrown into the sea."

And we afterwards find them, equally with Aaron, rivalling even Moses himself, and saying, "Hath the Lord only spoken by Moses? Hath He not also spoken by us?" The very possibility of such an occurrence argues a state of equality between the sexes much greater than exists in those countries. It may be said that among ourselves the emancipation of woman has been produced by Christianity, the elevating tendency of which we of course do not wish to question ; but we must allow that the Anglo-Saxons were not thus dependent. It is evident " the English in this period treated the fair sex with a degree of attention and respect which could hardly have been expected from a people so unpolished in their manners. This way of thinking they undoubtedly derived from their ancestors, the ancient Germans, who not only admired and loved their women, on account of their personal charms, but entertained a kind of religious veneration for them, as the peculiar favourites of Heaven, and consulted them as oracles. Agreeable to this, we find some of the Anglo-Saxon ladies were admitted into their most august assemblies, and great attention paid to their opinions ; and so considerable was their influence in the most important affairs, that they were the chief instruments of introducing Christianity into almost all the kingdoms of the Heptarchy."—*Henry's Great Britain*, bk. ii. chap. 7.

To the same purpose speaks Sharon Turner—" It is well known that the female sex was much more highly valued, and more respectfully treated, by the barbarous Gothic nations than by the more polished states of the East. Among the Anglo-Saxons they occupy the same important and independent rank in society which they now enjoy. They were allowed to possess, to inherit, and to transmit landed property ; they shared in all the social festivities ; they were present at the witenagemot, and shire gemot ; they were permitted to sue and be sued in the courts of justice ; their persons, their safety, their liberty, and their property were protected by express laws ; and they possessed all that sweet influence which, while the human heart is responsive to the touch of love, they will ever retain in those countries which have the wisdom and the urbanity to treat them as equal, intelligent, and independent beings."

And the Anglo-Saxons, having the wisdom and urbanity thus to treat the fair sex, ought not surely to be accounted less polished than the most civilised nations of the East from among whom they had come; but from none of whom, save their Israelitish ancestors, they could have learnt that truly just and generous propriety with which woman was treated among them throughout their various changes.

Notwithstanding this comparative equality of the fair sex (and in some respects superiority) among the ancestors of the English, every woman was placed under the care of some guardian or other, without whose consent she could not execute any legal deed. Thus the father was the guardian of his daughter; the husband of his wife; and the male heir of the husband was the guardian of his widow. The king was the legal guardian of those women who had no other.

When a young man made his addresses to a lady, one of the first steps he took was to secure the consent of her *mundbora* or guardian, by making some present suitable to his rank and that of the lady. In this way Laban profited by the disposal of his sister Rebekah to Isaac, and of his daughters Leah and Rachel to Jacob.

No marriage could be lawfully celebrated without the presence of the woman's guardian, who solemnised it by delivering the bride to the bridegroom, and who thus obtained the legal guardianship of the lady. From this we still retain the custom of giving away the bride at marriage. That of the bridegroom giving at the same time a ring to the bride seems also to have had an Eastern origin. It was a token of his endowing her with his property, and making her mistress of his house. In ancient times a seal was on the ring, by affixing which authority was given to a deed. Thus we read that when a king delegated his authority to a subject, he did so by "giving the king's seal;" which was done by putting his ring with such seal upon the finger of that person. And the bridegroom, by giving the ring at the same time, recognised his natural right to exercise authority, while investing the bride with the same under or along with himself. The large square piece of cloth, supported by a tall man at each corner over the bride and bridegroom in the after-part of the ceremony, when receiving the nuptial benediction, had the same Eastern origin.

The other marriage ceremonies—such as the bridegroom's party going for the bride in martial array, under the conduct of the groomsman, to conduct her in safety to the house of her future husband; the bride's procession in return led by the brideswoman, and followed by a company of young maidens called the bridesmaids; her betrothal when carried thus to the house of the bridegroom; the united rejoicing procession thence to receive the priest's benediction; the gladsome return, and subsequent splendid marriage-supper, all forcibly remind us of similar ceremonies prevailing in Israel, and intimated throughout both the Old and New Testaments (indeed they are still observed among the inhabitants of the Lebanon). The feastings and rejoicings continued for several days after the marriage, and seldom ended until all the provisions were consumed. To indemnify the husband, in some degree, for all these expenses, the relations of both parties made him some present or other at their departure. And this also, we find, was the case among the Hebrews, as is intimated in that exquisite nuptial-song (Ps. xlv.); which is beautifully illustrated by the Saxon ceremonies to which we have alluded, as they are also by it.

"Chastity in their youth," we are told by *Henry*, "and conjugal fidelity after marriage, may justly be reckoned national virtues of the Anglo-Saxons. Their ancestors, the ancient Germans, were famous for both these virtues. The intercourse between the sexes did not commence till both arrived at full maturity. The laws of matrimony were observed with great strictness. Examples of adultery were extremely rare, and punished with much severity. The husband of an adulteress, in the presence of her relations, cut off her hair, stripped her almost naked, turned her out of his house, and whipped her from one end of the village to the other. When the matrimonial knot was once duly tied, nothing but the death of one of the parties, or the infidelity of the wife to the marriage-bed, could generally have power to dissolve it. There were, however, instances of voluntary separations, and even divorces." This exactly corresponds with what we know of ancient Israel, with regard to whom the utmost care was taken in these particulars. Neither people were so perfect as could be wished; but they were far in advance of most other nations.

As among the Hebrew women, so among the Saxons, it was accounted a disgrace and great misfortune to be without offspring; and as seems to have been the case with the former, so also with the latter, mothers generally nursed their own children. When, after the introduction of Christianity, some Saxon ladies refused that labour, they were reckoned guilty of an innovation. Paternal authority did not extend to the power of life and death, as among the Gauls; but parents had a right to correct their children with becoming severity, to regulate their conduct, to sell their daughters to husbands with their own consent, and even to sell both sons and daughters into slavery, to relieve themselves from extreme necessity—all which we expressly know to have been the case with ancient Israel.

We know that in Israel the ties of kindred were very fully acknowledged beyond the mere domestic relations; and one of the claims of kindredship was the avenging of blood. The friends of the slain had a recognised right to slay the shedder of blood. This also was the case with regard to the Saxons. The custom degenerated into family feuds and bickerings, and private wars, which disturbed the public tranquillity, and prevented the regular course of justice; so that many laws had to be made on the subject, one of which provides that the murderer alone shall be obnoxious to the resentment of the relations of him whom he had murdered, and not his whole family, as formerly. Like Israel, they had places of refuge where the avenger could not enter.[1]

Like the Israelites, the Saxons seem to have been not a giddy isolated number of individuals. They had a strong tendency seriously to apply themselves to the matter in hand, and closely to combine one with another for the furtherance of a common object; not as being entirely submissive to a dictator, but rather as each exercising an independent although harmonious will in the matter. This led them to form free societies of various kinds, such as those for business in cities and burghs, some of which have been the strongholds of national liberty at all times, and still exist. They seem to have recognised the principle, " In the multitude of counsellors there is safety,"

---

[1] The Britons also had a law which declared—"There are three things free to a country and its borders,—the rivers, the road, and the place of worship."

while they acted with concentration, and generally with efficiency. Even their private ends they pursued in public bodies; yet not so as to sacrifice their individual rights by either cowardly following each other or tamely submitting to a leader. *Robertson* observes—"It was a fundamental principle of the Feudal system of policy, that no Freeman could be subjected to new laws or taxes, unless by his own consent. In consequence of this, the Vassals of every Baron were called to his court, in which they established, by mutual consent, such regulations as they deemed most beneficial to their small society, and granted their superiors such supplies of money as were proportionate to their abilities, or to his wants. The Barons themselves, conformably to the same maxim, were admitted into the supreme assembly of the nation, and concurred with the sovereign in enacting laws, or in imposing taxes."

Among the Anglo-Saxons this system of self-government appears to have prevailed, as much as was compatible with the military attitude they were obliged to maintain. The theory of their constitution seems to have been, that every ten men or heads of families should choose one from among them, to act for them in the council of their little community, generally consisting of ten such compartments or wards. Ten of these wards formed a Tything or parish. And ten of these Tythings formed a Hundred, the elders of which thus chosen were supposed to meet for the management of matters belonging to the ten Tythings in general, whilst each Tything took charge of the affair, that especially belonged to itself.[1]

The *county*, being still more extensive, corresponded to the *tribe* in Israel. The word seems to be derived from the

---

[1] The Swedes also had anciently the division of Tythings and Hundreds, or rather of twelve tens = 120.

Hebrew word קוֹם *koom*, signifying to "rise up," to "stand;" and refers to the rod or ensign of the tribe to which they congregated themselves in the larger assemblies of the people. In the earlier part of their history the Cossacks were called Comani, most likely in regard to their Tribes or Standards; as also they were anciently called Khazares, on account of their skill in archery, for which also the English were remarkable. The word *Shire* appears to be from the Hebrew word שַׁעַר Sha-ar, *the great gate of a royal city or palace,* and is still used in the country south of the Caucasus, in which Israel were placed by the Assyrians. "A shire" is a district of country connected with a principal city.

We have seen (Lect. V.) that the people of Israel at an early period of their national history, were given proper rules for their association, such as were equally adapted for large and small societies. The people exercised a mutual oversight of each other in tens: each ten had one who represented and enacted for them. The institution is very distinctly expressed in Deut. i. 9–18, and appears clearly enough to account for the peculiar constitution of the ANGLO-SAXONS, about the origin of which philosophers have been so puzzled, and such absurd notions have been entertained.

Here the people are enjoined to look out from among themselves men qualified for official situations, who are to be brought to the chief governor ruling "by the grace of God," and he gives them their authority, and the rules according to which they are to act. The people are divided into Thousands, the Elders representing which came to be denominated "the Thousands of Israel" (Num. i. 16; x. 36; Deut. i. 15 and 1 Sam. x. 19), and this subdivision of the people, and into hundreds and tens, is correspondent to that which existed among the Saxons from the earliest period ; and although the substance of the thing has been greatly lost, the terms *Hundred* and *Tything* still exist with regard to civil divisions of the people in England.

" In the Saxon times all were decenners, that is, ranked into several tens, each one being pledged for others' good abearance ; and in case of default, to answer it before the judge, that is, of the Hundred ; and in case of default of appearance, his nine pledges should have one-and-thirty days to bring the delinquent forth to justice : if this failed, then the chief of those decenners was to purge himself and his fellow-pledges, both of the guilt of the fact, and also of being parties to the flight of the delinquent. If they could not do this, then were they by their own oaths to acquit themselves, and come under a bond to bring the delinquent to justice as soon as they could, and in the meantime to pay the damage out of the estate of the delinquent, and if that were not sufficient, then out of their own estate. The master of the family was a pledge, or one of the ten, for his whole family. It was a building of great strength downward, even to the foundation ; arched together both for peace and war. By the Law of Decenners, wherein justice was the band, their armies were gathered not by the promiscuous flocking of people, but by orderly concurrence of families, kindreds, and decenners, all choosing their own leaders ; and so honour, love, and trust conspired together, to leave no man's life in danger, nor death unrevenged.

" It was a beautiful composure, mutually dependent in every part, from the crown to the clown, the magistrates being all choice men, and the king the choicest of the chosen ; election being the birth of esteem, and that of merit ; this bred love and mutual trust, which made them as corner-stones pointed forward to break the wave of danger. Nor was other reward expected by the great men but honour and admiration, which commonly brought a return of acts of renown. Lastly, it was a regular frame, in every part squared and made even, by laws which, in the people, ruled as *lex loquens*, and in the magistrates as *lex intelligens*, all of them being founded on the wisdom of the Greeks, and judicials of Moses. Thus the Saxons became somewhat like the Jews, distinct from all other people: their laws, honourable for the king, easy for the subject; and their government, above all other, like unto Christ's kingdom, whose yoke is easy, and His burden light. But their motion was so irregular, as God was pleased to reduce them by another way."—*Historical and Political Discourse of the Laws and Government of England*, p. 70.

So striking is the resemblance between the ancient Saxon constitution and that of Israel, that, nearly 150 years ago, a book was produced with this title: "An Historical and Political Essay, discovering the Affinity or Resemblance of the Ancient and Modern Governments, both in our Neighbouring Nations, as also in the Jewish Commonwealth, in respect to our English Parliaments," and from which we extract these few following remarks:—

"Selden allots to the great assembly or Sanhedrim of the Jews both a judiciary and deliberative power; to the first he refers their judgment of all matters relating to the payment of the annual tithes or revenues, and concerning all manner of sacrifices; to the last, of all matters relating to peace or war, to the amplifying of the temple or city of Jerusalem, to the enacting of any new laws, or the erecting of any inferior Sanhedrims. All which are things frequently treated of in our parliaments, the supreme judiciary power of the kingdom in civil affairs being also lodged in the House of Lords.

"It is farther agreed, that it belongeth to this great Sanhedrim, or Jewish assembly, to give all the necessary instructions and injunctions how firstfruits should be faithfully paid, and both sorts of tithes. Which course of making laws concerning the payments which the people were to make, as is shown before, is the proper business only of the Parliament.

"For the freedom of their votes, the king was not admitted into the College of the Senate; because it is a crime to dissent from him, and to contradict his words. In our Parliaments, whensoever the king came into the House of Peers, where his place and chair of state was, the house did forbear to proceed in any debate whatsoever in his presence, but only heard what he was pleased to say unto them. The reason is before given by these Rabbins, which doth suit with the usage and custom of our Parliaments, as it was the course in their great Sanhedrim, which was a supreme Council among them."

The author thereafter proceeds to prove, from a vast number of instances recorded in Scripture, that the representative system prevailed in ancient Israel as in the Anglo-Saxon Constitution.

To those who attentively study the institutions of Moses, and compare therewith those of the Saxons, so striking a similarity will at once appear as would lead to the conclusion that the Saxon commonwealth was thus framed after the introduction of Christianity. But this was not the case, as they left similar institutions among the people in the north of Europe, with whom they have been from time immemorial, and, as we have seen, also among the Cossacks of the Don and Ural. Yet, even granting this, we find *Millar* making the following remarks:—

"According to the early policy of the ANGLO-SAXONS, each of their villages was divided into ten *wards*, or petty districts; and hence they are called *Tythings* or *Decennaries*, as their leader was denominated a *Decanus* or *Tything* man. This regulation appears to have extended *over all the kingdoms upon the neighbouring continent;* and, in all probability, it originated from the influence of ecclesiastical institutions.

"As upon the first establishment of Christianity under the Roman dominion the form of church government was in some respects modelled by the political constitution of the empire, so the civil government in the modern states of Europe was afterwards regulated in many particulars according to the system of ecclesiastical policy. When the western provinces of the Roman empire were conquered by the barbarous nations, and erected into separate kingdoms, the conquerors, who embraced the Christian religion, and felt the highest respect for its teachers, were disposed in many cases to improve their own political institutions by an imitation of that regularity and subordination which was observed in the order and discipline of the Church.

"In the distribution of persons or of things which fell under the regulation of the Christian clergy, it appears that, in conformity to the customs of the Jewish nation, a decimal arrangement was more frequently employed than any other. By the Mosaic institutions the people were placed under rulers of thousands, of hundreds, of fifties, and of tens. A Jewish synagogue, corresponding to a modern parish, appears at a subsequent period to have been put under the direction of *ten elders*, of whom one became the chief ruler of that ecclesiastical division. A tenth part of the annual produce was appropriated for the support of the Levites; as the same proportion of ecclesiastical livings was claimed by the high priest. Hence we find that, in *modern Europe,* the members of a cathedral church, as well as those of a monastery, were divided into ten branches, each of which was put under a director, and the tenth of these persons, or *Decanus,* was entrusted with a superintendence of all the rest. Hence, too, the *modern institution of tythes, and the pretensions of the Roman Pontiff, the Christian high priest, to the tenth of all the revenues of the clergy."—Historical View of the English Government.* See also p. 171.

This writer seems to have been prepared to look upon the Saxons as being in a state of barbarism, and as if they had been obliged for everything to the Romans, to whom they were superior in arms, and to whom their descendants are certainly not inferior in intellectual power or moral dignity. Such writers are greatly at a loss to account for these Mosaic institutions existing in so perfect a state among a people they reckon so rude. By this (one of the most skilful of these writers) the conjecture is here hazarded that, without any concert, and even as separated into their minuter divisions, all these northern nations fell into this arrangement and coalescence, as copying *after* the ecclesiastical institutions then planted among them. Rather awkwardly for this theory, it happens that these institutions were most distinctly possessed by the Danes and Danish colonies, which were among the latest to receive Christianity, and that they became fainter the farther they departed from their early manners.

Kingsley, on the contrary, shows that the Romish clergy, being more or less permanently antagonistic to the

Teutonic nations, have pursued an inverse policy in these respects.

The great Olaus, Archbishop of Upsal, in his "History of the Northern Nations," printed at Basle, in A.D. 1567, and dedicated to the Archduke Ferdinand, brother of Charles V., says, " In Aquilonaribus terris ab antiquissimus seculis inter laicos, et eorum sobolem fuisse usitatem, videlicet quod pueri puellæque somnum, seu lectum petituri, ordine ætatum recitata Dominica oratione, paternam benedictionem accipiebant: atque adhuc sanctissimum eum morem, vetusta devotione susceptæ fidei sic introductum, servant. Maxima etenim cura parentum est, à maligna societate restringere filios, ne irreparabiliter corrumpantur. Fideles etiam amici non minus id prestant, quam veri parentes, ut domi forisue in bonis moribus, ac scientiis instituantur. Qualis autem benedictio sit in forma, vel modo, simili, laici discunt à predicantibus Parochis, sive Plebanis, et Curatis suis, ex cap. Numeri vi., ubi dicitur, Sic benedicetis filiis Israël et dicetis eis, Benedicat tibi Dominus, et custodiat te. Ostendat Dominus faciem suam tibi, et misereatur tui. Convertat Dominus vultum suum ad te, et det tibi pacem. Invocabunt que nomen meum super filios Israel, et ego benedicam eis. Nec certe falluntur in hoc sanctissimo ritu, cum ita obedientes maneant parentibus suis, ut nec verbo, nec opere, aut signis contraire videantur paternis præceptis. Novi ego homines adhuc mea ætate per patrem proprium, ob insignem contumeliam, et rebellionem illatam, à paterna benedictione exclusos fuisse; et continuò omnem infelicitatem, inopiam, calamitatem, et infamiam sunt experti." [1]

[1] "In northern lands, from the most ancient times, among the laity, it was the custom with regard to their offspring, for boys and girls, before they went to sleep, or sought their beds, in the order of age to recite the

To say the least, it is not very likely that these nations required to build up society from the very base, when previously, by their combined energies and wise counsels, they had broken down the strength and policy of Rome. This they did, not as individuals, nor even as small parties, but as nations. Was it likely that these people, acting thus successfully in concert, would all at once, as if with common consent, and yet without any concert, throw away their old associations into utter forgetfulness to adopt what was entirely new, whilst they retained the names of the Supreme Being which they used previous to their knowledge of Christianity, and also those of the days of the week and religious festivals? Had the author of the "Historical View of the English Government" been acquainted with our view of the case, he would not have been so puzzled in accounting for the planting of the institutions of Moses in the north, nor have been under the necessity of supposing such a simultaneous growth of

Lord's Prayer, receiving the paternal benediction; and hitherto they have preserved this most holy custom, thus introduced by the ancient devotion of godfathers in the faith. The greatest care also is taken by the parent to preserve his sons from bad society, lest they should be irreparably corrupted. Faithful friends, also, are not less anxious than real parents that from home they should be instructed in knowledge and good manners. Likewise the laity learn to bless, alike in form and manner, from their parish preachers (both common people and their overseers), from Numbers vi., where it is said, 'Thus ye shall bless the sons of Israel, and shall say to them, The Lord bless thee and keep thee. The Lord manifest His face unto thee, and be merciful to thee. The Lord lift up His countenance upon thee, and give thee peace. And they shall put my name upon the sons of Israel and I will bless them.' Nor truly have they been disappointed in this most holy rite, seeing that they remain so obedient to their parents, that neither by word, nor deed, nor sign are they seen to go contrary to paternal precepts. Besides, I have known men of my own age, by their own father, to be excluded from the paternal blessing on account of remarkable impertinence and rebellion; and for that reason experience all unhappiness, need, calamity, and dishonour."

like political constitutions, the most perfect in theory among many independent, and as he supposed, "barbarous" nations—a thing of which we have no example in history.

The same writer, it may be observed, has been led to acknowledge what is inconsistent with his own view of the case, and indeed deprives it of its only seeming foundation, viz., that it was in *modern* Europe that the ecclesiastical constitution and arrangements were assimilated to the Hebrew; so that this ecclesiastical change (equally favourable to our view) requires to be accounted for as much as the other.

Even granting, however, that the Mosaic institutions did exist among these nations anterior to their embrace of Christianity, it may still be objected that they had been given them by some legislator who had somehow been made acquainted with the writings of Moses. Neither will this objection stand. What is imposed upon a people as foreign to their former habits, exists only, as it were, in law. It is long before it becomes familiar to the every-day habits of the people, and acquires a perpetuity independent of the statute-book, so as to endure throughout all migrations and changes whatsoever of the people. What is *naturally* everywhere part of a people's political existence, and distinguishes them continuously through all their known history from all other nations, may well be supposed to have been *taught them in their infancy*, and to have grown with their growth. It has been early put into their very nature. But except Israel, we know of no people to whom this was done.

The presumption is certainly altogether in our favour. We find the English with these institutions in their earliest political history, and it remains to be proved how otherwise they received them. The theories hitherto formed to account for them have no foundation in history, and are too fanciful to be admitted as philosophy.

Our argument for the priority of the Mosaic institutions among the English, independent of the ecclesiastical institutions, is still more apparent when we consider that in the people's courts they followed their own customs and laws, the body of which was called the COMMON LAW, and had been handed down from time immemorial; whereas in the ecclesiastical courts, which were now for the first time allowed to the Christian priesthood, after the Israelitish pattern (in which the Levites had much to do in the administration of justice), there was no such favour shown to the Common Law, but rather of course to their own Canon Law, and also to the Roman or Civil Law.

The Common Law was not merely given in writing, but was engraven in the habits of the people, as in the rock for ever, so as to subsist throughout all the migrations, revolutions, and religious changes of this people, and is a perpetual witness to their having been under strict moral training in the earliest period of their history, and accustomed to the careful and regular administration of justice.

Nor was the manner of preserving the national records so imperfect as *Millar* has rashly asserted. Before their conversion to Christianity, in different parts of the country their priests seem to have kept distinct records in each section, according to their several knowledge of what was passing of a public and interesting nature. At the death of the king these different accounts were brought together, and consolidated into one general history of the nation during the period. After their conversion to Christianity, this business fell into the hands of the monks of the Benedictine order, in whose monasteries the district records were kept; and afterwards the whole were reduced into one statement by a chapter of the order. So regularly was everything of importance noted in this way, that it is said no history of the same period is so complete as that of the Saxons from their arrival in Britain until the Norman invasion.

We have the origin of all this in the Books of the Kings of Israel and the Chronicles of the Kingdom of Judah, written after the same plan, according to the lives of the Kings, and taking a religious view of men and events, noting particularly the hand of Providence in national affairs.

As the learned *Mr Ingram* has observed—" The Saxon Chronicle may be philosophically considered the second great phenomenon in the history of mankind. For if we except the sacred annals of the Jews, contained in the books of the Old Testament, there is no other work extant, ancient or modern, which exhibits at one view a regular and chronological panorama of a people, described in rapid succession by different writers, through so many ages, in their own vernacular language."

"The Scythians," of whom were the Goths and Saxons, are as clearly distinguished (Col. iii. 11) from the "Barbarians," as are the "Jews" from the "Greeks;" yet, at the expense of many inconsistencies, historians have been in the habit of confounding them. We shall close this line of argument with a quotation from *Turner*, who, having very gratuitously assumed that the Saxons were Barbarians, proceeds to give a statement of the results of their settlement in Europe, such as fully justifies his suspicion, elsewhere expressed, that the Saxons were not so barbarous as has been supposed, but were rather descended from some of the more civilised portions of Asiatic population—

"Yet from such ancestors a nation has, in the course of twelve centuries, been formed, which, inferior to none in every moral and intellectual merit, is superior to every other in the love and possession of useful liberty: a nation which cultivates with equal success the elegancies of art, the ingenious labours of industry, the energies of war, the researches of science, and the richest productions of genius. This improved state has been slowly attained under the discipline of very diversified events.

"The barbaric establishments were a new order of things in Europe, but cannot have been so prolific of misery to mankind as we have hitherto too gratuitously assumed, when, notwithstanding the discouragement of new languages and institutions, and ruder habits, they were preferred by many of the Romans to the country which was their birthplace, which had been so long consecrated by deserved fame, and whose feelings, mind, and social manners were congenial to their own.

"The invasions of the German nations destroyed the ancient governments, and political and legal systems of the Roman Empire, in the provinces in which they established themselves, and dispossessed the former proprietors of their territorial property. A new set of landowners was diffused over every country, with new forms of government, new principles, and new laws, new religious disciplines and hierarchies, with many new tenets and practices. A new literature and manners, all productive of great improvements, in every part superseded the old, and gave to Europe a new face, and to every class of society a new life and spirit. In the Anglo-Saxon settlements in Britain all these effects were displayed with the most beneficial consequences.

"The destruction of the Roman Empire of the West by the German nations has been usually lamented as a barbarisation of the human mind—a period of misery, darkness, and ruin—as a replunging of society into the savage chaos from which it had so slowly escaped, and from which, through increased evils and obstacles, it had again to emerge. This view of the political and moral phenomena of this remarkable epoch is not correct. It suits neither the true incidents that preceded or accompanied, nor those which followed this mighty revolution. And our notions of the course of human affairs have been more confused and unscientific by this exaggerated declamation, and by the inaccurate perceptions which have accompanied it."

Limited Monarchy, Constitutional Law, and Representative Government, an efficient Civil Police, and Trial by Jury, are among the most important legacies left the English nation by their Anglo-Saxon forefathers, which may all be easily traced to an Israelitish origin. And to this source, as we have seen, they have been traced even by those who were obliged, in rather an unphilosophical way, to account for the connection. It is indeed rather remarkable that so many of these institutions should have been allowed to remain as incontestable evidence that this people had been Moses' disciples. Equally does their social condition witness to this, as in our last lecture we saw that their personal appearance and character give full and explicit evidence to their being the children of Abraham.

XVIII.

ANGLO-SAXON ARTS OF PEACE AND WAR.

Dress of the Anglo-Saxons—At home on the Deep—Form of Battle—Use of Ensigns—Were Freemen while they were Soldiers—Agriculture—Architecture—Gothic Arch—Proficiency in the Fine Arts—Laws regarding Property—Poetry—Music—Their ancient Ideas of the Supreme Being.—Reception of Odin as the Incarnation of Deity—Symmetrical Arrangements of their Objects of Worship, as written in the days of the Week—Their great Temples, and Worship in Groves—Israelitish Days, Weeks, Measures, and Festivals—Their three Grand Convocations—Priesthood—Tithes—Retention of Israelitish Forms when they professed Christianity Seven Times, Lev. xxvi.—Gradual and continual Development of God's Favour to His Church in England.

THE DRESS of the Anglo-Saxons also witnessed to their Israelitish origin. Their garments are said to have been loose and flowing, chiefly made of linen, and adorned with broad borders of various colours. God had commanded them to wear a "riband of *blue*" around their garments (Num. xv. 38), to remind them of their duty; but having nationally lost sight of the thing signified, they had perhaps departed from the strict observance of this rule. Variety and elegance of dress appear to have prevailed among their women, as among the mothers of ancient Israel. They had also the same sort of muffling, wearing upon the head a hood or veil, which was wrapped round the neck and breast. And, as identifying these Anglo-Saxons with the people who built the tombs near the

Black Sea, to which we referred in Lecture IX., in one of which a large golden bracelet was found, it may be noticed that among them the men of consequence or wealth usually had expensive bracelets on their arms, as well as rings on their fingers. In an Anglo-Saxon will, the testator bequeaths to his lord "a beah, or bracelet, of eighty golden mancusa."

The Saxons gave very clear indications of being destined to the EMPIRE OF THE SEAS, even before they possessed the land which is blessed "for the deep that coucheth beneath." Thus they are described by an author of the fifth century (Sidonius, lib. 8):—

"This enemy is fiercer than any other. If you be unguarded, they attack; if prepared, they elude you. They despise the opposing, and destroy the unwary; if they pursue, they overtake; if they fly, they escape. Shipwrecks discipline them, not deter; they do not merely know, they are familiar with all the dangers of the sea; in the midst of waves and threatening rocks they rejoice at their peril, because they hope to surprise."

As foretold of Joseph (Gen. xlix. 23, 24), these people were remarkable for the USE OF THE BOW, success in which required that accuracy of eye in estimating distance and proportion so carefully cultivated in the fathers (Lect. V.), and still more profitably made use of by their children.

It may also be worthy of remark, that in the FORMATION OF THEIR BATTLE LINES the ancestors of the English were generally in the habit of constructing them something like the Greek letter Δ, the point of which was very sharp towards the enemy, and the sides gradually diverging, so as to become broadest at the rear. Curiously enough, not only was this the figure of their portion of Britain, but it was also much the form of their settlement of the land of Canaan, as holding military possession from the time of Joshua to the breaking up of their kingdom. The tribes along the border of the Great Sea formed the base; whilst part of the tribeships of Simeon, Judah, and Reuben formed the right side; and Asher, Manasseh, and Gad, the left; the main angle pointing eastward.

When an army was composed of several distinct battalions, or the troops of several different countries, the Anglo-Saxons often formed as many of these hollow wedges as there were battalions; each of which being composed of the inhabitants of the same country, were expected to fight the more bravely for the honour of their country, and in defence of their relations and friends.

And this farther supports our idea (Lect. XVII.) that the counties were so named from each containing those who belonged to a distinct standard; for, as in Israel, the different tribes or battalions had their different standards, with suitable emblems.[1]

---

[1] It appears, by the researches of a late learned writer, that the devices borne on the twelve Hebrew standards (Num. ii.), were the twelve signs of the zodiac (Job xxxviii. 32). "Josephus informs us that the twelve tribes of Israel bore the twelve signs on their banners, and the Chaldee paraphrase of a still earlier date, asserting the same, adds that the figure of a man was borne on the standard of Reuben, a bull on that of Ephraim, a lion on that of Judah, an eagle on that of Dan. The Targums also attributed to Dan a crowned serpent or basilisk."—*Mazzaroth by F. Rolleston*, 1862, ii. 48.

"The four signs of the four leading camps were also portrayed in the cherubic faces (Ezek. i. 10, x. 14; Rev. iv. 7), which thus symbolised the regenerated Hebrew nation in millennial times. It is interesting to notice how these signs have been preserved among the Gothic nations of Europe, the descendants of the lost ten tribes. Thus we find the twins under a wolf (Benjamin), in Rome derived from Etruria; the wolf again being the peculiar emblem in Normandy; the lion (Judah) in Scotland and Ireland and England; the bull (Ephraim) in England; the goat Naphtali) in Wales, the raven (a probable corruption of eagle for Dan)

And as the Israelites were emboldened by the presence of the Ark of the Covenant, so did the Saxon armies carry before them the insignia of their gods. When converted to Christianity, such as it then was, the heathen symbols gave way to the relics of the saints, or some other representation of their new religion; as did also the blessing of their arms by the heathen high priest, to the benediction of the Christian bishop. They used their arms with skilfulness as well as force, were equally prudent in negotiation as valiant in fight, and seem to have been scarcely more zealous in overcoming their enemies, than anxious to secure themselves against the oppression of those who led them on to victory. They were individually to be respected, as well as collectively to be feared.[1]

Like ancient Israel, the Anglo-Saxons were A PASTORAL PEOPLE. They seem to have been also well acquainted with AGRICULTURE, or, at least, as easily fell into this way of life as if it had not been foreign to their former habits.

---

in Denmark. The centaur (Asher) was the royal emblem of King Stephen, while in our ancient private families, the signs of the zodiac and the tribes are of constant occurrence."

[1] A singular invention marked at once the rudeness and the tactics which regulated the free militia of Lombardy. This was the Carroccio or great standard-car of the state.

It was a *car upon four wheels*, painted *red*, and so heavy that it was drawn by four pair of *oxen* with splendid trappings of *scarlet*.

It was an imitation of the Jewish Ark of the Covenant, and it was from its platform that a chaplain administered the holy offices of Christianity. It thus became sacred in the eyes of the citizens, and to suffer it to fall into the hands of an enemy intailed intolerable disgrace."—*Percival, History of Italy.*

"This custom became general throughout Lombardy, each city having its Carroccio."—*Macfarlane.*

Compare the great standard on wheels, used in Edward's wars with Scotland.

The lands seem to have been at once divided among the great leaders, and subdivided among their followers, upon such terms as implied a knowledge of the value of land, and the power of making use of it. And soon each soldier became a husbandman, or was otherwise usefully employed in the civil affairs of life. In converting their corn into meal, at first, like ancient Israel, they used only hand-mills, which were also turned by women.

As to ARCHITECTURE, consistent with the idea of their being Israel in dispersion, they seem to have used only wooden tabernacles for their more ordinary religious assemblies. But we are expressly told that, even before coming into Britain, their national temples were of the most splendid description. They were of the most curious workmanship, and glittered with gold. Like their descendants in North America to this day, they seem, in the northern wilderness, to have got much into the habit of building with wood, previous to which they had acquired a great predilection for the arch, observable in their early tombs, as described by Dr Clarke. (See Lect. XIII.) They had attained to great perfection in wood-carving, as well as in gilding on wood and the inferior metals; but this indeed, as coming up out of Egypt, they had from their fathers, even from the time of the erection of the Tabernacle in the Wilderness.

The ENGLISH CATHEDRALS appear to have been built after the fashion of the temples they frequented previous to their conversion to Christianity, and are evidently, it has been observed, built after the design of the Temple at Jerusalem, having their most holy place, their holy place, and their court outward from thence for the body of the people. The more minute parts and ornaments will in general be found correspondent.

The working in lead and iron must have been well understood by the Anglo-Saxons. Almost all their churches were covered with the former, and they had abundance of warlike instruments provided from the latter. They were also well skilled in the use of precious metals, which they wrought up into coronets, chains, bracelets, half-circles for dressing their hair upon, collars, and similar articles of usefulness and ornament—into such articles as we know to have been in use among the Israelites. Even the art of polishing and setting precious stones was not unknown among them. Nay, the English goldsmiths were so famous for their art, that the curious caskets adorned with gold, silver, and precious stones, in which the relics of saints were kept, became generally known as *Opera Anglica*. They also possessed the art of making gold and silver thread for weaving and embroidery; and the Anglo-Saxon ladies became as famous for their needlework as the English goldsmiths were in their department.

As they knew the value of property, and had skill to acquire, valour to defend, and prudence to make use of it, so were they equally well provided with laws for the regulation of matters of this kind, and indeed of almost every other. In criminal cases there was much effort at making compensation for the injury committed, both to the injured party, and to the king, as representative of the law—much the same as we find was appointed in ancient Israel. The farther we go back in the history of the Anglo-Saxons, we find their laws approximate more and more nearly to those of Moses.

If these were the descendants of Israel, we might also

expect them to have indications of their having been a race whose POETICAL GENIUS was great, and whose taste in this respect was highly cultivated. And after the examples of David and Solomon, it might be well expected that the employment of their genius in Poetry for the delight and improvement of mankind, would not be thought beneath the most exalted in character and station. And accordingly we read, that never were Poetry and Poets more admired than among the Anglo-Saxons. The greatest princes were no less ambitious of the laurel than of the regal crown.[1]

[An old *British* MS. (Grammatical Rules of Welsh Poetry) says—" This is the way to know, and to understand the measures of song, some of which were improved from the Latin, through the learning of *Einion* the priest; and *Dr Dafydd Ddû* gave authority to the metres so formed by him, and by others before, who had begun to praise GOD from the time of ENOS, son of SETH, the son of Adam, the first man who praised God; and invented figure, which in Latin is called FIGURA. The time when this began was about 600 years after the time of *Adam;* and from that time to the birth of Christ the Prophets carried it on, improving it in prophesying of Jesus. We obtained it through the Holy Ghost in our language when we received the faith in Christ, and calling on the Holy Spirit, promoted the muse, which vanishes through the commission of sins, and flourishes through the guidance of sciences and holiness. From the Seven Canons or Pillars of Poesy were formed the twenty-four metres of vocal song used by the Bards of Britain."—*Jones' Relics of the Bards*, A.D. 1802.']

---

[1] "The ancient seat of the poets was Caer-Siion, a British fort on the top of a mountain, north of Conway town."

ALFRED THE GREAT was not only a poet, but also never neglected spending some part of every day in getting Saxon poems by heart, and in teaching them to others. He made himself intimately acquainted with the wisdom of his Saxon ancestors; and thus, doubtless, after the preceding troubles were so many reforms produced in his reign, for the initiation of which he has in several important cases obtained credit.

CANUTE THE GREAT was also a famous poet. The ancient bards of the Saxon and Danish races are said to have produced the most astonishing effects upon those who heard them. To have had such power nature must have been vastly improved by art. They are said to have had an almost endless variety of kinds and measures of verse, the harmony of which did not consist, as among the Greeks and Romans, in only the succession of long and short syllables, nor as among the moderns, but in a certain consonancy and repetition of the same letters, syllables, and sounds in different parts of the stanzas, which produced the most musical tones, and affected the hearers with the most marvellous delight.

Much the same seems to be the genius of Hebrew Poetry, upon which the rules of ancient Saxon Poetry may be expected to throw considerable light.

As to MUSIC, for which the Children of Zion were so distinguished, and for which the descendants of that people have been so remarkable all over the world, we have the following account of the Anglo-Saxons :—

"Music was as much admired and cultivated as Poetry. The halls of all the kings and nobles of Britain rang with the united melody of the poet's voice and musician's harp; while every mountain, hill, and dale was vocal."

As an example, Alfred the Great excelled as much in

music as in war, and ravished his enemies with his harp before he subdued them by his arms. Music appears to have constituted a principal part of their heathen worship, for which, like the Hebrews, they had an immensity of songs; and after their embrace of Christianity, their public, and even private worship, consisted mostly of psalmody. In some cathedrals and large monasteries, perhaps as rivalling what had taken place in their heathen temples, and derived from their still earlier and purer way of worship, this exercise of singing was continued both day and night, without intermission, by a constant succession of priests and singers, with whom the laity occasionally joined.[1] Besides the harp, which was, as in ancient Israel, their most admired instrument of music, all the other kinds in use among the Israelites appear to have been equally possessed by this portion of the people who were to come of Jacob, and had been created for the praise of the God of Israel (Ps. cii. 18).

As to RELIGION, or the knowledge of the Supreme, and of the service more immediately required of Him, for which this people might be expected to be most distinguished, the Anglo-Saxons and their brethren in the north of Europe gave equally clear indications of their Israelitish origin. They are described "as having been acquainted with the great doctrine of one Supreme Deity, the Author of everything that existeth, the Eternal, the Ancient, the Living and Awful Being; the Searcher into concealed things; the Being who never changeth, who liveth and governeth during the ages, and directeth everything which is high, and everything which is low." Of this glorious Being they had anciently esteemed it impious to make any visible representation, or to imagine it pos-

[1] This also was the case earlier among the Britons.

sible that He could be confined within the walls of a temple.

These great truths, the same as we know were taught to Israel, had in a great measure become lost or obscured before these people came into Britain. But this of itself speaks of their origin, having chiefly taken place in consequence, it is said, of their receiving a mighty conqueror from the East as their God in human nature, correspondent to the expectation of Israel with regard to Messiah. This supposed incarnation of Deity is considered to have presented himself among these people about the same time as the true Messiah appeared among the Jews in the land of Israel, or perhaps shortly after, when the false Christs were deceiving the Jews (Matt. xxiv. 5).

The name of this pretender was Odin,[1] or Woden (Boden, or Godama, as he is still called by the Buddhists, and was anciently in some parts of Germany), the same word apparently as that from which we have Eden, and signifying *delight*. He was esteemed the great dispenser of happiness to his followers, as well as of fury to his enemies. When Woden was removed from them, they placed his image in their *most holy place*, where was a kind of raised place or ark, as if in imitation of that at Jerusalem, where between the Cherubim the Divine Presence was supposed to abide. Here, as if on the mercy-

---

[1] We may here recall the traditional descent of Odin, preserved by Snorre in the "Edda," and in his History. This great ancestor of the Saxon and Scandinavian chiefs is represented as having migrated from a city east of the Don, called Asgard, and a country called Asæland, which imply the city and country of the Asæ, or Asians. The cause of this movement was the progress of the Romans. Odin is stated to have moved first into Russia, and thence into Saxony, which is not improbable. The wars between the Romans and Mithridates involved and shook most of the barbarous nations in these parts, and may have imposed the necessity of a westerly or European migration.

seat or throne of the God of Israel, did they place the image of him whom they reckoned Immanuel, or God in our nature.[1] There also they placed the image of his wife Frigga, and between these two the image of Thor, who sat crowned in the centre. Outward of these three, by the side of Woden, was the image of Tuesco, and by the side of Frigga was Seater, or Saturn; outward of Tuesco was a representation of the Moon; and outward of Saturn was placed an image of the Sun. Thus Thor was in the centre; his father, Woden, from which we have Wednesday, and his mother, Frigga, from which we have Friday, were with armour on each side of him; whilst outwards from these were the more peaceful deities, Tuesco, from which we have Tuesday, and Saturn, from which we have Saturday; while outside of all were the two great luminaries, from which we have Sunday and Monday (2 Kings xxiii. 5). In the arrangement of these false objects of worship, and in the correspondent naming of the several days of the week, they manifested that same regard to symmetry in which ancient Israel were trained. These are the very same gods, it may be remarked, with which they had been threatened (Deut. xxxii. 17).

Before this elevation or ark on which the symbols of their worship were placed, they had an altar on which the holy fire burned continually, and near it a vase for receiv-

[1] "Over all Suithiod (Sweden) the folk paid tribute to Odin, for which he was bound to defend the land from hostile assault, and to sacrifice for a good harvest. After his death Niord maintained the sacrifices; and Frey, *his* son, erected the great temple in Upsala, whose sister, Freya, survived him, and superintended the sacrifices. (*Frey* is the Mœso-Goth c *Frauja*, Anglo-Saxon *Frea*, German *Fró*, and means 'Lord.') While Christianity had attained ascendancy in Gothland, the old sacrifices were still continued for a long time in Upsala, and the first Christians were compelled to purchase exemption from the obligation of attending at their performance, and contributing to their support."—*Geijer*.

ing the blood of the victims, and a brush for sprinkling it upon the people, reminding us again of what was done in ancient Israel (Exod. xii. 22).

They had generally one great temple for the whole nation, in one of which, it is particularly noticed, they had twelve priests, presided over by a high priest, who had under their charge the religious concerns of the whole people. It was at Upsala, in Sweden, and is said to have been of the most splendid description — of incredible grandeur and magnificence. In its neighbourhood is still preserved a pavement of eleven or twelve stones, where the person took his stand who conducted the election of the king among the people inhabiting that country.

It may be observed, that although Israel had one great temple for the whole nation, they had also their rural worship, which was generally in groves; and the Anglo-Saxons had the very same arrangement. We have, in short, every agreement of these people as to religion, except in those respects which have been anticipated by the spirit of prophecy.

Nor should we forget that these people had the Israelitish division of TIME. Their day was from evening to evening, and their weeks, like those of the Hebrews, consisted of seven days, which modern research has discovered to be the human proportion of a great cosmical system of chronology (Watchmen of Ephraim, i. 564; Our Inheritance in the Great Pyramid, 2nd edition, 1874; and the other able works of the learned Astronomer-Royal for Scotland Isbister & Co.)[1]

It may also be observed that the Israelites had THREE

[1] That the Anglo-Saxon chaldron wheat-measure of the time of Edgar the Peaceable should be of precisely the same capacity with that of the Hebrew Ark of the Covenant and the Laver is not at all surprising in

GREAT FESTIVALS in the course of the year, at which all their males were to present themselves before the Lord (Deut. xvi. 16, 17)—

> "Three times in a year shall all thy males appear before the Lord thy God,
> In the place which He shall choose;
> In the feast of unleavened bread,
> And in the feast of weeks,
> And in the feast of tabernacles;
> And they shall not appear before the Lord empty;
> Every man—according to the gift of his hand,
> According to the blessing of the Lord thy God, which He hath given thee."

(See also Exodus xxiii. 14–17; xxxiv. 18–26; and Lev. xxiii.)

Previous to their conversion to Christianity, the ANGLO-

---

the circumstances; nor that this people should have preserved through all their wanderings minor dimensions which had been provided for them with legal and mathematical exactitude by Him who gave them in the wilderness the command (Lev. xix. 35, 36)—

> "Ye shall do no unrighteousness in judgment,
> In mete-yard, in weight, or in measure.
> Just balances, just weights, a just ephah,
> And a just hin shall ye have:
> I, the LORD your God which brought you out of the land of Egypt."

The pertinancy of this oft-repeated motive becomes more apparent when we in some measure apprehend the history and metrological character of that great stone revelation set up in the great highway of nations, and executed under the eye and direction of their godly ancestor, who was emphatically called "My righteous king"=Melchi-tzekek, and whose filial piety caused his aged father to exclaim, "Blessed be the Lord God of Shem!"

Remarkable enough, even as a coincidence, is the cotemperaneous removing of the veil cast over lost Israel in the West, their excavated identifications in the East, and the opening up of their connection with the true and primeval service of the Living God. It is to be noted, also, that Sir Henry Rawlinson had his attention drawn to that which proved to be the alphabetic key to the Nineveh inscriptions in A.D. 1837, the same year that the late author's attention was drawn to the subject, and this book was commenced.

SAXONS had also THREE GREAT FESTIVALS, the first of which, called Eostre or Astarte, exactly corresponded in time with the Passover, the first of Israel's appointed feasts. Even after their conversion, the heathen name of the festival was retained, so that we still call it *Easter*. The second feast corresponded with the Hebrew Pentecost, or Feast of Weeks; when, upon the fiftieth day after the Passover, the firstfruits were offered with rejoicing. And hence it was called *White*-Sunday, because of their then appearing in garments that indicated rejoicing. The third great feast among the Hebrews was the Feast of Tabernacles.[1]

It is particularly noted that the Anglo-Saxons were in the habit of congregating to the Witena-gemote or GREAT PARLIAMENT THRICE IN THE YEAR, the two first of which assemblies exactly corresponded with the times of the first two great feasts of ancient Israel, and when all the males were supposed to be present, at least by their representatives. Nor did they appear empty, their principal object being to arrange with regard to the offerings to be presented to the king, as previously they had at such times paid tribute to their God, who was "King in Israel" previous to the time of Saul.

As in Israel, so among the Anglo-Saxons, the PRIESTHOOD was confined to certain families, and descended from father to son. They had possessions in land, and had

---

[1] This had been ordained for the Northern people by Odin; and it is related of Sigurd Thorson, a rich Norwegian, that "he had the custom while heathenism existed, of keeping three sacrifices every year—one at the commencement of winter, the second in midwinter, and the third towards summer. But after he had embraced Christianity, he preserved the custom of giving entertainments. In harvest he kept with his friends a harvest-home, in winter a Christmas revel, and the third at Easter, and many guests were gathered at his board."—*Sagas of Haco and St Olave*.

much to do in declaring the law. Their Church courts were given a degree of authority they did not before possess, and which they very speedily abused.

After the Israelitish pattern TITHES also appear to have been established in these countries, even under that corrupted form of worship which the Saxons brought with them into Britain. Upon their embrace of the Christian faith, the revenues of the former worship were appropriated to the use of the Christian priesthood; just as afterwards we find them taken from the Church as in connection with Rome, and given to the support of the Reformed worship. These tithes did not belong to the Church of Rome, but to the Church of the Anglo-Saxons. Popery purloined them for a time, but they have been so far recovered.[1]

When Gregory sent his missionaries to procure the adhesion of the English to the see of Rome, they were instructed not to destroy the heathen temples: only to remove the images of their gods, wash the walls with holy water, erect altars, and deposit relics in them, and so convert them into Christian churches; not only to save the expense of building new ones, but also that the people might the more easily be persuaded to frequent these places of worship, having been previously accustomed to assemble there. He directed them further to accommodate the ceremonies of the Christian worship as much as pos-

---

[1] We have seen (p. 171, that a tenth of the land was assigned for the support of the Druidical priesthood, and that King Lucius made over for the support of Christian worship all their rights (p. 261). *Sharon Turner* says (vol. i. p. 493)—"In A.D. 855, Ethelwolf (father of Alfred the Great), with the sanction of his Wit na gemote, made that donation to the Church which is usually understood to be the grant of its tithes. But on reading carefully the obscure words of the three copies of this charter, which three succeeding chroniclers have left us, it will appear that it cannot have been

sible to those of the heathen, that the people might not be much startled by the change; and in particular, he advises them to allow the Christian converts at certain festivals to kill and eat a great number of oxen to the glory of God, as they previously had done to what he is pleased to call the honour of the devil.

These sacrifices at such festivals, and the very possibility of making the new worship look anything like the old, argue such a similarity of the one to the other as we could not expect to exist between the Christian worship and any other save that of the Hebrews. Indeed, considering the changes which must have occurred during their sojourn in the northern wilderness, it is wonderful that the Christian worship could have been made so far like it as that the change in religion should not be much observed. Well may the English, as being the children of God's ancient people, acknowledge—

> "O God, we have heard with our ears;
> Our fathers have declared unto us
> The noble works Thou didst in their days;
> And in the old time before them."

---

the original grant of the tithes of all England.... Whatever was its original meaning, the clergy in after-ages interpreted it to mean a distinct and formal grant of the tithes of the whole kingdom." Comp. *Ingulf*, p. 17; *Malms.* 41; and *Matt. of West.* 306.

Asser says, "He liberated the tenth part of all his kingdom from every royal service and contribution," &c. &c. *Stuart*, in his "Laws of England," says the Council of Mascon, held in A.D. 586, under King Guntram of Burgundy, acknowledged tithes as an *ancient duty* due to the Church, and enjoined their regular payment. But the words of this law indicate that they were not to be solely appropriated to the clergy:—"Unde statuimus, ut decimas ecclesiasticas omnis populus inferat, quibus sacerdotes, aut in pauperum usum, aut in captivorum redemptionem erogatis, suis orationibus pacem populo et salutem empetrant." Charlemagne, in A.D. 778, *as due by a divine right*, established them throughout France, whence they soon passed into Germany and Italy.

Yea, well may the house of Israel now say—

> "Oh, give thanks unto the Lord,
> For He is good:
> For His mercy endureth for ever."

Their national change to nominal Christianity, and admission among them of the New Testament Scriptures, as well as recovery of their own Old Testament at the time of Gregory, was a partial restoration to the light and favour of God, and seems to have been about A.D. 592. Partial conversions had taken place previously in different portions of the Anglo-Saxon population through the influence of British, Irish, and Scottish Christians, about the middle of the space of time which has elapsed since the captivity of Israel.[1]

In Hosea vi. 1-3, it was said, "After two days He will revive us: in the third day He will raise us up, and we shall live in His sight." "A day with the Lord is as a thousand years." And immediately after two thousand years from the time of their captivity the Lord revived them by the dawn of the Reformation, when there was

---

[1] In Lev. xxvi. we read that Israel were given the Promised Land on condition of hearing and obeying the Word of the Lord. If they did not hearken to do all H's commandments, they should be visited with grievous disease and other plagues; and if they would not be reformed by these, they should be PUNISHED SEVEN TIMES FOR THEIR SINS.

They are also told that they should be visited with *famine*; and that if they still went contrary to the Lord, they should be PUNISHED SEVEN TIMES FOR THEIR SINS.

They are also threatened with *wild beasts*; and then, if they remained unreformed, they were to be PUNISHED SEVEN TIMES FOR THEIR SINS.

They are also told that a *sword* should be brought upon them, which should "avenge the quarrel" of His covenant; and that if they would not for all this hearken unto Him, the Lord would certainly PUNISH THEM SEVEN TIMES FOR THEIR SINS.

The word *times* is not in the Hebrew: the word is simply SEVEN. The

another recovery of the Scriptures, and release from the service of idols. There was also a clearer exhibition of the truth of the gospel than had ever been before enjoyed, which, however, they received with too great indifference. It required to be beaten and burned into them by the Marian persecutions, when they were taught the value of the doctrine of justification through faith in the crucified Redeemer, by its power in sustaining, amid suffering and death, in zealous devotedness to the service of God.

But there was a danger of the people leaving their religion too entirely in the hands of Government, when the sceptre and the sword were again wielded by the hands of Protestant piety; which accordingly is allowed sufficiently to evince its fallibility by separating from the Church many of the most zealous and conscientious of the clergy, who were thus left free to propagate the truth apart

---

"SEVEN TIMES" spoken of in Dan. iv., in relation to Nebuchadnezzar's punishment, are supposed to have been YEARS; and when a man represents a people (as in Num. xiii. 1-3, 25; xiv. 33, 34; Ezek. iv. 6), then A YEAR OF THE INDIVIDUAL'S LIFE IS PUT FOR A YEAR OF THE NATION'S EXISTENCE WHICH HE REPRESENTS. These seven years during which Nebuchadnezzar was to be cast out on account of his pride would thus represent the SEVEN TIMES 360=2520 years, during which Ephraim was to be lost among the Gentiles, and punished for his national pride and disobedience.

Israel had been trained to the primeval measurement of time by "seven" (and which may be seen in the teachings of the Great Pyramid). Every seventh *day* was the *individual's* Sabbath to the Lord; every seventh *year* was appointed by God as the *national* Sabbath; and at the *end* of every seven times seven they had another called THE JUBILEE, or great rejoicing; all of which were also typical of still greater epochs.

In B.C. 780 Hosea prophesied (chap. v. 7), "Now shall a month (of 30 years) devour them with their portions:" and Isaiah (B.C. 742), chap. vii. 8, "Within threescore and five years shall Ephraim be broken that it be not a people." The Assyrian began to "devour" Israel in B.C. 740, and in B.C. 710, or thirty years after (the prophetic "month" of Hosea), "he came up against all the defenced cities of Judah, and took them."

Take, then, B.C. 710 from the first half of the "SEVEN TIMES" threatened

from the State, and to provide more largely and earnestly for the religious instruction of the people than it alone could have done.

But in time this Nonconformist body undermined the Established Church, and despising many of the wise institutions of their fathers, were not merely content to do good in their own way, but they would also have their own way to be everything both in Church and State. They were allowed to try the experiment by the creation of a military despotism under Oliver Cromwell, after whose death a revulsion took place at the Restoration of the ancient mixed constitution.

Then there was a danger of the nation running into the opposite extreme; but again the most valuable portion of the clergy were disbanded by the State, to mix more familiarly among the people, and be supported by their free-will offerings. By these changes, also, the people were forced to spread abroad and plant their colonies; as, for

---

in Lev. xxvi.—which, of course, is 1260—and we come to A.D. 550, when the Angles gained their last settlement in Britain, and formed the seventh kingdom of the Saxon Heptarchy. The second half of the seven times is often alluded to in the Books of Daniel and Revelation, under the various formula of "time, times, and a half;" "time, times, and the dividing of a time;" "forty and two months"—or 42 times 30; "a thousand two hundred and sixty days," &c. Not till the Saxons had settled in England did the Bishop of Rome develop so decidedly the characteristics of the "Little Horn," "The Mother of Harlots," &c., which would account for the dates relating to Antichrist coming to just the same as the half of the SEVEN TIMES.

In Dan. xii. 12, it is said, "Blessed is he that waiteth and cometh to the thousand three hundred and five-and-thirty days," which is 1260 years, with 75 additional. 1260 added to A.D. 550 brings us to A.D. 1810, when the Pope began to lose his temporal power, and since which the great development of our race in all directions and aspects has taken place. See also Wilson's "Mission of Elijah;" "Watchmen of Ephraim," vol. ii.; "Our Inheritance in the Great Pyramid," by C. Piazzi Smyth.

example, in the New England States in North America, where they continue to spread and prosper, as they had been accustomed from the beginning.

At the Revolution the Church recovered partly from her downward tendency since the Restoration, but was sinking into a lethargic formality, when, by the violent shakings and sneers of infidelity, she was quickened into a deeper search for the intellectual foundations of her faith on the one hand, and on the other, by the loud voice and busy stirrings of Methodism in her midst, she was aroused to a more confiding faith in the One Foundation. By this and other awakenings all classes of Christians have been animated to a more earnest searching after the truth for themselves, and propagation thereof both at home and abroad. And ever and anon are bands of men raised up to give prominence to particular portions of the truth, so that what we might forget on the one hand, we are reminded of on the other. Latterly, from many quarters, our attention has specially been called to the consideration of Christ coming forth as the Chief Corner stone for the completion of that Building of which He is also the Foundation (Eph. ii. 19–22).

All this has been by the providence of God. Our business is therefore neither to overvalue nor undervalue our own position, or that of others, but rather to maintain the spirit of improvement which is the true characteristic of Israel, whereby we may ever receive advantage by all the Lord is saying to us and may be doing with us; like the shining light "that shineth more and more unto the perfect day." May all sections of the Church universal glory in the Lord, and strive to serve each other as brethren in Christ—as fellow-heirs of the promises made unto our fathers! The tribes of Israel and the truths of God have been alike widely "scattered abroad."[1] May He hasten the time when they shall all be gathered into one; when our Redeemer will clothe Himself with His people, as with a seamless robe of glory, woven from the top throughout; when the promise will be fulfilled—

> "Thou art my servant, O Israel!
> In whom I will be glorified."

---

[1] We are apt to overlook altogether the great advantage to England and Ireland from successive immigrations from the Continent of Huguenot piety, capital, and industry, driven out by the persecution of Spanish and French royal bigotry; and the vitality and success imparted to our own national protest against the usurpations of Rome over the intellect and conscience of Christendom, from the time of Edward VI., in 1550, before whom Latimer shrewdly observed of the distressed foreigners then beginning to flow into the country—"I wish that we could collect together such valuable persons in this kingdom, as it would be the means of ensuring its prosperity." By the year 1621, in London alone, 10,000 strangers were carrying on 121 trades. "They were not a peculiar people like the Jews, but Protestants, like the nation which had given them refuge, and into which they naturally desired to become wholly merged. Hence it was that by the end of the eighteenth century nearly all the French churches, as such, had disappeared" (Smiles' "Huguenots," 1868). And even by the Revocation of the Edict of Nantes, under Louis XIV., the flower of the French army was set free to assist in our own Revolution of 1688.

XIX.

FRENCH TESTIMONY AS TO THE ENGLISH CONSTITUTION AND HISTORY.

Rapin describes the great Change effected in Britain by the Saxons, Angles, and Jutes—The Heptarchy—The Angles—Distinguished Character of the Parts settled by them—Their Arrival under Twelve Chiefs—Their Kingdoms, East Anglia, Mercia, and Northumberland—Spread abroad by the Incursions of the Danes—English Constitution brought with them into Britain—Their Laws like the Law of God—Alfred only reformed and re-established the English Constitution and the Common Law, so like those of Ancient Israel—Acknowledgment of the *Abbé Milot*, as to the unparalleled Character of the English History—*Prévost Paradol* on the marvellous spread of the English race—*Victor Hugo* on the Positions held by England—The Discovery of the Lord's Truth and Faithfulness to Israel to precede the abundant bestowment of the Latter Rain.

THE evidence produced in these Lectures as to the peopling of England, especially by the race identified with Israel, having been chiefly supported by our own historians, it may be well to confirm it by the testimony of authors from among our French neighbours. We shall take four examples: one Huguenot Protestant, and the other three Roman Catholic. The former will give his testimony of the English at their settlement here, and of course previous to the operation of those causes of our national prosperity, to which enemies of the Reformation might suspect him of giving undue prominence in the later periods of English history, which we shall leave to be sketched by Romanists, who can as little be suspected of partiality in our favour.

Rapin's testimony with regard to the change effected in this island by the settlement of the Anglo-Saxons, is thus given at the commencement of his third book:—"The revolution caused by the conquest of the Anglo-Saxons introduced a new face of things in Great Britain. The country formerly inhabited by the Britons was now possessed by strangers. The very names of the towns and provinces were changed, and the country was divided in a very different manner from what it was by the Romans.

"The Saxons, Angles, and Jutes, who are all to be considered as one people, and comprehended under the name of ENGLISH, had conquered all the southern part of the island, from the Channel to the Wall of Severus, and a little beyond towards the east. This part of Great Britain possessed by these three nations was divided into seven kingdoms, whereof the Saxons and Jutes had four, namely, Kent, Essex, Sussex, and Wessex; the Angles alone had two, Mercia and East Anglia; but in Northumberland they were mixed with the descendants of the Saxons that first took possession of the country beyond the Humber under Octa and Ebusa.

"By the Heptarchy is meant the government of the seven kingdoms of the Anglo-Saxons as making but one body and one state. The Anglo-Saxons, as I said before, established in England a form of government not unlike what they had lived under in Germany—that is, considering themselves as brethren and countrymen; and being equally concerned to support themselves in their conquests, they conceived it necessary to assist one another, and act in common for the good of all. To that end they judged it proper to appoint a general-in-chief, or, if you please, a monarch, invested with certain prerogatives, the nature and number of which we are not fully informed of. Upon the death of the general or monarch, another was chosen by the unanimous consent of the seven kingdoms; but there were sometimes pretty long interregnums caused by the wars or divisions between the sovereigns who could not meet or agree upon a choice.

"Besides this monarch, they had also, as the centre of the heptarchal government, an assembly-general, consisting of the principal members of the seven kingdoms, or their deputies. This is what is called the Wittena-gemote or general parliament, where the concerns of the whole nation only were considered. But each kingdom had a particular parliament, much after the manner practised in the United Provinces of the Low Countries. Each kingdom was sovereign, and yet they consulted in common upon the affairs that concerned the Heptarchy; and the acts and resolutions of the assembly-general were to be punctually observed, since every king and kingdom had assented thereto."

It is worthy of observation that of the nations from the north of Europe which came into Britain, *the Angles alone*, who ultimately gave their name to this country, *left no known portion of their people on the Continent.* They seem to have merely passed through the country of the Jutes and Saxons, and to have almost entirely transported themselves into this island, after whom the whole southern portion of it came ultimately to be termed England. It would, however, be an error to suppose that only the south part of England was peopled by them. Partly by direct emigration, and partly by the scattering occasioned by the incursions of the Danes and the Norman Conquest, the same race which peopled first the central parts of the island, called in the times of the Heptarchy "East Anglia, Mercia, and Northumberland," spread out southward into the Saxon quarters, and even westward into Wales, as well as northward into Scotland. And thus the whole body of the people that remained after their first settlement here had the advantage of being leavened by a race which, with all its faults, is superior both as to intellectual capacity and moral power.

This is shown by the eminence to which those parts of England have attained that were first and most entirely peopled by the Angles. In their quarters are found the principal and most ancient seats of learning, such as Oxford and Cambridge; also the chief manufacturing districts, whether of clothes, metals, earthenware, or chemical preparations; as well as the greatest marts, with the exception of London, for the import of the fulness of the earth by sea, and for sending forth to all quarters of the globe the productions of English ingenuity and industry. They were all within the bounds of the Anglian kingdoms of the Heptarchy, even as distinguished from those which were called merely Saxon. Nor is it to be overlooked that from these same quarters London itself is still supplied with some main portions of its population which have carried literature, science, and art to such perfection, as well as mercantile and missionary enterprise to the bounds of the habitable globe.

With regard to the settlement of the Angles in Britain, *Rapin* thus writes in his first book — "About this time (A.D. 527) multitudes of Angles, *under the conduct of twelve chiefs*, all of equal authority, but whose names, except Uffa (of whom I shall have occasion to speak hereafter) are unknown, landed at some port on the eastern coast of Britain, where, without much difficulty, they possessed themselves of some post, those parts being ill guarded by the Britons. In time, as they were continually enlarging their conquests towards the west, they compelled the Britons at length to abandon the country along the eastern shore. The Angles, thus situated, had an opportunity of sending from time to time for fresh colonies from Germany, with which they founded a fifth kingdom, by the name of the kingdom of East Anglia, or of the East Angles. But as their first chiefs assumed not the title of king, the beginning of this kingdom is generally brought down to the year A.D. 571."

As to the kingdoms of the Heptarchy founded by them, he gives the following testimony in his third book:—
"The kingdom of the East Angles was bounded on the north by the Humber and the German Ocean; on the east by the same ocean, which surrounded it almost on two sides; on the south by the kingdom of Essex; and on the west by Mercia. Its greatest length was eighty, and its greatest breadth fifty-five miles. It contained the two counties of Norfolk and Suffolk, with part of Cambridgeshire. The chief towns were Norwich, Thetford, Ely, and Cambridge. I have already related how this kingdom was founded by the Angles that landed on the eastern coasts of Britain, under twelve chiefs, the survivor of whom, Uffa, assumed the title of king of the East Angles.

"The kingdom of Mercia was bounded on the north by the Humber, by which it was separated from Northumberland; on the west by the Severn, beyond which were the Britons or Welsh; on the south by the Thames, by which it was parted from the kingdoms of Kent, Sussex, and Wessex; on the east by the kingdoms of Essex and East Anglia. Thus Mercia was guarded on three sides by three large rivers that ran into the sea, and served for boundary to all the other kingdoms. Hence the name Mercia, from the Saxon word Merc, signifying a bound, and not, as some fancy, from an imaginary river called Mercia. The inhabitants of this kingdom are sometimes termed by historians Mediterranei Angli, or the Mid-land English, and sometimes South Humbrians, as being south of the Humber; but the most common name is that of Mercians. The principal cities of Mercia were Lincoln, Nottingham, Warwick, Leicester, Coventry, Lichfield, Northampton, Worcester, Gloucester, Derby, Chester, Shrewsbury, Stafford, Oxford, Bristol. Of all the kingdoms of the Heptarchy, this was the finest and most considerable. Its greatest length was a hundred and sixty miles, and its greatest breadth about one hundred." (Danmerk is "Dan's bound.")

And in page 47 :—"The kingdom of Northumberland was situated on the north of the Humber, as its name imports. It was bounded on the south, and parted from Mercia, by that river; on the west by the Irish Sea; on the north by the country of the Picts and Scots; and on the east by the German Ocean. It contained the present counties of Lancashire, Cumberland, Westmoreland, Northumberland, York, and Durham. The principal cities were York, Dunelm (since called Durham), Carlisle (named by the Romans Luguballia), Hexham or Hagulstadt, Lancaster, and some others of less note. This country was divided into two parts, Deira and Bernicia, each, for some time, a distinct kingdom of itself. Bernicia was partly situated on the north of Severus' Wall, and ended in a point at the mouth of the Tweed. Deira contained the southern part of Northumberland, as far as the Humber."

The Danes made most havoc of these three kingdoms, and by their incursions the Angles were much driven out into other portions of the Heptarchy, as well as into Wales and Scotland. Thus, in the reign of Ethelred, it is said of them—" They began with attacking Northumberland, of which they at length became masters. They proceeded next to East Anglia, which they also subdued; and after extorting money from the Mercians, they entered Wessex."

In speaking of the language of the Anglo-Saxons, *Rapin* writes, p. 162 :—" To say in general the Anglo-Saxons spoke English, or Saxon, would not be showing with sufficient exactness what their language was. To give a fuller idea, it will be necessary to distinguish the several tongues used in England after the arrival of the first Saxons. The English tongue originally differed but little from the Danish; since the ancient writers call them indifferently Cimbric, Scandinavian, Gothic; but this language was not the same with the Saxons. In the parts lying north of the Thames was spoken pure English or Danish; and south of the Thames, pure Saxon. Though these two languages were different, they so far agreed, however, as to be understood by both nations. In process of time, and especially after the union of the seven kingdoms, Saxon prevailed in all England, because the kings were of that nation. Thus pure English (or, the language of the Angles) was by degrees disused, or at least banished from common conversation.

" Afterwards the Danes, settling in England, brought their language, which was not the ancient Danish or English above mentioned, but a modern Danish, mixed with the language of several neighbouring nations of Denmark. This modern Danish was chiefly used in Northumberland, Mercia, and East Anglia, where the Danes were masters. Though out of compliance to the English, Canute the Great published his laws in Saxon, yet the Danish tongue was still retained in the north, where the people were mostly Danes. As it was also the court language during the reigns of Canute the Great and his two sons, it became necessary for the West Saxons, who adopted several words and idioms of it into their own language. But upon Edward the Confessor's accession to the throne, Saxon prevailed again at court. Hence the inhabitants of the north were under some necessity of learning it, just as the Gascons in France are obliged to learn French."

As to the origin of the Anglo-Saxon institutions, *Rapin* says :—" Great Britain was so overrun with Saxons, Angles, and Jutes, that hardly could any remains of the ancient Britons be discovered. It was very natural for these conquerors to establish in their newly-erected kingdoms their own country customs. And therefore it may be advanced for certain that the laws now in force throughout the greatest part of Europe are derived from the laws these ancient conquerors brought with them from the north. This might be easily proved with respect to all the countries concerned in this great revolution. But at present I shall confine myself to England alone. By what I am going to say, whoever has any knowledge of the British constitution will easily be convinced that the customs now practised in that kingdom are for the most part the same the Anglo-Saxons brought with them from the northern countries, and lastly from Germany.

" An English historian, by comparing the laws and customs of the Germans with those of the English, has plainly shown the English introduced into Great Britain the same laws that were in use in their own country. Nay, he affirms that till the Norman Conquest there was not so much as one law in England but what, in the main, the Germans had the same. 'Tis true, as the Anglo-Saxons consisted of three several nations, who had also their separate quarters in England, there might be some difference upon that account between the seven kingdoms of the Heptarchy. But this difference could not be very great, since the three nations were united in Germany before their coming into England, and made but one and the same people under the general name of Saxons. The laws and customs, therefore, introduced into Great Britain by the Anglo-Saxons, are to be considered as composed of the laws their ancestors brought into Germany, and of those they found among the ancient Germans.

"The Saxons had no kings in Germany when they sent their first troops to the assistance of the Britons under the conduct of Hengist. Their territories were divided into *twelve provinces*, over each of which a head or governor was appointed by the assembly-general of the nation, wherein the supreme power was lodged. This assembly was called Wittena-gemote, that is to say, the assembly of the wise men, and also the Mycel Synod, that is, the great assembly. Besides the governors of the provinces, there were others also set over the cities and boroughs.

"Though the title of king was not in use among the Saxons, it was, however, assumed by Hengist as soon as he was in possession of Kent. Indeed, it would have been difficult for him to have found any other so proper to express his sovereignty over that province. It is true the titles of duke and earl, or their equivalents, Heretogh and Ealdorman, were not then unknown; but they were not yet used to signify sovereigns. It was not till long after, that, certain dukes and earls being invested with sovereign power, these titles were made use of to denote the supreme authority. The other leaders who settled in Great Britain after Hengist, followed his example in assuming the title of king.

Thus, whereas in Germany the Saxon territories were divided into *twelve governments*, their conquests in England were parted into seven kingdoms; but with this difference, that in Germany each governor depended on the assembly-general of the nation, whereas in England each king was sovereign in his petty kingdom. However, this did not exempt him from all dependence on the Wittenagemote of his own state, which in conjunction with him regulated all important affairs. Moreover, by mutual consent there was established a general assembly of the whole seven kingdoms, where matters relating to all in common were settled. Hence this form of government, which considered the seven kingdoms as united in one body, was called the Heptarchy, that is, the government of seven."

And again, page 151:—" Among the Anglo-Saxons the lords had not the power of life and death over their slaves; nay, the laws provided they should not cripple or maim them without incurring a penalty. *They who made such laws imitated,* in some measure, *the law of God without knowing it.*"

And again :—" I have already observed, in the life of Alfred the Great, that this prince divided England into shires, the shires into trythings, laths, or wapentakes; these into hundreds, and the hundreds into tythings. However, it must not be imagined that in this division he introduced something entirely new to the English. He only settled the bounds of the former divisions, making some alterations for convenience' sake. At least, as to the division of the kingdom into shires, it is certain he only proportioned it in a better manner than before. This is evident from there being earls of Somersetshire and Devonshire in the reign of Ethelwulf, as Asser relates, who lived about that time; but Alfred, uniting all England into one monarchy, made a more exact and extensive division of his dominions. The shires contained a whole province subject to the jurisdiction of an earl or count, and were therefore called counties. Some of these shires, being divided into trythings, others into laths, and others into wapentakes, each of these divisions, which were the same thing under different names, consisted of three or four hundreds of families, and each hundred was subdivided into tythings. The courts of justice were formed with respect to these several divisions—that is, there was a court for each tything, hundred, &c.—to the end justice might be administered with less charge, greater despatch, and more exactness.

"If any person accused of a crime refused to appear, the other nine sureties were bound to see him forthcoming to justice. If he ran away, he was not suffered to settle in any other town, borough, or village, because no one could change habitation without a testimonial from his tything, for want of which they that received him were punished. By the laws of King Edward, the tything had thirty days allowed them to search for the criminal. If he was not to be found, the tything-man, taking two of his own, and nine of the three next tythings, these twelve purged themselves by oath of the offence and flight of the malefactor. If they refused to swear, the tything the offender belonged to was obliged to make satisfaction in his stead."

When we shall in truth obey the command delivered in the end of the Old Testament, "Remember ye the law of Moses my servant, which I commanded unto him in Horeb, for all Israel, the statutes and judgments;"—when this remembrance truly takes place, and the connection of these with the English Constitution is traced according as the evidence leads, the advantage of obeying the command will be felt, the value of the training given to Israel will become apparent, and it will be acknowledged that God hath spoken truly and wrought wondrously with His people (Mal. iv. 4, 5). See also The Mission of Elijah, by same author.

Rapin's testimony has shown that Britain changed its population, and of course its institutions and language, upon the settlement here of the Saxons, Angles, and Jutes, who formed themselves into a constitutional government called the Heptarchy, somewhat analogous to that of their Twelve Provinces on the Continent, and like that of the Twelve Tribes of Israel. The ANGLES occupied the most central position, and ultimately gave their name to the whole, although they have left least trace of their settlement on the Continent, consistently with the idea that they had mainly migrated to Britain. I have already noticed the distinguished character of those parts of England in which they chiefly settled, and the urgent occasion of their distribution from this central position into other parts of the island, to which they were first introduced under twelve chiefs.

Like Joseph, they were greatly afflicted in the commencement of their career, but have subsequently to a remarkable extent fulfilled the destiny of his younger son Ephraim, of whom was to come the promised "fulness or multitude of nations" (Gen. xlviii. 16-20).

Rapin has also testified that the English Constitution (bearing as it does the impress of Mosaic institutions) was possessed by the English previous to their coming hither. He also notices that apparently without their own knowledge their laws were an imitation of the Law of God, and that Alfred did not originate, but merely reformed and restored, the English Constitution, which had been thrown into confusion by the incursions of the Danes, and who seem to have indeed fulfilled the prophecy of Jacob respecting DAN (Gen. xlix. 16, 17).

> "Dan shall be a serpent by the way,
> An adder in the path,
> That biteth the horse-heels,
> So that his rider shall fall backward."

But all has been overruled for good. Soon may the Anglo-Saxon race prove themselves worthy of the interpretation which Gregory gave of their name in the Roman slave-market—" angels " = messengers. May they indeed be the " swift messengers " of the Lord, carrying forth in divine power like the lightning " His message unto all the nations!" (Isa. xviii.)

Upon showing "His Word unto Jacob, His statutes and judgments to Israel," it was to be discovered that " He hath not dealt so with any nation," as He promised to do with the people He hath chosen for Himself: that He might be peculiarly the Lord *their* God, the God of ISRAEL. But so far as we have come, we have found that He hath dealt with the ENGLISH people exactly as He promised to deal with ISRAEL; so that WE may well exclaim, as in Isa. lxiii. 7, "I will mention the loving-kindnesses of the LORD, the praises of the LORD, according to all that the LORD hath bestowed on US, and the great goodness toward the house of Israel, which He hath bestowed on THEM, according to His mercies, and according to the multitude of His loving-kindnesses. For He said, Surely they—my people (עַמִּי *Ammi*), sons (בנים *Banim*) that will not lie: so He was their Saviour."

Although men could not but see that the Promises were being fulfilled in them, they have failed to recognise them as the Children of the Promises. But even though Abraham be ignorant of them, and Israel acknowledge them not, their Father has recognised them as being "Ammi," *My people*. Amidst all their failings He recognised in them that integrity and trustworthiness for which they are so distinguished among the nations, and which He calls "an honest and good heart," wherein His Word might with advantage be sown.

He hath indeed been, both temporally and spiritually, "their Saviour," overruling all changes for their good. Most worthy of note is the manner in which they withstood the world at the commencement of this century, and have been enriching it with their wise institutions and useful inventions ever since. Not the supposed freaks of blind fortune have been manifested in their case, but the good providence of the God of Israel, who had promised to defend them, and so to cause them to be for blessing to all nations of the earth.

That this people have been dealt wondrously with is acknowledged by those who have had the best opportunity of judging, and who have studied their history in comparison with that of other nations. The Abbé Milot, Royal Professor of History in the University of Parma, a Frenchman, and a member of the Church of Rome, who had previously written a work on the history of France, wrote also "Elements of the History of England," from the preface to which I shall now quote. It is to be premised that this author wrote previously to the glory of the Georgian era, since which hath been the greatest bursting forth of power from this people on all hands. The Abbé unwittingly shows that in them the prophecy has been fulfilled, that they should be "a people terrible from their beginning;" and we ourselves have seen that this has been "hitherto." He thus proceeds:—

"No modern history, it must be confessed, presents to

our view so great a number of striking pictures as that of England. We see here a people free, warlike, unconquerable, and a long time ferocious, preserve the same characteristic qualities through a successive train of bloody revolutions. Depressed by the arms and by the despotism of the ambitious William, Duke of Normandy; gloriously governed by Henry the Second, the most powerful monarchy of Europe, though embroiled with the Church, they groaned afterwards under the tyranny of King John, and this very tyranny procured them the Great Charter, the eternal basis of their freedom. The English then gave their crown to France, drove out the French prince they had called to the throne, and became the terror of the monarchy of Clovis, which seemed on the point of submitting to the yoke. But France at length, after an interval of calamity and madness, displayed its resources, recovered its ancient glory, inseparable from the cause of its kings; triumphed over a haughty enemy, whose victories were the fruit of our fatal dissensions; and to revenge itself, had only occasion to leave it a prey to dissensions still more cruel. Two rival, yet kindred, houses, impelled to arms by rage and ambition, snatched from each other's brows a diadem drenched in blood; princes assassinated princes; the people massacred each other for the choice of a master, and England now became a theatre of anarchy and carnage. Under the Tudors we see tranquillity restored, and the national strength augmented, but liberty destroyed. A prince, violent and capricious, habituates to the chains of despotism this proud and restless nation. He domineers arbitrarily over religion itself; and Rome, for having opposed him, loses at one blow a kingdom which had ever been one of its most fruitful sources of services and of riches. Mary attempts in vain to restore, by severe punishments, a worship which, having truth (?) for its basis, ought to subdue minds by no arms but those of persuasion. She succeeds only in making inconstant hypocrites, or inflexible fanatics; she renders for ever detestable herself, and the faith she wishes to establish. At length Elizabeth reigns. Her genius enchains fortune, fertilises the earth, animates all the arts, opens to her people the immense career of commerce, and fixes, in some degree, in the ocean the foundations of the English dominion. Continually surrounded by enemies, either foreign or domestic, she defeats conspiracies by her prudence, and triumphs by her courage over the forces of Philip the Second; happy, if she had known how to conquer her own heart, and spare a rival whose blood alone tarnishes her memory!

"But how impenetrable are the decrees of Heaven! The son of Mary Stuart succeeds to Elizabeth; the scaffold on which his mother received the stroke of death, serves him as a step to mount the throne of England, from whence his son is destined to be precipitated, to expire on a scaffold also. It is at this period we behold multiplying rapidly before our eyes those celebrated scenes of which the universe furnishes no examples: an absurd fanaticism forming profound systems of policy, at the same time that it signalises itself by prodigies of folly and extravagance: an enlightened enthusiast, a great general and statesman, opening to himself, under the mask of piety, the road to the supreme power: subjects carrying on judicially the trial of a virtuous monarch, and causing him to be publicly beheaded as a rebel: the hypocritical author of this attempt reigning with as much glory as power; rendering himself the arbiter of crowns, and enjoying, even to the tomb, the fruits of his tyranny: the parliament, the slave of the Tudors, the tyrant of the Stuarts, the accomplice and dupe of Cromwell, exercising the noblest right which men can possess over their fellow-creatures, that of making laws, and maintaining their execution. At length from this chaos of horrors comes forth a form of government which excites the admiration of all Europe. A sudden revolution again changes the face of affairs. The lawful heir is acknowledged; his stormy reign develops the sentiments of patriotism; the imprudence of his successor alarms the national spirit of liberty; his subjects revolt, they call in a deliverer; the Stadtholder dethrones without bloodshed his timid and irresolute father-in-law; the usurpation is established by the sanction of the laws, but those very laws impose conditions on the prince, and, whilst he holds the balance of Europe, his will is almost without force in England. After him a woman presides over the destiny of nations, makes France tremble, humbles Louis XIV., and covers herself with immortal glory, by giving him peace, in spite of the clamours of an ambitious cabal. Anne, with less talents, and more virtues than Elizabeth, has merited one of the first places amongst great monarchs. The sceptre passes again into foreign hands, complicated interests embarrass the government, and the British Constitution seems declining from its original principles, till some favourable conjuncture shall arrive, which may restore it to its pristine vigour.

"To this very imperfect summary of the principal epochas let us add the detail of those laws, successively established, to form a rampart to liberty, and lay the foundation of public order; the progress of letters and of sciences, so closely connected with the happiness and glory of states; the singularities of the English genius, profound, contemplative, yet capable of every extreme; the interesting picture of parliamentary debates, fruitful in scenes, the variety and spirit of which equally strike us. The reader will easily conceive that *this history is unparalleled* in its kind. In other countries, princes, nobles, fill the entire theatre; here, *men*, citizens, act a part, which is infinitely more interesting to man.

"Since the publication of Rymer's collection, several able writers have availed themselves of the inestimable materials which that work supplies. Among these, Rapin de Thoyras, a French author, was the first who distinguished himself in this career. As a historian, judicious, exact, methodical, he exhausts his subject, he descends to the minutest particulars; but growing tedious by being too diffuse, he soon overburdens the imagination at the expense of what he ought to engrave on the memory. A more essential reproach which he deserves, is that of betraying a prejudice against his own country (which by the severities of Louis XIV. had incurred the resentment of the Protestants), and of favouring the sect of the Puritans, those dangerous enthusiasts, the system of whose religion tends only to render men savage, and their system of independence to make them factious and rebellious."

Rapin, from whom I have already quoted, is here admitted by his own countryman to be an unexceptionable witness, except in two particulars, one of which is an excellent fault in such an inquiry as that in which we are engaged, where truthful minuteness is required rather than philosophical generalisation or poetical embellishment. The other fault noted against him by the Abbé is his favour for Puritanism, which he insinuates has a tendency to render men savage. Unfortunately for this politic theory, facts tell quite another tale. That portion of history which we have been considering cannot be liable to this last exception of the Abbé, seeing it belongs to a period long anterior to the Reformation, and when the controversies connected therewith had not arisen to give that vigorous exercise to the human mind which has resulted in those splendid achievements in science and art that have since distinguished Europe.

To come to more modern times, the following view of this subject is by *Prévost Paradol*, who seems to have been very strongly impressed with the fact that our race is rapidly spreading abroad, filling up the waste places of the earth, and has, as it were, been given the master-key of the new countries appointed to dominate the world. He seems, however, to have had little knowledge of our real mission, and, perhaps, still less sympathy with it:—
"Two rival powers, but only one as to race, language, customs, and laws—England and the United States of America—are, with the exception of Europe, dominating the world. How is it possible not to recollect we could once have hoped that our race and language would be chosen by European civilisation to invade the remainder of the world? We had every chance on our side. It was France which, through Canada and Louisiana, began to embrace North America; India seemed to belong to us; and were it not for the mistakes political liberty could have spared to our forefathers, the language and blood of France would, in all likelihood, occupy in the world the place the language and the blood of England have irrevocably conquered; for Destiny has spoken, and at least two portions of the globe, America and Oceania, henceforth and for ever belong to the Anglo-Saxon race. Moreover, now-a-days, a book written in English is much more widely read than if it had been written in French; and it is with

English words that the navigator is hailed on almost all the accessible coasts of the earth.

"However, that actual predominance of the Anglo-Saxon race everywhere out of Europe is but a feeble image of what an approaching future has in store for us. According to the most moderate calculation, founded on the increase of the population during the last decennial period, the United States will number more than a hundred millions of inhabitants at the end of the present century—without speaking of the probable annexation of Mexico, and of the extension of the American Republic to the Panama Isthmus. Brazil and the several states of Southern America weigh very lightly by the side of such a power; and they will disappear when the masters of the northern continent think proper to extend themselves. The possible, though improbable, division of the American Republic into several states would very little affect that future; for, as soon as they would be separated, the fractions of that immense empire would soon feel the necessity of fortifying and extending themselves. For instance, had the secession succeeded, there is no doubt whatever that the new Southern Confederation would have invaded Mexico much sooner than the reconstituted American Republic will attempt. At all events, the American continent is, in its whole extent, destined to belong to the Anglo-Saxon race; and, if we take into account the increase of speed which is so very notable in human events, it is very likely that such an important change will be accomplished in the course of about a century or a century and a half.

"It is not the less certain that Oceania belongs for ever to the Anglo-Saxons of Australia and New Zealand, and in that part of the world the march of events will also be very rapid. No doubt the discovery of gold greatly contributed to the rapid increase of the English population in Australia, but immigration has not diminished since the production of wool has become more important than the production of gold. Agriculture will soon predominate, and the plough will soon convert the soil to pasture. Lastly, industry and the merchant navy will show themselves before long, for the Australians will soon be tired of selling raw produce which they can manufacture and ship themselves; already they announce, with some degree of pride, that they export coals into the ports of the far East. Most certainly, if the mineral industry is developed, the coals brought at so great an expense from Europe for the wants of eastern shipping will be unable to compete with the Australian products. Truly, it only suffices to look at the map to perceive the magnificent future reserved to the new states of Australia. Not only the European colonisation of the remainder of Oceania will be their own work (and some day a new Monroe doctrine will forbid old Europe, in the name of the United States of Australia, to have a footing on one of the Pacific Islands); but it is easy to foresee that China, to which they stand nearer than any other civilised nation, will acknowledge them masters sooner or later. It is also certain that the United States will play a great part in the East from the day when their coasts on the Pacific will be in full activity, and when San Francisco, already so commercially busy with the East, will have become a powerful rival in the same quarter of the ocean. But Australia can beat the United States in speed; in any case, she will ultimately contend with the United States for the commercial and political supremacy in the farthest East; for geography has its laws, and when two nations, equally civilised, contend for commercial or political domination over any part in the world, it is the nearest one which has finally the most chance of being successful. Therefore, in all probability, China will be for Australia what India has been for England; and should England collapse one day, it is not the less probable that her Indian Empire would fall into the hands of Australia. But let us put aside all those conjectures. Whatever power (the United States or Australia) may dominate in China, India, and Japan—it may be that England maintains her empire in those regions for a long time, or that she abandons it to the young competitors to whom she gave life—our children are not the less assured to see the Anglo-Saxon race mistress of Oceania as well as of America, and of all the countries of the farthest East that may be dominated, worked, or influenced by the possession of the sea. When affairs shall have reached that climax—and it is not too much to say that two centuries will suffice for it—will it be possible to deny, from one end of the globe to the other, that the world is Anglo-Saxon?

"Neither Russia nor united Germany, supposing they should attain the highest fortune, can pretend to impede that current of things nor prevent that solution—relatively near at hand—of the long rivalry of European races for the ultimate colonisation and domination of the universe. The world will not be Russian, nor German, nor French, alas! nor Spanish. For it can be asserted that, since the great navigation has given the whole world to the enterprise of the European races, three nations were tried one after the other by fate to play the first part in the fortune of mankind, by everywhere propagating their tongue and blood by means of durable colonies, and by transforming, so to say, the whole world to their own likeness. During the sixteenth century it was rational to believe that Spanish civilisation would spread all over the world; but irremediable vices soon dispersed that colonial power, the vestiges of which, still covering a vast space, tell of its ephemeral grandeur. Then came the turn of France; and Louisiana and Canada have preserved the sad remembrance of it. Lastly, England came forward; she definitely accomplished the great work; and England can disappear from the world without taking her work with her—without the Anglo-Saxon future of the world being sensibly changed.

"Even supposing that Russia should possess Constantinople, she will never be able to balance the naval power of the Anglo-Saxons, and her military progresses on the Asiatic continent will be at once stopped when she happens to meet either England in India, the United States or Australia in China. Furthermore, no power, however grand and potent, can pretend to firmly extend its race and blood by domineering over and deriving profit from submitted people, when it is impossible to assimilate them, or to expel them from their native soil, or to replace them on that soil. For instance, had the colonising work of England been confined to make profit of India, there would not be any reason, even now, that the world should belong to the Anglo-Saxon race. We must always distinguish a factory from a colony worthy of her name. India is but a factory; but Northern America, populated with emigrants, has been an English colony, as Australia is now, and it is through these two strong branches that the English race has taken possession of two continents. Russia could not do that, even in the supposition that her good fortune should encounter no obstacle. Firstly, there is nothing to prove that the Russian race is naturally emigrant and colonising; besides, the countries which can be usefully colonised, and that can still be occupied in the world, are without importance compared to the two American and Australian continents invaded and definitely acquired by the Anglo-Saxons.

"And it is owing to the second motive that united Germany cannot entertain the hope to counterpoise the Anglo-Saxon in the remainder of the world; for, on the one hand, Germany is popular and prolific for emigrants, and on the other—supposing that her great fortune should be completed according to her own wishes—she would have with Holland (as she has already with Hamburg) a navy and a population of sailors at her disposal. But Holland could bring to united Germany only factories like Java and Sumatra, and could give no space proper to the foundation of a truly German colony. Therefore it is very probable that the tide, so rich of German emigration, would continue to flow, without any profit for the metropolis, into the veins of the United States of America, which have absorbed them till now. Moreover, should Germany, always jealous and proud, resolve to direct that tide of emigrants towards some war-colony over which her flag should wave, that war-state, the situation of which is not easily to be ascertained, would never counterbalance the American and Australian continents, henceforth belonging irrevocably to the Anglo-Saxon race.

"Thus we can foretell through imagination that future situation of the world, and glance at that picture, the main lines of which are, so to say, already sketched by the hands of fate. And if we are inclined seriously to ask ourselves in what time earth shall have taken that new form, we shall easily perceive that two centuries are scarcely necessary to bring to its apogee the Anglo-Saxon grandeur in the Oceanian region as well as on the American continent. That greatness once established, no one shall be able to menace it from without, like Rome, which was surrounded on every side by a barbarous world. There are no more barbarous nations, and the race which will be invested with the guidance of mankind will have to fear neither the competition nor the appearance of a new race."

Victor Hugo, in Le Rhin, wrote thus in 1842:—

"England holds the six greatest gulfs in the world, which are the Gulfs of Guinea, Oman, Bengal, Mexico, Baffin, and Hudson; she opens or shuts at her pleasure nine seas, the North Sea, the English Channel, the Mediterranean, Adriatic, and Ionian Seas, the Archipelago, Persian Gulf, Red Sea, and Sea of the Antilles. She possesses an empire in America, New Britain; in Asia an empire, Hindustan; and in the great ocean a world, New Holland.

"Besides, she has innumerable isles upon all the seas, and before all the continents, like ships on station and at anchor; and with which, island and ship herself planted before Europe, she communicates, so to speak, without dissolving her continuity, by her innumerable vessels, floating islands.

"The English people is not of itself a sovereign people, but it is for other nations an empire. It governs feudally 2,370,000 Scotch, 8,280,000 Irish, 244,000 Africans, 60,000 Australians, 1,200,000 Americans, and 124,000,000 of Asiatics; that is to say, 14,000,000 of English possess upon the earth 137,000,000 of men.

"All the places we have named in the pages just read are the hooks of the immense net whereby England has taken the world."

The writer of the following does not trace the connection between the people to whom the Promises were given and the people to whom they are fulfilled; but he very strongly recognises the wonderful development of our race, and the magnificent work set before them:—

"Many signs betoken that, in a comparatively short period—it may be a century or so from the present hour—the world will have undergone a greater social revolution than any that has passed over it since the Christian era. We do not say that in a century the despotisms of the world will be supplanted by free governments, and all idolatries replaced by Christian churches; what we say is, that it is demonstrable that a greatly meliorated era is at hand, the immediate precursor of the world's evangelisation, if not that very evangelisation itself. There is an agency at work at this hour, of such steady and progressive force, that in a century or so it will inevitably create a new world around us. The agency in question is the growth and diffusion of the Anglo-Saxon race, perhaps the most remarkable social phenomenon of our times. A recent census of the increase of the population of the United States, founded on a long series of years, shows that the growth of the Anglo-Saxon race, in countries affording free scope for its trial and development, is in the ratio of forty per cent. every ten years. Taking into account only the colonies of England, and supposing the increase of the whole to be in the ratio of forty per cent. every ten years, we shall in fifty years from this time have between thirty and forty millions of British people scattered over the earth; and, in a century from the present hour, there will be some two hundred millions of Anglo-Saxons on the globe. This is irrespective of the population of America. This is the most powerful visible agency by which God is at this day changing the social and spiritual condition of the globe; and what an overwhelming importance does it give to home and colonial missions! Were the Anglo-

Saxon stock sanctified and holy, it would soon fill the earth with holy nations.

"How remarkable the fact that the *Anglo-Saxon* race should be the one only race that is expanding! What a sign of rich and manifold blessing to the world! It might have been the Muscovite, or the Spaniard, or the Hindu, or the Moslem, who had become the coloniser of the world. How terrible in that case would have been the prospect before the species! The blackness of darkness would have rested upon the future. We would have felt that we were rapidly and inevitably approximating the extinction of liberty, and that a revolution was in progress, which would as surely bring the world under the shadow of a universal tyranny and a universal idolatry, as the revolution of the earth on its axis brings it under the shadow of night. Happy is it for the world that the one race, which is the depositary of Christianity and liberty, is the one race that is expanding itself over the globe! Here is a revolution in progress on a scale as vast as its consequences must be blessed—a revolution which will as surely bring all 'the ends of the earth' into the light of Christianity and of all the civilisation which follows it, as the turning of the earth on its axis brings it out of night into day.

"Amazing phenomenon! On all sides dead or dying nations; one trunk alone, the Anglo-Saxon to wit, has life in it, but a life so vigorous that it is 'filling the earth with its boughs' (Gen. xlix. 22; Isa. xxvii. 6).

"It is a great truth, too little pondered, that to nations, as to individuals, the gospel brings life and immortality."

Those who deny that Protestantism, and freedom of discussion as connected therewith, have a tendency to invigorate and elevate the human mind, have the greater need of our theory to account for the manifest superiority of Protestant nations over those that have retained all the pretended advantages of the Papacy, which itself might have perished from the earth but for the vigorous interference of England; whereby the supposed rights of their ghostly father were protected, and also the throne was restored to "his most Christian Majesty" the King of France. How is it that England has been enabled to take such a lead among the nations, and to become such an emulated example of literary, commercial, manufacturing, political, and even military success—such an admired type of free institutions—if there be not something, either in their early or later training, to account for this; if, notwithstanding all the thunders of the Vatican, there be not under this people "the everlasting arms;" and if there be not with them the favour of Him who hath said to the outcast house of Israel, "No weapon that is formed against thee shall prosper, and every tongue that shall rise against thee in judgment thou shalt condemn"?[1]

It was predicted that, previous to the great promised outpouring of the Spirit in "the Latter Days," of which "the former rain" in apostolic days was an assured pledge, the Lord would be known as having dealt both kindly and wondrously with Israel; that He would be known as being in the midst of them for blessing, and around them for a sure defence. Thus it is written, Joel ii. 26-28—

> "And ye shall eat in plenty,
> And be satisfied;
> And praise the name of the Lord your God,
> That hath dealt wondrously with you:

---

[1] Ephraim and Manasseh were to be as types of blessing to their brethren (Gen. xlviii. 16 22).

And my people shall never be ashamed.
And ye shall know that I am in the midst of Israel,
And that I am the Lord your God,
    And none else,
And my people shall never be ashamed.
And it shall come to pass afterward,
That I will pour out my Spirit upon all flesh."

"HEARKEN unto Me, My People (*Ammi*, עַמִּי),
And give ear unto Me, O My Nation;
For a law (*Torah*, תּוֹרָה) shall proceed from Me,
And I will make My judgment to rest,
For a light of the Peoples (*Ammim*, עַמִּים).
My righteousness—near:
My salvation (*Yishuia*, יְשׁוּעִי) is gone forth,
And Mine arm shall judge the Peoples (*Ammim*, עַמִּים).
The ISLES shall wait on Me,
And on Mine arm shall they trust.
Lift up your eyes to the heavens,
And look upon the earth (*eretz*, אֶרֶץ) beneath;
For the heavens shall vanish away like smoke,
And the earth (*eretz*) shall wax old like a garment,
And they that dwell therein shall die in like manner:
But My salvation (*Yishuia*) shall be for ever,
And My righteousness shall not be abolished."—ISA. li. 4-6.

XX.

RESUMÉ OF THE EVIDENCE FOR OUR ISRAELITISH ORIGIN.

The Subjects discussed in these Lectures.—The Scriptures the Word of God and not of Man.—Language.—Useful Application of the Subject as revealing the true character, a God of Truth, Faithfulness, and everlasting Love: as accounting for the Desolations of the Land, and the Favours bestowed upon this People.—Their Tendency to Improvement, Adaptation for Universality, and singularly favourable Position for doing Good point out our Duty to the Jew on the one hand, and the Gentile on the other, equally our Brethren.

WE have now in some measure seen the unity of the works, word, and ways of Jehovah. We have observed that from the very beginning He indicated His gracious purpose with regard to "a peculiar people" (Exod. xix. 6); that when He laid the foundations of the earth, He had a particular respect to that portion of our globe which has since been called the Land of Israel—the most centrally placed with regard to all lands and races of men, and well fitted for becoming the meeting-place of all nations and the Throne of Universal Empire; and that as it was probably the site of Eden—that abode of blessedness which Adam lost by his fall into sin—so is it certainly to be the peculiar habitation of holiness, peace, glory, and joy during the approaching age. We have seen that prophecy anticipates important changes there, calculated to render it that happy land which is promised. We have seen that what was dimly intimated at first was more fully unfolded to the fathers, Abraham, Isaac, and Jacob, in whose names three great Birthright Blessings were written. These Promises, we saw, respect the land and the seed. They also imply the resurrection of the saints, seeing that to these fathers the land was promised as well as to their children; for although during their former lifetime they were not given "so much as even to set their foot on," yet after they were dead, God declared Himself to be "the God of Abraham, Isaac, and Jacob," as if He still intended to fulfil the promises made unto them, which He could not do but by raising them from the dead. And thus, indeed, our Saviour proves the resurrection (Matt. xxii. 31, 32).

The "seed," promised unto the fathers comprehended, as we saw, the one seed Christ, to whom the land was absolutely promised, and the multitudinous seed to be blessed in Him, and made a blessing unto all the earth. This latter multitudinous seed was to be distinguished from a merely adopted posterity, and also from the children of Ishmael and Esau; of the sons of Jacob, Joseph was chosen, and Ephraim of his sons to be the father of this chosen seed, this "multitude or fulness of nations," of which he was as truly to be the father as Judah was to be, according to the flesh, the father of the one seed Christ.

From the beginning God avowed His purpose of making this numerous seed a blessing to the nations. They were to constitute a kind of "measuring-line," or *cable* (see Heb.), by which one portion after another would be taken into the Lord's inheritance (Deut. xxxii. 9). For this they required a peculiar training, that they might be fitted for occupying all places and stations, for acquiring and communicating all knowledge to all the families of mankind, and especially the knowledge of God as presented in His Word.

This training, we saw, they were given progressively and continuously in the fathers, and after they became a nation, until the very eve of their departure from the land.

We saw that the purpose of God with regard to Israel, as avowed from the beginning, was not accomplished during their sojourn in the land. And we might have more fully seen, that when they were being taken away, as well as continually afterwards, God by the prophets recognised the Promises He had made, and declared they should yet be fulfilled. We saw that the Captivity was complete, except as to those who escaped from the land; and that those who were taken away captive were removed into the same quarter as that to which history traces the Saxon race.

We have adverted to the case of the other house of Israel, which as being left in the land, and having generally borne the name of "Jews," are supposed to have remained distinct from all other people. We have seen that the best portion of them must have become mingled among the Gentiles; and the worst of the Gentiles—the Canaanites and Edomites, children emphatically of the curse—having become one with them, they have become guilty of the sins of both, the curse of which they have been enduring; that they have nothing in the flesh whereof to boast, and cannot obtain possession of the land by the old covenant; that they can only obtain a peaceable settlement as being viewed in the One Seed Christ, and as being joined to the multitudinous seed to come, especially of Ephraim.

We then went forth in search of lost Israel, and reasoning from analogy as to the distribution of the three grand races of mankind, we were led to look northward among the children of Japhet. We saw, moreover, that the Word of God expressly points to the north as the place into which the children of Ephraim had gone, and out of which they were chiefly to be brought. In that direction we are also pointed by the great prophetic line of empires, and by the progress of Israel's punishment. Thither also tended almost invariably the journeys of all those who were divinely appointed to minister the Word, which was specially promised to " light upon Israel," and of which they were to be the great adminstrators to the nations; the preaching of Christ and His apostles, the Epistles, and the Apocalypse, all affording clearest proof of the peculiar and intense interest felt by the Great Shepherd of Israel in the north and north-west.

Having thus ascertained our course, we proceeded to investigate the localities north-west of those to which Israel had been carried, and immediately met with the "high heaps" raised by Israel in the way as they went, which upon examination were found to contain tombs, having every indication of being Israelitish. They are, moreover, said to be those of the ancestors of the Khazares or Co-mani, the ancestors of the Cossacks, who are of the same race with the Anglo-Saxons. We saw that the names of rivers between the Don and the Danube give also clear indications of Israel's sojourn there; and even Mœsia, the country south of the Danube, and ancient inheritance of the Getæ or Goths, with all else, seemed to tell that there had sojourned the disciples of Moses, who were there afflicted many a time. By the Persians, Macedonians, and Romans they were successively attacked, and more and more subjected to slaughter; till ultimately, by the Barbarians, they were driven in upon the Roman Empire, and obliged to occupy their present important position.

We took a glance at the most ancient poem which these

2 A

nations are said to possess, containing their traditional prophecies, and saw that it bears full evidence of their being children of the prophets who had foretold these calamities, and also the future blessedness of the "sons of the two brothers," in the house of their Father.

We then saw that Isaiah clearly foretells Israel's being brought out into these maritime parts; and whilst the nations their enemies would pass away from before them, they would be given place here in which to renew their strength. We saw that the great "whirlwind," described by Jeremiah as being raised up from the ends of the earth, and sweeping once and again, and a third time, around Jerusalem, ultimately spent its fury in the north, and describes that dreadful confusion which took place there at the time the Roman Empire was broken up; that the dreadful incursions upon the Germans, and subsequent breaking forth of the Gothic nations, are correspondently described in history. And we saw that the changes then produced in Europe of all kinds bore ample testimony to the truth that the new nations which then came into possession of these countries were the nations that were "to come of Jacob."

We took a glance at "the escaped of Israel," with regard to whom, although not so much is promised, yet much might also be expected, and saw that there was every reason to believe they occupied the place of "a measuring-line" to the Lord's inheritance in the first ages of Christianity, as those who have sprung from "the remnant" led captive are now appointed to be unto "the ends of the earth."

Philology has now the same voice as history with regard to our having been somehow connected with Media. *The language of a people is not an infallible test of their origin;* still it may do something, as indicating through what countries they have passed. It may speak of the tribes with which they have been connected, and the nature of their transactions with different peoples. It is remarkable that the Indo-Germanic languages are traced to Media as their common centre. As the Jews learned in Babylon to speak Chaldee, and the Normans in France learned to speak French, so Israel would learn the language of "the cities of the Medes."[1] Yet it was not likely that they would altogether forget the language of Egypt, which may account for a considerable portion of Coptic being found in the English. Neither were Hebrew words likely to be altogether ignored; and these remain, with Ephraimitish pronunciation. A good deal, also, of the idiom must have remained; and such certainly is the case, which is said to have been poured into the languages of Western Europe generally. A knowledge, therefore, of Hebrew, and of the different languages spoken by the nations dwelling along the route by which Israel came into Europe, and a comparison therewith of the English and kindred dialects of the Gothic, will be found most interesting and useful by those who have leisure and opportunity to pursue the inquiry. This *Sharon Turner* has already partly accomplished, and see Lecture XI.

We chose the ANGLO-SAXONS whereby to exemplify the truth of our propositions, showed that they came from the east of Europe, that they are even traced back into the very part of Asia to which Israel had been carried captive, and that they possessed all the physical, moral, and intellectual marks which were given to Israel as qualifying

---

[1] Prudentius (A.D. 380) in his *Hamartigenia* asserts that exiled Israel had even changed their language.

them for their important destined position among the nations, and for which they had been in training.

We saw, further, that their social, domestic, and civil arrangements were most minutely correspondent, and that all the peculiar excellences of the English Constitution came through a Saxon medium from their Israelitish forefathers. We also saw that their skill in the useful and ornamental arts—particularly those connected with religious worship—equally bore evidence to the truth that this was the very race which had been trained under Moses. Their religion itself, with all its predicted corruptions, we saw was equally full of the same decisive evidence; and the marvel came to be, that so much had been left to this people to bear such ample and undeniable evidence to the truth of their origin. We also saw that God's dealings with them since their embrace of Christianity exactly corresponds with the idea that the English are indeed the chosen people of God, "the cord, measuring-line, or *cable* of the Lord's inheritance."

We have yet to consider the abundant information which the Scriptures afford on the different subjects treated of in these Lectures. (See "Title-Deeds of the Holy Land," "Mission of Elijah," "Watchmen of Ephraim:" Nisbet & Co.; W. Macintosh & Co., London.) But we are already, I trust, more and more convinced that the historical and prophetical parts of the Old and New Testaments are worthy of a much more careful perusal than has yet been given them; especially by comparing one part with another as being all parts of one whole given forth by the same Spirit. (See also "The Gospel Treasury," compiled by Mr Mimpriss, but laboriously edited by the late author.)

Let us never forget that first rule, that "no prophecy of

Scripture is of any private interpretation." Let it not be confined to the supposed private thoughts, feelings, or circumstances of the individual who penned it; for it was not *his* word. Holy men of old spake not of themselves, but "as moved by the Spirit of God." God is a God of truth; just and right is He; and He will yet fully vindicate both His Word and His Ways. I trust that to this the view will be seen to conduce which we have been taking of Israel, whom the Word of God very much concerns; from the time the Promises were so surely given to the Fathers, throughout both history and prophecy, until they have issued in the promised "multitude of nations," which have, even so far, supplanted their enemies and been made a joy to all the earth.

God has made use of human speech and writing to communicate His will; and He has made His whole providential dealings with His people to bear witness to the truth of His Word, so as to make us feel and realise the more that we are in the hands of a wise and faithful Creator, who has been prospective of all that He has done and was about to do. (See "The Being of God," by the late author.)

"When God laid the strong foundations of the earth—deposited the iron beneath our soil, and produced that luxuriant vegetation which has been condensed into those immense coal-fields, which with the iron are now so much in requisition—He was preparing for *our* days of railways and steam-power.

"When He sprinkled the gold-dust over the earth, east and west, it was in order that it might draw out *our* population to the widest extent, and at the most fitting moment, just when we needed this outlet: even in very faithfulness to His covenant promise that EPHRAIM should become 'a multitude of nations,' and after *we* had been given uncommon facilities for availing *ourselves* of it.

"Nor was it until abundant provision had been made for the great increase of population that the gold was discovered. Australia had become to a large extent a food-growing country, and was covered abundantly with flocks and herds, before men's eyes were opened to see the gold lying underneath, or the hands of so many employed in gathering it.

"And so has it been with DIVINE REVELATION. Among the most remote and abundant predictions are those in Genesis, which relate, as we have seen, to our own people and time. From the beginning God foresaw and fore-appointed by revelation the people with regard to whom He hath dealt so marvellously in His providence, and most highly favoured by His works of creation.

"It is a grave consideration to me, my friends, that He has created *us* by His power, has instructed *us* by His wisdom, and by His goodness has furnished *us* with the means of blessing all nations; that thousands of years ago it was said of us, '*This people have I formed for myself; they shall show forth my praise*' (Isa. xliii. 21)."

This is one of the most powerful arguments in favour of the Divine inspiration of the Old Testament Scriptures, as clearly evincing that they are no Jewish imposture. Otherwise the Jews would not have given the Promises to a lost tribe, but would have taken care either to have secured their own right to them in the first instance (which is most emphatically not the case), or themselves constituted heirs to the people to whom these Promises were made, which the prophets do not at all allow; although the Jews themselves have been ever grasping at this, and we have very weakly conceded their claim, to the darkening of Scripture and hardening them in their unbelief.

No; let us look truth honestly in the face, and we have nothing to fear. He who has taken up his religion as a matter of worldly convenience may shrink from the investigation, through fear of finding the ground false upon which he is seeking to make himself at ease. But let him who firmly believes in a God whose "counsels of old" have been "faithfulness and truth" look to his standing, and find how sure it is. Let him endeavour to know what He hath purposed who knoweth the end from the beginning; and in the light of that knowledge let him look around to see what God hath *done*. Let him not endeavour to force the Word of God to his limited preconceptions of what it *must* mean; but, fairly receiving it for his teacher, let him look into the working of God throughout past ages, for the development of His avowed purposes, and he will find Him to be indeed a God of truth, "wonderful in counsel and excellent in working."

It is a most important movement that science has arrested the attention of those whose minds have been turned away from the Word of God; and I would very earnestly recommend the Christian and the phrenologist to take a closer and more impartial view of each other's labours.[1] When suspicion leads to strict scrutiny, so that

---

[1] I cannot but acknowledge my very great obligations to the science of mind, which infidelity has tried to make its own, and which many Christians have too weakly conceded to the enemies of the truth. So far as my experience goes, all true knowledge tends to confirm the Word of God; and no branch of science with which I am acquainted has this tendency more than phrenology, when rightly understood. Of this I have had many years' experience, and can truly say, that by this consideration I have been chiefly influenced in the attention I have for several years been giving to one of the most important branches of human know-

nothing may be received but what is truth, it is well; but its injury is incalculable when it turns away from the truth. No true science has anything to fear from free and full investigation, but much from misrepresentation and neglect. The abuse of phrenology should make us the more zealous in our endeavours to rescue it to the praise of our God, who is no less the Author of mind than He is of the Scriptures. If we have objections, let us honestly see whether they truly belong to that which we reject, or are not rather taken from the perversions or misrepresentations of others. Some there are who even sport with falsehood, and delight in deceiving the ignorant, or in pandering to their foolish prejudices. The sooner they are left alone the better.

And now, may we not more and more admire the faithfulness of the God of Israel, seeing that He hath fulfilled, or is fulfilling, exactly as declared from the beginning, all the Promises which He made unto our fathers and confirmed by His oath, and upon which so much, with regard to both our faith and hope, is built in the New Testament?

We see that these Promises were more than mere words, and that the use made of them in the reasoning of the apostles is more legitimate and conclusive than the whisperings of our unbelief would allow. Yea, saith Divine Wisdom—

ledge. The beautiful and minute adaptation of the Word of God to the mind of man—the value of that mental training which God has been giving to His chosen people, the distinction of races so constantly observed in Scripture, and that great law of Nature and of Providence whereby the child is viewed in the parent, and the parent is as it were dealt with in the child - could not have been so well understood without the true knowledge of our mental constitution. (See voluminous MSS. on this subject by the late author, now appearing in "The Standard of Israel.")

> "All the words of my mouth are righteousness,
> Nothing froward or perverse in them :
> They are all plain to him that understandeth,
> And right to them that find knowledge."

The seed of the Promises having been sown in the fathers, there was first "the blade" when Israel were brought out of Egypt, and were given possession of the land. This was an earnest of what was to come when there should be the greater redemption and more permanent possession. After that was "the ear," when, under David, the proper kingly type was given to the scattered form of the Israelitish commonwealth, and when the Ark was lodged in the glorious temple built by Solomon. This was the *form* of the fruit, not the fruit itself, which at length was given when the One Seed Christ appeared among men. He was "the full corn in the ear." Then was given the very substance of the Promises, and it has ripened unto the harvest when the multitudinous seed shall be made one with Christ, when He is in them "the hope of glory," when Ephraim shall be found the Lord's "firstborn" in Christ, who is the One Son, "the Heir of all things," by whom "the many sons" shall be "led into glory." Such is the glorious end at which we are to aim—

The Glory of God in the Salvation of Israel

—that they may be "vessels of glory" unto all the ends of the earth. Let us sow the good seed of the Word; and it will certainly prosper in that whereunto the Lord hath sent it. Let us prize every word. God hath not given a stone in place of bread to His children. If we think or feel as if it were otherwise, it is because we have not read the Word of God aright. Let us know that Word for ourselves, and make it known to others.

Christ, who hath fulfilled the covenant, is alone the rightful Heir of the earthly possession, as well as of the heavenly inheritance. True, His people will with Him "inherit all things;" but He hath Himself promised to come and give them possession. If, now, patiently continuing in well-doing, we seek through Him for glory, honour, and immortality, when He comes we shall live together with Him, and stand in His presence, being constituted "kings and priests unto God."

Now we may see why the north and west have been so peculiarly favoured; why it was that the journeys of the apostles and their epistles all proceeded in this direction, although the east and south were vastly more populous; how it is that many great empires are passed over, while those that run as it were in a line north-westward are particularly noticed in prophecy; how it is that so much is said about the *Isles* in connection with Israel; and how all the peculiar blessings of the God of Providence, as well as of redemption, have hence arisen or hither have been sent.

Thus we may account for the universal and continually-improving genius of this race, evidently designed to spread abroad and cover the globe, and in every respect fitted for universality, especially as the teachers of the world. They are a people "formed" by God Himself for the special design of showing forth His praise.

We may also see why all the varied instrumentality for acquiring and communicating blessings of all kinds to all parts of the earth has been bestowed upon these nations; and why such favourable positions, so widely scattered and so variously placed all over the globe, have been given to the British nation, the people of the covenant, in particular. The like hath not been done to any other nation; the position which is occupied by England is that unto which Israel is called, and for which they were gifted; and "the gifts and calling of God are without repentance."

And now behold the important position of these nations as being equally related to the Jew and the Gentile, that they should do good unto both, as God may give them opportunity, which He is doing abundantly. They have the Jews among them, and they are among the Gentiles; and the God of Israel, the Master of the Harvest, is looking on, and soon will appear, to the joy of those who have given themselves to His service.

Let us duly regard the claims our God has upon us for most loving and lively obedience; He hath been unceasing in His care, and marvellous in His love to the house of Israel. He is indeed fulfilling His Word:

> "In the place where it was said unto them,
> Not My People;
> There it shall be said unto them,
> SONS OF THE LIVING GOD!"

XXI.

PROVIDENCE AND PROPHECY.

I.

"Let them grow into a multitude of nations."—GEN. xlviii. 16.

[With the exception of a few letters, and part of Lecture X., the following was the late author's last writing, being prepared in the latter part of 1869, as notes for lectures to be delivered in aid of a mission to the Druses of the Haurân. The dying words of an old Lebanon Druse to one of the teachers had painfully reminded him of the cry of that remarkable people to the English Government, in the days of William Pitt, to send them English teachers, of which he had heard in his youth—"My hope is in Jesus! O schoolmaster, take care of my children!" and in much weakness he resolved to do what he could to stir the hearts of younger men in their behalf. Five schools have, since 1872, been established there, principally through the efforts of the Rev. W. Parry, D.C.L., and his late devoted wife; but what are these among so many? "Lift up your eyes, and look upon the fields."]

AT the commencement of the present century, just when the greatest development of our race was about to take effect, in some minds there was a fear of our multiplying more quickly than our means of comfortable existence. But the Author of our Being, who is also the God of Providence, has thrown contempt upon such niggardly philosophy, by opening up in all directions outlets for our surplus population, where they may pasture their families abundantly, or be provided with remunerative labour; where, also, those who have the genius to devise, the skill to execute, or the capital to be employed in any useful department of human industry, may have ample opportunity of turning to good account their various means of improving and multiplying the necessaries, conveniences, and elegances of life. God has given us a teeming population, and ample space for its development in all "the ends of the earth." He has given us hearts to desire good things for others, as well as for ourselves. He has also given us heads to plan, and hands to execute. We are the actual heirs of the rich inheritance of Old Testament revelation given to ancient Israel; and to us has been sent the gospel, so fully "confirmed" among and by the case of the Jews. The literature of Greece, and much for which Rome was remarkable; the traffic of Tyre, and the maritime highways of Spain; many things from many lands—yea, the treasures of the whole earth, have been freely opened to England.

We have abundance of shipping to convey our overflowing agricultural and artisan population wherever they are most needed for their own good as well as for that of others. We have engineering power, managed by ever-increasing skill, for the removal of all obstructions to their obtaining plentifully and distributing bountifully "the precious things of the earth, and the fulness thereof" (Deut. xxxiii. 16). Let us arise, and endeavour to occupy for the blessing of all nations that which the God of providence, according to His ancient purpose, hath bestowed upon us. Let us earnestly and with purpose endeavour to carry out the blessings of Christian civilisation wherever we can. If we do not use the means with which we have been entrusted by God for the purposes designed, we may be quite certain that they will become to us a curse instead of a blessing.

As military colonists the Anglo-Saxons, whom we have identified as Ephraim, came into England, settling along the south and east coasts of the island, which they gradually filled up. They also spread over Ireland from England, Scotland, and Wales, having previously supplied many of the Irish gentry with English wives, to which kind of union the former were extremely partial, long before Great Britain and Ireland were made one by Act of Parliament.

Having renewed their strength in these islands, our race proceeded still farther westward, crossing the Atlantic, colonising New England, Nova Scotia, and the eastern coast of North America, from French Canada in the north to Louisiana in the south. Thence, with some help from our brethren in Europe, we are spreading over the whole American continent, from the Atlantic to the Pacific. "There the glorious Lord," may be said to *have given* "unto us a place of broad rivers and streams," wherein no attack of foreign armament need be feared: "wherein shall go no galley with oars, neither shall gallant ship pass thereby." A peaceful highway for friendly and commercial interchange is secured, from the outgoings of the Mississippi and Missouri, until their waters mingle with the Gulf Stream, which is said ultimately to spread its genial influence over the British Isles.

We can rejoice in the welfare of our American brethren, even although they may lack some of the institutions for which we have a favour, such as our hereditary lawgivers, and our Queen; and without a grudge we can hear them say,

"The Lord is our Judge; the Lord is our Lawgiver;
The Lord is our King; He will save us."—Isa. xxxiii. 22.

So long as America sends by the Gulf Stream her joy-giving waters to kiss our shores, so long let us return the salutation in words of amity and deeds of kindness. Let us also say in warm-hearted associated effort, as carrying out our common mission of dispensing blessing to all mankind, "WE ARE ONE PEOPLE IN THE LORD!"

If from the Gulf of Mexico we look more immediately around, and think of Trinidad, Jamaica, and our West Indian possessions, and then pass on to the other extremity of America, where our rich aristocrats are beginning to pasture their flocks, we may see the rich provision which the Shepherd of Israel has made for all ranks and conditions of our men somewhere upon the earth. What a pity that more of our lady friends do not think of doing what they can to save their brothers from being lost in the wilderness, for want of sisters and wives to help them to build up English homes, whence Bible light, love, and healing might be diffused in the dark world around! Men and women come into existence in pretty equal proportions. Most certainly this law of our nature should not be overlooked in arrangements with regard to colonisation. The sexes are needful to each other for their mutual assistance and comfort. It is undoubtedly better that "every man should have his own wife, and every woman her own husband."

At present the mother-country abounds in that which is the most essential element of social happiness, but which is too much wanting in our colonies, and for want of which so many of our countrymen who have gone abroad to push their fortunes pine away in the midst of plenty, or take as their companions those who are no proper progenitors of the race chosen to minister blessing to all the families of mankind.

Let us lay it fully to heart, that mothers have fully as much to do in forming the mental and moral, as well as the physical character of a race or family as fathers. Our sisters have been accumulating at home; not always profitably to themselves, whatever it may have been to the community. Let them now think more of how they can best help to ameliorate the condition of things abroad. True, in many cases their home training has not been of a sufficiently practical nature; but those of the community who have the general welfare at heart might speedily remedy that evil in the rising generation, and even now contrive some way of educating young women to be good wives and mothers in our colonies, or at least for being useful in helping their brothers, husbands, and friends to the enjoyment of domestic comfort, and also in distributing blessing to the nations.

It must be a terrible hindrance, when the women who preside in the homes of our colonists, and who are forming the minds of those who are hereafter to represent us among the nations, are alien in religion and race; having therefore comparatively no sympathy with us in our great mission from God to the world.

None of us who remain at home would like to ask our lady friends to leave us. But why should we selfishly hold them back, when we know it is for their good that they should help to strengthen our brethren abroad? And surely those men who themselves go should take measures to facilitate compliance with their invitation, when they say "Come!"

In England our advantages are great. Climate, soil, freedom from "the plagues of Egypt," social privileges, religious and intellectual society, and, through the perfection of our postal, railway, and telegraphic systems, facilities for intercourse with the world. All that other countries possess, we may have, and much that is in a manner peculiar to ourselves. Our opportunities, not only of receiving, but also of doing good, are most remarkable. Whatever our means or ability, we can scarcely be without ample opportunities of using them in the spheres which we either might or do occupy at home. And therefore, there is no great inducement to emigrate, for those who have the best means of going abroad, to reach the best, highest, and most numerous enjoyments of life, or to possess in the greatest degree the luxury of doing good. And surely our own kindred, and those who have contributed to our wealth, or in connection with whom it has been bestowed upon us, and who either by nature or by Providence have claims upon our best efforts in their behalf, should be preferred to mere strangers. We do not *need* to go abroad to seek fields for the exercise of our benevolence.

Eastward we have spread out to India and China, where we have much for which to be thankful, on account of the means put into our hands of benefiting its teeming millions; but much also to repent of for the way we have used our power, notwithstanding God's wonderful manifestations of readiness to interpose in our behalf, when we honoured Him in speaking the truth and working righteousness.

Southward, we have Africa and Australia; round both of which we are rapidly planting numbers of states, which already, in the opulence of their cities, and the value of their productions, begin to rival those of our American brethren.

The dangers of excessive emigration ought, however, as well to be looked at, and which may easily be seen in the present condition of almost all the great empires which have dominated over the world. In the first place, it is to be considered that conquest itself must naturally tend to drain conquering countries of all native energy. Their men of ability and enterprise are given duties to perform, and posts to occupy in different parts of the world, where ultimately many of them leave their offspring; and thus not unfrequently their energy comes to be heired by others than those who planted them in the subject provinces. These coming to be possessed by the more active spirits of the race are apt to take the leadership from the more quietly disposed portion of the community which remain at home.

We have a great warning set before us in the state of those countries upon which the light of civilisation first dawned, where the greatest, most famous, and most populous empires existed, the most splendid buildings were erected, and cities most strongly fortified and most richly furnished. Now they are empty and desolate; the lands are left uncultivated and unproductive, and treasure, if possessed, is hid away in holes and corners. Even in those cities which remain in some measure inhabited, whatever of beauty or richness may be in them is in a manner concealed, and turned away from the public; the paths that lead from one house to another or to places of resort being left unwholesomely filthy. There is no consideration for each other's comfort or well-being. How has all this happened? We doubt not, from the causes assigned in the Bible.

The Governments looked upon themselves as the proprietors of the people and of their land and possessions, and let out the people to be fleeced by those who had no permanent interest in the good of the state, but who looked to present profit. Independently of those who are sent out in an official capacity to the colonies or other dependencies of an empire, and who may find inducements to settle abroad, there are of course many who voluntarily remove from a country where rents and taxation become oppressive, especially when men lose confidence in God and in each other, and cease to have the power of employing the artizan and labourer through the profits of their industry. Men become too wise to work together, and do their utmost to stand in each other's way. Manufactures are stopped, production ceases, commerce seeks another market as the consumer finds a substitute or learns to do without. Property becomes depreciated, houses tenantless, and lands uncultivated. There might still be much employment for the people; but money is withdrawn from circulation and left in comparative disuse, waiting for a more favourable opportunity or a safer investment. Those who have money upon lands or other property must wait to realise it. In the meantime those who have only their hands or wits by which to live, must make their way out of the country, and others who have something may be glad to favour the escape of the poor by whose labour all must live.

Sometimes the depopulation of city and country has been facilitated by war, anarchy, utter disregard of the laws of health, and the unprofitable cultivation of the land. Sometimes the land and people both have been farmed out to those who could squeeze the most out of them, without any regard whatever to the advantage of the people, or the protection and improvement of the property. Men are discouraged from sowing the ground, for they know not who shall reap. If they build, they must not invite the tax-gatherer or the robber by giving to their dwellings an inviting frontage; and if they have money, it must be carefully concealed.

II.

We have seen that our people have gone forth unto "all the ends of the earth." The central land for the whole world is therefore the most central for our race. That land into which God led our father Abraham at the beginning is the best for the reunion of his children, that their scattered lights being gathered into one, they may become what our Saviour said His disciples should be, "the light of the world." This, by His grace, they can best be, as occupying the midst of the space to be illuminated. Certain it is, that the central land should not be left, as it now is, in comparative darkness and confusion.

When we consider the advantages of the quarter we propose now to occupy, there is much that should induce us to look Zionward. And first, we should take this into view, that in going to the land of Israel we are not going from home, but *to* the country with which we have been most familiar from infancy. Our history and poetry, law and gospel—much that we look back upon with reverence in the past, as well as of what we hope for in the future—is connected with "the Holy Land." Here our father Abraham pastured his flocks, and talked with God; hither Moses led the children of Israel; here Joshua conquered, David and Solomon reigned, Elijah and Elisha walked and talked; and here the Son of God Himself passed the whole period of His sojourn upon earth.

For their rebellion against the Lord our forefathers were cast out of that which has been emphatically called "their own land." But the Word of God promises that after being spread out to "all the ends of the earth," they are at length to be brought back again in the fulness of blessing. To Jacob at Bethel, God said—

"And thy seed shall be as the dust of the earth;
And thou shalt spread abroad to the West and to the East,
And to the North and to the South:
And in thee and in thy seed
Shall all the families of the earth be blessed.
And, behold, I am with thee,
And will keep thee in all places whither thou goest,
And will bring thee again into this land;
For I will not leave thee
Until I have done that which I have spoken to thee of."
—Gen. xxviii. 14.

In blessing the sons of Joseph also, God plainly intimated that from an eligible position "in the midst of the earth" they were to grow "*as fishes do increase*," or to go forth in colonising shoals into "the ends of the earth;"[1] and that of Ephraim more particularly "a multitude of nations" was to come, unto whom were to be fulfilled "the promises made unto the fathers," which are "all yea and amen in Christ Jesus;" the letter representing which name in *Greek* is χ—the sign which Jacob made with his arms when he so emphatically "blessed both the sons of Joseph." In the *Greek language* the New Testament—confirmed by the personal ministry of our Redeemer—went forth unto "the Twelve Tribes scattered abroad,"[2] which, although lost as to name, we are assured by the word of prophecy were to be no more lost than the seed is which is covered in by the earth in which it is planted or sown. They were to be "sown" to the Lord "in the earth;" but they were to "take root downward," and so spread abroad upward, as to "cover the face of the world with fruit."[3]

[1] Gen. xlviii. 16.   [2] James i.; 1 Pet. i.   [3] Hosea ii. 23; xiv., &c.

With regard to that central land, out of which they were cast, and which is so much the subject of Old Testament prophecy and of New Testament history, it was predicted that after the Lord had cut off from it His people Israel by His "four sore judgments,"—the sword, famine, beasts of the earth, and pestilence,—and so had brought the land to utter desolation, then should "the land enjoy its Sabbaths," as it has been doing for ages[1] (Lev. xxvi.) "And yet for all that," while their own, the central land, has been lying waste and deserted, God has been, in the lands unto which they have been spread out, remembering, as He said He would, "the covenant of their ancestors;" "the covenant with Jacob" making them a supplanting people, "the covenant with Isaac" making them a rejoicing people, and also "the covenant with Abraham" making them a multiplying people. This He has been doing for them "in all the ends of the earth," where they have been growing into the promised "multitude of nations," have been made to occupy a leading position in the councils of the nations, and have been given the ministration of blessing to all nations.

But the Lord adds also, "AND I WILL REMEMBER THE LAND;" plainly implying that it is something in addition to His remembering them "in far countries," where also *they* were to remember the Lord, and to live with their children, and whence they are to return again.[2] Their spreading abroad in all directions where they were to become the Lord's inheritance, and their subsequent restoration under the guidance and guardianship of the Most High, was plainly implied in the promise to Jacob at Bethel.[3] And previously—when God entered into cove-

---

[1] Watchmen of Ephraim, vol. ii. pp. 109, 410.
[2] Zech. x. 9.   [3] Gen. xxvii-i.

nant with Abram, and contemplated his seed as being, like himself, justified by faith in Christ, in whom they were to be so made teachers of righteousness as to "shine as the stars for ever and ever"—they were spoken of as a migratory people.[1]

The land of Israel is a rich epitome of all lands; and of all countries it is the most centrally placed in respect to both land and water. Especially is this the case with regard to the different offshoots of the British Empire; so that in going there, we are, as already noticed, only removing into the midst of our family, to invite its several members to draw more closely around us. When the people are there who can take advantage of the capabilities and position of that Land so distinctly pointed out by the finger of God throughout all time; and now from the influence of the Old and New Testament, so much looked to from "all the ends of the earth"—when the people are there whose wants require the most extensive railway and telegraphic communication, these will be provided; and the Mount of Transfiguration, now called "Hermon" or *Desolate*,[2] will be found to be the heart of the habitable world, to and from which life will flow, to the enlivening and enriching of all between.

They will come from America, India, Australia, New Zealand, and the Cape; young, as well as old and middle aged. Very soon many of our people will find it more convenient to send their children thither for education, when more facilities are provided, and such as are already being implanted in the Land of our fathers.

[1] Gen. xv.   [2] Isa. lxii. 4.

III.

The Immigrants to the Land of Israel should, of course, be those who can justly free themselves from their connections and employments where they are; and who either because of what they are, or of what they have, are most needed there.

For some years past there has been a great derangement of the home money market; and there being so little confidence in the security of money lent out on interest, those who have it are apt to hoard it away, in place of letting it be used in the employment of labour; and thus it happens that many of our workmen must either starve or seek employment abroad. There is great waste in allowing so much capital to be idle at home, when it is required for carrying out the families of our labourers and artizans to the fields of labour which God has opened up for them in so many quarters, and where He has set before them a reasonable prospect of obtaining a living, as well as of being profitable to their employers; for the benefit not only of the people among whom they settle, but also of the mother country, which has trained and sent them forth.

The Rich should therefore consider the Poor in regard to their means of emigration and immigration; and as acting wisely and well in this matter, while making many rich, they will be themselves none the poorer. When Israel return, they are to bring "their silver and gold with them." Money is useful in the east as well as in the west; and it is desirable that our people should be obliged neither to borrow nor to beg. It is at least desirable that they should be able to purchase and possess land, and avail themselves of all real improvements and means of carrying out their mission. It is expedient that there should be some who can invest considerable sums in various undertakings. Much, however, may be done by many of moderate means uniting in one common object; making a kindly, economical, and industrial use of the means they possess, however small the sum contributed by each, as in the case of the proposed Wirtemburg Colonies.

In order to do this, it is well that there should be those who are able to give the best advice in gardening, farming, building, and road-making; and, as we are laying the foundation of a new state of society, physically as well as morally, it is well to have some regard to health, utility, and beauty in all agricultural and architectural arrangements. There are many economical and sanitary measures which, if adopted at once, or if provision be made for them at the beginning, will avert an immensity of mischief; and under the blessing of God, secure health, the means of enjoying life; and therefore of being able to employ it usefully, in place of being an uncomfortable burden to others.

The more of educated mind we can have in the Holy Land, well acquainted with the teachings of history, the principles of science, the practice of the various fine and useful arts, combined with thorough knowledge of the Scriptures and their true import, so much the better for that witnessing which is to take place therefrom in "the latter day." It is of the greatest moment that the ground should be thoroughly and at once occupied for God. None should even pass through that land without some effort having been made for their benefit; that so in their turn they may become blessings to others.

It is greatly to be desired that all who migrate thither should keep this steadily in view: That it is there pre-eminently we are to be obedient to our Saviour's injunction, "Seek first the kingdom of God and His righteousness." If in regard to what is most emphatically called "Immanuel's Land,"[1] we think we shall do better for ourselves, by seeking first our own things, we are likely to be most grievously disappointed.

We should go as benefactors to the Land and to the people. Those who are to return are described in prophecy as an ornament and enrichment to the Lord's Land:[2]

> "Lift up thine eyes round about and behold;
> All these gather together, and come to thee.
> As I live, saith the Lord,
> Thou shalt surely clothe thee with them all
> As with an ornament,
> And bind them on thee as a bride doeth."

Our people should go as employers of the present population:[3] "The sons of the alien shall be your ploughmen and vine-dressers." They should go as missionaries and teachers:

> "Ye shall be named the Priests of the Lord;
> Men shall call you the Ministers of our God."

We should endeavour to get the Scriptures opened, and to place in the hands of the Arabic-speaking population the means of becoming enriched with the wealth of English literature; that so in their turn they may hand out these treasures to the millions in Asia, Africa, and Europe. Thus the Holy Land may become indeed worthy of its name: a grand missionary centre in "the midst of the earth," such as England is or might be in the midst of the seas, for "the ends of the earth" generally.

Our American brethren were the first to take back the Gospel to the countries from and through which it came

---
[1] Isa. viii. 8. [2] Isa. xlix. 18. [3] Isa. lxi. 5.

unto us; and they have for a considerable time been quietly, but efficiently, labouring in schools, by the press, and by preaching, to make known the love of God throughout the Turkish dominions, to the various sects and nationalities. Latterly the Moslems also have been recognised by them as among those whose salvation should be earnestly desired. Our Government has at length interfered in behalf of the Turks; and procured from the Porte for them the right of following the truth, *though* it should lead them to abandon Mahometanism, which previously it was death for them to deny. And now throughout Turkey, so far as the Central Government is concerned, there is as much liberty of religious profession as in any other country of Europe, not excepting our own. Whereas *Christians* were not at liberty to purchase land, or even allowed to let their light shine, except at the risk of the lives of those who were benefited thereby, a recent firman commands all the Sultan's officials to help forward the efforts being made for educating the little children of all sects and parties, as well as adults; "more especially in the British Syrian Schools on Mounts Lebanon and Hermon."

A free way is thus presented for the Word of God to go freely forth throughout Bible Lands; along the whole line traversed by the Euphrates, from the Orontes to the Persian Gulf. From this line, southward to the Isthmus of Suez, the servants of the Lord may now "walk up and down in His name,"[1] and give forth light to all who come within the sphere of their influence.

We have still more intimately joined our American brethren in their work, by contributing funds for the support of their mission. "The Turkish Missions' Aid

[1] Zech. x. 12.

Society" has been formed mainly for this purpose; and other organisations, partly native, and some of them from the United Kingdom, have entered upon the same field of labour.

The Americans have been characterised by patient continuance in well-doing. They have been honestly labouring to introduce native co-workers, to whom they might leave the work when fairly commenced. Knowing that neither from this country nor from America can funds be expected for the permanent support of either scholastic or ecclesiastical establishments, they have been trying to initiate them into the payment of their own teachers and ministers. In many instances, however, perhaps, it might be better to allow of that liberty which the apostle of the Gentiles claimed: that of ministering the Word of Life freely.

Much will depend upon the constitution and first working of these native churches. I do not know whether the Americans have made the teaching of church polity any special object of their mission; but I believe they are evangelical in doctrine, reasonably attentive to science and the useful arts, well fitted to exhibit practical and protestant Christianity before the world, and willing to do their work as in the sight of God.

Therefore, when God calls our people back to the Central Land, we shall find those whom we can help, and who can help us in raising "the ensign" in the midst of the earth in the sight of all nations.[1]

It is desirable that those who go for some time to come should be able in an ordinary degree to take care of themselves. For labouring agriculturists and artizans, as well as for those who are able to direct and to give employment

---

[1] Isa xi. 12.

in all the useful arts, there will doubtless be ultimately plenty of occupation; but it is evident that the *poor* of the Lord's people are at length to betake themselves thither, and also that such facilities are to be provided, as that the lame, and the blind, and persons in the most delicate health, may be conveyed thither in company. Literally speaking (by the railways), "the valley shall be exalted, the mountain and hill made low, the crooked made straight, and the rough places plain;" and intelligence will not only be flashed across the Atlantic for the few, but also between the Central Land and "the ends of the earth" for the many.[1]

What was regarded a few years ago as a wild dream, is now merely a rational expectation. God has been preparing His work in "the ends of the earth;" and He will not fail those who honestly, as in His strength, endeavour to forward it in the place of His appointment.[2] Ample provision should be made for the reception of the poor and needy; but certainly they will not be brought together there to endure the curse of idleness. The work of God gives the joy of healthful exercise to all. Those who do the work should be supported in it; but care should be taken that the means are not absorbed by an expensive and inoperative agency

The Time has fully come when the Restoration of All Israel should take effect. The appointed "Seven Times"[3] have run their course. The two prophetic half weeks, each consisting of three and a half times 360, or 1260 years, making together 2520 years, during which Israel were to be punished by being excluded from the Land, are more than ended. The threatened desolations have

---

[1] Isa. xl. 4.   [2] Ezek. xliii. 7.
[3] Lev. xxvi.: Watchmen of Ephraim, vol. i. p. 100.

been accomplished in the east, the west, the north, and the south. In the Land itself, and in the surrounding countries, matters are exactly as predicted by the prophets. We are now invited to go and see how truthful God has been in the accomplishment of His threatenings; and to experience *in* the Land as we have done so wonderfully *out* of it, how faithful our God is in the fulfilment of His promises. It becomes the Lord's "witnesses"[1] to obey His call to "see what desolations He hath wrought in the earth:" and to see also how He bestows blessing, when He has a people there who really desire to be ministers of blessing.

There is no time to be lost. Let all who are free-hearted, and desire to devote themselves to God for the good of His people, prepare to go thither. This is the very time when God's "witnesses" should be found there, ready to see what God hath done, and will do, and to testify the same before all men in the great assembling of all the nations which have come of Jacob; who will then have found their union in the Son of God, as being constituted "sons of God" in Him.

> "Thou shalt arise and have mercy upon Zion:
> For the time to favour her, yea, the set time, is come.
> For Thy servants take pleasure in her stones,
> And favour the dust thereof.
> So the Nations shall fear the name of the Lord,
> And all the kings of the earth Thy glory."[2]
>
> — Ps. cii. 13.

Now let Britain carry back to Beyrout, not merely the blessings of commerce, but also that of which the names of both Britain and Beyrout seem to be expressive; and may Judah also be brought within "the bonds of the Covenant" (Lect. XI.)

---

[1] Isa. xliii. 10.   [2] See also the Title Deed of the Holy Land, &c.

Soon may Judah's voice be joined to that which already in Beyrout and over the Lebanon is preparing to unite with us in the song of welcome to our King; and may Britain, which has stood through so many trials, never prove false to her profession of the truth as it is in Jesus! After the signal displays which God has made here and hence of His faithfulness—in accomplishing the covenant "mercy sworn unto our fathers in the days of old," which He hath during these many ages been fulfilling unto us, their children, in regard to power, multiplicity, and means of blessing, may we now indeed arise to the duties of our high calling, in the use of these means; and labour and pray, that as God hath so liberally dealt with BRITAIN, according to the Covenant, *we may give* OURSELVES to the work so remarkably commenced at BEYROUT, until all the hills and vales of Syria shall be vocal with His praise, who loved us, and gave Himself for us, that we should joyfully give ourselves to Him.

IV.

We have seen that God's Covenant with Abraham, Isaac, and Jacob has been fulfilled to our widely-spread race, having been made sure to Ephraim, the younger son of Jacob, who was then constituted the heir of the promises in Christ. "The birthright is Joseph's" (1 Chron. v. 2), and from his son Ephraim chiefly was to descend that great nation pointed forward to in the name of the first great receiver of the promises, and also that "multitude of nations" referred to when his name was enlarged to *Abraham*.

At the disruption of the tribes, after the death of Solomon, Judah and Benjamin the younger brother of Joseph, together with many of the Levites and priests, adhered to the throne of David. But Ephraim, and the other tribes to the north, east, and west of the Jordan, separated from the Jews, and under the name of "Israel," or "All Israel," remained a distinct kingdom from that of Judah until the captivity of Israel, which began about 740 B.C., and was completed thirty years after, in the year B.C. 710.

Israel had been called near to the Lord, had been led about, instructed, and given abundant evidence of the justice and mercy of God, and of His determination to do all He had promised. But Ephraim had been a ringleader in rebellion to such a degree that the Lord had said (B.C. 742), "Within threescore and five years shall Ephraim be broken that he be not a people."[1] The curse was to take effect B.C. 677. Before that time Ephraim was to be lost among the Gentiles; and so it came to pass.

But even then there was one hopeful feature in Ephraim's case. It is the last view we have of him previous to his removal from the land, and it is as "bringing forth the fruits of the kingdom" (2 Chron. xxviii. 8-15).

The army of Israel had made war upon the Jews, and brought immense spoil and many prisoners to Samaria. Against the host thus returning a prophet of the Lord went forth; and the word of the Lord spoken by him was taken up by certain of the heads of the children of Ephraim, "expressed by name," who, acknowledging their own sins against the Lord, protested against adding to their guilt by being the wilful instruments of punishing their brethren of the house of Judah. The soldiery seem to have bowed to the word of the Lord as well as the civilians; so that they left both the prisoners and the spoils in the hands of the men of Ephraim; and the four who were expressed

[1] Isa. vii. 8.

by name rose up, and with the spoil clothed all that were naked among them, gave them to eat and to drink, anointed them, carried all the feeble among them upon asses, brought them to Jericho, the city of palm-trees, to their brethren, and then returned to Samaria. This seems to have been the original of the parable of the good Samaritan.

The Lord must have seen something of this when He said, "How shall I give thee up, Ephraim?"[1] And although the decree had gone forth that Ephraim should be cut off as a people, we may be quite sure that in thus bringing forth "the fruit of the kingdom" called for in the judgment of the nations previous to their being given to "inherit the kingdom" (Matt. xxv.), that practical exhibition of repentance towards God, and kindness to the poor and needy of the people whom the Lord of the Kingdom condescended to make His brethren according to the flesh, was not overlooked by "the Great Messenger of the Covenant" when sending forth the word of His grace by His apostles. May we not believe it was distinctly adverted to when He said to the Jews, after speaking of the very different treatment they had given to the Lord's messengers, "Therefore say I unto you, The kingdom of God shall be taken from you, and given to A NATION BRINGING FORTH THE FRUITS OF IT." This will be manifest when Ephraim becomes (what his name expresses), "I will bring forth fruits."

This saying of our Lord is like that in Jer. iii. 11—"The backsliding Israel hath justified herself more than treacherous Judah. Go and proclaim these words towards the north, and say, Return, thou backsliding Israel, saith the Lord; and I will not cause mine anger to fall upon you." The apostle testifies that upon the Jews of his

[1] Hos. xi. 8.

generation "wrath was come to the uttermost" (1 Thess. ii. 16); but this was not to be the case with Ephraim: "I WILL surely have mercy upon him, saith the Lord."

The Word of the Lord, to which at length Ephraim had shown a disposition to give ear while yet in the land, was sent after him "into the north country," after the nation to which he belonged had been given "a bill of divorce, and sent away" (Jer. xxxi). We are therefore not to look for Israel as still under the Law like the Jews, nor even as bearing their own name of Ephraim or Israel. *They were cast out among the Gentiles*, and were to become "a multitude of nations," or, as it is rendered by St Paul, "*the fulness of the Gentiles*" (Rom. xi. 25).

Let us then proceed in the direction in which the word of the Lord went forth from Jerusalem. Following the course of the great apostle of the Gentiles, we find that it was in this northern direction, and that each succeeding journey was more and more towards these "isles afar off," where we find a people dwelling "alone," who are also without number among the nations (Num. xxiii. 9).

Upon this nation, and the "multitude of nations" to whom they have given and are giving birth in all "the ends of the earth," has fallen the lot of ministering the word of the Lord to all the nations of the earth. God has done for them, and enabled them to do, great things for themselves and for others. But in nothing have they been more signally favoured than in this, that to them has been committed that which was taken from the Jews—the keeping of the oracles of God—the ministration of the Bread of Life to all people—the causing to be proclaimed in all languages "the wonderful works of God." Soon may the Spirit be poured upon us from on high, giving a clearer understanding of the words which have been uttered; so that all our lives and voices shall be attuned to welcome our returning King, who is about to come forth in glorious majesty to reign. "Come, Lord Jesus, come quickly" (1 Thess. iv. 16).

The People upon whom this pleasant lot has fallen came from the borders of the Caspian Sea, whither the Assyrians had carried the people upon whom it was promised the blessing should come. The destiny promised to Israel was special; and it is specially ours. "He hath not dealt so with any people." All things agree to confirm the word that God "hath remembered His mercy and His truth towards the house of Israel." "We are indeed His people, and the sheep of His pasture." May this be proved, not only by the Lord's kindness to us, but also by our making a right use of our privileges, and truly fulfilling our destiny in being for blessing to all the nations of the earth.

God is doing that which He said; and He remonstrates with us for not doing the part appointed to us, saying, "Turn again, O virgin of Israel; turn again to these thy cities. How long wilt thou go about, O thou backsliding daughter?" Not that all can be expected to cram themselves into Palestine, or even into Syria. "Place will not be found for them" there; but all who have the power are to use it, not obstructively, but as aiding those who desire to go with the view of promoting the cause of the Redeemer in that land which the Lord specially chose "to place His Name there," and from which is yet to go forth with power the word of His grace throughout the world.

Should this last great call to prepare for the coming of the Lord be attended to as it ought, the powers of darkness will be alarmed, and conglomerate in darkened masses to depress the influence of the truth, impede its progress, and, if possible, quench the light even in the central land. Then will be the rending of the heavens and of the earth at the return of our Lord in the clouds of heaven, and the resurrection of the saints.

Then also will be the descent of the New Jerusalem and the reception into their heavenly home of those who are to be as kings and priests with Christ, and reign with Him over the earth. They have the double portion. Their father Abraham was "the heir of the world," and they also shall inherit the earth. But the fact of his being appointed the "heir of the world," did not prevent Abraham from looking for that "city which hath foundations, whose Builder and Maker is God." He and his believing children "confessed that they were strangers and pilgrims on the earth, and that God hath prepared for them a city."

When the Son of man shall sit upon the throne of His glory, the Twelve Apostles shall sit upon twelve thrones, "judging the Twelve Tribes of Israel;" and all who in the present life have suffered loss for the cause of Christ will also have their reward.

Then will the Father have accomplished His promise of putting all rule and all authority and power under the feet of the Son.[1] "And when all things are put under Him, then shall the Son also Himself be subject unto Him who did put all things under Him." To them that are His He will appoint a kingdom, as the Father hath appointed Him, and they shall be "filled with all the fulness of God," "that God may be all in all."

At the close of the seventh thousand years of our world's history, a farther revolution will take place, and the last dread struggle between the powers of darkness and of light,

[1] 1 Cor. xv. 25.

when the present heavens and earth will pass away (Rev. xx. 7).

Not so the New Jerusalem, the heavenly abode of the glorified saints which abides for ever, even as the new heavens and new earth which are then created, and in which dwelleth righteousness. Whatever changes may take place, the children of God have nothing to fear. The Lord is their God: He is the strength of their heart, and their portion for ever.

But although we may thus rest in God through our Lord Jesus Christ, we are not to despise the thoughts of His heart as He hath been pleased to reveal them in the Scriptures of Truth. What He hath purposed in our Blessed Redeemer, and made known to us, we should endeavour to know. "To us and to our children" belong "those things which are revealed."[1] May the Spirit of Truth lead us into all truth, and enable us duly to improve and rightly to use the light so richly ministered in the Scriptures of Truth.

The masses of our people are being quietly enlightened and enlivened on the subject of prophecy respecting themselves and the Land, especially in connection with the gospel history, simply through the unbought diffusion of the truth by those who know, are able to defend, and are willing to be at sacrifices for the knowledge of what they are and what the Lord hath done for them.

By and by there will be a craving for the reunion of our race in the land of our fathers. A portion of the Royal Navy may well be employed in giving a free passage to and from the Land for such as a visit would be likely to benefit—not too much to ask, certainly, in behalf of those who have been giving their time, talents, and means for

[1] Deut. xxix. 29.

the good of the public; but especially such as are ministering the Word in various ways freely. The expense will be amply repaid by the improved method and spirit likely to be infused into their teaching, as such lessons in sacred and secular knowledge, and communion of varied and the best-conditioned minds are calculated to impart.

Meanwhile much may be done by private enterprise. Persons residing in the same neighbourhood may associate together to send out their representatives—enough to give tone to the society into which they may go or be sent, partly upon a recreative missionary tour; but also to see how things really are, and be the better able to advise others on their return. That even these may be accommodated, it is well that more of our people should be now settled in the Land. But this will take place naturally as opportunity serves. The great thing is to have the movement rightly directed.

From the experience of our dear old friend, Mr Lowthian, it may be seen what can be done by even one aged but faithful Christian.[1] Single-handed, he went to reside on the Lebanon, "alone, like a sparrow upon the house-

---

[1] Respecting Mr Lowthian, "A Handful of Corn on the Top of the Mountains" (London, Partridge & Co.) says—"In the month of August 1843, some lectures were delivered in Carlisle on the subject of 'The Lost Tribes of Israel; their progress in the ends of the earth, and their ultimate concentration in the land promised to their fathers.' Great interest was awakened in the study of prophecy, and many realised that the Bible is indeed a 'treasury,' out of which may be brought things new and old of surpassing interest and importance, even in a secular point of view.

"Among the most interested and attentive of the audience was a rather aged Cumberland farmer—a shrewd, industrious, and thoroughly practical Christian. He had worked hard all his life, and now, on the verge of seventy, had begun to think of rest from worldly toil. But, as the lecturer ('with the unmistakable air of deep conviction in his own soul') showed that the Christian nations who actually inherit the Promises are

top;" but he did not fold his hands and say, "I can do nothing." No, he introduced to the Lebanon improved seeds, implements, and methods of husbandry; and by proper management, especially as regards irrigation, he showed how the land may be made exceedingly fruitful. He taught the people sufficient English and learned enough Arabic to communicate with them, so as to give them some idea of God's truthfulness, even with regard to the Promises made unto our fathers. He opened the first of what are called the Lebanon Schools, of which there are now twenty-one, and encouraged the people to enrol themselves into little Protestant communities.

He was past seventy when his educational labours began on the Lebanon, yet he did much alone and in little time; and when no longer able to work, he came home to England, and quietly went to rest. But he has left behind him a bright example; though none can estimate the amount of good initiated or sustained by him both at home and abroad.

Like many others, he may not have accomplished all at which he aimed; and to some at the time his life may have appeared all but a failure. But results have proved that it was not so. And it seems to me that if good is to

the people for whom they were intended; that the 'Seven Times' of Israel, being scattered from the land of their fathers were ended; and as he spoke of the grievous physical and religious desolation of that land, and of its great need of Christian labourers, Mr Lowthian's honest heart responded to the involuntary appeal, and within two months he was on his way to see with his own eyes what could and ought to be done to prepare the way for making the Land of Israel what the Word of God promises it will yet be. The results of his observations he gave after his return in 1844, in his 'Narrative of a Recent Journey to Jerusalem,' which passed rapidly through three editions." In 1847 he returned, and soon commenced his very remarkable agricultural experiments and educational labours here alluded to.

be effectually done in the Land as elsewhere, it must be much as he did—by each, according to his or her ability, trying to make their ordinary calling an opportunity of conveying blessing to others. If he be a physician, let him make use of his healing power, of which there is ample need and opportunity; and so with agricultural and mechanical skill, or scientific knowledge. In any way whatever by which we can help to raise the present population to think and act for themselves, and to render the Land a school in which to learn what God hath said and done in past ages, and what He would have men, women, and children do in the present, in preparation for a full enjoyment of the future—let us work freely for Him who hath wrought all our works in us, and who "worketh in us, both to will and to do of His good pleasure."

And let us be encouraged by this thought: that not to anything is there the promise of greater and more glorious results than to the approaching great preaching of the gospel in and from the Land of Israel. Both by mercy and by judgment will the Lord bear witness to the truth of His word. Nor will the fulfilment of the Promises be long delayed in the return of our Blessed Redeemer, and His reign of righteousness and peace all over the globe. Then indeed shall His glory cover the heavens, and the earth be full of His praise.

> "They shall say no more,
> The LORD liveth which brought up the Children of Israel
> Out of the land of Egypt:
> But
> The LORD liveth which brought up and which led
> The seed of Israel
> Out of the North Country,
> And from all the countries whither I had driven them;
> And they shall dwell in their own land."
>
> Jer. xvi. 14, 15.

Emigration and Immigration will have accomplished their course, when our people, who came chiefly from the borders of the Caspian Sea, whither our Israelitish forefathers were carried by the Assyrians—when this people, so wondrously followed and accompanied by the blessings of Revelation, shall have gone forth and presented an open Bible to all the families of mankind of whatever tongue—when this people, having prepared their work without, and made it fit for themselves in the field, shall return from the west, the east, the north, and the south to the Central Land, with the riches of all countries and the improvements of all ages, there in the unity of the Spirit combinedly to use their various powers and endless resources for the good of all, and the glory of the Great King, in that Land which for their sins has been so long lying desolate, which now is found to burst forth in beauty, and to bear its fruit for His people of Israel, who heretofore were disobedient, but whose delight now is to honour Him with all they have in the place of His appointment. When that happens, God will acknowledge His people as they have acknowledged Him.

This long-predicted realisation of visible Unity is THE GREAT SIGN of the nearness of our Lord's glorious return, when Immigration shall be perfected in the transmission of the children of God to their Father's home above—" Our House Eternal in the Heavens."

THE RE-DISCOVERY OF OUR ISRAELITISH ORIGIN.

In all ages God has been communicating His will to man. In old time "holy men of God spake as they were moved by the Holy Ghost," which doubtless can and does still use special human instrumentality of different, or even of the same epochs, to unfold those former utterances for the instruction of their own times. The words of Scripture, the teachings of history, and the facts of science, are open to all; but evidently something superior to mere human intelligence is required to be able to recognise them as parts of one great system of revelation of the Most High, for whom it is as easy to influence millions, as one man to consider the same subject at His appointed time.

It was said by the wisest of men, nearly three thousand years ago, "There is nothing new under the sun;" and few scientific inventions of any great value have not haunted the imaginations of several dreamers before any *one* has been able to bring it to tangible realisation by the requisite mastery of the details of the complex machinery. Such was evidently the case with regard to the subject of this volume. Of late years one and another, without due inquiry, seem to have taken for granted that the late author, of necessity, must have received the clue to our Israelitish origin from Dr Abbadie (p. 136), of whose conjectures he did not even hear till some time in 1866, when an extract was sent to him by an esteemed correspondent. Mr Wedgwood's "Book of Remembrance," also, did not come into his hands till long after the publication of the second edition of "Our Israelitish Origin" (p. 160).

Within the last few months, a very able work, published nearly fifty years ago by Mr Nisbet, in 3 vols., 'Dialogues on Prophecy,' has come into the writer's hands, of which, evidently, also, Mr W. had heard nothing. In it occurs the following passage :—

"*Leander.*—An opinion has been entertained by some persons, that believers among the Christian nations are descendants of the Ten Tribes, and several passages of Scripture have been brought together in order to support the idea.

"*Anastatius.*—I have seen three papers in MS., drawn up by three persons, each of whom is unknown to the other, all maintaining the same position, but supported by reasoning derived from entirely different sources.

"*Philalethes.*—The coincidence of three independent testimonies is so remarkable, that I should like to hear how the view is supported.

"*Anastatius.*—I have two objections to laying it before you: first, *that I do not understand it well myself;* secondly, the little I do understand seems to be so ill borne out by Scripture, that it would be unprofitable to make the statement without examining its foundations, and overthrowing it where it was untenable; but this would take much time, and prevent our hearing what *Aristo* can tell us upon this very difficult subject," &c.

And it is curious, consistently with this disposition to complacently shirk the difficulty, how accurately afterwards the writer discriminates between Israel and Judah, and points out the requirements of prophecy as regards the descendants of Joseph; yet, like many later opponents to our Israelitish origin, he seems almost purposely to evade the truth. A master mind fully prepared to unlock the mystery was required.

Some of the late Mr Wilson's qualifications doubtless were, that he had an upright, quiet, godly ancestry, helpful to the welfare of others. His Bible-loving mother had encouraged him in all good things, and laid the foundation of his marvellous habit of extracting the essence of whatever literature came in his way, by rewarding him from her own library with any book he chose to be examined in thoroughly by her. By his seventeenth year he had acquired at least ninety-seven volumes, the contents of which he had in his memory—the book bearing that number being a very ancient copy of the "Life of Luther." The importance of the position assigned to Ephraim in Gen. xlviii. 16–20 (Watchmen of Ephraim, i. 175) was pointed out to him in his boyhood by her, and commended to his serious consideration.

He had early acquired such accurate acquaintance with the Scriptures (for which, to his latest hours, he had a most remarkable memory) as to find recreation, when others were asleep, in tabulating mnemonically their contents; in which though, perhaps from difference of mental constitution and previous education, he had comparatively few sympathisers, yet it is undeniable that he has pointed out some wonderful harmonies, correspondencies, and poetical arrangements generally unobserved.

He had most remarkable power of enthusiastically concentrating his attention, so that he seemed for the time being as "a man of one idea," whichever happened to be uppermost. When a youth, having made up his mind to go in for some college examination, within a fortnight of the time he discovered a certain knowledge of Hebrew was necessary, of which he knew nothing. Undaunted, however, he set himself to work, and passed with satisfaction to all concerned.

He had a great love of old people and old books; and, having ransacked many departments of literature on which had gathered the dust of ages, and kept pace with modern science, as well as thought originally, scarcely anything was new to him, or rather seemed as if he had seen it before; so that when he had time to work out a subject as it existed in his own mind, all that had been written upon it within his reach seemed to come forward and yield to his touch: the genial warmth of his genius so irradiating the pages referred to, as to bring out in bold relief exactly what was required at the time for the illustration.

He had a lofty sense of truth and duty, apart from selfish considerations, and in the school of Christ had acquired much faith, patience, and self-control. Notwithstanding his seeming abstraction from common affairs, he had a large capacity for friendship; and his tender reverence for both young and old doubtless often evoked from others the same feeling towards whatever he cared for. No womanly hands could perform kindly offices with more healing touch, nor feet move more softly or quickly on errands of mercy. Comparatively early, his power of teaching and persuading had been discovered, and was unceasingly cultivated to his latest hours. He was never without some gratuitous educational effort for those who wanted to learn what he could communicate. However young, poor, or ignorant they might be, he was always ready; and many he thus helped onward and upward. He had wonderful faith in young people, of which his address on one of "The Watchmen" covers is a fine example :—

"TO OUR YOUNG FRIENDS.

"It gives us no small pleasure to know that many of you are beginning to feel quite at home with us, so as to have increased delight in the study of Old Testament history and prophecy, and the parables of our Lord. You have found a freshness and beauty in the sacred page, such as the words of Divine wisdom might be expected to possess. You have found a unity and harmony in Scripture, something like what might be expected from a book, written indeed by men far distant from each other as to time and place, but all moved by one Spirit. It will give us true joy to know of you growing up in this full confidence in God, as the God of revelation and providence, the God and Father of our Lord Jesus Christ. We shall be glad that we can help you; and we shall also be glad to have your help. Whenever anything is suggested to you that you feel has a tendency to perplex, darken, or depress your mind, write to us, if you like ; and be sure to ask God, for His dear

Son's sake, to give us the power of helping you over the difficulty. And if you see or hear anything which you think may aid us in trying to be of use to others, make it known to us; and ask that we may profit by what you communicate. Think also of how you can make our labours useful to others in your several neighbourhoods, by letting the voice of THE WATCHMEN be heard whenever you can find a fitting audience. Propose our questions for examination whenever you can find those who either are or ought to be able to reply to them. You may do great good by following the example of Jesus. When a child, He was found among the teachers in the temple, both hearing them and asking them questions. Be sure you adorn the gospel by a meek and quiet spirit; but at the same time be brave, keeping by the truth firmly, and holding it out to others as God may give you opportunity. And may He add His blessing."

He had early learned to think for himself. Scientific research had encouraged the habit of observing the relation between cause and effect; and his practice of Christian phrenology, at the expense of being misunderstood by some whose esteem he valued, had won the confidence and brought him into sympathy with others of the best-conditioned and most accurately-intelligent minds in the sister kingdom, with whom he was able also to take counsel on "things touching the King." His own life was the best illustration of the principles he delineated in "The Mission of Elijah" in later years—"We greatly deceive ourselves if we look upon such means, and the improvement we can make of them, as our own. We must awake from this delusion, and in earnest act; not as seeking praise, or power, or wealth, or ease, or pleasure for ourselves, but as seeking with all our hearts to do good unto all as we have opportunity." "We owe it to ourselves, and to the Author of our being, that we cultivate our powers to the utmost degree consistent with our own health and the welfare of those around us. And to our fellow-men, in honour of God our Saviour, we are so to hold ourselves debtors, as to employ all that we are and all that we have in the furtherance of their greatest good—yea, of any good whereby we may be given an opportunity of saying, not by word only, but in very deed, 'Thanks be unto God for His unspeakable gift!'" Such were some of the characteristics of the man on whom was laid, as with the finger of God, the responsibility of scientifically opening out to the understanding and heart of the Church "the mystery of Israel among the Gentiles."

He set a high value, indeed, on Christian friendship; and one of his greatest sources of strength, doubtless, was that she who presided in his home was especially one with whom he could confer on most subjects—in whose intelligent, spiritual accuracy, tender, soul-refreshing, womanly sympathy, and restful self-control, he found the peace and quietness needed after long courses of lecturing and discussion of the same flippant objections one still hears repeated with parrot-like accuracy, and what some one has characterised as "the hopeless perversity of learned ignorance." "Let us work with the patience of hope for the rising generation," he used to say. "It always takes a generation for any newly discovered truth to take root and spring up as this must evidently do. Let us sow the seed broadcast in faith, and God will take care of it. We shall be away; but the work is for God, and will remain. It is as much, perhaps, as we need expect of the present generation, that in time they will be able to distinguish between Israel and Judah. If we succeed in awaking England to the fact that it occupies the place of Ephraim, it will be so much better." In a letter to her, dated March 24, 1843, he thus describes a lecture, and the opportunity which he always afforded of answering questions:—

"Last evening I gave my first lecture in Bristol. There was a large audience, to whom I gave an apparently satisfactory statement of the general view. At the close, the Rev. Mr T. (connected with the Jews' Society) was proposed as Chairman, and, the vote being put, was chosen. He, however, objected to the want of authority for the view, and waited for historical evidence. Of course, as I wished to answer this objection, I excused him from taking the chair; and as another could not readily be fixed on, I proceeded to answer to the entire approval of the audience. I pointed to the kind of evidence we had for the truth respecting the One Seed, Christ—the exact fulfilment of the prophetic word. I showed that we had the same here; and that we ought first to acquaint ourselves well with the designs of God, and then follow out the development of those designs in providence. This was what I had done—appealing to what was, from the beginning, broadly written throughout the whole inspired volume, and then to the circumstances immediately surrounding them, marking them out as the people with regard to whom the promises were made, and to whom the Lord might most truly say, '*I have* chosen thee, and *not* cast thee away.'

"Mr T. then rose to put a question, and being desired by the audience to go upon the platform, did so; when he asked if I really maintained that the term 'children of Israel' *always* in Scripture meant the English people? I *had* before explained that the term 'children of Israel' was a term common to Israel and Judah—that, of course, it included the branches of Joseph which had run over the wall of circumcision, and to whom the promise was to be sure through Christ, as well as to the other portion of the children of Israel which retained the name and some distinctive rites of Israel.

"Upon still further explaining, he went on to Hos. iii., to show that the term, 'CHILDREN OF ISRAEL' was used with regard to a people WITHOUT A KING, &c., &c.—the Jews; and that the prophecy there was not applicable to the English. I granted that he had explained that prophecy rightly, but that the people spoken of in chap. iii. were other than those spoken of in chaps. i. and ii.: 'Go YET love a woman,' &c. I showed that we were agreed as to that; and that, therefore, there was no cause of dispute. ' He stood thinking for some time, we all pausing for his reply; until sympathising with him in his position, I diverted the attention of the audience for a little until he should rally, when he said that he still waited for the historical evidence, and that perhaps it would have been well had he done so from the first. When he asked if any great men had embraced the view, I said I would not name any, although there were, as I wished to produce to them no substitute for a careful and impartial examination of the matter for themselves— that the view had nothing to recommend it to them but its self-evidence and abundance of proof of all kinds, which I would be ready to produce as required; although, indeed, I would prefer that to which they could most easily refer, most certainly ascertain, and

2 D

in which they could place the most reliable confidence—that of the Scriptures—which, I was ready to show, all bore witness most consistently to the truth of our Israelitish origin, as also did the whole working of Providence : each was a consistent half of one great whole."

The next (April 3)—

"Was a long lecture, but there seemed to be no wearying on the part of the audience ; and I had very little perception of the lapse of time. At the close, one of the 'Brethren' came up approving much that had been spoken, but blundering in the same way about Israel and Judah as Mr T——, quoting, 'LO, THE PEOPLE SHALL DWELL ALONE' (Num. xxiii. 9). I showed that he ought to have gone on to the next verse, where he would have seen that Israel's not being reckoned or numbered among the nations, was not because they were not among the nations, but because they were, according to the promise, *innumerable*. He also quoted Ezek. xxxvi., to show that the Jews were to be brought into their own land *before* having the Spirit given them ; and I quoted chap. xxxvii., to show that the 'Whole house of Israel' were rather to be brought to life OUT OF THE LAND. He referred to the union of Israel and Judah IN the land, when they were to be 'no more two nations ;' and I showed that, seeing they were but two nations when before in the land, and were to be but *one* upon their return, Ephraim's being 'a multitude of nations' must take place in the interim—must have now taken place. So you see I have very different kinds of opposition. I have not met with any here who seem not to be weakened in their opposition when the matter is brought near to them. It is astonishing upon what feeble grounds it has been kept at a distance."

"The Carlisle Patriot" of September the same year says of the lectures :—

"By those best acquainted with the Christian Scriptures, Mr Wilson was at once felt and acknowledged to be a skilful workman, needing not to be ashamed, and *rightly* dividing the word of truth which he handled with a power and clearness of exposition that, we are assured, appeared to many to be most rare and incontrovertible ; while those to whom many of his considerations were novel, felt a warm interest in the inquiry springing up in their minds."

His wife had encouraged him to go out on that course of lecturing, with general free admissions, so that none might be excluded; and one thinks tenderly of the little circle of loving friends who there rallied round her, some of whom met daily to pray with her, and to hear of his progress, especially of the dear "mother in Israel," nearly related to generations of clergymen, who waited till after his departure to make to her the proposition, that if he had faith to go forth to lecture in the circumstances, she would throw in her life for the comfort of the little household, that the self-denying wife and mother might have less carefulness.[1] A frequent expression in his letters was, "My hands, I doubt not, have been greatly strengthened and upheld by your prayers." She always knew the hour of his lecture, and if not able to be present, was asking for him direction and strength. The connection between these heart-to-heart pleadings, and the marvellous help, renewed strength, and spiritual blessing received that year—the various results of which may not be known till the great day—may be questioned by some; but he himself has said ("Watchmen of Ephraim," iii. 233), "There is a beautiful chain of promise and fulfilment, of revelation and providence, which links human destiny to the Throne of the Eternal—the God and Father of our Lord Jesus Christ. Man requires to see that God is, and that He is the Rewarder of all them that diligently seek Him, in order that he may be induced to seek unto the Source of all blessing for skilfulness and strength to wrestle with the great enemy of God and man so as to prevail." Those who are left think with gratitude of several friends who, that year and since then, were raised up for the promotion of this work; from the devoted sisters, who sacrificed ease and pleasure to work harder during the London season than any paid secretaries, and disposed of their jewels

---

[1] A correspondent writes, October 2, 1875:—"Well do I remember his lectures in Bath, and also his kindly coming to our village Bible-meeting, and giving the most thrillingly beautiful speech on the Word of God I ever heard!"

to meet the heavy expenses attending public lectures, and otherwise making the subject known; and good old Mr Lowthian who at once set off to work out the problem of Israel's restoration; to many another who long remained helpful (see "Handful of Corn," and "Watchmen of Ephraim," i., ii.)

Perhaps the highest tribute he could pay to the accuracy of his wife's criticism was, within a few weeks of her departure, in re-writing *nineteen* times these closing paragraphs of Lecture XIV., in the "Mission of Elijah" (the object of which volume was to correct crude notions about the Restoration). So far as she was aware, these ideas were new to the Christian world, and she had a great dread of his meaning being misapprehended. "If, as has been suggested, Elijah's last journey upon earth before his translation was a foreshadowing of his ministry in the Apocalypse, which conducts the view onward from the apostolic age to the time of the saints' reception into glory, then it follows:—

"(1.) That the scenes through which we are now being led are not to be viewed merely in reference to the present and the past, but also as possibly foreshadowing 'the things which must be hereafter.' They may, even as to the trains of ideas which they suggest, be a preparation for more important service in a higher state of being.

"(2.) That Revelation is not extemporaneous on the part of God. Like Creation, it gradually and majestically rises into maturity. Nearly a thousand years before the Apocalypse was ministered, its germal thoughts were placed in that mind, which was to be employed in developing this wondrous manifestation of the Divine foreknowledge."

His usual mode of request—"Agnes, I have a matter here in which I want your full sympathy. Have you time now, or shall I wait a little?"—was enough to secure her best attention. She fully realised the dignity of the work to which he had evidently been appointed, and the honour of being contributive to its efficiency. And better than anybody else she knew that he had no by-ends to serve. The help she gave in many ways *must* have made his labours infinitely more practically helpful. Every line written by him for the 8vo " Gospel Treasury" passed under her review at least four times, and she verified all the references in it, as well as in the smaller Harmony.

Her daughter says—" I think my mother must have purposely set herself to train me to sympathise with my father by her own precious example of heart-interest in all that concerned him, as well as by encouraging my acquiring knowledge of what would be helpful to his work during his absence, so as to have companionable repose on his return."

It is worthy of observation, that early in 1837 (the same year as Sir Henry Rawlinson discovered the alphabetic key to the Nineveh inscriptions), for months Mr Wilson was accumulating by purchase from stalls and auctions such a variety of curious old books as would have taken many leisurely lives to read; and one summer morning he said, " I had a most remarkable dream last night. A history of England was placed before me unlike anything I have ever seen, giving the various aspects of the different epochs distinctly, which I think I am intended to write. It would be a most useful thing. It is greatly wanted." With great glee she used to tell how mistaken she had been in saying, " Narrative is not your *forte*. You had better mind your own business, which that is not at present, my good man."

But forthwith he wrote out the plan as seen in his dream, and afterwards went to a book sale. A pile of books was being passed round, on the merits of which the salesman was descanting. He was so astounded to find they belonged to a historical work following a similar plan to that he had seen in his dream, that, much to the auctioneer's surprise, he refrained from " bidding." That evening, however, seeing the same set of books on a stall, he bought them. Some weeks after he was waited on by another old book-dealer to tell him of a work, respecting which it had been so impressed upon his mind that " it would be of use to Mr Wilson," that he had resolved to come to offer it to him and take no denial. So a second copy of "Henry's History of Great Britain" was in the house.

Soon after he went to Cork on professional business. Various Christian friends received him as their guest from Saturday to Monday mornings. One Sunday, soon after his arrival, he was asked by the late Miss Cummins, of Glanmire, "What is the meaning of this, Mr Wilson; 'His bow abode in strength?'" In reply he gave some ordinary explanation, which he always said was very unsatisfactory to himself, and seeing her look of disappointment, said, "The passage requires farther consideration. Let us find out all we can about Joseph, and compare notes when I come again."

Wisdom is promised to him who "applies his heart to understanding." During the following week his spare time was given to the study of the Scriptures respecting Israel; and on his return, finding some of the family in the drawing-room, engaged in making children's scrap-books out of some old Saturday Magazines, to which mutilation he had always an objection, he playfully remonstrated, and, taking up a printed scrap, said, "Dear me! what is this?"

"Cressy, Poictiers, Agincourt—indeed, most of the great victories gained over the French—mainly resulted from the unrivalled skill of the English bowmen, nor were they less successful on their own soil. Truly was it said by Sir John Fortescue, 'That the might of the realme of Englande standyth upon her archers;' indeed, all our old writers are agreed upon the vast superiority of the English bowmen over those of other nations."—Vol. v. p. 126.

"Is it possible? What can they have had to do with Joseph?" he exclaimed, as a bright flash of light, which he often described, seemed to illuminate the passages of Scripture he had been just reviewing. The circle in which he was then visiting had been previously keenly investigating the early history of Ireland, and were ready to help him by their sympathy. Forthwith he sent for some of the books which had been so persistently brought before his notice, and began what he soon saw must become his life-work. Friends caught the spirit of his enthusiasm, and he remained for weeks unfolding to others as God taught himself out of His Word and Providence.

While the snow was on the ground that winter, he gave his first course of lectures in one of the Dublin theatres. Soon after, the late Rev. P. Roe of Kilkenny called to ask what had lately occupied his mind? On hearing his story, he said, "Yes, go on. That *is* most important. I have a book which will be a great help to you. It is not well known, but I received it as a college prize." "What is it?" "Henry's History of Great Britain!" To him the first MS. course of eight lectures was submitted; and he replied that he wished they could be delivered in every city and town in Ireland.

To Mr Wilson, as well as to others, it was often strange how the evidence came to his hand, and the books seemed to open at the right page, when at the close of some branch of the inquiry he turned to refresh himself among them. A *habitué* of the College library made it his daily business to sit with him to catch up the thread of his thoughts when they were interrupted by professional visitors, and otherwise help him in any way.

In the summer of 1838, the late Rev. H. Nixon, of Booterstown, offered the use of his Infant School for a course of lectures. "We have had Phrenology last year. Now let us have Israel, if you please." Respecting these lectures he afterwards wrote to a friend: "I was greatly pleased; nor could I hear a dissenting or cavilling voice from any one of the many who attended them." His assistant, the Rev. E. Leet (afterwards of Dalkey), with large-hearted enthusiasm, disposed of tickets and acted as secretary,[1] and before me lies the following:—

---

[1] Three-and-twenty years after he joyfully arranged for a similar meeting for the same purpose in his own School-house at Dalkey.

"We, having heard Mr Wilson lecture on the Modern Nations of Europe as related to ancient Israel, are convinced that his views on the subject are well worthy of being heard and seriously considered.
(Signed) "WALLSCOURT.
"PARNELL NEVILLE KEARNEY, Clk.
"R. J. L. M'GHEE, Clk.
"GUY CRAWFORD."

Evidently this document, not being signed by either Revs. P. Roe, H. Nixon, or E. Leet, was intended for more general signature; but he was unmindful of the importance to others of such matters, besides being almost studious to avoid leading any to commit themselves to a course of action, respecting which they had not fully counted the cost. A semi-official message also came from some who had attended, bidding him not be disheartened by either apathy or opposition; that it was clearly his duty to go forward; for though not exactly prepared to accede to his propositions, none of the College people had found anything to refute them.

Mr Wilson had thought so much of the divine and apostolic journeys all taking a north and north-westerly direction, as seriously to have talked of having a map made describing these for his lectures; when one day Mr Mimpriss walked in with an introduction from a friend, and on being spoken to about it, immediately opened out one of his maps of the Acts of the Apostles ready for use, and as if it had been constructed expressly to illustrate that Law of Providence.

From chronological investigations, the late W. Cunninghame, Esq., of Lainshaw, had indicated that "the years 1830-1840 would bring us to the termination of one of the great dispensations of God, and the commencement of another."—See "Conference on Israel for 1872," p. 65. Whether Mr Wilson knew of this or not, he wrote to ask if Mr Cunninghame had any light upon Israel, and received the following:—

"LAINSHAW, 23d *March* 1839.

"DEAR SIR,—I am very unwilling to appear wanting in Christian courtesy by leaving unnoticed your letter of the 16th inst., and yet

I am so weighed down by labour of various kinds connected with my own chronological enquiries (which are still proceeding and issuing in new discoveries), and also with various other duties, that all I can possibly do is to thank you for your letter, and to wish that God may prosper your labours for the elucidation of the truth. The time, I believe, is exceedingly short, for the coming of the Lord draweth nigh. I certainly do not believe that we are descended from the Ten Tribes; but I shall be willing to consider any evidence on this and other subjects which you may submit to the public. I have, however, not strength for my own duties, and therefore I cannot take any share in the labours of others.—I remain, &c., &c.

"WILLIAM CUNNINGHAME."

In his preface to the third edition of this book, Mr Wilson says:—

"In 1839 I gave several courses of lectures on the subject, especially in the North of Ireland. Objections were here and there presented, which, when examined, uniformly resulted in additional confirmation of the views I advocated. In 1840 I delivered several courses of lectures in the neighbourhood of Liverpool,[1] chiefly to schools, when I had opportunity of seeing how clearly the subject could be apprehended by the minds of youth of both sexes; and how usefully it might be made the basis of very much of that knowledge which it becomes us to possess, both as inhabitants of this world, and as expectants of the world to come. I also delivered public courses, both in Woodside and in the Medical Institution, Liverpool. Several of the most eminent clerical students of prophecy attended. One of them had previously expressed his dissent from the view; and said that, after having examined my evidence, he would speak out if he found me in the wrong. He did not do so; and I suppose that the Rev. Hugh M'Neile is not a man who would fail to fulfil his word: but, otherwise, I have no sure evidence that he yet sees along with me in the matter. In addition to lecturing, he had recommended this other means of laying the information before the public; and accordingly, in the same year, I published the first edition of my lectures on 'Our Israelitish Origin.' From many different parties, I have received evidence of the usefulness

---

[1] Here he early made the acquaintance of the Rev. Jacob Tomlin, who has so ably followed out the subject of Language in his "Comparative Vocabulary of Forty-eight Languages."

of that book; and many are the quarters in which I have beheld the influence of the views advocated therein, even when that influence has not been acknowledged."

Many urged him to publish indeed; but one dear old friend asked for the printer's estimate, and then offered to bear the immediate responsibility. With similar liberality he placed a slip of paper in his hand when parting with him for a lecturing tour, to be kept in his pocket-book, with words to this effect, "If Mr Wilson should, in any of his journeys, require money, please say so to ——," &c., &c., &c.

A few mutual friends in London, who had exerted themselves much in the promotion of female and infant education among the Jews, while endeavouring to draw their attention to the Messianic Prophecies, had their own eyes opened to the existence of Israel among the Gentiles, and then to pray for their discovery, conversion, and restoration. The late H. Innes, Esq., at the 1872 "Conference on Israel" said, "I recal with deep interest my own intercourse, associated with some dear Christian friends, amongst that people, here in London in those closing years of 1830-1840. We resorted to their synagogues to pray for them on their great feasts; they welcomed us to their houses; they received us in their place where the Rabbis met. And on those occasions they rose to receive, and even to bless us, though we went unto them expressly, and told them we came in the name of the Lord."

One morning in the latter part of 1839, one of this party of friends received a note from a now deceased Rabbi, requesting her presence on important business, and which he thought would gratify her. The late Mrs Boyd of Williamstown Castle, county Dublin, in her eagerness to get the subject of "Our Origin" brought before the London world, took it for granted that a Rabbi was the most suitable medium for making known anything respecting Israel, and had written to him on the subject. Such was their reward for promoting the welfare of his people, at the same time their initiation to what subsequently became *their* most successful life-work in behalf of the adult deaf and dumb, and Mr Wilson's introduction to the great metropolis. That little praying circle of friends received him in the Lord's name, and remained faithfully helpful and encouraging, under all circumstances, to their lives' end. They got up his first London meeting in 1841, at which Dr Alexander, then just appointed Anglican Bishop in Jerusalem, took the chair; and there was a singular appropriateness in the last great meeting in which that party of friends were able to have any share, being presided over by Bishop Gobat. It was held at Mildmay on June 24th, 1872; and soon after the principal promoters "fell asleep," having in the most solemn manner delivered their united testimony by speech and writing to the charge of the Church of God. To them also is due the introduction of the subject in 1850 to the late Dr Holt Yates, the founder and chief supporter of the Suediah Mission, who became a warm advocate of our Israelitish origin, and a devoted personal friend.

The following, written by Mr Wilson immediately after the departure of the Rev. W. Marsh, D.D., may perhaps encourage some who may be refraining from identification with a truth which seems still to be in its infancy:—

"The late Rev. Dr Marsh was rightly regarded as the father of the London Jews' Society, and doubtless had much influence in regard to the formation of thought on prophetic subjects among evangelical members of the Church of England, lay and clerical. I remember his telling me, that when he first mentioned the personal reign of Christ on earth to the Rev. E. Bickersteth, the latter laughed: so little at that time did he understand those views of which he was afterwards a distinguished advocate; and Dr Marsh mentioned this as an encouragement to hope that he might yet see cause to come over to our side on the subject of Israel, as he already had in respect to Millenarian doctrine. Without mention of names, this conversation is alluded to in my 'Reply to Rev. E. Bickersteth.'

"I afterwards heard he had modified his views; but he did not acknowledge any change in reply to my enquiry.

"Dr Marsh was himself very favourably inclined to the subject; saw nothing in it opposed to the truth of Scripture, and much profit to be derived from its investigation as conducted in my lectures.

So early as 1840, a public meeting in Leamington was brought together very much through his instrumentality, the Hon. and Rev. F. Powys in the chair, at which he 'heartily expressed his gratification in hearing the interesting statements by the lecturer. He adverted to several points of the evidence as being very convincing, and the whole line of argument as being, to appearance, unanswerable. He could not say that at a moment's warning he could altogether accede to the view, yet could he see nothing to object to it. Everything seemed to be in its favour. At any rate, the inquiry, he was convinced, must do good ; and he warmly recommended the book the lecturer had published on the subject as being, even independent of this particular view, deeply interesting and profitable. He also alluded to the practical bearing of the subject, as being at the present moment most important.'—*Leamington Courier.*[1]

"Next day I received the following :—' Understanding you are to lecture at Warwick this day, I take this note in case I should not find you at home. I was much interested in your lecture, and I should like to have some further conversation upon the subject ; and should you be disengaged either to-morrow or Thursday evening, I should be happy to see you, and to introduce you to a few friends of the cause, &c., &c. W. M.'

"When I was going to Cheltenham I received from him the following written message to various friends there, inviting them to a consideration of the subject, to some of whom he also wrote privately :—

"'MY DEAR FRIEND,—Doth our law judge any man before it hear him ? Pray hear Mr Wilson. His book is worth reading, independently of its startling hypothesis. He is a truly Christian man, and has been considering the subject of Israel for the last twelve years, I understand. His books have been found very illustrative of Scripture and history. He appeals particularly in one part to Sharon Turner's "History of the Anglo-Saxons."—Yours ever affectionately, W. M.'

"I acknowledge I did not make much use of this note. I have ever had a difficulty in calling upon individuals ; and, besides, there

---

[1] About this time the Hon. and Rev. M. Villiers (afterwards Bishop of Durham, invited Mr Wilson to lecture at Kenilworth, "after which he expressed himself in the name of the audience as greatly gratified, and disposed to enter with spirit into the study of the prophetic word and the practical results of the inquiry."

were some things in it which might have led to mistakes, such as that I had been considering the subject of Israel *twelve* years; whereas our Israelitish origin had been before me only three or four. I had indeed been about twelve years engaged in the study of prophecy; and during that time had been looking at the case of Israel in different aspects. I saw that the Christian nations were dealt with and spoken of as Israel; but not for half that time had I any idea of finding them *literally* descended from those unto whom the promises were made. The first to whom the note was addressed (then Vicar of Cheltenham), there was some difficulty in my seeing at the time, and never did in reference to the subject; with which, however, I heard otherwise, he declined intermeddling. This, I dare say, was wrong. It is not the only thing which I ought to have done, and have left undone.

"I had the happiness of again meeting Dr Marsh on a visit to Malvern in 1842.[1] I think he was the chief speaker at a meeting of the Jews' Society. At that time it seemed as if a movement were taking place among the Jews all over Europe; and supposing him to have received the view of our Israelitish origin as being at least probable, I was surprised to hear him dilate upon the 'resurrection of the dry bones' in Ezek. xxxvii. as illustrative of the case of 'the Jews!' On taking occasion afterwards, in private conversation, to remark that I had thought he believed in our Israelitish origin, he replied that he did not know he had said anything inconsistent therewith. I then referred to the use he had made of Ezek. xxxvii. 1–14, and showed that the resurrection spoken of was the raising up of ALL-ISRAEL, not of 'the Jews;' and that in ver. 16, 'All the house of Israel' are represented as being 'the companions of Ephraim,' as distinct from 'the children of Israel,' 'the companions of Judah,' ver. 19. The passage evidently applies to a people who were *lost* (ver. 11; Is. xlix. 20) with regard to whom Ezekiel *required* to be informed that they were *Israel;* not a people who, like the Jews,

---

[1] A letter, dated August 30, 1842, says: "I have had a great many conversations with Dr Marsh, who has shown every disposition to forward my views; and when I parted he most kindly wished me every success, and asked for communion in prayer. He has introduced me to a circle of very good people here. I had, at a pretty large party, considerable argument on the subject of Israel: and Dr Marsh stood valiantly by me against an M.P."

had retained their organisation, but a people who required to be given newness of life by the Word and Spirit of God—the very instrumentality employed in our own reformation, so far as it successfully proceeded.

"After this we had comparatively little familiar intercourse, although it did not seem as if this arose from any estrangement of feeling. I had been very much pleased with the clear distinction made between Israel and Judah in his 'Plain Thoughts on Prophecy,' as recognised by Moses in Deut. xxviii.: 'Their captivity,' he says, 'is twice referred to, at verses 36 and 68; and the peculiarities of these two descriptions appear to me to refer to what has since been realised—the separate captivities of the Ten Tribes and of the Two Tribes:' and I had been given to understand that when he republished his 'Letters' he would take some kindly notice of 'Our Origin.' He has edged it in, rather sparingly, when speaking of the distinction made in Isa. xi. 11, 12, between 'the outcasts of Israel and the dispersed of Judah.' He mentions the former as being in some unknown situation; whether among the North American Indians, or the Afghans in Persia, or the inhabitants of the interior of Africa, or among the chief of the nations; agreeably to the promises to Ephraim (Gen. xlviii. 16; Deut. xxxiii. 17), or in any other part of the world: in a footnote to which he adds, 'See a curious book by Mr Wilson, entitled "Our Israelitish Origin,"' &c.

"Evidently he wished our view to be known; though, perhaps, in the state of the argument, or of his own health, he did not wish to be responsible for it. Men must make their choice of topics. There are life engagements to which they must almost exclusively attend. He had many; and at his period of life was doubtless careful not to identify himself very prominently with what might threaten to bring him into collision with those who had been labouring with him in the Gospel.

"When in 1844, I began to publish 'The Time of the End Prophetic Witness; advocating the Israelitish origin of the English Nation,' &c., he wrote: 'I like the paper much. Send me one every month, and one to my son, &c. I have a little doubt whether I should have announced the Israelitish origin in the *title*, though discussed in the work. May a blessing attend all means used to enlighten the nation, and stir up the Church to the consideration of the Great Coming Events!—Yours very truly, W. M.'

"The last note I received of any length is dated Nov. 2, 1852, and was written before leaving Brighton, where he had been for a short time. Speaking of Palestine, he says: 'I cannot but hope that light begins to dawn upon that Land. From thence, eventually, light will go forth into all the earth. We must pray the Lord to hasten it in His time. If He say, 'I come quickly,' we may well echo, 'Yea, come, Lord Jesus!'

"In 1837 he had preached the Anniversary Sermon of the London Jews' Society, from the text Luke xix. 41 : 'When He was come near, He beheld the city, and wept over it.' The *compassion* of Jesus he placed under three heads; as excited

    I. by their inflexible obstinacy ;
    II.   ,,   invincible hostility ;
    III.   ,,   impending judgments.

And his concluding appeal was, 'Look on them as Christ looked :

    I. in a spirit of sympathy for their present condition ;
    II.   ,,   faith as to their predicted restoration ;
    III.   ,,   gratitude for the inestimable privileges into which we have been grafted in their stead.'

"His own life was a reflection of this discourse. Dr Marsh looked upon the Saviour, who when He was about to 'bear our sins in His body on the tree,' wept over the case of the Jew, and he was changed into the same Image, causing that melting tenderness which persevered in showing him kindness and endeavouring his deliverance, notwithstanding much discouragement. He was one of those upon whom 'the spirit of grace and supplication' having been poured, they 'look upon' Jesus, and become assimilated to Him. They fulfil this anticipation, which doubtless was part of 'the joy set before Him '—the assimilation to Himself of His people in grace and supplication, in love and intercession (Zech. xii. 10). One and another of those annual short prayers, which may be said to have become universal, were written by him. In the annual call to united prayer for the outpouring of the Holy Spirit he deeply sympathised ; and when that veteran, the Rev. Haldane Stewart, was taken home, he very naturally took his place.

"His first Jews' Society Sermon was preached in 1827, under very remarkable circumstances. Soon after, at Colchester, he had the happiness of introducing to the Hebrew New Testament, M. S. Alexander, educated for a Jewish Rabbi, who afterwards became the first Anglican Bishop in Jerusalem ; and who just after his appointment introduced by prayer my first lecture delivered in London on the subject of our Israelitish origin."

On October 28th, 1845, Mr Wilson received his first letter from the Rev. F. R. A. Glover :—

"Sir,—I have been greatly gratified, as well as instructed, by your lectures on 'Our Israelitish Origin,' and what makes them the more interesting to me is that, from certain things connected with Irish Antiquities—by which I am led to believe that Judah (probably of the first captivity) took refuge and found rule in Ireland. I was led to conjecture that England might be Joseph to the nations ; seeing the literal acting out of the prophecy of Joseph, which God has committed to this our people.

"Accident, as men speak, made me buy a leaf-tract of your answer to Mr Bickersteth, and caused me some time after to buy your book ; and now I find that what I had *conjectured* is indeed the reality of the case, and also that my idea of Queen Victoria—i.e., the royalty of Britain or Anglia gathering up the promises of Judah and of Joseph, has strong confirmation. If it be any satisfaction to you to hear it, I have pleasure in informing you that this view of her position and responsibility has gone to Her Majesty, and has been presented to her as a 'a striking thing,' by a nobleman of the highest rank and undaunted courage. What effect it may have, God knows. We may hope, while seeking, that she may be allowed to have the book. . . .

"Allow me to suggest a question, which I am sure you will feel is done in friendship, and with the earnest desire that the difficulties in the way of the general reception of what I feel to be truth, may be gradually removed. How do you account for the entire absence of the rite of circumcision on the whole of the descendants of Israel after the flesh ? This difficulty was mentioned to me by Dr Russell, Canon of Canterbury, who had the advantage of being an auditor of some of your lectures in London. [For reply, see "Popular Difficulties."]

"Allow me to say in conclusion, the subject, opened up with much power and ability in your lectures, seems to derive every day confirmation from the reading of the Minor Prophets, where every page seems to receive flashes of life from the action of the mind upon the subject of your labours. I have been particularly struck with this during the last month, when this portion of the Word of God has been read daily in the Church.—I am, Sir, with respect, very faithfully your obliged, F. R. A. GLOVER."

Mr Glover's book, "England, the Remnant of Judah," &c.,

was not published till 1861, immediately after which Mr Wilson received a copy.

In the winter of 1846–47, he lectured at Hastings, and there made the valuable acquaintance of Dr George Moore, who has successfully followed out the inquiry in his "Lost Tribes; or, Saxons of the East and West" (1861), and "The Ancient Pillar-Stones of Scotland" (1867), whereby the early connection of Britain with India is clearly established from Asiatic monuments, literature, and character—the first notice of which Mr Wilson gladly received from a friend unacquainted with Dr Moore, who sent him a copy of a review, saying, "The work before us is distinguished for scholarship, intellectual activity, reverence for the Bible and the Author of it, and a certain enthusiasm which is apt to prove contagious to the reader. The author adopts Mr Wilson's conclusions, which he endeavours to establish by further evidence, to complete the chain of argument."

Of "Our Israelitish Origin," Dr Moore says (Lost Tribes, p. 94)—"This was too much opposed to the views of popular expositors to be received with the candour it deserved; but it must be acknowledged that Mr Wilson in that work has done much more to meet the requirements of prophecy than any that preceded him," &c.

In 1847 a number of friends united for the publication of the "Tracts on Israel," and about the same time the Rev. Robert Polwhele, of Avenbury, being convinced of the truth, simply on his own responsibility, had printed on cards the "Queries on our Israelitish Origin," which he has continued steadily to circulate, and otherwise quietly, but firmly, to promote inquiry into the subject.

In reviewing these and many another chivalrous word and deed in behalf of our Israelitish origin, two thoughts have presented themselves to the writer: That God makes use of human instrumentality to work out His greatest purposes and designs; and that our generous, large-hearted, sympathetic action may be necessary to develop some great result from apparently insignificant beginnings. We know that "His people shall be willing in the day of His power," but always some brave heart has to begin work in the grey, cold, cheerless dawn. To "live before one's day" *is* a trial of faith, and the author felt it sadly enough in many ways. If a first opportunity and desire of serving the cause of God by helping some such tiny effort, which has little to show for a long time in answer to the querulous, cold cynicism, "What is the good of it?" be overlooked or despised, seldom does the same person have another, however much it may be desired. When human comfort, however, seems farthest away, the consolations of Christ are most abundant. And blessed be His name, who neither in shade nor in sunshine allowed His servant to feel utterly lonely in this work, but raised up from time to time, as absolutely required, such genial help as carried it forward in peace and quietness, without exciting the envy or the needless antagonism he so studiously avoided. The responsibility of withholding the knowledge from our nation was perilous; but the ordeal through which he had sometimes to pass with adverse circumstances, ill health, and want of hope, to him was painful to the last degree in his own soul.

With profound thankfulness he read the following in August 1865, from the beginning of which year he had begun to realise that the thought of our Israelitish origin had struck its roots deeply into the heart of society, from the fresh impulse it seemed to receive in various directions, without any one being able to tell exactly how or why; twenty years after it had been supposed by some other learned men to have been cut up, root and branch, dead, buried, and forgotten (see *Leisure Hour* for July 1872):—

"DEAR SIR,—When recently in the city of Cairo, in Egypt, your book on 'Our Israhtish Origin' was mentioned to me by the worthy chaplain there, the Rev. Buchan Wright, as containing a clue towards the explanation of the discoveries which appear to have followed the late Mr John Taylor's theory of the Great Pyramid, when treated by his peculiar method of religious analysis, begun by him in his work, 'The Great Pyramid; why was it built, and who built it?' followed by myself last year in 'Our Inheritance in the Great Pyramid.'

"Since coming home, I have accordingly procured your said book, and find that it does, indeed, tend to supply an important link in the pyramid discoveries; and at the same time I could hardly help thinking that the pyramid developments supplied an additional and more precise character of proof to the many which you have brought together, respecting your soul-strengthening idea of our Israelitish origin. I write this, therefore, earnestly inquiring if you have published anything further on your subject since 1844, and if so, where it is to be found; or, if you have in your own mind in any way modified or altered the views there expressed, or have any still further proofs of them. Hoping that you will kindly excuse my brusqueness by reason of the powerful effect your theory, or rather illustration of what Israel is, has had upon me, I remain yours very truly, C. PIAZZI SMYTH."

The author's labours "in season and out of season," his joyful welcome of all available opportunities of either increasing his own knowledge of the various ramifications of the subject, or helping others of any age, sex, or condition to a fuller knowledge of the Word and Ways of God, would require a volume. But we may quote his opening address to the readers of the January " Watchmen of Ephraim," 1866 :—

"Throughout the different sects and parties holding the cardinal doctrines of Christianity, our views have been quietly making their way; but our constituency has at present no collective voice, no concentrated action.

"So soon as individuals became convinced that the Anglo-Saxon race occupies the place of the Firstborn, they looked to what they had in hand, that they might use it heartily in the Lord's service for the common good; and if they were not already employed, they have looked about for something worthy of their high calling, into which they have thrown their energies, no longer waiting for another people to accomplish the work appointed for themselves.

"They have seen that there was much to be done preparatory to their Lord's return, and that, although there may be more time to do it in than some prophetic interpreters have allowed to the present dispensation, still they know that it is theirs to work while they may, without being content that their Lord should find

His people unprepared to meet Him. They have not regarded themselves as a sect, but as intended to help all who are doing the work of the Lord, whether in behalf of the Jew, the Gentile, or the Israel of God.

"Our views have thus proved themselves to be thoroughly practical, except in respect to united action in the propagation of those truths which have been found so 'soul-strengthening' and stimulating to every good work.

"There has been a long time of comparative silence, during which, however, a work has been done which could not perhaps have been performed, except in retirement, and for years we almost entirely ceased even from ordinary correspondence with friends. This was wrong, and has been misinterpreted by some, as if we had seen cause to abandon our views respecting Israel. The work in which we have been engaged will, it is hoped, be ultimately found preparatory to the universal diffusion of the truth. Our views have been proved most useful, not only in regard to Old Testament history and prophecy, but also in opening up the treasures contained in the gospel history; and many of our most earnest youth are being trained, in all sections of the Church, to publish with one heart and one voice the whole truth and manifold wisdom of God."[1]

Ten years earlier, the late John Fenwick, of Newcastle, wrote to Mr Wilson—"Well, you have been most usefully

---

[1] Mr Mimpriss remarks, in referring to Mr Wilson's labours in preparing "The Gospel Treasury," for the press, that "whatever excellence there is in the book, the compiler most unfeignedly acknowledges is due, not to himself, but to others; especially to the valuable contributions, and disinterested and laborious revision and superintendence, of a dear Christian brother. (The gatherings of many years, most carefully and impartially sifted, are here offered to the Christian public, and with an earnest prayer that God will add His blessing to what is His Own.)"

And to the latest edition in 1865—"The flattering and nearly unanimous commendation given to 'The Gospel Treasury' by all who have used it, makes it my very grateful duty now to record, with unfeigned thanks, that the dear Christian brother above referred to is John Wilson, author of 'Lectures on the Israelitish Origin of the English Nation,' without whose serviceable and almost gratuitous aid, and most valuable contributions, in notes, practical reflections, &c., the volume would probably have had no existence." See also the Preface to "The Title-Deeds of the Holy Land," &c.)

employed, and you and our friend have the high satisfaction of giving an immortal work to the Church of the living God. The more I examine it, I like it the better, and feel thankful that any friends of mine have given such a fearless enunciation of truth."

In connection with "The Treasury," a remarkable circumstance occurred in the summer of 1847, which may as well be mentioned, as bringing out the characteristics of the two men. The first twelve sections had been sent out in paper covers as a "feeler," or rather like Noah's dove; and they were resting from their writing. Meanwhile a great crisis came in the money-market, which threatened to cripple everybody's exertions. It was no time for lecturing in the provinces, and Mr Wilson grudged to see the summer passing without doing anything for London, for which funds were required. But one evening a stranger called to entreat of him to give two lectures daily for some weeks, on a Model of Jerusalem, at the Egyptian Hall, *for which he would be paid*, and should have the liberty of giving as many gratuitous invitations as he pleased, for the evenings, to those likely to be benefited. After much anxious thought, he took the message as from God, in answer to his yearnings for some way of making known the truth, and with his usual force of character began anew to study the topography of the Holy Places, with much profit to students of the "Treasury." The scene of the Transfiguration came up, and he became fully convinced it had *not* been on Mount Tabor. Not so much was then known about the Holy Land, and Mr Mimpriss might have kept back our Scripture-knowledge clock, if he had chosen, for many a long day; but upon Mr Wilson pointing out to him the reasons for his conviction that Hermon was the true Holy Mount, the scene of the Transfiguration, and of the Great Commission, as well as the great Sion of the future, just as he has given them in the "Treasury," he at once, at great expense, had all his Map and Manual plates altered, and the maps in stock cancelled.

Respecting this part of his work, he thus wrote in 1862:—

"Even in the present time, the object of one's life is sometimes attained without the world being aware of it, *and by means which the individual may, at first, have regarded as an interruption to his work.* . . .

"Knowing this truth (of Israel), and feeling somewhat of its power, I was, of course, anxious to impress it upon others, and to propagate it widely. I wished to hasten forward that restoration of Israel which I saw was coming, and which is to have such an important bearing upon the destinies of the human race generally, and our own family of nations in particular. I would have delighted to lecture on the subject extensively, and to have agitated immediately for a reoccupation of Palestine.

"I was too apt to forget that, in order to the restoration being effected happily, and with the desired results, the people's hearts must be prepared. A better knowledge of the gospel history, and of the teaching of our Lord, must be diffused, along with the other truth —that we are indeed *the people* who were appointed to be conformed to the Son of God. He must have His life impressed upon those who are to learn Him, and who are to show Him forth when 'the manifestation of the sons of God' takes place (Rom. viii. 19; Rev. xiv. 1-5); when 'as the stones of a crown, they shall be lifted up as an ensign upon His land' (Zech. ix. 16).

"In a measure I had seen this, but had little thought of submitting to the drudgery of being so intimately connected with the production of the means appointed, to fashion after the image of God's dear Son, 'the people which shall be created to praise the Lord.'

"But my way by Providence was most effectually hedged in, and blocked up, so that I could not do otherwise; and I was, as it were, taken by the shoulders and set down to work at books designed to teach teachers the life of Christ; wherein they might learn, week after week, and year after year, to communicate more clearly and fully that knowledge which is needful to be possessed, in order that the end I had in view—the discovery and restoration of Israel— might be happily attained.

"This work I would have been well enough pleased to leave to others, and yet it was that for which my previous training had remarkably fitted me. And the result has been the production of books reckoned, by men familiar with these matters, as the most perfect of their kind—books not to be read once, and then cast aside, but to be continually pondered by those most diligent in doing good, and who are most anxious to learn, in order that they may teach others also. Here, without excitement, and without being seen in the matter, I am teaching and preaching much more extensively—both in this country and the colonies—than I could possibly have done, in the way I desired, by personal address. . . .

"What I know of the difference between outward seeming and the reality, would incline me to be not hasty in judging of success or defeat, of happiness or unhappiness, in the case of others. Had my own desire been granted, it is not likely that I would have been so usefully employed, and my words would not then have taken such a permanent form, nor have been sown in peace so widely over the world. I have studiously avoided being the object of envy or jealousy, and have been allowed more quiet than was at one time likely to be my lot in life." . . .

On Saturday evening, January 22, 1870, the revered author, having completed his testimony, sweetly fell asleep in Jesus. Almost the last words he spoke were deliberately delivered, as to a great multitude: "And—when—the witnesses—had—completed their testimony, they ascended — up to heaven. And L——, the testimony is completed." To his latest hour his loving trust in the faithfulness of our covenant-keeping God remained unshaken, and his discernment undimmed to the rapid development in our own day of the ancient designs of Providence unfolded in the foregoing pages, as expressed in the advertisement prefixed to this volume in 1867.

It was his privilege to know that his mission was increasingly recognised as having been that of directing the national mind to the minute recognition of God's hand, as guiding the world's history to the fulfilment of ancient prophecy. He had the great joy of seeing the partial development of what he had long regarded with the eye of faith—the people of this our nation awaking to their special duties as the children of those fathers to whom the "Promises" were made, through a more intimate knowledge of Him who became our Elder Brother, that to us they might be confirmed.

The success of wise and earnest efforts for the redemption of the Land of Promise from its long desolation of idolatry and ignorance were daily causes of prayer and praise. But to the education of our home population for their high destiny his life was consecrated; and the memory of his unceasing and self-denying labours in the great mission of "turning the heart of the fathers to the children" will long live in the hearts of many, and energise the efforts of those with whom he was longest associated, and who knew him best.

An instance of his earnestness in caring for those who are "out of the way," recurs to the writer's mind as most characteristic. His own account is dated March 18, 1855:—

"On Monday evening I stumbled upon a nest of atheists near King's Cross. I had met with two or three exceedingly active in disturbing other people's meetings, both in and out of doors. One of them I had begged to be quiet, and not interfere with other people's business (it was an anti-Mormon meeting), and if he chose, I would discuss his own subject by itself. He mentioned their place, and another person less precipitous was willing to accept the challenge. I had some conversation afterwards with a third on our way home, and got him somewhat tamed, and willing, I hope, to examine. I had occasion to walk a long way with a fourth, who had said almost nothing, with whom also I had much conversation. His father-in-law, I learned, was an old man of eighty-two, a deist, as I understood always. . . .

"On Monday evening I went to their place, and finding it open, I went in. It was a meeting of the Society of Unemployed, and was just breaking up. They profess to keep the two objects apart, but the meetings are in the same place, and are conducted by the same parties, as in the case of Atheism. The man's father had been a Methodist preacher, and his wife had been a Sunday-school teacher. Her father had belonged to the Tabernacle. I told those that remained my errand: that I had been challenged to a discussion, but did not see the parties there. The person to whom the place belongs, and who is the lecturer, took up the subject, and I replied; and so we went on till about twelve o'clock, the people who were present at the beginning continuing to the end. They seemed exceedingly interested, and evidently would like to have the matter out. So I drew out my thesis, and handed it to them yesterday. Will you be so kind as look over it, and tell me what you think of it?

"There is evidently a great work for some one to do here. It is rather thankless labour; but it begins to gain ground with me that it is for work like this I have come up to London. It is curious that it was said in that letter I got before leaving C——, 'If, therefore, you are called to wait upon the Lord concerning the Land of Israel, this He will show according to your faith and ours, that it is with the opening of the graves—yea, graves—that He will manifest the glory of ancient Israel, whose the land is, who shall tread upon it in His name, who shall take possession through the power of the blood of Jesus.' I had been literally invited to wait upon the Lord concerning the Land of Israel, when these dens of death, in which multitudes of our people appear to be fast hastening into corruption, were opened to me, and exhibited wretchedness certainly very much in contrast to the glory of ancient Israel, calculated to humble us in the dust on account of the condition, physical and spiritual, of masses of our people. May the Lord direct!" &c.

And so he followed the matter up thoroughly to the end, night after night taking notes of their difficulties, just as they are given in the little book, "The Being of God,"[1] that he might more accurately consider them at his leisure, and write out fully his answers; in which his son, one day at least, found he had been occupied upwards of eight consecutive hours, utterly unconscious of the lapse of time.

He never knew here the ultimate result of his single-handed conflict. So far as he could ascertain, he was the only Christian present at these discussions. When he next visited London, they had changed their place of meeting, and he was not able to follow them up. But on their last evening together, it was acknowledged that no one who had ever come among them had so well met their difficulties. One who had passed fourscore took his hand between his own, saying, "Sir, if any one could have convinced me that there is a God, it would have been yourself; BUT IT IS TOO LATE: I AM TOO OLD TO CHANGE."

[1] London: James Nisbet & Co.; W. Macintosh & Co.

His own life was the best illustration of his belief, expressed in the following lines, wherein may be retraced the great secret of that wondrous heart-rest whereby his outer and inner life were so perfectly harmonised for the Master's service :—

"Let our joy be that which does not fade with the perishing things of time, or depart with our capacity for the enjoyment of mere sentient existence. Let it be that which comes nearer, the farther we proceed in life, and which becomes brighter as all others are fading from our view.

"Let us seek conformity to the Son of God, who hath bought us for Himself with His own blood. Thus, having become 'meet for the inheritance of the saints in light,' we shall, in the morning of the resurrection, have not only our proper dwelling in the heavens, but shall also inherit the earth; and even now, all things needful unto us will be added by our heavenly Father.

"The *possibility* of such things being true may not much affect either conduct or happiness, *but the full persuasion of them must.* The REALISATION of their being truly ours in the Divine Promise must incite to the work of faith, and labour of love, and patience of hope. If human beings can trust in each other, wait patiently, and count no labour or toil which may bring them for a few short years into intimate fellowship in the present very uncertain, and sometimes very unsatisfactory, life, how much more should we come under the influence of that faith which has the whole Word of God, and His working in Providence, throughout all ages, to rest on! The Hope of that life is as certain as our own existence so clearly foretold to our fathers thousands of years ago ; as certain as the Resurrection of the Saviour, and as the Descent of the Spirit sent to teach us the Love of God, and prepare us for our Lord's glorious Return.

"May the Son of God, who bought us for Himself with His own blood, perfect us in love and in patient continuance in well-doing, introducing us into the fuller enjoyment of that *life* which is the highest happiness and the truest *wisdom* we can reach upon earth!"

INDEX

OF

BOOKS, AUTHORS, AND SUBJECTS.

Abbadie, *Theological Works*, 136, 411.
Abdiel, *Jewish Expositor*, 170.
Abraham's vision, 4.
Agreement of Oriental and Welsh traditions respecting the White Island of the West, 170, 279.
Alaric, 236.
Albigenses, 155.
Albinus, 203.
Alcuin, 291.
Alexander, Bishop, 427, 431.
Alfred the Great, *Commonplace Book*, 262, 346, 348.
Allemani, 237, 269.
All-Israel, 100.
Ancient Music of Ireland, 145.
Andrew, Dr, *Hebrew Dictionary and Grammar*, 190.
Anglo-Saxon wheat measure, 82.
Anglo-Saxon identification, 273.
Angus, *Bible Handbook*, 205.
Annales Fuldensis Monasterii, 168.
Anquetil, *Zend-Avesta Translated*, 185.
Antonio a Tempo *On Poetry*, 262.
Apocalypse, 133.
Aristotle, 170.
Arthur, King, 173.
Aryan languages, 195.
Asher and Etruria, 151.
Ashmole, *Order of the Garter*, 173.
Asiatic Researches, 211, 279.

Asser, *Life of Alfred*, 330.
Assyrians, 2, 8; used as an axe to punish Israel, 180.
Astyages, 207.
Attila, 234.

Baal-worship in Scotland, 164.
Balaam's prophecy, 85.
Babylonians, 2, 8.
Bards, 172.
Beauty of the Angles, 283.
Bede, *Ecclesiastical History*, 208-210.
Belgæ in Ireland, 168.
Beni-Israel, 212.
Betham, Sir William, origin of the Welsh, 168.
Beth-Omri, 181.
Beyrout and Britain, 160.
Bickersteth, Rev. E., 427, 432.
Bilerium, 159.
Bird, *Historical Researches*, 143.
Birds of all countries on Hermon, 38.
Birthright, our, 57.
Black Sea, shores of, 217.
Blackwood, *Magazine*, 197.
Bohemian heads, 156, 165.
Book of Remembrance, 160.
Bossuet, 136.
Boulogne, 154.
Boulaq Papyri, 36.
Breaking up of the Assyrian Empire, 198.

Britain, origin of the name, 160.
Buddhism in Scotland, 225.
Bunting, *Ancient Music of Ireland*, 145.

Cable, Israel the Lord's, 31, 82, 409.
Cæsar, Caius Julius, *Commentaries*, 278.
Cambria Formosa, 172.
Carlisle Patriot, 1843, 418.
Cassi, 278.
Central position of the Land of Israel, 37.
Certainty of the recovery of Israel, 114.
Chaldee Targums, 194.
Chemarim, 181.
Chivalry, 258.
Christianity first made the religion of England, 261.
Cisner, 210.
Clarke, Dr, Travels in Russia, Tartary, &c., 217, 221, 291, 293, 294, 319.
Combe, 165.
Completeness of Israel's captivity, 104.
Continuance of Israel's captivity, 105.
Connection of Beyrout with Britain, 161.
Constantine, 161.
Cornwall, 157.
County, Saxon, 263.
Covenant with Abram cannot be made void, 14.
Covenant with Noah, 21.
Crusades, 260.
Cubbees, Kelts, Chaldai, and Galatians all one people, 174.
Cumberland, 171.
Cumri, origin of the name, 170, 182.
Cunningham, Major, *The Bhilsa Topes*, 219.
Cunninghame, William, 424, 425.
Cuvier, *Regne Animal*, 170.
Cyaxares, 205.
Cyrus, 207.

Davia, 232.
Dan, blessing of, 1, 7.
Dan, losing of, 143.

Danes, 140, 281.
D'Aubigné, *History of the Reformation*, 173.
Davies, Rev. E., *Mythology of the British Druids*, 277.
Defoe, Daniel, 285.
Deioces, 201.
Demetrius, 223.
Dialogues on Prophecy, 412.
Diodorus Siculus, 159, 276, 279.
Dispersed of Israel, 147.
Don Carlos, 139.
Don Cossacks, 291.
Druidism and Buddhism, 171.
Dutch, 153.
Ddu, Dr Dafydd, 322.

Early British Church, 173.
Early connection of Britain with Eastern lands, 157.
Earth and world, 45.
Ebrard, Professor, 175.
Edda, 241, 324.
Eden, 34.
Edom, Dukedoms of, in Spain, 109.
Education and training of the Patriarchs, 70.
Eginhartus, 108.
Egypt, 8, 77.
Egyptian Commonwealth, 145.
Einion, 322.
Eldad, *Memoirs of the Ten Tribes*, 143.
Empires point in the direction of lost Israel, 22.
Encyclopædia Britannica, 185.
English heraldic emblems on ancient Buddhist monuments, 170.
Epistles sent in the same direction, 133.
Esaksa, rebellion of the, 226.
Escaped of Israel, 137.
Etruria, 119.
Eutropius, 209.
Evangelical religion in Italy, 151.

Families of Abraham according to the sons of Noah, 119.
Ferrers, *Progeny of the English Monarchs*, 208.
Feudal system, 257.

INDEX. 445

Fishbourne, Admiral, *Missing Link*, 171.
Florentine Town Council, 153.
Fo-kweki, 277.
Formal introduction of Christianity to the Anglo-Saxons, 261.
Forster, Dr Charles, *Primeval Language*, 215.
Freemasonry, 259.
Fruitfulness of the land of Israel, 39.
Future changes in the land of Israel, 40.

Galen, 39.
Garden of God, 34.
Gawler, Colonel C. J., *Our Scythian Ancestors*, 165.
Geijer, *History of Sweden*, 139, 221, 325.
Geneste, *Parallel Histories of Judah and Israel*, 113.
Gesenius, *Hebrew Lexicon*, 269.
Gibbon, *Decline and Fall of the Roman Empire*, 236, 280.
Gildas, 171.
Glover, *England the Remnant of Judah*, 60, 166, 167, 432.
Gobat, Bishop, 427.
Good Samaritan, 97.
Gospel in the ten generations from Adam to Noah, 20.
Gotha, 141.
Goths, 234.
Govett, *English Derived from Hebrew*, 190.
Grammatical Rules of Welsh Poetry, 322.
Great Empires, 8, 122.
Great Pyramid, 82.
Grecian Empire, 8.
Grimm, German law, 268.
Gwawd Lludd y Mawr, 277.

Handful of Corn on the Top of the Mountains, 406, 420.
Haxthausen, Baron, *Trans-Caucasia*, 215.
Henry, Dr, *History of Great Britain*, 296, 297, 300, 422, 423.
Henry of Erfurd, 210.
Hanseatic League, 253.

Heads, similarity of English and Jewish, 284.
Hebrew and Highland music, 173.
Hebrew basis of English language, 189.
Hebrew ark of the covenant same as Anglo-Saxon wheat measure, 82.
Helena, Empress, a British princess, 161, 297.
Heraldry, 259.
Herder, *Philosophy of Man*, 271.
Hermannus Contractus, 168.
Herodotus, 144, 146, 182, 191, 199, 202, 209, 231, 271, 275, 276.
Himalayas, 188.
Historical connection of the languages of Europe, 179.
Historical and Political Discourse of the Laws and Government of England, 305.
Holinshed, *History of Great Britain*, 172.
Homer, 275, 279.
Hu the Mighty, 170, 223.
Huet, 187.
Hugo, Victor, *Le Rhin*, 337, 364.
Hundreds, Saxon, 304.
Huns, 234.

Identity of the Galatians with some of the Germans, 175.
Ingram, 312.
Ingulf, *Chronicle*, 330.
Innes, Henry, 426.
Inquiry concerning primitive inhabitants of Ireland, 168.
Ionian Commonwealth, 146.
Irenæus, 173.
Irish Church, early, 169.
Israel and Judah, distinction between, 99.
Israel in Egypt, 144.
Israel's grave the Saxon's birthplace, 267.
Issachar, 153.

Jacob's pillow, 166.
James, Epistle of, 132.
Jerome, 175.
Jewish Intelligencer, 1875, 225.
Jews greatly mixed, 109.

Joel, 141.
Jones, *Relics of the Bards*, 321.
Josephus, *History*, 107, 109, 141.
Journeys of our Saviour and the apostles all north-westward, 130.
Juhadah the mighty, 223.
Julian, Emperor, 39.

Karaim, 222.
Keith, 278.
Keppel, 184.
Khorsabad, 181.
Kingsley, *The Roman and the Teuton*, 256, 268, 280, 303.

Lacedemonians, 141.
Lamp in the Wilderness, 163.
Land promised to Abraham, 13, 32; never yet occupied as a seat of universal empire, 47.
Language, historical connection of, 184.
Latimer, Bishop, 335.
Leamington Courier, 425.
Leisure Hour, 431.
Lewis, *British History*, 163, 172.
Life of Luther, 413.
Lion, the ancient standard of Ireland, 146, 167.
Lombard laws, 268.
Lorimer on the Culdean Church, 175.
Lost Israel to be looked for among the descendants of Japhet, 134.
Lowth, Archbishop, 189.
Lowthian, *Narrative of a Recent Journey to Jerusalem*, 406, 407, 420.
Lucius changes the national religion from Druidism to Christianity, 251.

Maccabees, 141.
M'Crie, *Annals of English Presbytery*, 173.
M'Neile, Hugh, 425.
Magi, the, 211.
Malmesbury, *Chronicle*, 330.
Maraveh, 161.
Mara-Zion, 157.
Marcellinus, 203.
Mariette, *Hymn to Amen*, 36.
Mariner's compass, 264.

Marriage customs of the Anglo-Saxons, 298.
Marsh, Rev. Dr, 427, 430.
Martial, *Epigrams*, 172.
Matthew of Westminster, 330.
Median monarchy, 200.
Messiah the Prince, 223.
Millar, *Historical View of the English Government*, 307, 309, 310, 312.
Milot, Abbé, *Elements of English History*, 336, 337, 350.
Mimpriss, *Gospel Treasury*, 130, 131, 393, 421, 424, 436, 437.
Ministers of religion, provision for, 257.
Ministration of judgment, 12.
Mœsia, 230.
Montalembert, *Monks of the West*, 175
Moore, Dr, *Ancient Pillar-Stones of Scotland*, 225, 227, 433.
Moore, Dr, *Lost Tribes*, 143, 144, 164, 169, 170, 186, 188, 191, 211, 226, 228, 274, 279, 433.
Morgan, *British Kymry*, 171, 262.
Music, identity of Hebrew and British, 173, 197, 262.
Mystery of God finished, 1.

Neander, *History of the Christian Church*, 173.
Nestorians, 227.
Newton Stone, 225.
Normans, 282.

Objections answered, 104, 115.
Ogygia, 168.
Olaus, *History of the Northern Nations*, 309.
Old Testament prophecy all points north-westward, 135.
Oliphant, *Russian Shores of the Black Sea*, 255.
Origin of the name Britain, 159.

Palestine and England, 157.
Pallas, 220, 221.
Parable of the Good Samaritan, 97.
Parable of the Lost Son, 265.
Parable of the Lost Piece of Silver, 267.
Paranzabuloe, 159.
Parkhurst, *Hebrew Lexicon*, 31, 189.

INDEX. 447

Pass of Dariel, 215.
Patrick, 169, 174.
Pechts, or Picts, 280.
Pehlevi, 185.
Penine, *Historical Drama*, 187.
Persia, 8.
Persia, language of, 185.
Peter, *Epistles of*, 133.
Petrarch, *Sonnets*, 262.
Phraortes, 204.
Pinkerton, *Early History of Scotland*, 176, 281.
Pirie, 189.
Pliny, 277–279.
Pocock, 136.
Poetry, 241, 262.
Polwhele, Rev. Robert, 433.
Prevost, Paradol, 336, 337, 355.
Prideaux, *Connection of Old and New Testaments*, 109.
Primitive Inhabitants of Ireland, 168.
Principles of Government, 79.
Prinsep's *Historical Results*, 162.
Procopius, *De Bello Gothico*, 136.
Progress of Israel westward, 212.
Promises made to the fathers, 51.
Proportion of Israel to the families of Noah, 118.
Protestantism in Spain, 140.
Prudentius, *Hamartigenia*, 371.
Psammiticus, 145.
Ptolemy, 208, 210, 215, 226, 277.
Puranas, 279.

Quæstor, Fabius, 209.
Quarterly Review, 1846, 161.

L. N. R., *Missing Link*, 1873,
Races of Mankind, 23.
Rapin, *History of Great Britain*, 336–338, 340, 343, 344, 348, 354.
Rawayah, 185.
Rawlinson, Sir Henry, 181, 191, 327, 421.
Rawlinson, Professor, 191.
Rees, *Cyclopædia*, 39.
Rejoicing multitude, 69.
Resemblance of ancient Egyptian to English furniture, 77.
Results of Israel's training in the Anglo-Saxons, 286.

Revival Paper in Italy, 152.
Revolt of the Medes, 200.
Rock Temples, 143.
Robertson, *History of Scotland*, 250, 302.
Rolleston, *Mazzaroth*, 318.
Romans, 2, 8.
Romanism and Druidism, 171.
Rymer, *Fœdera*, 354.

Sagas of Haco and St Olave, 328.
Sailman, *Researches in the East*, 143.
Sakai, 211, 277.
Samarina, or Samaria, 181.
Sanskrit, 185.
Sargon, or Sargina, 181.
Sarum, or Sarou, 163.
Saturday Magazine, 422.
Savary, *Travels in Egypt*, 145.
Saxon Chronicle, 312.
Saxons called Syrians, 279.
Saxon, true origin of the name, 210.
Saxon women, 296.
Scythians, 276.
Selden, 305.
Serpent-worship, 220.
Silence of the Druids, 163.
Simeon, 146.
Smiles, *The Huguenots*, 335.
Smyth, Professor, *Life and Work at the Great Pyramid*, 194.
Smyth, Professor, *Our Inheritance in the Great Pyramid*, 83, 221, 326, 333, 435.
Snorre, *History*, 324.
Social and political relations of the Anglo-Saxons, 290.
Sonnets, 126, 262.
Sons of God, 19.
Spain, 139.
Speed, *Chronicle*, 208, 210.
Spirit of deep sleep, 10.
Standard of Israel, 376.
Star-banner on ancient Buddhist temple, 170.
State of Europe subsequent to northern invasions, 246.
Steam power, 264.
Stillingfleet, *Antiquities of British Churches*, 172.
Strabo, 209, 275.

Stranger who joins himself to the Lord to have part with Israel, 16.
Strathclyde, 173.
Stuart, *Laws of England*, 330.

Temple, Sir W., *Miscellanea*, 252, 258, 263.
Tertullian, 173.
Teutonic Order and League, 258.
Time of the "Horn" of Israel budding forth, 183.
Tin-mines, 153.
Tithes, 171.
Toland, 174.
Tomlin, *Comparative Vocabulary*, 190, 425.
Traces of Dan in Europe, 139.
Tracts on Israel, 433.
Traditions, 210.
Training and education of the Patriarchs, 70.
Training and education of Israel under the Judges and Kings, 84.
Trelawney, *Perranzabuloe*, 159.
Trident, &c., 170.
Tristram, Canon, 38.
Turks, 2.
Turner, Sharon, *History of the Anglo-Saxons*, 176, 184, 250, 275, 276, 281, 313, 329, 372.
Tyndal, 190.
Tyre, 163.
Tyrsenia, 149.
Tything, Saxon, 302.

Ulphilas, *New Testament*, 191, 236.

Varada and Mateya, 279.
Vetus Chronicon Holsatica, 139.
View of the State of Europe, 252.
Virgil, 150.
Vision of All Israel, 3.
Voluspa, 229, 241.
Voyage to the Land of Israel, 32.

Wadilove, Rev. W. D., *Lamp in the Wilderness*, 163.

Waldensian Confession of Faith, 156.
Waymarks, Get thee up, 229.
Wedgwood, *Book of Remembrance*, 160, 163, 412.
Welsh Archæologia, 277.
Welsh of Israel, 169.
Was the House of Israel ever restored? 105.
Where Israel were lost, thence came the Anglo-Saxons, 274.
Why did Dan remain in ships? 138.
Williams, *Ecclesiastical Antiquities of the Cymri*, 171.
Wilson, John, *Answer to Mr Bickersteth*, 432.
" *Being of God*, 441.
" *Time of the End Prophetic Witness*, 430.
" *Mission of Elijah*, 272, 333, 348, 372, 415, 420.
" *Our Israelitish Origin*, 278, 397, 421–437.
" *Title-Deeds of the Holy Land*, 17, 37, 121, 372, 390, 398, 436.
" *Watchmen of Ephraim*, 39, 68, 73, 122, 123, 126, 190, 232, 326, 333, 372, 413, 414, 415, 419, 420, 435, 436.
Wittena Gemote, 187.
Wood, Dr, *An Inquiry Concerning the Primitive Inhabitants of Ireland*, 168.
Women of the Saxons, 296.
Wylie, *Dawn in Italy*, 153.

Xenophon's Retreat, 211.
Xenophon, *History of Cyrus*, 279.

Yankee Doodle, 177
Yates, Dr Holt, 427.
Ynglyngasaga, 221

Zamoxis, 231.
Zebulon, 153.
Zend Avesta, 195.

INDEX OF SCRIPTURE TEXTS.

GENESIS.	PAGE
iii. 15,	18
vi. 2,	19
ix. 25,	109
ix. 25-27,	28
xii. 1-3, 7,	53
xii. 2,	138
xii. 7,	14
xii. 7-9,	56
xiii. 10,	36
xv.	1, 391, 3
xv. 4, 5,	54
xv. 15-17,	11
xvi. 12,	120
xvii. 3-8,	55
xviii. 19,	75
xxi. 6,	67
xxi. 12,	273
xxi. 12,	119
xxii.	51, 72
xxii. 16-18,	56
xxii. 18,	67
xxiv. 35,	138
xxv. 2, 5, 6,	119
xxv. 20,	279
xxvi. 2-4,	51, 58
xxvii. 28, 29,	59
xxviii.	390
xxviii. 12-15,	59
xxviii. 14,	68, 389
xxviii. 15,	60
xxxv. 9-12,	61
xlviii. 3-7, 19,	63
xlviii. 15-20,	14, 164
xlviii. 16.	380, 389, 430
xlviii. 16-20,	348, 413
xlviii. 16-22,	363
xlviii. 19,	94, 159
xlix. 4,	212
xlix. 5, 6,	146
xlix. 10,	94, 126
xlix. 13,	153
xlix. 16,	137

	PAGE
xlix. 16, 17,	349
xlix. 17,	140
xlix. 22,	53, 363
xlix. 22-26,	14, 62
xlix. 23, 24,	317
xlix. 24,	123, 211
xlix. 26,	102

EXODUS.	
iii. 2-4,	165
iii. 5,	36
xii. 22,	326
xv. 21,	296
xix. 5,	174, 178
xix. 5, 6,	91, 96
xix. 6,	54, 367
xxiii. 9,	287
xxiii. 14-17,	327
xxviii. 31,	172
xxxiv. 6,	80
xxxiv. 18-26,	327
xxxix. 22,	172

LEVITICUS.	
xiii.	257
xix. 35, 36,	327
xxiii.	327
xxvi.	390, 397
xxvi.	316, 331, 333
xxvi. 18, 21, 24, 28.	102
xxvi. 42, 43,	40

NUMBERS.	
i. 2,	269
i. 16,	303
x. 36,	303
xiii. 1-3, 25,	332
xiv. 33, 34,	332
xv. 38,	316
xvii. 5,	277
xxii.-xxiv.	85

	PAGE
xxiii. 9,	402, 418
xxiii. 18-24,	86
xxiv. 2-9,	87

DEUTERONOMY.	
i. 9-18,	79, 303
viii. 7-10,	38
xiii. 3,	183
xiv. 2,	61
xx. 17, 18,	110
xxvi. 5,	279
xxviii. 36, 68,	430
xxviii. 62,	183
xxix. 29,	405
xxxii.	30
xxxii. 8,	134
xxxii. 8, 9,	17
xxxii. 9,	82, 178, 368
xxxii. 10,	70
xxxii. 17.	139, 265, 325
xxxii.-xxxiii.	96
xxxiii.	85, 137
xxxiii. 13-17,	62
xxxiii. 16,	381
xxxiii. 16, 17,	165
xxxiii. 17,	163, 430
xxxiii. 25,	151

JOSHUA.	
vii. 26,	214
viii. 29,	214
xxi.	138

JUDGES.	
v.	151
v. 14,	154
v. 15, 16,	6
v. 17,	138
xii. 5, 6,	191
xviii. 27,	137

1 SAMUEL.	
x. 19,	303

INDEX OF SCRIPTURE TEXTS.

2 Samuel.

Ref	Page
v. 5,	100
viii. 3,	279
xviii. 17,	214
xix. 15,	92
xxiii. 11-33,	143
xxiv. 18,	110

1 Kings.

Ref	Page
vii. 13,	95
xi. 25-38,	94
xii.	179
xii. 1, 3, 12, 16, 17, 20,	269
xii. 16,	99
xii. 16-20,	100
xii. 28,	94
xii. 28, 29,	137
xvi. 24,	181
xviii.	271
xviii. 16,	181
xviii. 19, 20, 30, 39.	269
xviii. 26,	164
xviii. 30,	273
xix. 8,	217

2 Kings.

Ref	Page
vii. 17,	105
xv. 29,	103
xvii. 6,	103, 198
xvii. 18,	99
xvii. 23,	105, 106
xviii. 4,	222
xviii. 9-12,	103
xviii. 26,	99
xxii. 8-20,	210
xxiii. 5,	182, 325
xxiv.	47
xxv. 12,	105

1 Chronicles.

Ref	Page
i. 1-4,	21
iv.	138
v. 2,	63, 399
v. 26,	103, 226
vi.	138

2 Chronicles.

Ref	Page
ii. 14,	138
viii. 3,	279
xi. 12-17,	101
xxviii. 8-15. 66, 97, 400
xxviii. 12-15,	66
xxx. 10,	193

Ref	Page
xxx. 11,	101
xxxvi. 15, 16,	194

Ezra.

Ref	Page
i. 3,	48
viii. 17,	217
ix.	240

Job.

Ref	Page
ix. 23,	193
xi. 6,	288
xxx. 24,	278

Psalms.

Ref	Page
ii. 8,	158
ii. 12,	159
xxiv.	45
xlv.	299
xlv. 16,	61
xlvi.	32, 43
xlvi. 1-4,	40
xlvii. 8, 9,	38
l. 16-23,	125
lix. 13,	102
lxviii. 13,	9
lxviii. 18,	34
lxxviii. 71,	91
lxxx. 6,	193
xc. 2,	45
xcii. 15,	96
cii. 13,	398
cii. 18,	323
cx. 3,	92
cxviii. 22, 23,	167
cxix. 99,	30
cxli. 7,	234
cxlvii. 19, 20,	66

Isaiah.

Ref	Page
v. 8,	332
vi. 10,	87
vii. 8,	400
viii. 8,	394
ix. 8,	7
ix. 8-12	126
ix. 8-21,	114, 126
ix. 13-17,	126
ix. 18-21,	126, 242
x. 1-4,	114, 126, 129
x. 5,	113
x. 5-15,	34
x. 13, 14,	180
x. 20,	138, 143
xi. 1, 2, 5,	124
xi. 1-10,	114

Ref	Page
xi. 6,	8
xi. 6-10,	125
xi. 11,	112, 430
xi. 11-16,	113
xi. 12,	50, 396, 430
xi. 13,	166
xviii.	349
xviii. 3,	50
xix.	166
xxiv. 1,	46
xxv. 4,	234
xxv. 7,	133
xxvi. 20,	163
xxvii. 6,	115, 363
xxviii. 15-17,	160
xxviii. 18,	227
xxviii. 22,	211
xxviii. 29,	167
xxix. 2,	1-3
xxix. 10,	10
xxix. 11,	269
xxx.	32
xxx. 25,	40
xxx. 25, 26,	43
xxxiii. 6,	92
xxxiii. 20, 21,	43
xxxiii. 22,	382
xxxv. 1,	28
xl. 4,	397
xli. 1,	163
xli. 1-16,	246
xli. 2,	90
xli. 5-9,	247
xli. 9,	102
xli. 10-12,	248
xli. 13-16,	248
xliii. 10,	398
xliii. 9, 10,	101
xliii. 21,	263, 374
xlv. 11,	269
xlix. 1,	27
xlix. 18,	394
xlix. 20,	429
li. 46,	366
liv.	21
liv. 1-8,	244
lvi.	1
lvi. 6-8,	16, 116
lviii.	288
lx. 8,	9
lx. 21,	155
lxi. 5,	394
lxi. 6,	96

INDEX OF SCRIPTURE TEXTS. 451

	PAGE
lxi. 7,	288
lxi. 9,	28
lxi. 9-11,	115
lx. 2,	6
lxii. 3,	179
lxii. 4,	391
lxiii. 7,	349
lxiii. 16-19,	266
lxvi. 19,	33, 157
lxvi. 19-20,	160

JEREMIAH.

i. 5,	167
iii. 11,	285, 401
iii. 12-19,	211
iii. 17,	37
iii. 18,	112
xvi. 14,	121, 408
xvi. 16,	48, 90
xxiii. 7, 8,	121
xxv. 15-33,	246
xxx. 11,	275
xxx., xxxi.	17
xxxi.	402, 121
xxxi. 7,	26
xxxi. 8,	50
xxxi. 8, 9,	122
xxxi. 9,	15, 63, 180
xxxi. 9, 10,	101
xxxi. 16, 17,	97
xxxi. 18, 19,	66
xxxi. 21,	229
xxxi. 22, 23,	106
xxxiii. 24,	166
xli. 2, 3,	166

LAMENTATIONS.

iv. 7,	27, 73

EZEKIEL.

i.	92
iii. 15,	211
iv. 6,	332
xi. 15,	99, 269
xi. 15, 16,	179
xiv. 22, 23,	12
xvi. 3,	110
xvi. 46,	112
xvii. 6,	226
xix. 14,	226
xx. 40,	296
xxvii. 16, 17,	139
xxviii.	32
xxviii. 12,	163

	PAGE
xxviii. 13,	34
xxviii. 14-16,	35
xxix. 17,	183
xxxi.	32
xxxi. 3,4,8,9,16,18.	35
xxxiv.	130, 144
xxxiv. 10-16,	179
xxxiv. 12, 13,	38
xxxvi.	418
xxxvi. 11,	107
xxxvii.	429, 418, 140
xxxvii. 11-16,	99, 182
xxxvii. 1-14,16,19.	429
xxxvii. 16,	68, 269
xxxvii. 22,	102
xxxviii.	32
xxxviii., xxxix.	87
xxxviii. 20,	40
xxxviii. 20, 21,	42
xxxix.	32
xxxix. 21, 22,	42
xxxix. 28, 29,	107
xliii. 7,	397
xlv. 8,	257
xlvii.	32, 42
xlvii. 1-12,	40
xlvii. 21-23,	117
xlviii.	141

DANIEL.

ii.	57, 122
iv.	331
vii.	8, 177
vii. 7,	249
vii. 8-12,	125
xii. 3, 5,	5
xii. 12,	333

HOSEA.

i.	175, 417
i. 1, 6, 7, 9, 10,	102
i. 3,	170
i. 4,	115
i. 9, 10,	265
i. 10, 11,	135
i 16,	241
ii.	417
ii. 3,	29
ii. 16,	164
ii. 18,	7
ii. 23,	148, 389
iii.	417
iv. 17,	228

	PAGE
v. 7,	332
v. 9-13,	99
vi. 1-3,	331
vi. 2-3,	104
vii. 11,	9
viii. 8,	228
ix. 3,	265
ix. 3-9,	144
ix. 17,	95
x. 5,	182
xi. 5,	145
xi. 6,	226
xi. 8,	401
xiii. 12-14,	182
xiv.	389
xiv. 4-7,	45

JOEL.

ii. 26-28,	364
iii.	32
iii. 4-8,	141
iii. 9-18,	41
iii. 13-18,	42
iii. 16-18,	40

AMOS.

vi. 6,	21
vii. 9-16,	226
vii. 16,	99, 210, 278

OBADIAH.

i. 16,	109

MICAH.

ii. 12, 13,	176
ii. 13,	57
v. 3,	106
vi. 16,	181

HABAKKUK.

ii. 3,	4

ZEPHANIAH.

i. 4,	182

ZECHARIAH.

i. 17,	102
ii. 5,	80
ix. 7,	111
ix. 12-16,	101
ix. 12,	288
ix. 14,	141
ix. 16,	13, 438
x. 7, 8,	183
x. 9,	390

INDEX OF SCRIPTURE TEXTS.

	PAGE
x. 12,	395
xii. 10,	431
xiv.	32
xiv. 4-3,	40
xiv. 8-10,	41
xiv. 11,	107

MALACHI.
i. 4,	108
iv. 4,	269
iv. 4, 5,	348

MATTHEW.
xv. 24,	120
xvii. 5,	183
xxi. 44,	123
xxii. 31, 32,	367
xxii. 32,	84
xxiv. 5,	324
xxv.	401
xxv. 31,	97
xxvii. 25,	109

MARK.
xiii. 1,	109

LUKE.
x. 30,	97
x. 30-35,	66
xv.	66, 130, 265
xv. 8,	179
xv. 12,	180
xix. 41,	431

JOHN.
vii. 35,	147
viii. 56,	55, 74
x.	130
x. 4,	179
xi. 52,	53

ACTS.
vi. 7,	108
xvi. 9,	33, 131

ROMANS.
	PAGE
i. 28,	108
iv. 13-18,	51
iv. 17,	52
iv. 23, 24,	4
viii. 19,	438
viii. 19-22,	2, 135
viii. 32,	17
ix.	64
ix. 23,	96
xi.	64
xi. 12-15,	96
xi. 25,	64
xi. 25,	95
x., xi.	64
xv. 8,	56
xv. 24,	131, 132
xvi. 10,	171
xvi. 13,	172

I CORINTHIANS.
xv. 25,	404

GALATIANS.
iii. 15-29,	13
iii. 16,	54
iii. 39,	57
iv. 27,	244

EPHESIANS.
ii. 14,	28
ii. 18-22,	156
ii. 19-22,	334

COLOSSIANS.
iii. 11,	113

1 THESSALONIANS.
ii. 16,	402

2 THESSALONIANS.
ii. 4,	156
ii. 8,	125

2 TIMOTHY.
	PAGE
iv. 21,	131
iv. 21,	172

HEBREWS.
iv. 12, 13,	7
xi. 8,	73
xi. 8-16,	46
xi. 10,	74
xii. 23,	69

JAMES.
i. 1,	389
v. 16-18,	273

1 PETER.
i. 1,	389
ii. 5-9,	96
ii. 9,	61
ii. 9-10,	102
ii. 10,	91, 174

2 PETER.
i. 19,	10

REVELATION.
i.	12
i. 17, 18,	4
ii.	12
v.	17
v. 8, 9,	51
v. 10,	91
vi. 2,	141
vii.	51, 68, 138
x. 1-7,	1
xi. 14,	129
xiii.	123
xiv. 1-8,	438
xv. 2-4,	131
xvi. 1,	40
xx. 7,	405
xx. 7-10,	244
xxi. 1,	46

www.ingramcontent.com/pod-product-compliance
Lightning Source LLC
Chambersburg PA
CBHW022106300426
44117CB00007B/613